REINHOLD
CRAFT AND
HOBBY BOOK

REINHOLD CRAFT AND HOBBY BOOK

Günther Voss

Translated by Thomas E. Burton

REINHOLD PUBLISHING CORPORATION
NEW YORK

Originally published in Germany under the title "Knaurs Bastelbuch"
©1959 by Droemersche Verlagsanstalt Th. Knaur Nachf. Munchen, Zurich

Type set by The Photo-Composing Room
Printed by Mutual Lithographers, Inc.
Bound by Van Rees Bookbinding Corporation

CONTENTS

FOREWORD

The best time of the day is surely the evening, a time of relaxation and recreation. For some this simply means rest and passive entertainment, but for others it means a chance to cultivate a skill or talent for which there may be no outlet in the daily routine of job and office. It is for these, the active ones, that this book is intended.

The interests of the craftsman and hobbyist should not be confused with those of the handyman, who is primarily concerned with material improvements to the home or garden. Apart from any material ends, the craftsman takes his chief joy in the exercise of his imagination and creative powers, and there is a spirit of playfulness in his work which the handyman would find it hard to appreciate. Accordingly, our guide to the fascinating world of crafts and hobbies does not take the form of a rigid set of rules and regulations, but of hints, examples, and encouragement to each one to develop his own personal resources.

No one, however, can turn out really satisfactory work unless he is well informed about tools and materials, and aware of the full possibilities of his chosen medium. For this reason the early chapters of this book are devoted to a thorough discussion of craft principles. The examples that follow do not call for an excessive amount of technical skill and are not likely to prove too difficult even for complete beginners or children, particularly as the descriptions are so clear and given in such detail.

Woodwork and metalwork, toy making, handmade jewelry, weaving, ceramics, electrical gadgetry, and home-made aquaria are just a few of the many topics discussed within the covers of the REINHOLD CRAFT AND HOBBY BOOK, a truly lavish source of interesting ideas and useful tips and suggestions, with numerous illustrations, most of them in color, that make even the trickiest operation easy to follow. May it bring you many hours of rewarding leisure.

Günther Voss

A FIRM FOUNDATION

Anyone who has worked at one time or another with wood or metals knows that craft hobbies are a form of creative activity. Whenever, in a free, untroubled moment, he can take up a tool, and use it, he leaves a workaday world that all too often is overconcerned with theory, to find contentment and liberty in working with his hands. He may soon come to the conclusion that theory tends only to undermine the walls that would keep him safe, and to diminish the value of all that he does. Therefore he wants no more to do with it: rules and bleak formulas cease to attract him, for they limit the freedom of his own decisions, and a shadow will fall over the pleasure that he rightly expects to find in his human occupations.

If you enjoy handling tools, you like to build. You take a genuine pride in seeing a job well done. The delight to be found in craftsmanship is therefore twofold: it arises in part from the activity itself, and in part from the contemplation of the finished work. The more satisfactory the job you have done, the greater and the purer will be the pleasure that it gives. There are, of course, many persons to whom experiment and research, the eternal quest for whatever is new and strange, will offer stronger attractions than those of ownership; the creative workman delights in making things and is completely satisfied by his work of creation. Others may wish both to make and to own, and this also is perfectly permissible. But neither can create with real pleasure, where a basis of knowledge is lacking, knowledge of the principles and understanding of the materials of the craft. Without this basis, any craft will necessarily prove laborious, troublesome and unrewarding. Naturally, therefore, you wish to acquire your craftsman's knowledge as easily and quickly as possible, and you want to learn how to put that knowledge to practical use.

Now, handicrafts are, by definition, activities requiring some degree of manual skill and dexterity. The amateur craftsman is not, of course, expected to produce work of a very high professional standard, nor is he obliged to observe the rules of a medieval guild or a modern trades union. But if his occupation is to be of lasting value, even to himself, the budding craftsman will be careful to apply some of the principles, and make use of processes, which have been used by craftsmen since the very earliest times. The ready acceptance and application of old and tried techniques will ease the path of every handyman. Another useful piece of equipment is a good knowledge of the handiest tools, their purpose and uses, and a familiarity with the properties of the commoner craft materials. The craft worker who makes himself master of these things will make light work of analyzing the processes required for any job that comes into his hands, and he will soon know by instinct which tools he should use. He will know the causes of defects, and how to avoid mistakes, and why a particular project is not a success; and he will be in no danger of false starts and blind alleys.

The first section of this book will summarize for the craftsman all this necessary information, without laying on him a burden of useless knowledge. A concise description of the various materials and a review of tools and equipment will give him all the essential information on the subject, and a glossary of craft terms in common use will be found useful for understanding the day-to-day expressions connected with tools and processes. The glossary will also make it easy to survey the crafts related to the one he is following. None of this information will cloud the craftsman's pleasure in his own inventive improvisations, but it will provide a secure foundation for his work, so that he can make rapid progress on sound methodical lines towards a clearly perceived objective.

THE CRAFTSMAN'S MATERIALS 1

The true craftsman has enterprise in his blood. If he possesses the creative urge, he will seldom be defeated by the problems he encounters in the course of his craft activities. The object of his work is practical: to create some useful or decorative article out of commonplace materials and with ordinary tools. But even simple skills have to be acquired. Practice is necessary, and the craftsman-beginner must be willing to learn from his own mistakes.

Most of the ordinary products of Nature will supply you with fragments on which you can practice, and even waste materials will provide a challenge to your skill in working and shaping. Whether your chosen medium be wood, metal or paper, leather, stone or fiberboard, your material will have its own secret essence to be revealed only to the craftsman who brings to it much patience, and also something akin to love. Even the scraps and waste that craft activities necessarily leave behind may serve some useful turn. It is by the intimate feeling that he acquires for his materials, the respect with which he treats them, that the true artist is known. He has an eye that can see the form hidden in the mass of clay, in the curious growth of a log, or in a buckled sheet of metal—and once he has seen it, he will know no rest until the idea has been made a reality.

The first principles of a craft have to be carefully and patiently acquired, and the beginner will be wise if he "makes haste slowly," familiarizing himself with the materials best suited to his purposes. Nowadays, the range available to the craftsman is very wide: he must therefore learn to use his judgment and avoid expensive mistakes.

Wood

Civilized life first began when wood was used to light a fire. It may not be strictly accurate to say that it was the lighting of that first fire that ended the Ice Age (because it melted the ice), but there are reasons to believe that the cave-dwellers who first set fire to wood by striking a spark from flint or horn were not long in making the further discovery that similar primitive implements could also be used for shaping wood.

For craftsmen, wood is one of the most interesting of all the substances supplied by Nature, because of its workability, its clean lines, and the pleasing appearance of the finished product. That some mysterious spirit certainly does reside in a piece of timber is something we shall soon learn from experience, and we shall not be long in discovering that the laws of its being are purely mechanical. Science tells us that all earthly phenomena are subject to universal laws which govern growth and decay. Timber is not exempt from these laws: it is a living substance having clearly recognizable characteristics. Even when felled, sawn and seasoned, timber retains something of the vigor of the tree from which it came. Wood knows no "state of rest," it goes on "working" and never tires. It is this extraordinary ruggedness that distinguishes wood from every other natural substance readily available to the craftsman.

It is a normal feature of every craft material that it offers a certain resistance to the shaping and abrading action of the tool wielded by the craftsman—a reminder, perhaps, of primeval strife as order emerged from chaos. We craftsmen, however, are trying to avail ourselves of the friendly offices of wood, and we are certainly not at enmity with it: the greater the respect with which we treat it, the more docile it will be in our hands; and the more dependable the results of our work.

Wood:
its structure and nature

All the characteristics of wood are due to variations in its cellular structure. Its strength and elasticity depend upon the direction and length of the fibers, its moisture content, and its density. It should be borne in mind that the compressive strength of sound wood is only about half its tensile strength. These mechanical properties are largely conditioned by the species, the age, and the habitat of the living tree from which the timber was cut. Climate and certain other conditions of growth are also important factors. Further, it is quite important to know whether the wood we select for a job came from the heartwood or the sapwood of the log. The mechanical properties of flat-sawed lumber, which is taken from the young, soft, mostly light-colored sapwood, are greatly inferior to those of the older and darker heartwood. Therefore heartwood should always be chosen by the craftsman wherever it can be had, though not all timber-trees produce it.

The anatomy of timber can be studied in a sawn tree-stump; the surface visible to the eye is known to the lumberjack as the "cross-grain" or "end-grain" timber, and to the carpenter as the "crosscut." A longitudinal "heartwood cut," however, will yield a board from the heartwood or *duramen* of the log, while a "chord cut" will produce a "slab" or outside board from the sapwood timber. Clearly distinguishable as zones of color, alternately light and dark, on the cross section of a log, are the annual growth rings, concentric with the pith cylinder or *medulla*. These rings are due to seasonal changes in the rate of growth of the tree. When the process of growth begins anew with the coming of spring, new and branching bundles of fiber cells appear beneath the bark, providing the tree with its moisture supply. It is the rapid, open growth of the spring season, the spring wood, alternating with the slow, condensed growth of the summer season that gives rise to the annular marking which indicates the increase in girth in each year. In the dry summer season the cells become thick-walled and more closely packed, and the dark ring of the "late wood" is formed. It is this layer which gives the wood its strength and stiffness. At the end of the season the growing process stops, and there forms over the new ring a wall of cell tissue, the *cambium,* which will in time serve as a bed for next season's growth of new wood, and which, by making it possible to distinguish the number of annual growth rings, provides an estimate of the age of the felled tree. It is clear that the width of the annual rings will have a bearing on the appearance and quality of the wood: the shorter the growth period of the ring, the harder and more close-grained the wood. For most craft purposes, however, we shall pay more attention to the appearance of the wood than to its strength.

Corresponding to the annual growth rings observed in a cross section of the log is the grain of the long-cut plank. The pattern of the grain varies according to the point at which the long cut was made in the trunk. It is much more diversified in an outside than in a heartwood board, and where the grain is cut through at a sharp angle, it yields an attractive finish much prized by furniture-makers and known as "veining." The heartwood board is cut from the very core of the trunk, and in this case the annual rings are seen as lines, more or less straight,

logs, however, this wood can be used for making crates and boxes or for lathing; if not, it can at least be sold for firewood.

Hardwoods are generally dealt with as untrimmed logs, and cut up into flat-sawed planks and boards in the sawmill. Boards

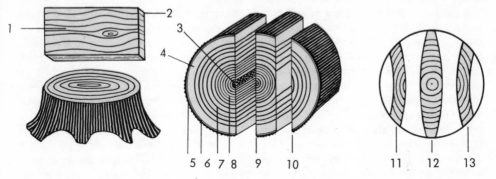

The structure of wood: 1—grain, 2—end grain, 3—pith cylinder or medulla, 4—sapwood, 5—bark, 6—inner fibrous bark, 7—annual growth rings, 8—heartwood or duramen, 9—radial cut, 10—chord cut, 11, 13—outside, flat-sawed boards, 12—heartwood board.

parallel and close-set. A very sharp-eyed observer may also detect in the lighter-colored annual rings of cross-grain timber a number of very fine holes. These are resin ducts or tubular vessels that carry the sap by capillary action from the roots to every part of the tree. In certain commercially valuable trees, these vessels are tapped for natural rubber and birch tar. The *wood* or *medullary rays* are cellular structures extending radially from pith cylinder to bark and serving to store food for the tree and to transport it horizontally within the trunk.

If a cross-grain cut be made through a log of elm or pine, the boundary between the heartwood and the sapwood can be detected by the clearly marked color zones. The sapwood is sheathed in a very thin layer of inner fiber, and this in turn is covered by the outer bark of the tree. When timber is squared, the four rounded outside slabs are usually discarded as waste. In the case of large

containing the pith cylinder are known as heartwood boards. Boards cut from the middle of the log are much stronger than outside boards, and may be identified by the close, straight grain. A board, like a human being, has its right side and its left side, which does not depend on the position of the observer. The "right side" of a board is the side towards the pith cylinder, and it is recognizable by the conformation of the annual rings. Even in the heartwood board the annular ring is intersected, so that it forms a segment about the axis of the end-grain. The "left side" of a board is on the side farthest from the pith, facing the bark. Where a flat-sawed board contains both heartwood and sapwood, the heartwood section is always the right side.

Greenwood newly felled contains 40–60% water, expressed as a percentage of the kiln-dry weight. This moisture has to be removed by a long drying process, until the timber is well seasoned, and becomes a matured and useful material. In this process it loses volume, shrinking most across its width, that is, in the direction of the annual growth rings. The loose cellular tissue of the cambium and sapwood retains considerably more moisture than the compact heartwood, so that the outside boards containing the larger cells which have stored more water will shrink much more than the inside boards, and they will also shrink more on the left side than on the right. The consequence is that an outside board will warp to the left, away from the pith cylinder of the tree. The left side of the board will cup and the right side will arch like a bow; and the farther the board lay from the center of the log the more pronounced the deformation will be. Outside boards shrink more than inside boards. But here again the heartwood board breaks the rules: instead of being concentrated on one side, as in the outside boards, the sapwood structure extends right through it at both ends. Maximum shrinkage therefore occurs at both ends of the heartwood board, while the middle remains comparatively stable. The heartwood board bulges like a lens on both faces: therefore it has two "right sides."

Thus, wood shrinks while it is being seasoned, but its moisture content and also its size will continue to change after it is put to use, because it is hygroscopic: this means that in damp climates it will absorb moisture from the atmosphere. Water thus absorbed is held in the cell walls. This results in a compensatory movement of the cell structure, and the wood swells, exerting a remarkable force. Where drying has been too rapid, the wood may split as a result of the lengthwise separation of the tissues along the medullary rays. Both swelling and splitting are due to the fact that wood is a natural product with a cellular structure, and should

not be regarded as defects. They are not necessarily serious, and storage under suitable conditions, together with careful preservative treatment, will keep them within tolerable bounds. They must be borne in mind, however, when work starts with the tools.

For the carpenter, then, the First Commandment is: Right side of the wood on top! Secured in this position to a suitable base its warping tendencies will be reduced, and the edges of the board at least will lie true (see illustration). In general, the custom is not to work with the full width of flat-sawed boards, but to cut them up into planks. When gluing planks together, lay them right side to right side and left side to left side. If you want to glue two narrow planks edge to edge, so as to obtain a broader surface, remember that the rule is still: "Right to right, left to left." If you glue pieces of long-cut and cross-cut timber together, you must not be surprised when they part company, as they are bound to do sooner or later, because the wood will work more in one direction than the other.

Defects and diseases of wood

As a business transaction, buying timber is next in dignity to horse-dealing. If you lack experience in this branch of trading, take with you someone familiar with lumber, and follow his advice. Timber is liable to attract wood-destroying fungi, and the early stages of the decay resulting from their activities is often very difficult to detect. If, when you tap the wood with your knuckle, it gives out a dull, flat note; if it is discolored; if it gives off a musty smell; or if you can easily dig into it with your finger-nail—leave it where you found it! A common disease in spruce timber is indicated by a reddish striation known as nail hardness. Nail-hard timber is harder to work than sound timber. Apart from the fact that it is difficult to drive in even a single nail, it tears easily and will distort in every direction. As with crooked-grain wood, the only thing to be done with it is to use it for firewood.

Most crooked-grain wood comes from trees which have grown to maturity in isolated positions, where continuous resistance to the wrenching action of high winds has caused the timber to grow up twisted like a corkscrew. This twisting tendency is also observable in the fibers of boards cut from the logs of such trees, and nothing can be done to make good the damage. Crooked-grain timber will go on twisting: no ingenuity will cure it.

Natural wood and plywood

All unprocessed lumber is classifiable as "natural timber." Carpentry throughout the ages can be expressed in terms of a struggle between the workman and the perverse behavior of his material, which is apparently not disposed to submit itself without a fight to the wishes of mankind.

But carpenters have from the beginning been resourceful as well as artistic, so that they were bound, sooner or later, to bring to an end the chronic state of war between the man at the bench and his stubborn material. They found out how to make themselves independent of the warping of natural timber—by using plywood.

A sheet of plywood looks much the same as natural timber, but is in fact of totally different composition. Plywood is made by bonding together three or more thin sheets of wood under high pressure, using a waterproof adhesive. The important point is that the grain of alternate plies is laid at right-angles. Therefore, an odd number of plies must be used, as the grain of the back layer must lie in the same direction as that of the face layer. The adhesive strength of the bonding agent puts an end to the natural life of the wood: the layers can no longer warp, and the cells of the wood fibers are practically prevented from "working." As a craft material, plywood is inert.

In lumber-core plywood a thicker middle layer consisting of narrow strips of pine,

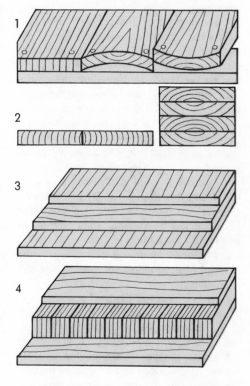

Warping can be counteracted by positioning the boards correctly: 1. When nailing down boards, the right side should always be on top. 2. When gluing boards edgewise, the right sides should all lie in the same direction. Boards glued one on top of the other should lie right side to right side or left side to left side. 3. Plywood. 4. Lumber-core plywood for cabinet-making.

alder, beech, birch, or poplar, is bonded between thin face veneers of similar wood.

With the discovery of ways of making hardboard and chipboard, the lumber industry revolutionized its handling of its raw material. For chipboard, wood is reduced to shavings, for hardboard, it is shredded into fibers. Next—as with paper-making—an adhesive or binder is added to the mass, and the mix is formed into sheets by rolling under heavy pressure while hot and very plastic. Hardboard made by this process is enormously strong and stable.

Various types of plywood and laminated board have been universally adopted for decorative and paneling applications, and have practically driven natural timber off the market. Hardboard provides the craftsman with a very handsome and versatile structural material. It is sold in all the standard grades and thicknesses. It is considerably harder than the pine and fir hitherto so widely used, and it is just as easily sawn, planed, drilled and joined.

The chief element in plywood and laminated board is the *veneer*. By this term we generally understand thin plies separated from the log by sawing, knife-cutting, or peeling on the lathe principle. It is usual to classify wood laminates according to the method of production, as sawn, knife-cut, or peeled veneers.

Sawn veneers are the best and the most expensive, but peeled veneers are the more finely figured, taking an exceptionally good finish, comparable with that of the veining of flat-sawed planks. These peeled veneers are very widely used in the furniture trade in the production of highly-polished paneling. Where hardwood face veneers, such as mahogany, walnut and rosewood, are used the deception is almost complete. It is always at the edges of the work that the difference between laminated material and the

honest cross-grain of genuine natural timber can be detected. It is here that the laminated structure has to be concealed, possibly by gluing on a thin strip of the same veneer.

Species of wood

Of all the many timbers produced by Nature, only a few are really useful to the majority of craftsmen. The "softwoods," spruce, fir, pine and larch, are best for all construction work.

The wood of the spruce is white with a yellow tinge; it is cheap and easy to work. Like all the softwoods it splits easily, it is resinous, light in weight, soft and springy. It is extremely strong, and is very suitable for all the simpler woodworking operations.

In characteristics and appearance, common fir resembles spruce as one twin resembles the other.

Pine, unlike fir and spruce, is a heartwood tree. Its timber is harder and more resinous, with a better resistance to decay. Its strongly marked veining yields a fine surface finish, and it is the favorite wood of every carpenter.

The larch, too, is a heartwood tree, with a wood yellowish to orange-brown in color, with characteristics similar to those of firwood, and strongly resistant to decay.

In the great majority of cases where he wants to produce shaped surfaces in solid wood, the craftsman will be well advised to choose one of the "hardwoods," which are available in much greater variety than softwoods. Like some of the evergreens, only a certain number of broad-leaf trees show a distinct boundary line between the heartwood and the sapwood. The line is very clearly marked in oak and ash, whereas in linden and beech the heartwood and the cambium are scarcely distinguishable to the eye. Such timber comes from mature trees. Native broad-leaf trees may be classified as soft, hard and very hard.

The ideal carving wood for the craftsman, whether he be an expert or a beginner, is basswood. White to yellowish-red in color, it is very soft, yet it gives a remarkably firm line, and will cut "like butter" in any direction. The annual rings are scarcely visible, so that the finished surface is mat and uniform in texture.

Softer and lighter even than basswood is poplar, but it would be a mistake to assume that these qualities make it an easy wood to work. Short-fibered and large-pored as a mushroom, it is extremely unstable and will crumble under even the sharpest blade. Its surface is soft and fleecy, and it should only be used as a filler for veneers, for which purpose it is well suited. Other woods with similar characteristics are chestnut and alder. The latter, especially, is a great favorite with turners, on account of its attractive red-brown color, and its uniform close grain. It is somewhat harder than basswood, and both woods will split easily, even when not fully dried out. Alder wood is more liable to develop checks.

The medium-hard woods are birch, walnut and pearwood. Pearwood is firm and close-grained, light to dark brown in color, and with a not very attractive grain. Its smooth surface makes it very suitable for smaller pieces, while the strongly marked, wavy veining of walnut requires a large surface to be seen to advantage.

With the noble oak we come to the hardwoods proper. The oak is a heartwood tree and is one of the best decay-resistant timbers used by man. The heart timber presents a handsome appearance and is extremely hard, rigid, and strong, but the sapwood is soft and easily penetrated by woodworm. It should not be used for structural work.

There are more than four hundred varieties of oak. One variety, Quercus sessiliflora, is exceedingly brittle, and so extraordinarily hard that it will blunt the tools of even the best craftsman. More easily worked, but still hard to cut, is American white oak, which is less brittle and lighter in color. This wood is one of the most handsome and durable that the carver or sculptor could desire.

Ash is very hard, and behaves well under the cutting tool. Tough in texture, it is usually straight-grained. Much finer in structure are the red beech and the very beautiful maple. The wood of the latter is almost without pores, so that it does not shrink or swell to any great extent. Thus it is an ideal material for kitchen articles and table services.

Among the hardest woods available are plum, hornbeam, and boxwood. Any craftsman who wants to make toys or models with wooden wheels and axles, or pastry-rollers, or wheels and spindles for a spinning-wheel, should certainly choose hornbeam.

For woodwork and carving of the very finest quality, hard, bright-yellow boxwood should be used as it is uniform in texture and finely figured. Even the end-grain wood will give an extremely sharp cutting line and a beautifully marked surface. Boxwood is the most desirable of all woods for the sculptor. It is also the most expensive.

The basic requirement for every variety of timber is that it be well seasoned and dried before it is touched by any carpenter's tool. This requirement is easily satisfied in the case of thin boards of softwood, but dense, hardwood in the log is another matter. There is an old rule-of-thumb among carpenters that an oak log must be seasoned by air-seasoning for one complete year for each half inch of its diameter. When this is borne

Metals

in mind, the suspicion aroused by timber supposedly "guaranteed dry" and the high price of thick oak planks are easily understood.

Metals

The second large group of materials supplied by Nature is that of the metals. If necessary, the carpenter can obtain his material by going into a forest and felling timber, but for the metalworker the question of supply is not so easily solved: he cannot just dig into the ground and find his copper rod or his iron bar "ready for use." Most metal has to be gotten out of the earth by procedures that are more or less laborious and complex. Then it must be dressed, purified, and in varying degrees refined, and subjected to a succession of smelting and machining processes, before the crude ore is converted to a form suited to the varied requirements of industry.

Further, pure metals are rarely suitable for use as the raw material of manufactured articles. In practice—and particularly in craft metalworking—we are usually dealing with alloys obtained by combining two or more metals in a process of smelting or casting. Metals are solid crystalline bodies, and their atoms are arranged in clearly defined orderly space-lattice formations. The components of alloys exert a mutual influence on each other's lattice structure, so that by selecting the right components a new alloy material can be made to withstand a wide range and variety of stresses. Alloys are classified according to composition, characteristics and their intended application; we can also classify them as magnetic, acid-resistant, heat-resistant, etc.

It is characteristic of all metals that in varying degrees they reflect light. They can therefore be given a high polish. They are also conductors of heat and electricity, and they can be subjected to plastic deformation by rolling, forging, drawing, and hammering.

The more important metals

In view of the steady demand, the large reserves available, and the resulting low prices, the place of honor among the heavy metals must continue to go to iron (chemical symbol: Fe). In a table showing all the elements composing the crust of the earth in the order of the frequency with which they occur, iron would occupy the fourth place.

To be accurate, the metal commonly known as "iron" is not iron at all, but structural steel. The engineer reserves the term "iron" for a metallic ore of high carbon content containing traces of other elements such as sulfur, phosphorus, silicon or manganese; for the pig-iron produced by smelting this ore in the blast-furnace, an impure product, low in tensile strength and non-malleable; and for brittle cast iron.

Iron ore is smelted in a Bessemer converter or a Siemens-Martin furnace, or by the Krupp-Renn process, to produce a steel which can be rolled, forged and machined, and possesses strength and ductility. Structural steel is very strong in compression, shear, and tension and highly shock-resistant. It also has the valuable properties of malleability and weldability. It is therefore not surprising that we see it wherever we go, and in a great variety of applications, ranging from shoe-horns to iron bridges.

The great versatility of steel is due mainly to the proportions and grain-structure of its carbon content. Heat treatment and alloying with other metals will considerably increase its strength. Tempering and quenching will improve its hardness and ductility, as will cold-working. The addition of chromium and nickel will reduce its tendency to corrode. The addition of vanadium produces a high-grade alloy of great hardness.

Aluminum (chemical symbol: Al) is the most important of the light metals. It is found as a hydrated oxide, known as bauxite, which is widely distributed in many parts of the world. It is estimated that 8% of the solid crust of the earth consists of bauxite. Aluminum, however, never occurs in the pure state. To obtain the metal, the ore is refined by treatment with caustic soda, the resulting aluminum hydrate is calcined, and the pure alumina thus obtained is then electrolytically reduced to metallic aluminum.

Pure aluminum is soft and ductile. It can be hardened by the addition of certain alloying elements until it is almost as strong as steel. Aluminum alloys possess great strength, and low density. The extraordinary chemical properties of more than three thousand aluminum alloys have given aluminum a secure place in the forefront of the industrial metals.

The first scientist to succeed in producing metallic aluminum from bauxite was a German, Friedrich Wöhler. That was in 1827, and for many years thereafter the metal was more expensive than silver. Today it is the principal metal used in the aircraft industry, and it is even a threat to the leading position held by iron in the world metal market. It is much cheaper than copper, with good thermal and electric conductivity, so that it has found ready acceptance as a substitute for the latter metal in instrument-making applications. The resistance of aluminum and its alloys to atmospheric corrosion is a further interesting feature. This is due to the protective effect of a spontaneously forming moisture-resistant oxide film. All in all, aluminum is an ideal metal for the home workshop and the craftsman. It is light in weight, cheap in price, has good mechanical properties, is easily worked, and in general it offers a good surface for decoration.

Lead (chemical symbol: Pb) is one of the softest of the known, and the heaviest of the base, metals. It is so soft that it can be scratched with the finger nail. Lead was formerly used for writing and drawing, but nowadays our pencils are filled with graphite, a form of carbon. The melting point of lead is low (327°), so that it is widely used for casting "tin soldiers." Industry is a large consumer of lead. It is used in batteries, for printing type and tin solder, as a sealing material, for cable sheathing, and for many other purposes. Sheets of lead are also used as shock-absorbing "cushions" in press-tools for punching and stamping work. All those who work with lead are exposed to certain risks, because all compounds containing lead, including lead oxides and lead dust, are poisonous.

Zinc (chemical symbol: Zn) is a soft, greyish-white, shining metal. In the pure state it can be hammered cold, and rolled into very thin foil. Its resistance to acid attack is poor, but it will stand up to severe climatic conditions, and is very tolerant of solder. It is therefore the principal metallic material used by plumbers and sheet-metal workers in the fabrication of roofing, weathering, gutters, rainwater leaders, and flashing. Zinc is expensive, and it is customary to substitute galvanized steel sheet for the pure metal. Protective coatings of zinc on iron and steel render these metals resistant to corrosion and to alkali attack.

Silver-white, shining tin (chemical symbol: Sn) is only a little harder than lead. Its

Metals

melting point is low (231.8°). It is therefore a good casting metal, and is widely used as a solder. Tin is very flexible, and it can be hammered into foil almost as easily as gold. We find it in our bathrooms as toothpaste tubing, and in the food industry as packaging for chocolate. Tin is highly resistant to corrosion, and tinned sheet iron (tinplate) is used for the countless containers required annually by the canning industry. The metal, however, is sensitive to cold: at very low temperatures the pure metal will disintegrate into a white powder. This singular characteristic, known as "tin plague," is liable, in a cold winter, to ruin the pipes of church organs, and to spoil the beautiful medieval plate negligently left in the display cases of cold museums. A peculiar feature of this metal is known to tinsmiths as "tin cry," a crackling or rustling sound emitted by the metal when being cut by the shears.

Copper (chemical symbol: Cu) is the only red metal, and one of the most important of all natural products. It takes a good polish, is comparatively soft, ductile and malleable. It can be hammered into thin foil, and drawn into fine wire. These technological advantages, together with the handsome appearance of the metal, make copper one of the most attractive of all materials for hammered work. It tends to harden when rolled or hammered, but annealing will restore its plasticity. It is easily hard or soft soldered, brazed or fusion-welded, and in a damp atmosphere it will sometimes form its own corrosion-resistant film, the "patina" so often seen on the roofing of churches and civic buildings. As a good conductor of heat and electricity it is surpassed only by silver. Copper suffers from certain disadvantages: it is a poor casting metal, and when used for kitchen vessels it is a danger to human life. Acids, such as fruit juices, re-

act with the metal to form the toxic verdigris.

Copper may be alloyed with many metals, the resulting products being classified as completely new materials.

The most important of these non-ferrous alloys is that of copper and zinc to produce brasses and bronzes. Red brass, a copper-base zinc alloy containing 90% copper, is known as tombac, a term borrowed from the language of the Malay States. By altering the zinc content, the color of brass can be varied over a wide range with the most attractive results: ranging through red-gold, yellow-gold, greenish gold, yellow ocher, and pale yellow to a delightful silver-gray. This very great variety of colors, combined with easy workability and the fact that it will take a very high polish, makes brass a very popular material with art-metalworkers. Brass, and its wrought alloys, is a splendid hammering metal, hardening rapidly under the tool.

Copper alloyed with tin yields bronze, a metal with a high coefficient of expansion, easily worked, and attractive in color. Bronze, like copper, forms its own protective coating in humid conditions. It is highly resistant to abrasion, and on account of its rugged strength it is the most prized of all metals for casting work.

Gold (Au) and silver (Ag) are precious metals. Gold is seldom used in the pure state except by the dentist. As a rule, the craftsman will only need these expensive metals for making jewelry, decorating glass and porcelain, and gilding bookbindings, and his requirements will in any case not be so heavy as to endanger his standard of living. A little gold goes a long way: an ounce of the metal can be beaten into 1,600 extremely thin leaves, covering an area of

105 square feet.

Silver also takes a very high polish. We shall need it only for jewelry and small pieces of chased work. It is very ductile, and its hardness number lies mid-way between those for copper and gold. Silver may be hardened by adding copper: most table silver contains 20% copper. The familiar "800" stamp on silverware indicates that the alloy (considered to be 1000 parts) contains 800 parts of pure silver to 200 parts of copper. Silver is the best of all metallic conductors of heat and electricity.

Commercial forms of metal

Before they can be put to further industrial or commercial use, all metals and their alloys must be in saleable condition as normally required by the customer. They must be rolled, drawn, forged, or cast into bars, tubes, profiles, sections, sheet, wire, and other semi-finished products, in a great range of dimensions and thicknesses. The dimensions, the grain structure, and the proportions to be observed in the case of alloys, are all carefully controlled by national consultative committees, with a view to standardizing the terms used in bidding for contracts and placing orders, and to maintain the quality of the materials offered to the public.

The most important semi-finished products for the ordinary craftsman are wire and sheet, for he will rarely wish to tackle proc-

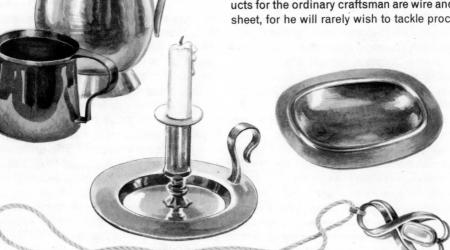

A skilful metalworker can make many beautiful things.

esses other than cold-working. Where some piece of construction has to be carried out in structural steel, he will find that any good steel-yard carries a sufficient range of ready-made sections.

Plastics

Plastics first appeared on the market shortly after World War I. At the time they were regarded as "substitute materials," but the description has long been obsolete.

The discovery of plastics was due to an intensive search for new materials, which began in chemical laboratories more than a century ago. Industrialists were looking for substances which would supplement the diminishing world resources of mineral wealth, and would also have equivalent or better characteristics in respect of mechanical strength, physical properties and chemical resistance. Having found the key to the mystery of the molecular structure of matter, the investigators proceeded to reproduce that structure by artificial means. They made their products increasingly synthetic, relying more on simple chemicals and common industrial by-products and less on substances found in nature. Today, most plastics are produced synthetically, though the starting chemicals are derived from the breakdown of natural products such as coal and oil.

Any metal, or any alloy-forming element, retains the characteristics of the starting material, very often in a clearly recognizable form. No one, for example, would describe bronze as a plastic substance. But the case is altered when chemistry takes a hand, and uses constituents which are perhaps little better than industrial waste, to produce completely new and exceedingly useful materials as though by magic. In most of the new plastics it would be impossible for even the trained eye to distinguish any of the characteristics of the starting materials. Coal. air and water bear no resemblance to a tough fabric, yet the plastics engineer can transform them into one that can be used to make a very solid and efficient gearwheel. Similarly, carbon, hydrogen, oxygen and nitrogen can be polymerized and drawn through a die to form a spinnable thread. Clearly, therefore, it is quite permissible to describe these end-products as "man-made" or artificial. It would serve little purpose to investigate the definition further, or to describe the truly vast range of plastic materials now available to world industry.

The most important sector of the plastics industry is that concerned with the production of synthetic raw materials from coal, by the processes of polycondensation and polymerization developed by industrial chemists. The first of these involves the formation of chain polymers from cyclic compounds. The second term includes any chemical process resulting in the formation of large molecules consisting of repeated structural units, the large molecule (polymer) having the same percentage composition as the original substance, i.e. no by-products are found.

One of the most important end-products contributed by organic chemistry to modern industry is the group of plastics known as synthetic resins, which depend upon both the techniques mentioned. This group supplies the raw materials for well over half the output of the entire plastics industry. It is little wonder, therefore, that in common usage, "plastics" and "synthetic resins" have become interchangeable, although they are in fact very far from meaning the same thing.

Synthetic resins, like natural resins, are amorphous: they are not crystalline in form, the molecules are not arranged in a space-lattice pattern, and they show no cleavage planes. They are viscous or refractory, semi-hard or solid, and their flow qualities (softening points) are so varied as to make possible a wide range of applications. They fall broadly into two families: the "thermoplastics," which are not chemically changed by the application of heat; and "thermosetting" materials, which become permanently hard and unmoldable when heated.

Polyvinyl chloride (PVC), a composition produced by polymerization, has found applications without number in the industrial world. We see it everywhere, in the form of phonograph records, table tops, cups and saucers, window blinds, bottle caps, floor coverings, upholstery in automobiles, garden hoses, lampshades, soap boxes, raincoats, and a thousand other astonishing applications. The whole of this amazing range of everyday things is made from a combination of hydrochloric acid and water.

The versatility of PVC is in part due to the fact that it can be used either as a polymer or as a composition produced by hot-mixing the polymer with plasticizers, to give materials in a wide range of hardness and flexibility. It is tough, has good weathering properties, and is resistant to chemicals. It is tolerant of acids and alkalis, alcohol, benzene, and the majority of gases. It is non-flammable and has color possibilities. Brittle and hard, PVC is easily machined.

The craftsman will normally use plastics in the form of laminates or sheets. In some laminates the plastic functions as the bonding agent for multiple layers made up of a great variety of fibrous fillers. They can be worked with ordinary carpenter's tools. They are very suitable for practical applications where appearance is not the primary object. They make a very good surfacing material, and are splendid structural elements for the craftsman to use; unfortunately they are not cheap.

Plastics can also be prepared in the form of sheet and film. These are used for a variety of decorative and protective purposes, for example, as attractive upholstery fabrics or crease resistant cloth, and in their finest form as plastic bags. The many valuable characteristics of this class of plastics have resulted in their being adopted for use in trades as various as house-decorating, upholstery and bookbinding. The many plastic fabrics are durable, color-fast, washable and hygienic. The range of colors available is dazzling.

With so many useful characteristics to recommend them, the craftsman will certainly find a great many uses for these materials. As decorative surfaces they have many attractions. They can be cut with a knife or scissors, and they can be joined by adhesives better than by sewing. When using them follow carefully the instructions issued by the manufacturer, and remember that, although a plastic fabric may look very much like a woven textile product, it is nothing of the kind. A plastic surface is solid and continuous.

The craftsman will also make great use of another useful product of the plastics industry: adhesives. Synthetic resins and silicone rubbers provide very stable adhesives. A very wide range of these products is available. The use of plastics in solution form as adhesives and bonding agents has driven the old casein glues and starch-based pastes off the market.

We have said a great deal in praise of the new adhesives, but the beginner should treat them with considerable respect. First, many brands require the addition of special thinning agents, and when in the fluid state these mixtures are highly inflammable. Weigh up all the factors, therefore, before

Synthetic adhesives

you decide to use them. The vapors they exhale may irritate the lining of your nose. Therefore, before you start any big job of sticking, make quite sure that you have adequate ventilation. Finally, it is important to find out whether the bonding agent you are going to use is a synthetic resin, a synthetic rubber (such as Neoprene), or a silicone. These adhesives must always be used with the most careful attention to the maker's instructions, or they will fail to work. Never attempt to mix one adhesive with another with a view to "improving" the bonding strength. This is the greatest of all breaches of the bonding rules, which should be regarded as—binding!

Other materials

It goes without saying that the craftsman will find a use for many other materials besides wood, metals and plastics. The list can be stretched like a rubber-band. Rubber, by the way, should certainly be found in the workroom, as bands and ropes for holding tools and securing work, and in membrane or sheet form.

The contribution of the mineral world is also important. It includes clay for modeling, and plaster-of-paris for casts and molds. Many kinds of stones can be used for carving, or in tiny pieces for setting in jewelry. Organic substances like leather, paper and textiles can be put to so many uses that whenever we take them in hand we are reminded of the boundless resources and liberality of Nature, and we may reflect that she is still well able to meet competition from the laboratory. The range of raw materials offered to the craftsman by Nature is almost infinite: he can find a use for such varied articles as straw, nutshells, and dried-out bones. A library might be filled with descriptions of such things, and of their uses. But we are practical men, rather than theorists, so we will leave the subject for the present. If any special product of nature attracts our notice in the later chapters of this book, we will deal with it in detail when we discuss its particular applications.

THE CRAFTSMAN'S TOOLS   2

Our materials are constantly on the move through the workshop. After a flying visit of a few days or weeks they take their leave as finished articles or as waste. Our tools, however, are permanent residents. Materials are passive, but tools are active, the instruments of the craftsman's creative activity.

Every home contains a few simple tools, even though sometimes nothing more than a pair of pliers and a hammer. In many cases these are seldom used and spend most of their existence in some forgotten drawer, in poor condition for any hard and conscientious job of work. Such tools are merely tolerated: they are kept because they "might be wanted sometime". It is therefore not surprising that the face of the hammer is chipped, the pliers loose; the file, if there is one, has probably given up completely and is quietly rusting away, while the screwdriver is in such a poor state that it might as well end its days doing duty as a gimlet, or for levering off box lids. To the craftsman who means business, tools in this condition are worse than useless; and if they were also cheap and shoddy articles to begin with, he will certainly have nothing to do with them.

Hammer and pliers are part of the iron ration, the minimum kit, in any workshop. Add a saw, a screwdriver, a couple of wood chisels and a cold chisel, a plane, a file, a gouge, and a wrench, and you have the basic equipment for meeting the ordinary emergencies of the home. This list contains all the tools essential for working in either wood or metal, and you will be able to carry out ordinary simple repair work to your complete satisfaction. But such a kit and such occupations will scarcely satisfy the craftsman: he will want to go very much further, and his activities are going to demand the finest tools his money can buy.

The operations involved in the working of wood and metal will impose their own systematic scheme for the purchase of tools. Not only are metals and timber the most important of the craft materials, but most of our tools came into existence precisely to simplify the work involved in handling them.

The useful effort that can be applied by means of a tool does not depend upon its size, but upon its design—the thought and skill that were put into the shaping of its parts—and its quality. Make up your mind before you begin that you will spare yourself the vexation and disappointment that inevitably come of buying cheap tools. The inferior steel in a cheap cutting tool quickly loses its edge, and frequent grinding shortens its life still further. In the long run, cheap tools will cost you more in frustrated work and wasted material than good ones can ever do. There is truth in the old saying: "A good tool does half the work".

For the keen craftsman then, only the best will be good enough. Remember also that handicrafts are meant to be therapeutic, not a burden, a true recreational pleasure, and not mere slogging and hard work. Do not sour yourself by purchasing tools that are needlessly heavy. You ought never to need a sledge-hammer, for example, or a big wood saw, or a pipelayer's wrench as thick as your arm, since your raw materials will normally be bought in handy sizes, ready for you to use. In exceptional cases, you can prudently avoid the needless use of your own tools, and the risk of doing them damage, by resorting to a little diplomacy: take your large, heavy pieces to some friendly workshop nearby, and have them cut up the material on their large machines. You will then more quickly reach the point at which, free from needless fatigue, you can cheerfully and profitably begin to apply your talents to your own creative work.

Now, what material will you normally be using? If all your skill and inclination is centered on one material, whether it be wood or metal, your workshop will obviously be specially fitted out for it, and your tool-kit will comprise only the tools essential to the particular processes involved. You will, however, want your equipment to be as complete as possible. Most craftsmen will find as they go on that their interests are not so severely limited. They will venture into more than one specialist's territory, and so they will want a workshop fitted out with equipment for a variety of tasks and skills: there must be no artificial limitations on the creative mood.

Let us therefore make a methodical beginning, and plan the purchase of our tools according to the demands of the principal materials in which we propose to work.

Woodworking Tools

The most universal of all tools is the human hand, but its original functions of striking and holding have been taken over, so far as the carpenter is concerned, by hammer and pliers.

A carpenter's hand hammer not exceeding eight ounces in weight will provide adequate hitting power for all our work. Even when we need to restore our peace of mind by smashing to pieces something that has gone wrong, a hammer of this weight will do. People call such behavior "lack of restraint", but it should rather be seen as a healthy expression of self-criticism. It is always much better to destroy a piece of work which is obviously unsuccessful, than to preserve it as a monument to failure.

A carpenter's hand hammer differs from a mechanic's hammer in several points. For example, the peen is tapered on one side only. The peen may be called the tail-fin of the hammer head, and in ordinary hammering work it will be turned upwards. The face of the hammer is the part making direct contact with the head of the nail. The claw-hammer differs from both the carpenter's and the mechanic's hammer in that its peen forks into a curved claw, each tip of the claw tapering to a thin edge. This is the hammer to use for splitting thick boards and drawing awkward nails.

A short shaft is not an insurance against bruised fingernails. To ensure a firm, safe blow, the handle of the hammer should be about 12 inches long. Grasp the hammer firmly near the end, and swing it with a free, confident movement. An oval shaft will lie more comfortably in the hand than a round one.

Some important woodworking tools: 1 carpenter's hammer, 2 end-cutting nippers, 3 end-cutting nippers with compound leverage, 4 plane (patent plane), 5 dovetail saw, 6 bit brace, 7 center bit and countersink, 8 push drill, 9 chisels, plain and bevel-edged, 10 skew chisel and gouge, 11/12 bent and straight carving tools with range of profiles, 13 carving knives, 14 spoke shave blades.

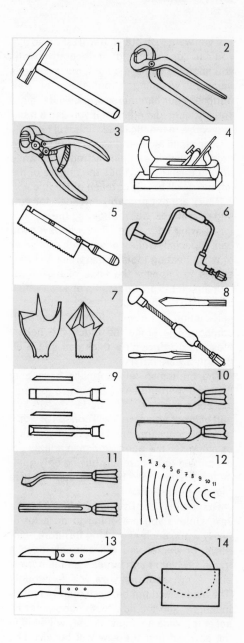

If you want to fit out your workshop so that you can cope with a lot of decorative work, you should also have a light, glass-cutter's hammer, weighing about three or four ounces. Your hammered work will be more speedy, neat and efficient if you use a hammer with a magnetic head. This will not only pick up small tacks and screws, but will also hold small nails and pins as required, while driving them home. Thus the fingers of the left hand will be out of reach of trouble.

Pliers are not primarily intended for cutting operations, but for holding the work or for drawing nails. Use pliers whenever you can, especially while working with a hammer or when heating tools or materials. When it comes to clipping the ends of a wire, or nipping off the protruding tip of a nail which is too long for the board, use wire-cutters or end-cutting nippers. If you have a pair with compound leverage, so much the better: they will go through a thick nail shank as though it were cheese.

The craftsman will normally have only limited opportunities for bending and forming solid wood, so that by far the greater part of his shaping work will consist of wood removal. Since this must be done by cutting or chipping, the good workman will select his cutting tools carefully buying only quality tools, which can be relied upon to give him the best service.

First on his list of cutting tools will be the saw. Unless you are going to do a lot of heavy work, such as making furniture, windows, or doors, you will scarcely need a frame saw with teeth larger than the normal size. A crosscut handsaw will be enough. The blade need not be more than 14 inches in length, and the saw teeth should not be set at too wide an angle, or they will bind in the saw cut and the saw will buckle. The handsaw is also useful for cutting up larger sections of plywood, since it has neither a

back nor a tensioning frame to limit the width or length of the cut.

For smooth, accurate cutting and snug-fitting, well-matched joints, instead of the coarser handsaw we use a dovetail saw or a back saw, which is really a thin crosscut saw with fine teeth, stiffened by a thick back. The range is wide, and you should select one with a reversible handle so that it can be used for either right-hand or left-hand work. Although a little more expensive than the ordinary back saw, this model is very much more versatile.

If you want to build up a really extensive set of saws, you should get one of the new patent pistol-grip saw handles, with a complete nest of interchangeable blades for cutting wood and metal: both coarse and fine compass saws, and the very wide range of small blades available for keyhole saws.

On no account forget to provide stable, sturdy frames for the coping saw and fret saw, with an adequate supply of blades of various sizes. These are ideal tools for fine straight saw cuts and for cutting out any unusual or irregularly curved shape. When fitted with the appropriate blades, they can also be used for fine metalwork.

There are many tools working on the boring principle, but the gimlet from the kitchen drawer will very quickly be discarded in favor of a handy bit brace with a set of auger bits and twist drills in various sizes. For very deep drillings we must have single-twist bits, and for large-diameter holes with clean-cut walls and a flat bottom we shall require a center bit.

All these bits are inserted into the steel jaws of the self-centering chuck, which locks, guides and drives them through the wood. The same chuck will also take a counter sink, which is not strictly a drill at all, but a milling cutter, useful for enlarging the head of the hole to seat wood-screws.

If your taste and skill in woodwork lie in the direction of fine, small work, you will not regret the purchase of a good push drill for use with small drill points.

A spiral-ratchet screwdriver is a similar tool. It has a straight drive-spindle acting on a spiral ratchet which is rotated right and left by the up-and-down movement of a sliding barrel element. With a suitable screwdriver bit inserted in the chuck, this tool makes possible a very neat job of setting decorative rows of screw-heads by hand.

Before the invention of machines, the ordinary mechanical needs of the woodworker had resulted in the development of planes of many different types. Only two of these are of real importance to the modern craftsman: the jack plane and the smooth plane. The jack plane may be adjusted for coarse or fine work, by turning the adjusting nut in front of the handle. It is a general purpose plane for taking off thick or thin shavings and trueing up lengths of lumber prior to finishing. The plane iron or cutter is covered by a steel cap of the same width, which leaves the merest fraction ($1/16''$) of the cutter uncovered. The cap curls and breaks the shaving and prevents cross-grain wood from splitting in front of the cutting edge. The smooth plane is used to plane broad surfaces and prepare them for final sanding. It can also be used to plane edges and ends. It is smaller than the jack plane, varying between 6″ and 10″.

Never grudge the price of a good plane. If you want to be quite sure that you have got a good tool, see that it is a plane of standard size, and that the cutter is of the finest steel, scientifically hardened and tested and about 2″ wide.

The first attempts at planing are never easy, and the first shavings will not be effortlessly produced or smooth as silk. An easier tool to handle is the spoke shave, which works on the same principle as the plane but is drawn towards the body instead of being pushed away from it. The spoke shave can be fitted with a variety of blades and is useful for smoothing concave faces or for cleaning up flat surfaces.

The razor-sharp cutting edge takes off an even shaving as fine as a silken thread. On small surfaces a similar fine finish could be obtained with a fragment of window-glass, suitably mounted in a handle. Note that it is easier to smash a window-pane for this purpose, than it is to sharpen a spoke shave cutter. It is less troublesome to fit a new blade.

It is the common experience of beginners that smooth facing tools are best used on flat surfaces. With plain-edged and bevel-edged chisels we can begin to shape our wood in a third dimension: we can chisel out slots and all kinds of holes, and we can cut notches, mortises, and rabbets for jointing work. The function of both types of chisel is in principle the same. They differ only in one respect: the cross-section of the plain chisel is rectangular, while that of the bevel-edge chisel has sloping sides.

When you buy a set of chisels, choose the bevel-edge type, because these are much easier to use than plain-edged chisels and they are unquestionably better suited to the light work involved in craft carpentry.

The number of chisels we need, and the range of sizes, will depend on the kind of work we intend to do. A set of three chisels, with blades $3/8''$, $1/2''$ and $5/8''$ wide, should be enough for all ordinary needs. When selecting a chisel, pay careful attention to the quality of the steel, but be sure that you also examine the shoulder, handle and head. A chisel handle with top and bottom surfaces slightly flattened, so as to be parallel with the working direction of the iron, is more easily controlled by the hand than a round handle. Note that the handle should be reinforced by an iron or leather tip and by a ferrule at the end of the blade. It is frequently necessary to increase the cutting power of the chisel by using a mallet, and unprotected chisel heads will not long survive heavy mallet blows or other forms of rough treatment.

As soon as you leave the simple cutting of flat surfaces for the shaping and molding of curves, you leave the domain of the carpenter for that of the wood carver. You will therefore have less need of the flat chisel, and will require instead carving knives, gouges and veiners. It is at this point that the woodworker has to make up his mind about the sacrifices he is prepared to make to his creative urge, since here, as in all other handicrafts, success will not depend simply upon a fine array of tools. An assortment of chisels and gouges, when tastefully suspended on a peg-board, makes a very striking impression on the casual visitor, but the display will serve no useful purpose until dexterity carefully acquired, and talent patiently fostered, have put the amateur carver in a position to compete honorably with the professional. It is quite unnecessary to collect a large tool-kit before you begin creative work. The only advantage to be gained from any tool-kit is the lightening of labor—and the operative word is labor.

The knives and gouges used by the wood carver for fine work differ from a carpenter's chisels in two respects: they are very much lighter in the hand, and the eight-sided handles have no reinforcing tip or ferrule. These reinforcements would be superfluous on small gouges, since the mallet is not normally used on them: they are forced through the wood by the carver's unassisted hand.

Carving tools do for the wood carver what the pen does for the calligrapher: they facilitate fine work on a small scale. The rougher,

heavier starting work, however, should be done either with a large, ferrule-protected carpenter's gouge, since this tool will tolerate a heavy blow, or with a strong, broad chisel with a skewed cutting edge.

For the craftsman with wood-carving ambitions, the gouge is an important tool. Gouges are made with a great variety of cutting edges, from the flat for rough dressing to the U-shaped for lighter and more accurate work. The bent or spoon gouge is useful for finishing touches and for chipping surplus wood from inaccessible corners, deep slots and grooves.

Gouge irons are normally stamped with a number which indicates the shape of the blade. Numbers 1 to 4 are reserved for flat or gently-curved irons. Numbers 5 to 8 are true gouges, and numbers 9 to 11 are sharply curved, U-shaped blades. Skew chisels, with edges sloping at an angle to right or left of the cutting line, are driven into the wood with a light mallet or with the ball of the thumb, and the wider ones are ideal for marking out and starting the work. A useful tool for making deep and narrow grooves with clean edges is the veiner or V-tool, which has an angular V-shaped blade. This tool, which is more useful to the block-maker than the carver, is very difficult to sharpen.

Thus a great variety of flattened, curved or U-shaped blades is available, and this very profusion may explain why so many craftsmen who take up wood carving with enthusiasm are inclined to give up in despair. The prudent learner will severely limit his purchases of cutting tools until he has gained a fair knowledge of how to use them. He must realize that he has a long road to travel before he reaches proficiency, and he should be willing to start with a bare minimum of equipment. His starting kit will be adequate if it contains the following items:

two skew chisels, one $^3/_8''$ and one $^5/_8''$, two flattened No. 4 straight gouges, one $^3/_8''$ and one $^1/_2''$, and two No. 10 U-shaped gouges, one $^3/_{16}''$ and one $^1/_4''$. If we add bent versions of the narrower of the two flattened gouges and of both the U-tools, we shall be very well equipped to tackle even difficult problems. We shall, moreover, prolong the life of our expensive chipping tools, and work more quickly, if we use a broad and sturdy carpenter's gouge to hack out the crude shape of our design.

Our set of cutting tools should be completed by adding one or two carving knives with short, strong blades. These are handy for incised and chip carving and for small impromptu carved work.

There are some marginal activities connected with wood carving where continuous work with the gouges might be altogether too tedious, the rounding and smoothing of pins and studs, or the trimming of a hammer handle, for example, might very well be done with a half-round, pointed wood rasp. For smoothing the inside faces of hollow forms, use a shoemaker's rasp, a special tool with two short, half-round or spoon-shaped rasps at either end of a common handle, like the twin blades of a kayak paddle.

Small Hand Tools
Auxiliary Tools

In addition to the primary tools already named, a whole series of small auxiliary tools has been developed to meet practical needs and lighten the craftsman's work. One of these is the nail set, used on heavily nailed joints for driving the head of the nail below the surface of the wood. Another small, but useful tool is the scratch awl for marking the positions of pins, nails, and drilling points, and for indicating dimensions. If it is necessary to drill a large number of holes to a uniform depth, it is very useful to have a bit gage to guarantee this uniformity. This is a simple attachment to the bit that prevents it from penetrating too far. The depth of hole required is pre-set before starting to drill. Any handyman can make a simple instrument of this kind for himself. All he needs is a block of hard wood and a few short lengths of stiff wire.

A carpenter should know how to sharpen and set the teeth of his saw. He will need a three-cornered saw file, a saw set, and a saw vise or filing clamp to hold the saw blade. A satisfactory home-made saw clamp can be constructed from a 6-inch board with a saw cut along one edge extending about three-quarters of the way through the wood. This will make a sufficiently sturdy filing board. Secure it in the bench vise with the saw cut on top. Fit the back of the saw blade into the saw cut, and you will be able to file the teeth as required. Move the saw blade through the saw cut as you work, so that filing and setting are always done over the board, where the saw is held tightest.

Every woodworker must have a good bench with a satisfactory means of holding the work. If you expect to do only light work or lack the space for setting up a regular carpenter's bench with a full-size bench vise, you can improvise a makeshift worktop out of any rugged and expendable table. In doing so you will have to utilize the clamp, one of the most versatile of the woodworker's auxiliary tools.

Clamps are available in many shapes and sizes, from small spring-operated clips that are prised open and slipped over the work to huge bar clamps capable of exerting quite considerable pressures. Clamps are made of both wood and steel, but the steel ones will generally give more satisfaction. The length of the thread and the maximum jaw clearance are selected according to the requirements of the work in hand. The C-clamp renders an important service whenever gluing jobs have to be done. The jaws will hold the parts together under just the right pressure until the glue has set. Clamps can also be used in planing two or more boards to the same dimensions, in drilling matching dowel holes, and in a variety of other operations where parts have to be held temporarily, but firmly together.

By means of a few clamps you can convert any rugged kitchen table into a useful makeshift work bench. Since the clamps can be fixed to both the front and the back of the table, they can be arranged to form a substitute vise, capable of holding all the ordinary sizes of work that the home craftsman is likely to meet. It is preferable, however, to make a detachable work-top to protect and reinforce the kitchen table during your woodworking sessions. This could be constructed of a beechwood plank some 2 inches thick, 16 inches wide, and slightly longer than the top of the table itself. Very much more serviceable than a single plank would be a wide, flat work-top made of several narrower planks glued together at the edges. For example, a useful top can be made by joining five four-inch planks to form a continuous, flat surface. This has a great advantage over the work-top consisting of a single plank in that it will certainly never warp, for, hard as it is, beechwood has an unfortunate tendency to deform under stress, and it should go without saying that our work bench, since it is literally the basis of all our work, must be perfectly smooth and flat.

Mount your beech planks on two stout cross pieces, positioned so that they fit closely against either end of the table top and prevent the working surface from slipping. If the table is completely expendable, drill matching holes through both work-top and table and clamp the two together with heavy bolts and wing nuts. If you cannot afford to sacrifice the table, you will have to make do with C-clamps. The work-top will be sitting correctly if it projects three inches beyond the front edge of the table.

The reason for this will be clear when we come to provide a means of holding the work in place. A clamping force directed in one direction only is useless if there is no resistance strong enough to withstand the pressure it exerts. The standard woodworker's bench is fitted with a steel bench stop specially designed to provide such a resistance. This is the principle we shall apply in constructing our makeshift work-top.

Instead of going to the lengths of forging steel, we shall simply use a length of tough beechwood measuring $1^1/_4'' \times 1^1/_4''$. This will form the stem of our bench stop. Into the top of this stem a small iron bracket is recessed so that its projecting leg is flush with the end face of the stem. The vertical leg of the bracket should be long enough to take two screws. Before screwing on the bracket, cut a vee-notch in the projecting leg to form two sharp tongues, each of which should be beveled on the underside.

The bench will now have to be slotted to receive the bench stop. Make this slot on the left hand side of the bench, $1^3/_4''$ from the front edge and $2^1/_2''$ from the side. It is better to wait until this slot has been cut and its walls checked to make sure they are perfectly vertical, before planing down the stem of the stop to its final thickness. When the stop has been inserted in the slot, any board on which you are working can be held firmly in place by forcing it against the sharp tongues of the iron bracket.

The thicker the workpiece, the further the bench stop is pulled out to retain it. In order to make the bench stop hold in any position without slipping, a leaf spring can be screwed to the back of the stem. A strong piece of clock spring or a strip of steel cut from an old saw blade is suitable for this purpose. The screws should be located near the bottom of the stem. The necessary tension is obtained by inserting a small wooden wedge between the spring and the stem just above the fixing screws.

A somewhat cruder bench stop for small work can be made from a discarded fret saw table. A short nail is driven into each fork of the vee-notch. Then the heads are nipped off and the shanks filed to a point. The converted saw table is clamped to the left hand side of the work-top, where it will render the same service for thinner stock as the adjustable bench stop does for thicker pieces. The same device can be used for thicker material if it is mounted on a block of wood to give the nail points more clearance.

Positive pressure is provided by means of a screw clamp. This will have to be a large and expensive one with an arm at least four, and preferably six inches longer than the work-top is wide. The best arrangement is to let the arm of the clamp rest against the left hand side of the work-top so that the workpiece is gripped solidly between the jaw of the clamp and the front edge of the bench. A small piece of waste inserted between the clamp and the workpiece will prevent the latter from being crushed. Admittedly, this is a crude improvisation, but we can refine on it by chiseling out a groove in the side of the work-top designed to receive the long arm of the clamp. If a similar recess is formed in the back of the work-top for the short transverse arm, we not only gain an inch or so of extra clearance in front, but the clamp as a whole will rest securely in the bench. It is now possible to release the clamp without any fear of it dropping on our foot. The situation will be even better if

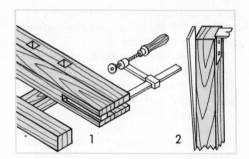

Makeshift workbench made of several planks: 1 clamp with recessed arm, 2 home-made hardwood bench stop.

the work-top is composed of several narrow planks laid side by side. The recess of the transverse arm of the clamp can then be formed in the back of the second or third plank from the front, before the work top is glued together. The assembled top will thus contain a slot long enough for the clamp to be slid in from the left. Apart from its neatness, this solution has the advantage of enabling us to get away with a much smaller screw clamp.

Those who feel disinclined to go to these lengths will find that hardware stores sell a number of lightweight vises and handy clamping tools which will serve much the same purpose as those described above. For serious work, however, there is no real substitute for a well-built bench and a sturdy woodworker's vise.

Marking and Measuring

The professional finish of sharp, clean lines and the sturdy service of a well-made article are only obtainable by working carefully to measurements. Therefore the selection of our measuring and marking tools should be a leisurely and careful process. It is better to measure and mark out your principal dimensions with the time-honored

Measuring tools

folding rule than to rely on a simple straight rule or a push-pull metal tape. The best rules are made of hornbeam.

The most important angle for any workman is the right-angle, and this is guaranteed for him by the try-square. This tool has two arms, the thick handle serving to hold and reinforce a thin blade for marking-out. The blade should be of steel with a glass-hard edge, and it should be firmly riveted into the handle. When scribing an angle of 45° use a bevel square. To cut the bevels marked out by this tool we need a miter-box

—a long, open-ended box with perpendicular slots cut at various angles through the walls to guide the blade of the back saw. The box thus functions as both an angle-setting device and a tool guide. An adjustable bevel square will enable you to mark off any angle between 0° and 180°.

Of equal importance to the worker in wood is the marking gage, used to scribe all lines parallel to the length of the board. This tool consists of a flat head through which slide one or two adjustable scales. These are set to the width to be measured. A dimension line is scored in the surface of the wood by applying pressure to the scriber in the sliding arm of the gage. The point of the scriber is set to lead into the work.

Of the caliper-type instruments, the dividers are perhaps the most important for a carpenter. Dividers are used for scribing an arc, a full circle, or a combination of both in laying out a curved design. Dividers are much more useful in a workshop than a compass with a pencil. If you plan to do a lot of wood carving, which will require checking outside diameters (and sometimes inside diameters), you should add to your range of instruments a pair of inside calipers and a pair of outside calipers. A precision instrument for taking quick and accurate outside measurements and for determining the thickness of materials is the micrometer caliper. A very sophisticated tool of this type is used by engineers. It allows the direct reading of both inside and outside measurements on one instrument. Before you buy this rather expensive model, take stock of your activities and be quite sure that you will really need it.

The same remark might also be applied to the level, which is undoubtedly of the greatest value for determining that a surface is truly flat or truly vertical. Whether you would be justified in adding a high-quality level to

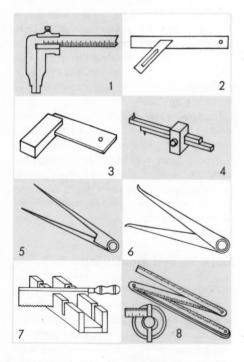

Marking and measuring tools: 1 sliding calipers, 2 bevel square, 3 try-square, 4 marking gage, 5 dividers, 6 inside calipers, 7 miter-box, 8 folding rule and tape rule.

your equipment will depend upon the type, size and amount of craftwork you have in mind.

Metalworking Tools

The marking and measuring tools used for woodworking are employed in precisely the same way in the metalworking shop. We need not, therefore, repeat what has been said above, but will describe some alternative or additional tools.

Cutting lines on sheet metal can be marked out with a scriber or scratch awl. Use a center punch to mark the position of individual points. This tool has a 90° hardened steel point. It is also used to mark the starting position for drilling so that the point of the drill will not slip on the smooth metal surface. The pin punch has a round flat end. It is used for knocking out pins and rivets or for punching small holes in thin sheet metal.

Of the shaping tools used to remove surplus material, the file is undoubtedly the most important. There is no need to lay in an elaborate set of files immediately; we can make do for a start with an ordinary flat file of medium fineness about 8 inches long. For fine metalwork, a smooth-cut key file or a pointed needle file will be very useful. These are similar in shape to locksmiths' files, but the blades are only 4 inches long, and can be used with or without handles.

In metalworking the cold chisel serves much the same purpose as the carpenter's chisel in carpentry. Four types are made, but for us the most useful one will be the round-nose cold chisel, for chipping medium sheet metal. The flat cold chisel, used for cutting steel plate or thick sheet metal in a vise, is of secondary importance. The cape chisel is only used for taking off heavy chips, an operation we shall seldom per-

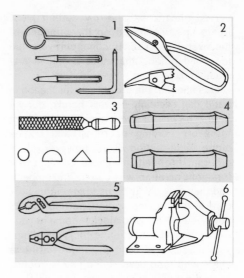

Indispensable tools for the metalworker: 1 scriber, pin punch, center punch, reamer, 2 tinner's snips, 3 files with different cross sections, 4 cold chisels, round-nose and flat, 5 gas pliers and side-cutting pliers, 6 bench vise.

form, so that we do not need to add this tool to our kit.

Sooner or later, however, we shall need something for cutting through a pipe, or tube, or a steel bar, or for slicing the head off a thick rivet. For these operations we use a hack saw with an exchangeable blade. Like the woodworker's coping saw, the hack saw cuts by impact, having very fine chisel-teeth which cannot be sharpened. When the blade becomes dull, it must be changed for a new one. When sawing soft material use a coarse-tooth blade of non-ferrous metal. It is important to have on hand a reserve of special blades for your metal saw.

We shall frequently need to cut thin sheet metal, and for this purpose we shall use tinner's snips. For cutting straight lines or following outside curves, use shears with straight, broad jaws, but for cutting out holes and following inside curves, use curved shears with narrow cutting jaws. Pliers are also based on the principle of the lever. They are an uncommonly versatile tool, and among the most useful in any metalworking shop.

Gas pliers of the proper size for the job in hand can certainly be very handy, but we should be on our guard against using them for every holding operation that comes along. Side-cutting pliers, however, are a different proposition. These combine the functions of tongs, wire cutters and nippers, and they may safely be used for eighty percent of the holding and supporting operations you are likely to meet. If some of your work involves delicate and tricky handling, you should also have a pair of flat-nose pliers with long jaws, and a pair of round-nose pliers with tapered jaws. You will then be in a position to tackle really difficult work requiring both manual dexterity and technical skill.

For some classes of work a sturdy pipe wrench, if not too clumsy, will be found very useful. The jaw clearance on these tools can be adjusted by a simple movement of the knurled nut, so that the tool can be set to apply gripping forces acting roughly in parallel. In an emergency, a pipe wrench will perform the work of a simple open-end wrench, but however you apply it, you must use it correctly: while turning, the top jaw must grip and pull, the lower jaw must push. Otherwise, if the work is hard, the jaws will slip, and your knuckles will suffer.

Every workshop has at least one unvarying law: loosen your nuts with a wrench of the correct size. Nuts loosened with the wrong wrench (or, even worse, with pliers or pincers), will soon lose their sharp edges, and they will be even more difficult to move. Where nuts and bolts are in regular use, a set of first-class plain wrenches in all the standard sizes is indispensable. They should be made of hardened chromium steel. If you seldom use nuts and bolts, you will find that a single adjustable offset wrench will meet all your needs. Remember that the same rule applies to it as to the pipe wrench: the top jaw pulls, the bottom jaw pushes.

Our screw sizes will generally match a standard screwdriver with a grooved or flattened handle and a $1/4''$ blade. Twisted wood screws with ploughed-up slots can give a lot of trouble, so treat your screws with respect, using only a screwdriver that has been kept in good condition. When you start work, select a screwdriver with a blade of the correct length and width for the job. The sides of the blade should be practically parallel, and the working edge should be dead straight, neither rounded nor beveled, or it will slip out of the slot. The tip should be a good fit in the slot, reaching to its full depth. Thus it will be securely bedded, and the whole of the twisting force exerted will be effectively applied.

A good general-purpose hammer for the metalworking shop is a ball-peen hammer with a chamfered, hardened and tempered head weighing about 12 ounces. This, however, is not a suitable hammer for all the jobs that come along. For stretching thin sheet we need a cross-peen (or straight peen) hammer, and for straightening thin material on the anvil we should use a wooden mallet or a rubber-faced hammer. Soft-faced hammers allow a certain recovery of the metal, thus avoiding the otherwise inevitable weakening and thinning of the metal structure under the impact of the tool.

Some metalworking processes will require a yielding surface, others a hard anvil. Punching, stamping and chiseling are operations best carried out on a semi-hard bed, for which purpose the end grain of a hardwood block would be ideal. A small planishing block of smooth steel is useful for light work requiring a hard bed, but this is no substitute for a lightweight anvil. A small bench anvil weighing not more than 11 or 12 lb will be sufficient for all the heavy work we are normally likely to get. A couple of feet of old rail makes an excellent substitute.

We now come to an essential piece of equipment—the bench vise. Several patterns are on the market, but we shall only be interested in one of these, the sturdy steel bench vise, with jaws made of hardened and tempered steel; it is secured to the bench by four bolts passing through a rugged bed-plate. A hand vise has the advantage of being portable and less bulky, but is only suitable for holding small pieces.

We shall need a couple of small hand tools for riveting work; a pair of rivet tongs, and a rivet set. Use the tongs to draw the parts of the work tightly together on the stake or anvil before inserting the rivets. On one side of one end of the rivet set there is a spherical depression which serves to finish off the rivet ends, giving them a uniform, exact shape and great durability. When preparing thick metal for riveting, drill the holes by machine or hand-drill. Thin sheet can be punched by hand. Use a reamer to round off the hole and remove the burr. An angular reamer, four- or six-sided, is a very useful tool for this purpose.

Those planning to do some coppersmithing jobs involving cold-working procedures will need a certain amount of special equipment to deal with two important stages of the work: stretching and upsetting. It is necessary to have quite a series of miniature anvils or stakes, with flat, curved and angular surfaces. When in use, the stake is held in the vise or stands in a square socket in a special stake-holder or bench plate. The first item in your series of stakes should be a simple bending stake. This is handy for many purposes, and is especially useful for bending edges and angles on sheet metal. The half-moon stake is ideal for bending edges on curved shapes, either to form a hem or for the purpose of making a seam. The square stake has a flat, square face and is used for planishing thin sheet and for bending and riveting. The common T-stake has a rounded end for raising bowl-shaped forms, while the other arm of the T forms a long, narrow anvil for small work.

The active counterpart of our array of stakes is the hammer. Metalworkers' hammers have a special feature: they have no peens. Instead they have two faces, and they take their names from the varied shapes of these faces. Thus, the planishing hammer has one square and one round face, while the raising hammer has two hemispherical faces and is used for raising dome-shaped forms. The half-round faces of the creasing hammer can be used for stretching work.

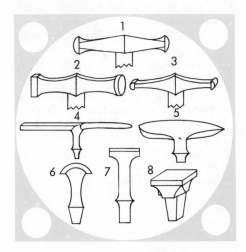

Special hammers and stakes for metal work: 1 raising hammer, 2 planishing hammer, 3 hollowing hammer, 4/5 T-stakes, 6 half-moon or flanging stake, 7 bending stake, 8 square stake.

Soldering tools

In the entire vast range of metalworking processes there is only one form of hot-working that will be of interest to readers of this book. This is soldering. Our principal tool is of course the soldering iron, formerly a copper bit heated in a brazier. Nowadays the iron is heated electrically by means of a built-in resistance, giving a better job with cleaner conditions of work. A good iron of this type has an adjustable heating head and screw tips which can be replaced. With a modern iron very fine work can be done even in recesses that are difficult to reach.

The ordinary pointed soldering stick or copper bit is much cheaper to buy. Either tool can be heated over a bunsen burner, a gas-ring, or a blow-torch. A blow-torch can also be used to warm the work so that the solder does not cool and set too quickly. A blow-torch needs to be used with prudence, since it is in fact a miniature flame-thrower and can develop temperatures quite high enough to reduce an entire workshop to ashes in a few minutes. It should however be tolerated for another property much more serviceable: where prolonged hammering has hardened a metal, the blow-torch can be used to anneal it and restore its ductility.

We may complete our soldering equipment by adding to it a triangular scraper for the removal of flux residue, and a soldering brick (solid sal ammoniac) for cleaning the tip after use. Fluxes and soldering tin in stick, block, and wire form will not be described in detail, because, like nails and screws, they belong among the consumable stores of the workshop, and not among the tools.

Care of Tools

A good tool deserves careful treatment. Even the best and most expensive tool will very quickly deteriorate if it is not put carefully away when not in use. It is not desirable to pile your tools into a box: keen edges will be dulled, and the hammer head will be chipped, or else it will knock the teeth out of the saw. If a tool chest is unavoidable, let it be a flat one, with plenty of straps and pockets in which each tool can rest with comparative safety.

When your stock of tools increases beyond the capacity of a chest, it is time to provide a permanent and comfortable home for them in the form of a tool board. Thus each tool will have a place of its own, and all tools will be plainly in view. Design your board with a view to maximum use of storage space, but be careful that no one tool is concealed by any other—there should be no contact between any tools when hanging on the board. Drills and other small pieces should be placed in a drill stand, and all chisels should be arranged according to size and with the cutting edge downwards. Chisels should always be suspended by clips between shoulder and handle. Always press the chisel into the clip from the front: never try to insert it from above. Aim at instant accessibility for every tool in the rack, so that you can take the tool you want without delay and with one hand, and replace it as easily when you have finished with it.

Wood-carving tools and knives can be stored in handy folding wallets made of sailcloth, leather or plastic, in which each tool fits into a separate pocket. Thus the cutting edges cannot be damaged by contact even when the wallet is rolled up and put away. This is a very useful gadget for the carver who carries his tools about with him.

The greatest enemy of tools is humidity, which plays a major part in the corrosion of iron and steel. Where tools are used out of doors, they are, of course, much more exposed to attack by damp. A common example is the saw used for felling timber or cutting up green lumber. All such tools should be dried and cleaned immediately after use, and the entire surface of the metal coated with a light film of oil. All tools should be regularly coated with bone-oil or vaseline. If flakes of rust appear, in spite of these precautions, they should be removed with a little kerosene. Do not use sandpaper, as the results obtained with it are deceptive: the emery scores the surface of the metal or scratches the plating, providing many new points for corrosive attack; thus rusting is actually promoted by this method of cleaning. All the moving parts of a tool, and all sliding parts in contact, must be regularly greased: the mechanism of a drill, the screw of a vise, and the joints of pliers are instances, and the conscientious craftsman will not wait until they begin to squeak or jam, before he attends to them. There is

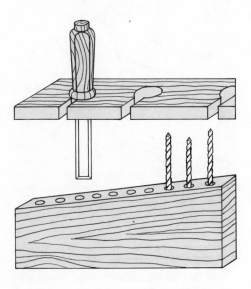

Tool rack and drill stand.

only one steel tool which objects to oil or grease of any kind, and that is the file. The work of a file is not done by sliding, but by biting—and it can only bite effectively if the blade is most carefully protected from contact with grease. Even a finger-print on the blade will leave a zone of dullness. Use kerosene and a wire brush to clean an oily file, and bear in mind that files, like other tools, need to be cleaned after every working session if they are to do a satisfactory job with their properties unimpaired.

The work involved in cleaning tools must be regarded as an indispensable activity. Provide time for this job, and your tools will reward you by giving you better service. Grease, dust, and metal filings are ingredients that will form an abrasive deposit on exposed metal surfaces. Even small amounts can have a considerable abrading effect. Now and then, the bottom of the plane is bound to pass over a resinous patch on the surface of the work, and the contact will foul it. Glue, paint or lacquer spilt on the wood will also foul the work surface, and if allowed to dry they will form a hard, horny patch which will, of course, make smooth, clean planing impossible. Therefore—always keep both the working surfaces and the tools perfectly clean, and lightly oil your tools before you begin to use them.

The teeth of the saw will be very much more efficient if they are given a regular and vigorous "toothbrush drill", especially after sawing green wood. Metal saws, coping saws and fret saws should always be allowed to rest after use, that is the blades should be slackened.

The moment you notice the slightest trace of abrasion or burring on a tool—for example on the edges or shoulders of chisel irons, on the backs of plane irons when they have seen good service, on punches and nail sets, on the edges of steel bench hooks which have suffered misuse as anvils—you must immediately deal with it, if only for your own safety. Any tool that is battered and damaged, or shows signs of wear, not only is a poor testimonial to its owner's interest in the condition of his tools, but may actually be dangerous. If a ridge of metal is left on the face of a tool, it may cut like a knife—in the wrong place. Under the impact of a hammer blow it may fly with the speed of a bullet—into your eye. The heads of tools struck with the hammer should be filed down at the edges to a narrow chamfer.

It is wrong to suggest that the great variety of modern tools is a device of the makers to extract money out of the poor craftsman. There may be cases in which some particular feature is overrefined, but in general the rule holds good, that a tool is designed for a given purpose, and must be used for that purpose alone. Do not attempt to do the work of a screwdriver with a framing chisel, or hammer nails with your pliers. Handle your tools carefully and correctly, and you will be able to do with them everything for which they were designed; treat them badly, and both you and they will very soon cease to do good work.

The sharpening of plane irons and other cutting tools is undoubtedly the most important duty in the care of tools. A dull blade is worse than no blade at all, for it sends up the accident and injury rate.

A moderately hard medium-grit grinding wheel is probably the best general purpose sharpener for a craft workshop. When you buy a wheel of this type, select one of fairly large diameter and not too narrow. If your wheel is too small, the curvature of the grinding surface will be too steep, and the result will be the removal of too much metal, and a hollow bevel on the blade. Your iron will still cut, and it will do so quite efficiently

for a short time, but the edge will soon be lost: your dull blade will have to be ground again, and frequent grinding soon wears out the tool. We may put the warning in another way: a small wheel eats the tool, and though cheap to buy, is very expensive in the long run.

Any iron, whether it is a plane iron or the blade of a chisel, cuts with its bevel as well as with its cutting edge. The bevel must be neither too steep nor too flat. If the bevel is too steep the iron will jam in the wood; if it is long and thin, it will certainly cut, but it will wear out quickly, will be weak, and will tend to nick. There is no generally acceptable grinding angle for the sharpening of cutting tools; this is one of the details which is only learned by practice. As a generalization, the bevel should be a little longer for the softwoods than for hardwood timbers. Carpenters have a rule of thumb for the bevel: it

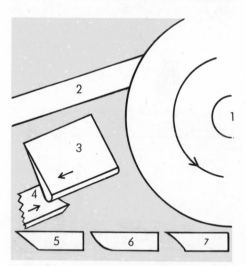

Correct sharpening of tools: the grindstone (1) rotates against the blade of the tool (2). The hollow face of the gouge (4) is rubbed with the rounded edge of an oil stone (3) in the direction of the handle. 5 correctly ground bevel. 6 convex cutting edge. 7 concave cutting edge.

should be a little longer than twice the thickness of the iron.

The ideal bevel is a mathematically plane surface. A dished or concave bevel is a lesser evil than a convex one. An iron with a convex bevel will never cut well, however sharp it may be, because the iron will tend to slip over the surface of the work. This defect is the usual explanation for the bewilderment of the novice, when in spite of the most energetic grinding he cannot get any edge on his iron, though he wears himself out, and grinds the blade right down to the crown.

Only the bevel is ground, never the flat side of the plane iron. The grinding wheel should turn against the iron. Since the wheel runs dry, grinding must proceed very carefully at every stage. The finer the grit in the wheel, and the faster the wheel turns, the greater the amount of heat generated by grinding friction, until at the point when grinding is almost finished, the blade glows a dull blue color. This color will persist until the metal cools. Cooling must be rapid, or the steel will be brittle and have no cutting edge. Therefore, while you are grinding your irons, have a quenching tank near at hand: a bucket of cold water in which the irons can be dipped as often as necessary, so that they can make a good recovery from the strain and rough handling they have had on the abrasive wheel.

Continue the grinding process until a uniform thin wire edge is formed along the flat face of the blade. Remove this wire by a final fine honing on the oil stone. Your stone should be perfectly flat and not too hard. Arkansas stone, composed of pure silica, makes a good natural oil stone. Artificial oil stones have the advantage of cutting faster and being available in any degree of fineness.

Use sufficient oil on the stone to keep the surface moist. First rub the flat face of the iron with a gentle rotary movement over the stone, then bring the bevel into contact and move it backwards and forwards in a straight line parallel with the long edges of the stone. Since whetting is a finishing process, apply only a very moderate pressure to the iron, and continue alternately as above until no shiny area, bluntness or grinding wire remains visible on the blade. While the oil stone is in use, clean off the grinding slime occasionally. Never attempt to whet your irons on a dry stone. A thin flat oil stone is obviously useless for whetting the curved edges of gouges. You can whet your gouges on a special stone with rounded sides.

It is often useful to whet an iron on a corundum stone before the final honing on the oil stone, as this will prolong the cutting life of the blade. Test the sharpness of the edge by shaving off the hair on your forearm: if the blade gives a close and instant shave, it is ready for use.

Before you put the finishing touches to carved woodwork, give the edges of your carving tools a few strokes on a leather strap touched with a trace of solder or black lead. This small attention will improve the iron greatly, and it will produce a remarkably fine, clean cut under which the grain of the wood will be plainly visible.

Saws must be set before they are sharpened. If you look at a saw blade, you can see that alternate teeth are bent to right and left of the cutting line. By this means the kerf is made wider than the thickness of the saw blade, so that the teeth can carry away the sawdust and the saw blade does not bind in the saw cut. The more pronounced the setting, the wider will be the kerf, and the greater the "play" for the saw blade. Be careful, however, not to make the saw cut too wide: it should not exceed one-and-one-half times the thickness of the saw blade. Secure the saw blade in a saw vise or filing clamp, so that it cannot spring or slip, and set the teeth with a saw set, bending first all the left-hand teeth, then all the right-hand teeth. The setting must be perfectly regular and alternate, or the blade will leave the cutting line.

It is quite commonly believed that the setting of saw teeth is a job to be done once and once only in the lifetime of a saw. This is an error. Every time a saw is sharpened, a minute quantity of metal is abraded from the points of the teeth, and at the same time the gullet depth tends to increase. In addition, the set itself is gradually flattened out so that the blade will tend to bind in the saw cut, particularly if the saw is unskillfully used. When the teeth have been set, they must be sharpened in a filing clamp with a three-cornered file. Begin at the free end and work tooth by tooth along the whole of the blade. File back and breast of adjacent teeth simultaneously. Never try to sharpen a saw with any tool other than a three-cornered file, and put both hands to the file, the right hand grasping the handle, the left hand on the point, to raise it slightly at the end of the stroke. You will not want the cutting edge of your saw to look like a scenic railway, so give each tooth space the same number of filing strokes without varying the pressure. Inspect the finished work for worn points. If there are none, the saw has been properly sharpened and is again ready for use.

WHAT'S THAT?

3

A Glossary of Terms in Common Use Amongst Craftsmen

A

Acetone. A colorless, easily inflammable liquid with a characteristic smell; evaporates even at room temperature on account of its very low boiling point (56°C). Acetone is obtained from the dry distillation of wood. It can be mixed with water, alcohol, and ether. It serves as a solvent for organic and inorganic substances used in the manufacture of paints and adhesives and as a starting material for many other products. Caution: because of its inflammability acetone should always be kept in well-stoppered containers.

Adjustable Cutter. Knife with a strong narrow four-bevel blade ground to a sharp point. Useful for cutting paper, foil, leather, cardboard, etc. The adjustable blade is held by a clamping screw in the handle.

Aggregates. See mortar.

Alabaster. See gypsum.

Ampere. The practical unit of electric current (written amp.or simply A).

Anchor. A term applied to a wide range of devices that can be embedded in walls and ceilings and from which objects of various kinds can be suspended. Mirrors, picture frames, and similar light loads can be hung from masonry walls simply by inserting round wooden dowels into predrilled holes (carbide drill), which are then plugged with plaster or cement mortar. Heavier loads call for wedge-shaped dowels with a broad base narrowing towards the top. A hole is chiseled out and the dowel is inserted base first and cemented in place. In this case plaster will not be strong enough. Screw anchors, molly bolts, and expansion shields of various kinds are versatile and sophisticated types of anchors, all of which work on the same principle. Driving in the screw or bolt forces the material of the anchor apart and compresses it against the sides of the hole. For this reason the hole must not be made too big, but should exactly match the diameter of the anchor. Special drills can be purchased for this purpose.

Animal Glue. A glue obtained by boiling animal matter (bones, hooves, hides) in water. Its action depends on the ability of the proteins (glutin) to gelatinize. Swells in cold water and dissolves in hot water. The best known animal glue is joiner's glue which is sold as flakes or in powder form (fish glue from fish waste, skin glue from animal hides). Edible gelatin is a pure form of glutin.

Arkansas Stone. A stone used for sharpening cutting tools. Also called oil stone because the honing is done with oil rather than water. Oil stones should not be allowed to dry out, but should be kept in kerosene.

B

Balsa Wood. Yellowish-white, soft to medium hard species from Central and Northern South America. The lightest timber in the world, it is used by the natives for building boats and rafts. Balsa is used in the aircraft industry and as an insulating material. The craftsman can make good use of it in building model aircraft and ships.

Bastard File. See Files.

Bevel. A bevel is formed on a piece of wood or metal by cutting off the edge on the slant. Typical examples are the bevel-edged chisel and the sharp edges of all cutting tools. These tools may have a single bevel (wood chisels, plane irons) or a double bevel (knives, cold chisels).

Binders. In general, substances used to hold solid particles together. In paints the binder is the nonvolatile part of the vehicle. The most important paint binders are linseed oil and boiled linseed oil for oil paints, natural resins for lacquers, emulsions of water and oil or synthetic resins for emulsion (water-base) paints, and size for distempers. The binder is responsible for the formation of the continuous film in which the pigment is trapped when the paint dries.

At the same time it serves to develop a strong bond between the paint and the surface to which it is applied.

In building, the cement and lime in mortar and concrete can also be described as binders, since they serve to hold the sand and gravel together in a solid mass.

Block Plane. See planing.

Body Colors. In contrast to colored light, all colors that only become visible when light falls on them, hence all colors mixed with other substances or applied to an object in the form of a thin coating (paints).

Bow Saw. Saw with a coarse-toothed blade and a strong curved tubular steel handle for heavy duty bucking and working in cramped quarters. The triangular teeth are sharpened on both faces and the saw cuts in both directions.

Bunsen Burner. A gas burner designed by the German chemist and scientist Robert Bunsen (1811-1899), the principle of which is the same as that of the burners of a kitchen range. The gas flowing from the vertical tube of the Bunsen burner sucks in air through an adjustable opening, with the result that the temperature of the flame is considerably increased. If the air supply is correctly regulated, the Bunsen burner burns with a faintly luminous flame.

C

Carbon Tetrachloride. A colorless, easily boiling, incombustible liquid. Good solvent for resins, oils, fats, and waxes. Used as a cleaning agent. Caution: the vapors are harmful.

Cellophane. Trade name for cellulose film. Consists of hydrate cellulose made flexible by the addition of certain plasticizers. Non-waterproof. Coated with lacquer will serve as a versatile packaging material. Often used as a substitute for the highly inflammable celluloid.

Cement. A binder for concrete and mortar consisting of fine-ground limestone, clay and marl. The most important type for building purposes is Portland cement. The quick-setting roman cement is similar in character, but contains more lime and is not suitable for concrete. White cement, obtained by removing the iron impurities, is used where white concrete or white joints are required.

Chalk. A fine, white limestone. Chalk is used for drawing, cleaning, and polishing. It is also an ingredient of putty and is sometimes added to priming coats.

Chlorinated Rubber Varnishes. These varnishes are highly resistant to chemical action. They are sold in the form of solutions of chlorinated rubber in organic solvents. Since, unlike natural rubber, chlorinated rubber is very brittle, special plasticizers have to be added. Chlorinated rubber varnishes are used with special thinners and primers specified by the manufacturers. They are very quick-drying.

Chrome Glue. Joiner's glue (animal glue) made waterproof by adding chrome. To prepare, dissolve about two parts by weight of potassium dichromate in ten parts of water and add to hot joiner's glue. Since chrome glue is sensitive to light, it must be prepared and applied in a darkroom (red light). It should also be stored away from the light. When the glued parts are later exposed to the light, the glue and the chrome form a compound that will not dissolve in water.

Circuit Diagram. Wiring diagram. A schematic drawing of the electric circuit of a piece of electrical apparatus, showing both the arrangement of the wires and all the circuit elements and accessories, represented by standard symbols.

Clay. A sedimentary earth resulting from the weathering or alteration of aluminous or silicate rocks. The ceramic clays consist mainly of hydrous aluminum silicates (kaolinite) with admixtures of quartz, feldspar, mica, and calcite. When breathed on, the very fine-grained, dull clay body develops the characteristic clay smell. It absorbs water readily and in the moist state is more or less plastic, depending on the nature and amount of the admixtures present. According to the amount of pure clay material and non-plastic substances, we can distinguish between fat and lean clays. By firing in the furnace, shapes modeled in moist clay can be given permanence and strength. Loam is a sandy clay colored yellowish brown by the presence of iron hydroxide. Kaolin, called after the Chinese mountain Kau-ling and better known as China clay, consists mainly of the mineral kaolinite with admixtures of quartz and feldspar and is the raw material for porcelain.

Concrete. See mortar.

Coping Saw. A saw with a short, narrow blade held at both ends in a deeply recessed handle, for cutting curved shapes.

D

Dextrin. White or yellowish starch gum powder; completely soluble in hot water. Makes a paper paste when mixed with borax and alkali.

Dies. Tools for cutting external threads on cylindrical bolts and pipes. The most common type of die is the round split die, which can be adjusted for either a tight or a loose-fitting thread. The device used to hold the die while the thread is being cut is called a die stock.

Drawing Knife. Draw knife. A heavy two-handled knife with a straight or curved blade at right angles to the handles. Used for shaping spokes, cutting tool handles, removing the bark from logs, etc.

Drier. Added to the vehicle of paints and binders that contain drying oils to speed up the drying process (by absorbing oxygen). Organic salts of heavy metals such as lead, cobalt and manganese are those most commonly used. Most paints are now manufactured with the correct amount of drier already added.

E

Earth Colors. See pigments.

F

Farad. Unit of capacitance. The farad is too large for ordinary use and capacity measurements are usually made in terms of microfarads and micromicrofarads (or picofarads). The microfarad is one millionth of a farad and the micromicrofarad one millionth of a microfarad.

Files. Tools for smoothing and cutting metal, wood, plastics, and other materials. The work of abrasion is done by teeth formed by parallel furrows scored in the face of the file. These furrows are known as the "cut". We can distinguish between single and double cuts, depending on whether the furrows all run in the same direction or cross each other at a definite angle. Single-cut files are used for softer, double-cut files for harder materials. Rasps are coarse files, the teeth of which consist of individual projecting points rather than vee-shaped ridges extending across the face of the file. The harder the material, the finer the cut. Depending on the fineness of the cut we can distinguish between bastard files, smooth

files, and supersmooth files, the latter being used for the finest work and for finishing purposes. Files are also classified according to the shape of the cross section as flat, half-round, three-square, etc. Riffle files are double-ended and bent files useful for reaching inaccessible areas. Jeweler's files, used for delicate work, have no tang. During filing the workpiece should be clamped rigidly in the vise. Hold the file in the right hand with the thumb on top. The end of the file is guided by the heel of the left hand. Material is removed on the push stroke. Work steadily and evenly: push the file forward slowly under heavy pressure and pull it back quickly with the pressure removed. Always hold the file straight, never allow it to tilt or wobble. In working large pieces the file is guided over the surface in a roughly diagonal direction and shifted sideways by an amount not quite equal to its own width during each forward stroke. The direction of attack is continuously changed as the work proceeds. Watch each stroke carefully to make sure that the entire surface is being evenly abraded. Accurate filing calls for frequent checking with try-square and calipers.

When filing shoulders and dowels, the workpiece is clamped in the vise in such a way that the jaws are level with the base of the projecting part (see drawing). Use a flat file, the smooth edge of which will slide easily over the face of the material. In forming round dowels first file out a square shape, and then progressively remove the edges, until an exactly circular cross section is obtained. Never file against the hard jaws of the vise. During the first stages of the work a round washer can be placed over the rough dowel to keep the jaws of the vise and the file apart.

Keep files free of all forms of oil and grease. Do not touch the surface of the

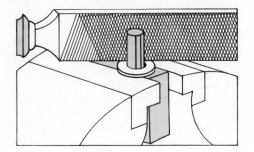

Shaping a dowel with a flat file. The face of the material is protected as long as possible by means of a washer.

workpiece with your fingers. While filing brush the face of the file occasionally with a wire brush.

Finishing is done with a smooth-faced file. Fine-cut files are not pushed back and forth, but rubbed over the surface broad side on. Chalk rubbed lightly into the file will reduce its tendency to fill with metal particles and score the wood.

Fixative. Transparent, lacquer-like protective coating for easily smeared drawings (in chalk, charcoal, pastel). Ordinary fixatives consist of resins or resin-like substances in easily evaporating solvents. They are sprayed onto the drawing with an atomizer, thus "fixing" it. Valuable originals can also be protected from smearing by spraying on several coats of zapon varnish (q. v.).

Flashed Glass. Cased glass. Unlike opaque glass, which is colored all the way through, flashed glass is made by coating or "flashing" the surface of a piece of clear glass with a thin layer of colored glass. Usually found in stained glass windows.

Float. A plasterer's tool consisting of a flat board of pine or poplar with a handle on the back. Used for laying on plaster and smoothing plaster surfaces. A somewhat lighter board padded with felt is used for rubbing

down fine-grained plasterwork. Steel trowels with strong, polished steel blades and wooden handles, are used for giving cement surfaces a dense finish.

Folding. The process of bending sheet metal to form a sharp or, in the case of thicker material, a slightly rounded fold. Sheet metal can be folded in a folding machine or over a stake, the jaws of a machinist's vise, the edge of an anvil, or any other convenient square steel edge.

Fore Plane. Jointer plane. Long bench planes used for dressing large flat surfaces; see also planing.

G

Glazing Colors. Transparent colors applied to a surface or parts of it in a layer so thin that the ground shows through. Also applied on top of an already painted surface to modify the tone.

Glycerin. Glycerol. A trivalent alcohol. A clear, colorless, syrupy, sweet liquid. Strongly hygroscopic. Obtained by saponification of fats in the soap industry. Can be mixed with water and alcohol in any proportions. Added to printing colors to keep them soft; may be used to freshen up dried out plasticine.

Graphite. Elementary carbon. Used in the manufacture of pencils, electrodes (arc lamps), smelting crucibles, as a lubricant and sealant, and in atomic reactors.

Gypsum. A whitish, sometimes colored, plastic, coarsely crystalline mineral. Alabaster is a very fine-grained form of gypsum. Plaster of Paris is made by grinding gypsum which has first been heated (calcined) to drive off the chemically bound water. The plaster of Paris used for modeling and casting purposes has had about 75% of the water of crystallization removed. Depending on the water content, which varies with the calcining temperature, we can distinguish three principal types of gypsum plaster: ordinary gypsum plaster for interior walls and ceilings, Keene's cement—a hard finish plaster, and high-strength gypsum plaster for plaster block and decking. A double-calcined form of gypsum impregnated with alum is used to fill the joints between wall tiles.

Gypsum sets by absorbing water (gypsum plaster). The setting process can be slowed down by adding borax or bone glue, which also increases the strength of the plaster. Adding alum, waterglass and Glauber's salt results in a considerable increase in hardness, whereas milk makes the plaster unusually plastic.

H

Hard Soldering. See soldering.

Hemming. Folding over the edges of a piece of sheet metal, either to form a seam or to avoid sharp edges. The material must be bent over with a wooden mallet. A wire may be introduced into the fold to strengthen the edge.

Hinge. Hardware element on which doors and windows, cabinets, etc. swing or turn. The commonest types are the strap hinge, the T hinge, and the angle hinge for heavy doors, the butt hinge and the piano hinge for lighter duties. Hinges may be concealed or exposed. The pin hinge is a concealed hinge for modern flush-face cabinets. Loose pin butt hinges can be dismantled simply by knocking out the pin. The pins of nonrising pin butt hinges and piano hinges are fixed.

J

Japan Lacquer. The resinous sap of the Japanese lacquer tree, Rhus verniciflua. Previously much used, especially for fine cabinet work, on account of its handsome luster and resistance to chemical action. Now largely displaced by oil and synthetic-resin varnishes.

Jaw Chuck. A device for clamping tools or workpieces. There are two-, three- and four-jaw chucks, the individual jaws of which can be adjusted with a key and hold the tool or workpiece in their common grip. The chucks used in braces and drills work on the same principle. They consist of a tapering threaded sleeve which, when screwed down, radially compresses the conical jaws, thus clamping the bit.

Joiner's Cement. Mixture of hot joiner's glue and chalk. Also serves for filling holes and cracks in wood. Joiner's cement shrinks somewhat on drying, and must therefore be applied thickly. Excess cement is rubbed down after drying.

K

Kaolin. See clay.

Kilowatt. A thousand watts, see watt.

L

Lac. A reddish brown resin exuding around incisions in the twigs of certain South Asian trees caused by the bite of the female lac insect. Shellac varnish is a solution of refined lac resin in denatured alcohol, which dries quickly by evaporation of the alcohol. It is available in white (bleached) and an orange color range. Shellac is used as a clear finish for woodwork, to seal knots and pitch stains in wood painting, and to seal bituminous coatings before applying pigmented paints. Should not be kept more than six months in liquid form.

Lacquer. A term frequently applied to any coating that dries quickly and only by evaporation of the solvent. A true lacquer has nitrocellulose as the basic nonvolatile ingredient and is characterized by a distinctive odor. Lacquers are available clear or pigmented. The film they form is tough and thin, but not as durable as a high-grade varnish when exposed to sunlight and moisture.

Light Metals. Any metal or alloy with a density of less than 4. Among the materials in this group aluminum and magnesium and their alloys are of particular importance.

Lime Plaster. A mixture of lime putty (slaked lime) and sand. A preferred finish plaster for interior walls and ceilings because of its permeability and elasticity.

Linoleum. Trade name for a floor covering. Can also be used for desk tops and counter tops where heavy wear, grease and cooking spillage occur. Linoleum backings may be a strong burlap (jute), onto which a colored mixture of linseed oil, resins, cork, wood flour and various mineral fillers is rolled. The finished linoleum is matured for several weeks in vertical steam-heated stoves. High-grade linoleum is elastic and very hard-wearing.

Loam. See clay.

Luffa. Luffa sponge. The fibrous skeleton of a cucumber-like, elongated fruit, chiefly cultivated in Japan. The skeleton of the ripe fruit, from which the husk and flesh have been removed, is dried and sold as hard, sponge-like raw luffa. The raw luffa is stamped into the most varied shapes and worked into bath sponges, bathroom slippers, etc. When colored makes all kinds of decorations, toys, and facings.

M

Mat Finish. Matte. A flat or dull finish giving little or no reflection. The addition of turpentine dulls otherwise glossy paints. Tempera colors are naturally mat.

Mercury Switch. An electric switch made by placing a large globule of mercury in a glass tube having electrodes arranged in such a way that tilting the tube causes the mercury to make or break the circuit.

Metal Saw. See saws.

Milk Glass. See opaque glass.

Mineral Spirits. A hydrocarbon obtained from petroleum. A cheap substitute for turpentine. Inflammable.

Miter Joint. The joint formed when two pieces of wood or metal of identical cross section are joined at the ends and the two ends are beveled at equal angles (usually 45°). Miters may be cut in a miter box. The joint formed when the two parts meet at right angles is called a true miter (picture frame). The parts are either simply butted one against the other or the joint may be reinforced with a thin plywood spline. A mitered mortise and tenon joint is particularly difficult to make.

Mortar. A plastic mixture of binders, aggregates and water that hardens into a stonelike mass. Used for laying bricks or as stucco. Binders include lime, cement, gypsum and clay. The aggregate is usually sand (river sand, pit sand) of various degrees of fineness. Special additives will make the mortar waterproof. The proportions in which binder and aggregate are mixed depend on the nature of the binder and on the strength desired. Mortar for common masonry work is always mixed in proportions of 3:1 (sand: cement). Pure clay, gypsum and lime mortars are called air mortars, since they set by simple drying (clay mortar) or by the absorption of carbon dioxide from the air (lime mortar). Cement mortar, on the other hand, will also set under water. Concrete is a cement mortar with gravel used as an aggregate as well as sand. By using other aggregates (pumice, expanded shale, cinders) the concrete can be given a variety of different properties (light weight, thermal insulating value, fire resistance, etc.).

Multipurpose Power Tool. A portable power drill which can be adapted to perform a variety of operations such as drilling, grinding, buffing, polishing, turning, etc. The chuck of the machine is designed to hold any of a number of tools the action of which depends on rotation. Can be used as a hand tool or mounted on special stands. Power can be transmitted to circular and jig saws by means of a flexible shaft.

N

Nail Drawing. The process of removing nails from nailed joints by means of pincers or, in the case of heavy nails, a claw hammer.

Nailing. A joining technique in carpentry employing wire nails and brads. If the point of the nail is very sharp, it should be flattened slightly with the hammer before being driven to prevent the wood from splitting. For the same reason rows of nails should, as

far as possible, be staggered, rather than straight; this relieves the individual fibers. Driving nails on the slant increases their holding power. Nail heads should be driven below the surface of the wood with a nail set. Never use bent nails. Very small nails that are hard to hold can be controlled by pushing them through a slit in a piece of cardboard. If the left hand is not free to hold the nail, the point can be stuck in position for hammering with a small piece of plasticine. When nailing hardwood, it may be advisable to predrill a hole to start the nail and grease the nail shank lightly. Do not use unnecessarily large nails. The points of nails that have been driven right through the wood should be removed with a pair of end-cutting nippers and the ends upset, placing something hard underneath the nail head (hammer head or pliers) to prevent it from being forced out. If the joint has to bear a heavy load, drive the nails right through and hammer the projecting points back into the wood. First bend the tip of the nail into a hook over the triangular tang of a file placed against the shank. The descending part of the hook should slope in the direction of the grain. After removing the tang of the file, drive the point of the nail firmly back into the wood. Again place something hard underneath the nail head. When drawing nails always insert a piece of wood underneath the pliers or hammer head to prevent them from crushing the surface of the nailed member.

O

Opal Glass. See opaque glass.

Opaque Glass. Milk glass. Opal glass. Glass made nontransparent by adding substances (fluorine compounds, phosphates) capable of producing turbidity. The glass may be delicately tinted or dense, like porcelain, depending on the nature of the additive. No more than 69% of the light is transmitted. Among the opaque glasses are milk glass, colored milky white by cryolite, and opal glass, obtained by adding bone ash. Because of its light-diffusing qualities, opal glass is much used in glass painting and for lampshades. The color effects resemble those obtained with natural opal.

P

Paint Removers. Old coats of paint and varnish can be removed with the aid of caustic soda or organic solvents or a combination of the two. Solvents are generally applied with an old brush. After allowing a certain time for the solvent to do its work, the softened paint is removed with a scraper. Caustic soda solution is a strong lye that saponifies the oil in the paint; it cannot be used on nitrocellulose lacquers, or on alcohol and synthetic-resin varnishes. It is better to treat veneered or natural wood surfaces with solvents rather than lye, since the latter darkens the wood. Moreover, solvents do not require any aftertreatment. After using caustic soda paint removers, the ground must be carefully neutralized with a weak acid and washed clean. Apart from chemicals, the blow-torch is a good means of cleaning broad, flat surfaces. It is used to scorch old coats of paint, which can then be scraped off while they are still hot and soft.

Pigments. According to origin and manner of preparation we can distinguish between natural pigments (obtained from minerals, or vegetable or animal matter) and synthetic pigments, for the most part coal tar dyes. Earth colors are pigments obtained from natural or artificially prepared minerals or colored earths, for example, ocher, sienna, umber, green earth, etc. Pigments are absorbed by, but not dissolved in the binder.

Pin Vise. Hand vise. Essentially a tiny split chuck on a hollow length of metal comprising the handle. Thus, it is possible to insert a length of wire into the chuck, as the wire extends through the hollow handle. The end of the wire protruding from the chuck can be sharpened with a file for use as a pin or turned over as a rivet head. With a small broach the pin vise forms a miniature hand drill.

Planing. A method of smoothing or dressing surfaces, usually flat, by removing shavings with a hand plane or planing machine. In working with a hand plane, always plane in the direction of the grain with the cutting edge of the blade projecting only slightly and strictly parallel with the base of the tool. To plane properly, grasp the large handle in the right hand and wrap the left around the knob in front. Push the plane forward over the board in a series of straight, parallel strokes. The blade should not follow the irregularities of the surface, but remove all the high spots until the surface is perfectly flat. As the plane reaches the end of each stroke it should be lifted by bearing down on the rear handle. Otherwise it will tend to drop and the final surface will not be flat, but sloping. At the start of the stroke, the plane is set down so that the blade is clear of the end of the board and can thus begin with a good bite. At this point the tool should be pressed down in front, with the left hand. Pressing down with the right hand would again result in a sloping surface. Where it is necessary to plane against the grain, for example in the neighborhood of knots, a short smoothing plane will do a better job than the longer jack plane. The large fore and jointer planes, which vary from 18 to 24 inches in length, are intended for dressing long, straight boards or for smoothing the edges of several boards in a single operation. Skill in handling these rather clumsy tools can only be acquired by practice.

Narrow end-grain surfaces are planed with the board clamped in a vertical position and the end projecting slightly above the jaws of the vise. To prevent the wood from splintering at the edges, plane only to about the middle of the end face, from the left and then from the right. If the cross section of the board is very small, it is safer to clamp it between two other pieces of wood of the same thickness, the faces of which are slightly beveled. The small block plane, which can be held in one hand and has a sharp blade set at a low angle, is particularly suitable for smoothing end-grain surfaces. The scraper plane, which cuts on the pull stroke, can be used for the same purpose.

Plastic Film. Plastic film of various thicknesses is made by casting or rolling the molten or dissolved raw material. Transparent films of the cellophane type are mostly used for packaging purposes, but soft colored, printed and embossed films are being increasingly used as textiles owing to their highly decorative effect, hygienic advantages, and durability. Thin plastics also make attractive draperies, upholstery fabrics, and wall coverings.

Plasticine. Slow-drying modeling compound made of kaolin, gypsum and oil, and generally colored by the addition of various earth colors. Dried out plasticine can be made flexible again by adding glycerin.

Plastic Wood. A commercial wood putty for repairing holes and defects in wood work. A home-made substitute can be prepared by mixing very fine, sifted wood flour (fret-saw dust) with joiner's glue, cellulose adhesive or shellac solution.

Priming Coat. First or preparatory coat applied to a surface to protect it from corrosion or mechanical damage or to reduce the absorbing power of the ground (canvas). If the ground consists of very porous material (wood, wall plaster), the primer (linseed oil with or without the addition of chalk, size, etc.) will close the pores, saturate the material, and, when it has dried, help to form a strong bond between the paint film and the painted surface.

Proportional Division. The dividing of a

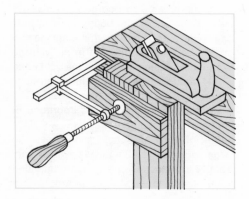

Trimming end grain. The piece of waste prevents splintering.

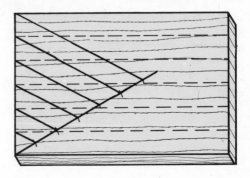

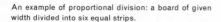
An example of proportional division: a board of given width divided into six equal strips.

given line into a number of equal parts with no remainder. Practical example: A board of given width is to be divided into six equally wide strips. The correct width is determined by first dividing the right angle formed by one corner of the board in two, preferably so as to form two angles of roughly 45°. The dividing line is carried well over the face of the board and six equal segments of any convenient length are marked off along it with the dividers, starting from the corner of the board. (If it were desired to divide the board into seven equal parts, seven equal segments would have to be marked off along the dividing line). A line is drawn from the sixth and final mark to the other corner of the short side of the board, which now forms the base of an acute-angled triangle. If lines parallel to the first one are drawn through the five other points marked off along the dividing line, the base of the triangle, i.e. the short side of the board, will be divided into sixths. It then remains to take a marking gage and score five cutting lines parallel to the long side of the board.

Putty. Glazing compound. A soft cement made of chalk and linseed oil. Used for glazing windows and filling holes in wood (for example, over nail heads before paint-ing). A useful home-made putty consists of an intimate mixture of 8 to 10 parts by weight of prepared chalk (whiting) and 1 part of boiled linseed oil. Store in an airtight container, preferably in oiled paper or under water. Stale, hard-to-work putty can be refreshed by adding more linseed oil. To remove very hard putty from old joints, first soften with a concentrated solution of caustic soda.

Q

Quenching. The rapid cooling of red-hot workpieces in a water, oil, or salt bath to develop unusual hardness. This is one of the processes in steelmaking.

Quicklime. Calcium oxide. See slaked lime.

R

Red Lead. Minium. Lead oxide (Pb_3O_4). Base of a heavy, rust-inhibiting paint for iron and steel. A bright, orange-red powder of great hiding power. Insoluble in water. Like other lead compounds, it is poisonous. The non-poisonous red ocher or raddle (an iron oxide) is cheaper and more weatherproof than red lead.

Riveting. A joining technique employing rivets, mainly used in metalworking. Rivets may be distinguished by the shape of the head as round-head, flattened or flush countersunk. Rivets are made of steel, brass, copper, and the light metals. The easiest to work are aluminum rivets. The commonest riveted joints are the lap joint, between straight or tapered plates, and the butt joint. In the latter the edges of the two parts to be joined are butted one against the other and riveted through cover plates placed over the joint on either side.

The rivet holes are drilled or, if the material is thin enough, punched. They must correspond exactly to the diameter of the rivet shank. If the shank is loose in the rivet hole or if the holes do not properly coincide, the joint will not hold. Clamp the parts together and if the rivet rows are fairly long put in a temporary holding rivet at each end. In the actual riveting process the manufactured head is placed in a rivet set held firmly in the vise and the projecting shank is upset with a vertical blow of the hammer. Then a rough head is fashioned with a series of oblique hammer blows. Before the head is upset, the two parts being joined must be driven together with a rivet setter. A second rivet set is now placed over the rough head

of the rivet and struck with the hammer until a uniformly rounded head has been formed. The head must be exactly centered on the shank. A correctly rounded head will be obtained, if, after the parts have been brought together, the shank of the rivet projects beyond the hole a distance equal to its own thickness. In flush riveting (only possible with fairly thick material), the rivet holes must be countersunk using a countersink, after which the rivet is headed over and filed flush. If the material is very thin, rivet burrs (a kind of washer) must be placed under both heads.

Riveted parts can only be separated by destroying the rivets. This is done by knocking off the head with a blow from a flat cold chisel, delivered from the side, and punching out the remains of the shank between the jaws of a partially open vise.

S

Sandalwood. The fragrant heartwood of any of a number of Asiatic trees, used for ornamental carving and luxury goods.

Sandblasting. Method of artificially aging wood surfaces. After the surface has been carefully scorched, the soft parts of the wood are removed with a sand blast. The hard fibres that have resisted the action of

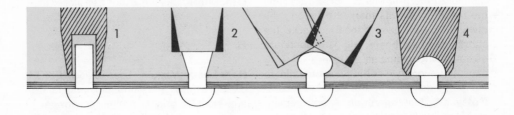

Riveting: 1 the parts are brought together with a rivet setter, 2 the shank of the rivet is upset, 3 the hammer is used to form a rough head, 4 a rivet set gives the head its final shape.

the flames remain. Particularly effective when used on strongly grained woods (pine).

Sawing. Method of cutting or forming slots, particularly in wood and metal. Wood saws may be divided into rip saws and crosscut saws for cutting along and across the grain, respectively. Use of crosscut saw: Start the cut by placing the end of the blade nearest the handle on the work and drawing the saw towards you. This forms a groove from which the blade will not escape during the first cautious forward thrust. In sawing, the blade should be held at an angle of about 45° to the board. Never saw on, but always alongside the mark; otherwise the width of the cut or kerf will reduce the dimensions of the material. To guide the saw, place the thumb of the left hand close to the cut and allow the side of the saw blade to run against it. Never carry a saw cut right through from one side to the other. A short notch made from the other side will prevent the last piece of wood from splintering off. In order to avoid the risk of splintering when cutting very thin material—especially veneers and plywood—the line of the cut should be covered on both sides with a strip of adhesive tape. The tape is sawn through together with the wood and removed after the sawing is complete.

If you have to saw in the direction of the grain, the work should be set up in a vertical position and cut with a rip saw or a frame saw in which the blade is clamped at right angles to the frame. Alternatively, the plank can be set up horizontally, and the saw worked straight up and down. If the saw jams during a long cut as a result of stresses inside the wood, its path can be opened up by driving a narrow wedge into the cut directly behind the blade.

In sawing metal the cut is started with a three-square or knife-edge file. Again do not begin by pushing the saw forwards, but draw it backwards two or three times, until the blade gets a firm enough hold on the metal. Metal saws or hack saws are worked with both hands, the right hand around the pistol grip, the left hand in front on the tensioning screw. Long cuts are made with the workpiece clamped vertically and the blade set at right angles to the frame. Hollow workpieces (tubes, channels) are not sawn through in a single cut, but turned repeatedly in the vise before the saw penetrates right through the metal wall. Otherwise the teeth may break when the blade is driven against the inner edges of the wall. Always clamp the workpiece in the vise so that the saw blade passes as close as possible to the jaws. Use special blades for non-ferrous metals. Place the blade in the frame with the teeth pointing away from the handle. Do not oil the blade during sawing. Always release the tension on the blade after use.

Setscrew. A small cylindrical, headless screw with a slot for the screwdriver formed directly in the sharp upper end. Used to clamp two metal parts which would otherwise slide one along the other.

Setting. A general term for the drying and solidifying of mortar and cement. The duration of the chemical setting process and the final strength of the product depend on the water content of the mix. The term setting is also used to describe that part of the operation of sharpening a saw consisting in bending the points of the teeth outwards with a tool called a saw set. The object of setting is to ensure that the teeth of the saw will not bind in the kerf. Particular care must be taken to see that the set is regular.

Shellac. See lac.

Shooting Board. A planing aid. In its simplest form two dressed boards, one fastened to the face of the other so that the long edge of the lower board projects a few

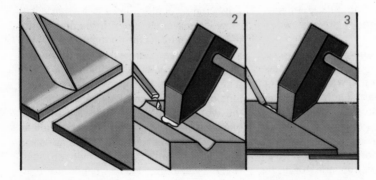

Soldering: 1 scraping the edges of the joint, 2 tinning the soldering iron on a sal ammoniac brick, 3 working the solder into the tinned and pickled joint with the hot soldering iron.

inches in advance of the corresponding edge of the upper one, this projection forming a bed or guide for the plane. The object is to hold the plane at 90° to the work so that after planing the edge of the work will be square. In shooting an edge the work is held against a stop fastened to one end of the shooting board, which is itself held in place on the work bench by means of a bench hook at the other end.

Siccative. See drier.

Slaked Lime. Calcium hydroxide, formed by "slaking" ordinary lime (quicklime) with a controlled amount of water and then air-separating and sifting it. It has the advantage of being dry yet, when mixed with other ingredients, ready for use in plastering in a much shorter time than quicklime.

Soft Soldering. See soldering.

Soldering. Method of joining two or more metal parts by means of an easily melted metal alloy, solder. The solder, generally an alloy of lead and tin, is melted by heating it with the soldering iron. Soldering with soft solders (melting point below 400°F) is called "soft soldering." The melting point of the hard solders used in "hard soldering" is more than 1200°F. Because of the very high temperatures required, the latter method will rarely be used by the amateur craftsman.

Where soldering is mentioned, soft soldering is always intended.

The very strong joint between the solder and the metal parts is the result of a surface alloying, which, however, will only develop its strength if the surfaces are completely free of impurities and oxide layers. The cleaning or pickling is done with fluxes (soldering fluid, soldering paste). Soldering fluid consists of zinc filings dissolved in dilute hydrochloric acid (mixed with water in the proportion of 1:1), to which ammonia has been added. The flux most commonly used for lead, brass and copper soldering is a rosin paste. These metals are soldered with solder in the form of a hollow tin wire with a rosin paste core. This technique is particularly useful for wiring low-voltage circuits. For zinc and zinc sheet a 50% solution of pure hydrochloric acid is enough. The easiest metals to solder are tin and tinned sheet; aluminum and its alloys can only be soldered with great difficulty, using special soldering materials. How to solder: Scrape the surfaces to be joined bright and clean with a scraper or a file (preferably not sandpaper). Then immediately brush with soldering fluid (pickle) and "tin." Tinning is done with the tip of the hot soldering iron, which is used to spread a thin film of molten solder over the joint. After tinning, apply more soldering fluid. Like the metal being soldered, the tip of the soldering iron should also be cleaned and tinned. When the iron is hot, its tip is freed of scale with an old, rough file and rubbed bright. It is then tinned by being smeared with a drop of solder in a groove formed in the top of a brick of sal ammoniac. The iron must be retinned from time to time during soldering, since repeated heating causes the tin film to evaporate.

In soldering zinc or zinc sheet, it is possible to dispense with tinning and allow the solder to flow directly into the joint. Soldered joints should be arranged to lie at right angles to the ends of the work. In the case of smaller joints the hot soldering iron is used to take individual drops of solder from the wire and work them into the joint. Where the joint is a long one, bring the wire close to the joint and make it drip into the joint with the heat from the soldering iron. If necessary the wire can be thinned out somewhat with a hammer. The solder must penetrate the entire joint, since only solder lying between the parts will hold them together. The thinner the flux, the better. In no case should the parts be allowed to warp. Where they are being soldered, they should be pressed together with a block of wood. It is important to have the soldering iron at the right temperature. If it is too hot the solder will burn or boil. The result will be a porous seam. If the iron is too cold, the solder will not penetrate far enough into the joint.

When the joint has been soldered, it and the metal around it are carefully rubbed with a soda solution to neutralize any remaining traces of soldering fluid. Only then is the excess tin, lying outside the joint, neatly scraped away, since it contributes nothing to the strength of the joint.

Spatula. A broad, flat, more or less flexible blade with or without a handle for spreading plaster, paint, adhesives, etc.

Squaring. The smoothing or leveling of a piece of material by planing, sanding or grinding. In carpentry rough-cut boards are squared by being passed through a planing machine from which they emerge with the sides strictly parallel and the edges all true right angles.

Staining. Wood surfaces may be stained when it is desired to give them a dark color without masking the grain. There are three main types of stain: water stains, alcohol stains, and oil or chemical stains. The best known is walnut stain, a dark brown, granular substance that can be dissolved in water or alcohol. Soda is added to increase the permanence of the stain, liquid ammonia intensifies its coloring action. After staining, the wood surface is rubbed down and treated with wax or shellac. Wax stains, which can be purchased as prepared solutions with a wax additive, give a mat finish if, after drying, the surface is simply polished vigorously with a horsehair brush. Working with chemical stains is difficult and requires much experience.

Strip Steel. Steel sheet 12″ or less in width. Material more than 12″ wide is known simply as sheet. Sold in rolls.

T

Taps. Pieces of round tool steel with a thread on one end and a square shank on the other. The threaded portion is fluted with grooves cut across the threads parallel to the axis. These grooves form cutting edges and a space for the removal of chips. Used to form threaded holes (tap holes). The tap wrench is a handle used to hold the tap.

Thermostat. A temperature regulator. Any control element built into a heating or cooling system to maintain a preselected constant temperature by controlling the fuel supply (gas, electricity, oil). Electric thermostats use thermocouples or resistance thermometers as the temperature pickup. The energy supply is controlled by means of a mercury switch or a bimetallic strip that activates a regulating valve in the supply line.

Turpentine Oil. Turpentine. An essential oil prepared by steam distillation of the oleoresins obtained from various coniferous trees, particularly pines. Thinner and solvent for paints, varnishes, disinfectants, etc. Inflammable. Keep the container firmly closed and store in a safe place.

V

Varnishes. Combinations of resin (natural or synthetic), drying oil, drier and solvent. A brushed or sprayed coating that dries to a high-gloss or mat finish and offers protection against chemical attack and mechanical damage. Varnishes are usually clear, but may be pigmented. They harden by evaporation of the solvent (turpentine, mineral spirits) followed by oxidation and polymerization of the resins and drying oils. Asphalt varnish is a cheap, opaque iron varnish. Enamels are clear varnishes with white or colored pigment added. Copal oil varnishes are used as rubbing varnishes. Clear spar varnish forms a very hard-wearing coating.

Veneering. Method of embellishing the surface of wood or plywood by covering it with a very thin layer of more handsome wood with a distinctive grain or color. Veneering large surfaces is quite an exacting gluing operation for which numerous auxiliary devices and special presses are required. Consequently, it will usually be beyond the range of the average craftsman. Smaller surfaces are more manageable, particularly if the new cold synthetic-resin adhesives are used instead of the traditional joiner's glue. The following rules should be observed: the veneer should be applied so that the grain runs in the same direction in veneer and base. If the base is plywood, the grain of the veneer should run at right angles to that of the outer ply. Both sides of the base must be covered with veneer of the same thickness, otherwise it will warp. Waste veneer or cheaper material can be used on the back.

If the sides of thicker pieces are also to be veneered, the veneer is applied to these areas first, so that the face veneer will overlap and conceal the edges. If it is necessary to make a butt joint between pieces of veneer, the two ends are overlapped (right side on top) and cut through simultaneously by drawing a very sharp knife along the edge of a steel ruler. Try to make sure that there is no interruption in the continuity of the grain. A butt joint running at an oblique angle to the direction of the grain will be less conspicuous and stronger than one at right angles. If strips of veneer meet along their length, the edges must be neatly planed and perfectly straight. It is best to clamp the two pieces of veneer between two boards placed edgewise and work with a jointer plane. The plane iron should be sharp and should project no more than is absolutely necessary. The shaving should be as fine as a hair.

Before the adhesive is applied to the back of the veneer and the surface of the base, both must be rubbed perfectly clean and flat. Holes that may be present in a solid wood base should be filled with plastic wood or a home-made chalk-glue paste (see joiner's cement). Never use oil putty. Then apply synthetic-resin adhesive to both sur-

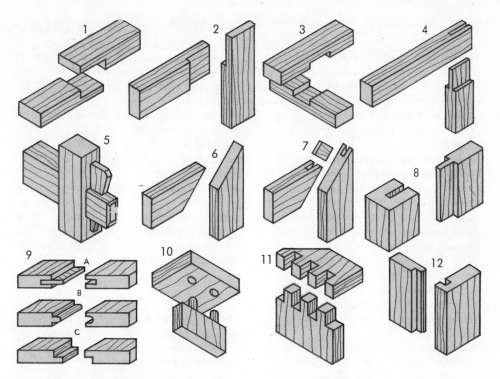

Typical wood joints: 1 half lap, 2 end lap, 3 cross lap, 4 corner mortise and tenon, 5 wedged tenon, 6 plain miter, 7 miter and feather, 8 stub tenon, 9 three types of continuous joint: A spline, B tongue and groove, C shiplap, 10 doweled corner, 11 dovetailed corner, 12 tongue and groove corner.

faces. End-grain surfaces should be given a thin preliminary coat of adhesive to seal the pores. Scrupulously observe the instructions of the maker of the adhesive, especially as regards the time the adhesive should be left exposed to the air (this varies between about 5 and 15 minutes, depending on the make of adhesive and the room temperature). When the adhesive is ready, place the veneer over the base and rub it down hard with a cloth or the face of a hammer, working from the middle towards the sides. Special care is required at the edges and joints. Synthetic-resin adhesives harden very fast and when they have set errors can no longer be corrected. The veneer should always be slightly larger than the base; after the adhesive has set the projecting edges are trimmed off with a chisel and smoothed with a block plane. The finished surface is leveled with a scraper plane and rubbed in the direction of the grain with very fine sandpaper wrapped around a sanding block. If the veneer is to be stained, it should be moistened with a damp sponge after the first rubbing and again rubbed down after it has dried.

Volt. Unit of potential of an electric current (V). One volt is the electromotive force that will send one ampere through a resistance of one ohm.

W

Waterglass. Sodium silicate. An amorphous powder or thick heavy liquid, soluble in water. It is used as an adhesive in the paper industry, as a binder for cold water paints, as a bleacher and cleaning agent, as a protective coating, and for many other purposes.

Waterproofing Compound. Added to concrete and cement mixes to reduce the capillary attraction of the voids and hence the permeability; will not keep out water under pressure; useful for cellar walls and other concrete in contact with the earth or exposed to the weather.

Watt. The practical unit of electric power, calculated from the relation voltage x current = power or V x A = W. 1000 watts make 1 kilowatt (kW). A kilowatt-hour (kWh) is the work done by 1 kilowatt of power in one hour (h).

White Lead. An important mineral pigment for exterior paints with good hiding power. Very weather-resistant, but gradually darkens. Like all lead compounds, white lead is poisonous. For this reason it is best avoided; for craft work the non-poisonous zinc white can be used in its stead.

Whiting. Prepared chalk. Chalk ground and purified by washing. Used as a pigment extender and with size and water in whitewash. Also a polishing agent and tooth powder.

Wood Cement. A composition for filling joints, holes and defects in wood and for making good chipped wall surfaces. Made by adding gypsum to hot glue water (3.5 ounces of joiner's glue to a quart of water).

Wood Joints. See drawing on page 65.

Z

Zapon Varnish. A high-quality, clear nitrocellulose lacquer. Serves as a protective coating for shiny, but easily tarnishing metal surfaces (brass, copper).

WITH HEART AND HAND

People who in their spare time pick up a tool and create something for their own personal use are the last real individualists of this era of machinery.

Most of us do not really care what material our household furniture or the many utensils we use daily are made of, and yet they bear witness to the style and way of living of each individual. The general attitude is that an object should fulfill its purpose and look reasonably good. Whether it is made of wood, metal or ceramics makes little difference; plastics are best, because they are practical, usually nice and bright, and hard-wearing. The discussion of form is mostly empty enthusiasm about what can now be done with machinery.

The feeling of affinity with the raw material and the sense of form are steadily disappearing. Stereotyped conveyor-belt culture rules even the most intimate aspects of our life. It is evident in the mass consumption of mechanically reproduced music, in factory-made furniture, and in the molded, synthetic marble ornaments in innumerable china cupboards. Nevertheless, the ordinary consumer feels quite happy surrounded by such things because standards have changed, and the value of an object is usually judged solely by its price. But the intrinsic value of an object or a utensil starts not with its price, but with its quality or characteristics. True luxury is found in uniqueness, in exceptions, in individuality. The great joy of possession, which induces us to return again and again to an object, to appreciate it in quiet contemplation, arises out of the honesty of its material, out of its natural straightforwardness and genuine form. The secret of shape or form is that it respects the individuality of the material from which it grows. Therefore it can only be present if there is a real understanding of the essence and purpose of the object created. For this reason there are few things that one can really admire. Most of these are the loving work of a craftsman. Success depends on two things: the heart and the hand.

MADE OF WOOD

4

The close relationship that has existed from the earliest times between mankind and wood is not due solely to the ready availability of this raw material in the forests and the ease with which it can be worked, even with primitive tools. Primitive man recognized in the growth and decline of the trees the image of his own life. The structure of wood, in which the nature of growth is preserved, the ever-changing ornamental grain with its characteristic and expressive figure, continues to stimulate our imagination, in the same way as it did a thousand years ago; we are tempted into shaping this most natural of all natural raw materials and feel the desire to give the object made from wood a decorative role that goes beyond pure functionalism.

To a large extent wood carving consists of overcoming the resistance which this natural raw material offers to all attempts to shape it. After all, the natural growth of the wood is governed by laws completely different from the demands which man, with his purposeful way of thinking, may make upon it. All sorts of things can be made of wood, and it will stand up to practically any treatment; only one thing must be avoided: the use of force. Even the simplest piece of wood will always, in the true sense of the word, remain loyal to its family tree and will never allow itself to be forced into shapes which are inconsistent with its natural inherent characteristics.

It is as well to be aware of these facts before picking up the chisel and mallet hastily in order to attack the wood. To be sure, no glory is gained by following well-trodden paths and imitating prescribed models, but we should look with gratitude to the masters, who were at work long before us. From them we can learn how the technical problems are solved. To ignore tried and tested methods, developed by diligent and honest men and handed on as a precious gift from generation to generation, would be foolish. Anyhow, even if we follow these tried methods, we shall still have to pay for our experience!

Hollow Forms: Bowls and Plates

Let us start practicing on one of the oldest hollow shapes, one which man was forced to produce when he got tired of that delightful state in which his drinking water or his midday millet seed trickled between the fingers of his cupped hands. We refer to the bowl or dish, the shape of which is inspired by and imitated from the shape of hands extended in offering. Luckily, we need return to prehistoric times only in our thoughts. From the point of view of technique we have long ago passed the age of the flint chisel. All the tools required for our task are cutting tools: a saw, a chisel, and one or two rasps. This is because we work in the round, from a board or a block that holds the shapes we are looking for. Our object will be to feel our way to this shape by carefully removing parts of the material.

With regard to the type of wood to be selected we offer this rule of thumb: choose hard wood for small work and softer pieces for larger shapes. Also bear in mind that small objects should not show too distinct a grain. This would break up the form and would dissolve the outlines of the object, acting like camouflage. Wood with a strong grain should be used only for shapes with large surfaces. If a surface, say the edge or walls of a bowl, is to be decorated, choose a piece of wood with a fine and not too noticeable structure.

In general, the wood of broad-leaf trees is better suited for hollow shapes than that of evergreens, as the latter have an irregular structure and very strongly defined annual rings.

It is best for the beginner to start on linden wood (basswood) which is easy to work, or—if his self-confidence is strong enough for a sporting fight with the material—with a plank of close-grained common oak. But please, don't rush things. Don't tackle a man-sized block of tough mountain oak at the start of your hopeful career as a woodcarver and go at it like a busy woodpecker. Notchy, broken chisels and splintered wood will not help to maintain your enthusiasm for the work.

Do not start by shaping the outer surface, like the turner on his lathe, but first carve the inside wall. For this purpose outline the circular shape of the bowl and the thickness of the wall as a double circle on top of the block that forms your raw material. As soon

as you have fixed your still square piece of wood to the left hand corner of your working table with one or two screw clamps, you will realize why we start with the inside surface, for if we had cut away the outside wood as far as the face of the wall, we would have had no material left with which to clamp the work down.

The first step in carving a bowl is to cut into the wood along the inside circle. This is best done with a gouge, the curve of which corresponds exactly with the curve of the circle. If such an ideal tool is not available, it is advisable to choose a gouge with a slightly sharper curve than that of the circle. Should such a tool not be available either, then we must cut a short distance inside the final edge in order to preserve some thickness of material for the final finishing. The first rough cuts are made with the widest and strongest gouge at our disposal—starting from the center. This gouge should have a slightly curved cutting edge. A flat chisel would very soon get stuck. Those who want to be ambitious and start by tackling oak must use a mallet. Soft wood, however, is more easily worked by hand. The right hand is used to grip the handle of the tool and supplies the necessary driving force, while the left hand guides the blade from above. The chisel is not just forced through the wood like a plough being drawn through a field: while the right hand is driving it forwards, it is simultaneously rotated lightly about its own axis by the left hand. Only in this way can the correct cut be achieved. Try to get used to this technique right from the start; firstly, it is easier, and secondly, you obtain a cleaner cut. It is not really difficult work at all, but should any difficulty arise, it will be where the side walls of the bowl pass gradually, with a soft curve, into the bottom. The deeper the bowl, the more skill is required in making this transi-

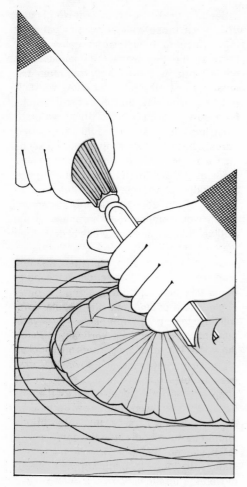

very deep goblet-shaped vessel with steep sides, care must be taken to avoid carving out a funnel. Just keep the tool firmly vertical when cutting the wall.

Similar rules apply when making plates, but here especially exaggerated shapes should be avoided. It is true that in designs with horizontal edges the transition to the deeper parts should be marked by a distinctly recognizable boundary line, but be careful to avoid sharp-cornered forms. These are not in harmony with the material and belong rather to the art of ceramics. The basic shape of the wooden plate is a flat, shallow depression. If you stick to this, you will not feel uncomfortable or disappointed when you see the finished work.

In a plate the transition from the side wall to the flat bottom is usually shorter and therefore more rounded than in bowls. The bend between the sharp edge and the plane, which can be so pleasing to the eye and the sense of touch, is again best carved with a bent gouge. In order to check the regularity of the curve, a template can be made with a fret saw from a piece of plywood or tin; the curve can then be continually checked by applying this template. It is also wise to

First cuts and position of the hands in carving a round bowl.

tion. It is advisable to use a tool bent at an angle and to stick to a curve, at least at the beginning, which follows the curve of the angled tool.

In principle it is the same whether we carve a flat bowl with a shallow curve, a deep rounded bowl, or a plate; the working technique does not change. When making a

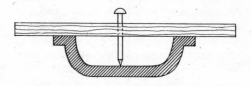

Makeshift gage for controlling the depth of a flat-bottomed dish.

71

construct a simple depth gage from a stick two-thirds longer than the outside diameter of the plate with a nail hammered through its center. By laying the stick across the edges of the plate it is possible to scratch all the parts that still have to be removed with the point of the nail, which has been previously adjusted to the correct depth. If the nail is inserted in the stick in such a way that the latter can be laid edgewise, even greater precision will be possible, since the stick will be less prone to sag.

A surface cut with the proper, really sharp tools can hardly be improved by the most careful sanding. But not everybody will achieve such perfection at the start. Therefore, once the carving tools have done their job, we must sand. The first stage of the work is best done with an angled cobbler's rasp, an oval spoke shave or a so-called swan's neck, a kidney-shaped spoke shave, particularly suitable for this type of work, because its varyingly graded contours—similar to a French curve—are so adaptable. The final smoothing is done with the finest sandpaper which is wrapped around a shaped sanding block of soft wood, or better still, cork or rubber. A particularly smooth surface can be obtained if the wood is moistened several times before the final sanding. This makes the loose "woolly" wood fibre stand up and it can then be grasped better by the sandpaper after the surface has dried. At all events, this treatment is to be recommended for soft woods and for wood which is to be stained; it will prevent the surface from becoming unduly rough as a result of the application of the stain. Sections where the end grain comes to the surface may offer some resistance. This resistance cannot be overcome by force, but only by cunning and perseverance, by never sanding against the grain, but always in the direction of the fiber.

Sanding the end grain of soft woods can drive even those with enormous patience to distraction. It just won't come clean, because the fine wood dust immediately settles into the pores and frustrates the most earnest efforts. Don't allow yourself to be carried away: quickly cover the stubborn surface with a quick-drying varnish! Once this has dried it will toughen the wood fibres. These will then drop off during sanding like a good growth of beard under a new razor blade. Be careful when sanding the inner ridge of vessels with a flat rim. Do not rub off the edge through carelessness, which would impair the sharpness of the outline; this is much more easily done than you may think.

Once the inner profile is finished, we must start molding the outside curve. If the material is too thick for cutting along the outer circle with a coping saw, the circular form will have to be gently approached by several tangential cuts passing vertically through the wood. The resulting corners are knocked off with a framing chisel. It is advisable, however, to keep one of these corners in the shape of a narrow bridge so that for the time being, the hollowed block can be held by this corner in a screw clamp. This bridge should be cut off only after the carving is so far advanced that a screw clamp with a sufficiently long clamping arm can be employed to grip the bowl by the bottom.

If auxiliary cuts into the round from the side are required, such as are useful in forming a plate rim, it is important that the cut be uniformly deep. The simplest way is to mark these cuts by drawing a line on the saw with a wax crayon parallel to the teeth of the blade. Therefore, for this type of work the back saw with its broad blade or the dovetail saw is right. People who prefer to work according to feel rather than visually can clamp a narrow lath to the saw blade

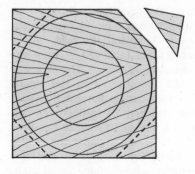

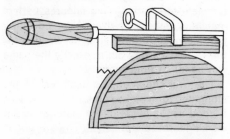

From the square block to the round: vertical saw cuts define the rough shape; for cuts made from the side use a dovetail saw. A stick clamped to the saw serves to control the depth of the cut.

When used for working sharply curved surfaces, the flat chisel will take a better bite if held mirror-side down.

which will then act as a depth gage. This procedure is more foolproof, and the correct penetration is obtained, even when working in a half-light, because the lath acts as a stop by automatically preventing the saw from penetrating too deeply.

As soon as enough wood has been cut away to reveal a distinctly rounded form, we can put away the gouge and the mallet and continue working with a broad flat chisel. A skew cutting edge is preferable, but this is not absolutely necessary. With the flat-ground chisel the cutting effect is not achieved by turning it about its axis, as with the gouge, but rather by a slight parallel displacement during the forward movement. The closer we approach to the final shape of the bowl, the sharper the curve that turns away under the blade of the tool; thus, the shaving it grasps gets smaller and smaller and at the same time it becomes more difficult to guide the tool on the bevel edge. Therefore, it is easier to work with the wrong side of the tool on convex surfaces; that is, to hold it with the mirror side to the wood and the bevel edge uppermost.

Don't try to get the wall of your bowl so thin that it rivals a china tea cup for transparency and fragility. A certain heaviness is inherent in the character of wood, but this by no means implies a lack of charm. The charm of wooden objects is derived from their graceful lines and the striking beauty of their surface.

The outside is polished in the same way as the inside, but this time we use a straight rasp, and after that again the spoke shave and sandpaper. It is questionable whether polishing is necessary in every case. Boldly outlined cuts can enliven the surface very effectively. But on no account should such cuts be timid, and never should they be added on purpose, by superfluous cutting with a gouge.

Oval Shapes

Oval shapes are even more in tune with the nature of wood than round ones, since the effect of the raw material having actually grown is more evident; also the fibre, the natural structure of the wood, is not cut up

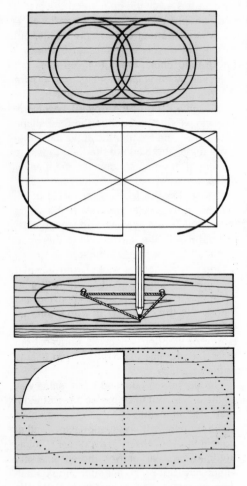

Development of oval shapes from a circle or rectangle, and how to draw an ellipse by means of a loop of string, a pencil, and two nails.

so much as in circular forms. To obtain an oval, or a shape based on the oval, we can use a paper template; the oval can be developed from a rectangle or from two slightly overlapping circles. The trick with a pencil and a loop of string, laid around two nails set at a certain distance from each other, can also help us to obtain an oval form. Once a satisfactory shape has been obtained, it is cut out in paper and divided into four parts. One quarter is used as a template for transferring the external shape onto the wood, by applying the quarter template four times. This ensures perfect matching of the two halves. After indicating the thickness of the wall by an inside line, the work is carried out in exactly the same way as for a round shape.

The oval shape adapts itself well to the elongated form of the plank, and in this way, if good use is made of the material, larger working forms are obtained. The oval shape goes well with deep hollows and steep walls if distinctively grained wood is used. In the event of the desired depth necessitating a block so thick that the "heart" of the tree has also got to be used, we draw our starting oval on the right side of the wood and lay it down with this side uppermost. In this way the close annual rings at the narrow ends of the bowl can be cut away to a minimum. On no account, however, must the actual medullary ray of the tree, which is quite pronounced in some types of wood, be left.

A good effect is achieved if the oval of a bowl or even a rectangle is tapered off into two handles at the narrow ends. It is true, however, that by describing them as "handles" we ascribe a purpose to these shapes which in reality they do not possess. They are not intended to be grasped when lifting the bowl off the table to take it away. The bowl has been shaped in such a way that it fits cleanly into the two open hands and

Some attractive bowls and dishes developed from square and rectangular blocks. Note the sparing use of ornament.

thus cries out to be picked up in this manner. There is nothing eccentric or mysterious about this; there are wooden bowls the beauty of which only becomes apparent in all its harmony when we hold them in our hands. The handles, then, have an esthetic, rather than a practical purpose. To a certain extent they repeat the shape of the bowl, gently absorbing its broad outlines. Essentially, they are no more than a deliberate rounding off of the whole. This should always be borne in mind when designing such handles, which can even take the shape of a stylized animal head. Avoid angular transitions, which look as though they had been stuck on, and also non-organic ornamentation that is in formal disharmony with the main lines of the bowl.

Ornament

Human beings have an almost irresistible decorative instinct. The smooth edge of a wooden plate seems to cry out for adornment in the form of a continuous ornament or a scroll. The bottom of the plate also can be enlivened by a chip-carved motif. Only the outside walls of deep oval or round bowls can be used for decoration. Such ornamental elements can be added by chip or incised carving. The techniques and appropriateness of ornamentation are discussed in Chapter 5. Here we shall merely

75

Straight scoops

emphasize that mastery is shown by restraint. Do not spoil good work by overloading it with frivolous ornament. The
temptation is great. But steel yourself and
resist. A few bold motifs, set sparingly in
the right place, are better than an elaborate
display. And above all: ornament should
only be added to quiet, calm surfaces. When
working in wood with a strong grain or
flamelike veining, the beautiful play of lines
should not be interrupted by "artistic" addi-
tions. Ornament must never degenerate
into being an end in itself and decorative
lines should never run counter to the true
shape of the object. As far as possible, the
carved form should be enhanced by the
ornament, which should never minimize or
obscure its basic shape.

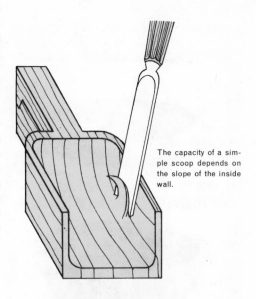

The capacity of a sim-
ple scoop depends on
the slope of the inside
wall.

Scoops—Ladles—Spoons—Forks

The way to a man's heart is through his
stomach, according to the proverb at least.
Thus love is tied up with the quality of food.
Food, however, is brought to the table in a
bowl and is conveyed to the stomach with a
spoon. Thus, there are secret connections
between bowls, spoons and love. And, in
fact, there were times when the spoon,
especially one carved by the lover himself,
was a much honored love token. "Let spoons
speak" was the saying then, and when all is
said and done there is really hardly any object as expressive as a spoon. By carving
appropriate symbols into the handle, binding promises of love and faith were given,
and the size indicated discreetly, but quite
unmistakably, what sized portions would be
expected from the beloved, once she had
become the mistress not only of the donor's
heart, but also of his kitchen. We, too, have
reasons enough to take a closer look at this
charming branch of wood carving. We need
no more tools than we have used so far. Soft

or strongly grained wood, however, will no
longer give us good practical results. Although, as a rule, we probably will not eat
with the spoons we carve, they will have a
rather delicate shape which requires strong
materials; moreover, the surface will have
to be resistant. We shall hardly want our
products to miss the purpose of their existence by being mere ornaments. They can
lead a useful life as salad servers, salt or
sugar spoons, flour scoops or ladles.

We therefore need hard wood. Red or
common beech is suitable for objects which
will usually either always be kept dry or
constantly dipped in water. Beech does not
stand up very well to continual changes.
Hornbeam *(Carpinus betulus)* is excellent
and durable, as it is very hard, but because
of this it is very difficult to carve. The wood
that serves our purpose best is maplewood.
It is white, non-porous, smooth, hard, and
neutrally grained.

It is advisable to start with a simple scoop.

This, in principle, is a hollow form, open on one side and with a handle at the closed end. The depth of the scoop will determine the thickness of our starting material, if we plan to make only a straight or slightly bent handle.

First, we draw a center-line on the surface of the block with a hard pencil and this will give us a reference for applying a paper template representing the shape divided in two lengthwise. After having determined the thickness of the wall of the scoop blade, we start working on the hollow interior. Make sure that the slope of the wall is sufficiently steep, in order to give the scoop as large a capacity as possible. Avoid all sharp transitions to the bottom and keep the shape gently rounded. The back wall needs to be carved very carefully, because here we have to deal with end grain wood. And end grain wood always involves finishing problems. Finishing is done by the methods already described, for example, with a swan's neck and sandpaper. Remember the advantages of a shaped sanding block for the transitional curve between the wall and the bottom of the scoop.

Once the inside shape has been established, the outside shape is cut out of the block with a fret saw. Should the block be a thick one, it may be better to use a coping saw. When you start adapting the rough outside shape thus obtained to the interior form, your work is nearing completion. The side walls taper off towards the front and swing around gently towards the straight or possibly slightly rounded front edge of the bottom. Make sure that the walls are not unnecessarily thick and clumsy. The front edge should be neither angular nor too sharp. You can round it off with sandpaper and then give it a very slight chamfer from the bottom. A too finely tapered handle for a scoop or ladle is annoying, because it can easily slide off the edge of the bowl into the soup. Make use of the available thickness of the material and carve at the end of the handle a decorative downward-pointing knob, beak or simple hook. This will not only stop the scoop sliding, but will support it when it is laid flat. You can also hang the scoop up by it, and, moreover, it will add to the beauty of the design.

Altogether, the handle of the scoop is the part where we can really go to town. The above-mentioned hook can be made into a horse's head or a flamingo beak, but, apart from that, the critical zone where the hollow shape of the scoop blade harmoniously flows into the elongated form of the handle, can also be used for ornamentation. When shaping this part of the scoop there is a great danger that beginners may imitate the shape of metal forms which have been soldered on. This must not be allowed to happen, because our raw material is wood, and the shapes formed out of it should correspond to the law of its growth.

If you are working on a very large scoop, you will find that cutting away the outer material with a carving knife is both a laborious and a time-wasting business. You will therefore think of ways and means of fixing the bulky piece to your work table so that you can carve the outside with a framing chisel. However, before you place your work in a screw clamp and tighten it up, remember that the wood has already been hollowed out on one side and has therefore been considerably weakened. For this reason, place a block of suitable thickness inside the hollow, otherwise you may hear a crack—and there are easier ways of obtaining firewood!

If you want your scoop handle to bend upwards at an angle to the blade, you will need a block which can accommodate the depth of the scoop blade plus the height of the angle formed by the handle. You must

Spoons and forks

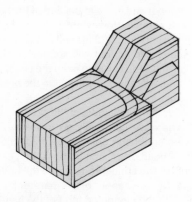

Bent-handled scoops call for a thick block. Before hollowing out the blade, saw out the slope of the handle and the shoulder of the scoop.

also bear in mind that these shapes are not meant to be flat little pans with which to sweep the crumbs off the table, but rather deeply hollowed cavities for a hearty dip into the flour or sugar bin. The first terror of the thick block is removed by forming a shoulder for the bend of the handle with a saw. Only then is the half-outline of the top transferred onto the surface of the block by means of a paper template. A profile sketch of the shape drawn on the side wall of the block will help you to stick to the correct measurements when cutting away waste wood with the saw and a wide chisel. All subsequent work is carried out in the manner already described.

As already mentioned, with such scoops the blade will assume a deeply hollowed shape. This will no longer run out more or less flat and level, but will rise slightly at the front. The greatest depth will be approximately two-thirds of the way towards the back of the blade. In working such scoops the blade can also be closed in front to form a continuous bowl, and extremely attractive

shapes can be achieved in this way. Such scoops, designed to taper gradually towards the front, may be constructed with slightly thicker walls.

It is only a small step from the scoop with a closed blade to the spoon. If the blade is made smaller and the handle elongated, we arrive at the typical spoon shape. The carving of a spoon will present no difficulties, as the work will be based on the skill and experience already acquired.

The shape of a flat spoon, the handle of which is on a level with the comparatively flat blade, can be cut out of a relatively thin piece of wood. A sound plank about $^5/_8''$ to $^3/_4''$ in thickness is sufficient as starting material for a flat pair of salad servers. A clever carver, who knows how to make use of his material, can make a small salt or sugar spoon from wood only $^3/_8''$ to $^1/_2''$ thick.

A pair of salad servers can be obtained from two identical spoons. When making a spoon with a bent handle, both the slope of the blade and the slope of the handle are defined with saw cuts before the blade itself is carved.

Scoops and spoons carved from different thicknesses of wood.

Larger dimensions are required for a bent handle combined with a tilted blade. We treat the rough block in the same way as we did for a scoop of the same general shape. First, we form shoulders to provide for the bend of the handle and the slant of the blade. Then we outline the shape as seen from above, and carve out the hollow of the blade. Only then do we saw off the angular edges of the rough block and start shaping the handle and the outside curve of the blade.

When planning a bent handle, make sure that the flow of the wood fibers is adapted as much as possible to the lines of your shape. This will not only make your work easier, but your handle will also be extremely durable. With the spoon, as with the scoop, the place where the handle joins the blade is a critical point, which might tempt the beginner into all sorts of tricks. Always bear in mind that the spoon is a practical utensil; its appearance should therefore be simple and its surface smooth. Naturalistic ornament in the form of allegorical shapes

or plastically modeled joints is contrary to its nature.

Only the upper side of the handle is suitable for very sparing, and definitely not naturalistic, simple chip-carved ornament. Ornamentation on a spoon which is in daily use becomes a problem for the most prosaic reasons. Spoons must be washed from time to time, and smooth surfaces are easiest to clean. When shaping the blade, avoid too deep a hollow and too pointed a form. Keep the curves on the top of the blade as nearly round as possible. Pay special attention to the edges of the blade to make sure that they do not get too thick. A sharply indicated transition from the edge to the back of the blade gives the spoon its distinctive profile.

Salad servers are rightly popular among home-made utensils. For these, however, we need a fork as well as a spoon. If you want to tackle salad servers, you will be well advised first to make two spoons of the same size and shape. The blades should not be too deep, they must not be too elon-

Hollowing out the block

gated and on no account too pointed. The
prongs of the fork can be cut out of one
of these spoons with a fret saw. But remember, more than three prongs will give you
not a salad fork, but a garden fork. Once you
have cut and polished the rough edges of
the prongs, your twin spoons will have
been transformed into a useful set of salad
servers.

Boxes from a Block

In the same way as we carved round, oval
or rectangular bowls from a square block,
we can also carve boxes and small jewel
cases. A practical model for this purpose is
the simple wooden pencil box as used by
schoolchildren, with the lid sliding in a
groove. Another form of construction for
the loose lid is the simple rabbet, and finally
for ambitious skilled do-it-yourself fans
there is the fixed lid swinging on a hinge,
with or without a rabbet. But going to a hardware store, buying a hinge like a piano hinge
in brass, and simply fixing it with screws is
out. Your work should be one hundred percent in tune with the material. Metal hardware on our little case represents a crime
against the spirit of the wood. Therefore the
hinge must be worked in wood too. To be
sure, this is not quite so simple any more,
but your pleasure will be all the greater
when you succeed. After all is said and
done, on some occasions we do need to
put our skill to a real test.

But first let's go back to the block and the
hollowing out operation. Only wood with a
fine structure can be used, such as basswood, pear or walnut. The learner would be
well advised to use basswood, which is
easier to work and also cheaper; moreover,
its completely neutral surface will be suitable for close decoration, which is in keep-

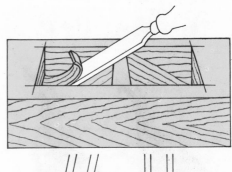

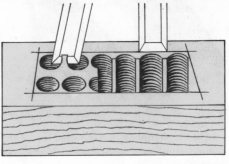

Chipping out the inside of a box. Either cut away the
wood from the middle towards the sides or drill out the
unwanted wood, chisel away the ridges between drill
holes, and clean up the inside face.

ing with the severe shape of the completed
box.

Be careful in your choice of wood. It must
be reliably dry and should come, if at all
possible, from the middle of an inside board.
Only then can you be sure that the lid which
has been shaped to close tightly will not jam
and thus spoil your precision work.

The inside walls can be vertical, but need
not necessarily be so, though a cigarette
box with a cylindrical bottom, where only
the two end walls are vertical, will tempt a
guest to help himself to a handful of ciga-
rettes.

However, even with vertical walls on all
sides, rounded corners are attractive. The
easiest and most uniform way of achieving

this is by spot drilling them using a large bit. In any case, a lot of hard labor can be saved by drilling away unwanted wood. However, don't forget the depth adjustment for the drill. After the drill has done its work, cut away the remaining ridges between the various drill holes and clean up the side walls. This is done with a wide flat chisel which is driven downwards vertically with the mirror side to the wall of the box.

Leveling the floor is hard detail work. The best procedure is first to take the two narrow sides down to the correct depth. This will give you a boundary line on the right and left hand sides and the base level in between. For the time being, however, this is so much theory, because the central mass of wood, which the drill did not reach, still rises well above this base level. This mass will be all the higher and more rugged, if the individual drill holes have not been taken down accurately and evenly. We now hold the chisel slanted at a shallow angle and cut away from the center towards the sides of the box; on completion of this process there will be only a single ridge left in the middle, with the bottom of the box sloping away towards the narrow ends on either side.

We can use the same technique when we have no drill available for a preliminary drilling operation, and are forced to strip away the compact central mass of wood with a framing chisel. In this case the ridge left in the middle will still be the same height as the thickness of our block after the correct depth at the sides has been reached. We start cutting down this ridge from its crest, provided the length of the inside of the box permits a slanting chisel cut. What remains must then be cut away in very fine slivers right down to the base level, starting at the left narrow end and holding the chisel vertically. The mirror side of the chisel will point towards the central ridge, that is in the direc-

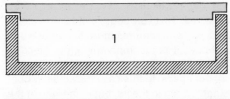

Two forms of rabbet: 1 in the lid, 2 in the wall of the box.

tion of cutting. On reaching the middle, the box is turned around and we start working in the same manner from the side which had previously been on the right. The final carving is much easier if done with a bent gouge. This applies in particular to the leveling off of the bottom. At all events, always try to achieve a neat surface with the carving tool itself. Smoothing with a block and sandpaper is a long and laborious process in the confined interior of the box.

Lid with rabbet and hinge

The loose lid definitely requires a rabbet that will prevent it from slipping off the box. The simplest method is the sunk rabbet, a step formed all around the lid and as wide as the wall of the box is thick. Such a lid will fit tightly and is easy to make, but cannot be called exactly elegant. The very massiveness of the joint makes the lid rather clumsy. Besides, there is another disadvantage: the rabbet takes up part of the precious space inside the box, on which we have not toiled

Glued lining

so hard just to accommodate a rabbet on a lid.

Accordingly, the second method of tackling the problem of the rabbet is to be preferred. This solution is a little more complicated, as it requires more accurate work. However, it is incomparably more elegant, gives a closer fit, and does not eat into the interior space. In this case the actual rabbet is not formed in the lid, but in the wall of the box, by cutting away half its thickness from the outside. This requires very accurate marking out of the rabbet and a scrupulouslously exact right-angle cut, because the final fit between the lid and the box must be like a "mirror image". This means that the lid should always fit, no matter which way round it is put on.

Thus, all the care taken in working out the rabbet on the box will be in vain if the corresponding projection on the lid, which fits over the rabbeted edge and gives a tight closure, is not worked out with the same precision. In this case it is necessary to work down to two or three hundredths of an inch, an activity that calls for more patience in constantly testing, putting on the lid and sanding, than if you were angling for fish in a rainwater tub. The principle of working from the inside to the outside, which we followed when carving bowls, also applies in a modified form to making boxes. It is true, the outside shape is approximately determined from the start, but the final detailed dimensions are only settled after the interior has been completely hollowed out and the problem of the rabbet has been solved. It is best, at the start, to choose a piece of wood for the lid big enough to project slightly beyond the walls of the box on all sides. Only after the fit of the rabbet is satisfactory do we assemble the two pieces, i.e. the box and the lid, lock them tightly in a screw clamp, and start the final treatment of both parts.

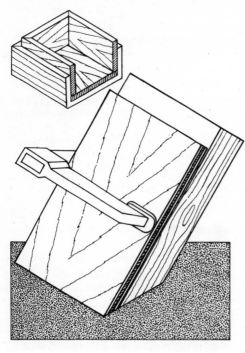

The lined box. Use a guide block to miter the walls.

If by ill luck during our work on the rabbet —in spite of all the care we exercised—we had an accident, for instance if the short fibres on the end-grain wood of the side wall broke off, this would be regrettable, but by no means a reason for despair. In such circumstances we could make a synthetic rabbet. Our box might no longer be an example of the finest craftsmanship, but from the outside it would look as beautiful as ever. The healing process starts by removing the ruins of the rabbet completely from all four walls. Then the whole interior of the box, i.e. the bottom and the walls, is lined with thin plywood, starting with the bottom. The plywood on the sides is made higher by the height of the rabbet than the outside walls of the box. A genuine mitered joint will give the cleanest detail in the corners. The 45° chamfer which this requires is sanded down on a flat piece of sandpaper. For this purpose clamp the plywood onto a thicker piece of solid wood which has been cut to the right miter angle. This will serve as a guide for the plywood lining. As soon as the lining has been glued in, the damaged box will have grown a new and quite acceptable rabbet. It will look even nicer if the upper edges are finished off by rounding from the inside.

An attractive, craftsmanlike device, in keeping with the material, is the snug-fitting lid that swings open on a wooden hinge. The mechanical action of the whole thing becomes clear when we look at a multi-tab hinge joint. This system, where the individual tabs engage each other like teeth, must be applied to the back wall of the box and the edge of the lid in such a way that one half of the hinge is carved out of the lid and the other half out of the box. For this purpose we leave a square projection along the top of the upper rear wall, the cross section of this projection being roughly twice as thick as the box wall; this is left rough and shaped later. A projection of the same dimensions is also left along the back edge of the lid, on the inside. So right at the start we must take care when measuring the piece for the lid. In its original form it must be at least twice as thick as the finished lid, which in this case should be the same thickness as the walls of the box. Besides this, the rough lid must be longer than the bottom of the box by at least the thickness of the projection. The second stage of hinge construction is to notch out the two square projections to form hinge tabs so that the lid sits neatly on top of

the box. For the sake of appearance the hinge should be finished off with an outside lid tab on the right and on the left. This is only possible if we make an uneven number of tabs. Let us assume that there are five tabs all told, of which three are pin tabs on the lid and two socket tabs on the back wall of the box. We therefore divide the projection on the lid into exactly five parts. This is done by proportional division. Those who can't remember how to do this from their school days, should look it up in the glossary under the heading "proportional division."

When the five parts have been marked off, we can start notching. Make vertical cuts (exactly vertical!) with the dovetail saw and then chisel out the unwanted wood. First cut along the base line with the chisel, so as to get a clean cut. It is wrong to try to knock out all the waste with one blow. Just pare away a little bit at a time. When this notching is complete it is transferred to the projection on the box wall by fitting both parts together and tracing the outline of the notches onto the hinge block with a sharp hard pencil.

After the notch outlines have been carried over the back edge of the hinge block, the two wall tabs are sawn out and the wood between and on either side is cut away with a chisel. Take care always to saw inside the part of the wood that is to be removed, otherwise the joint will be too slack.

Now for the next stage, which requires courage, self-confidence and great accuracy with the drill. The hinge tabs, which have now been fitted together, still have their square profile. At either end of the hinge the intersection of the diagonals drawn across the outer faces of the two outside lid tabs forms the starting point for the drill; we now drill a fairly broad hole through these two outside tabs right into the wall tabs on the other side (start working

The hinge tabs

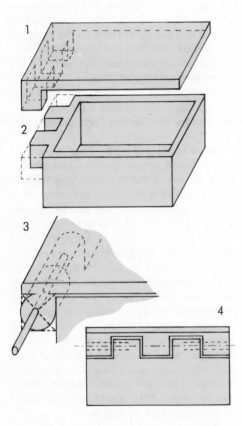

The hinged lid: 1 lid projection with three tabs, 2 two tabs left on wall to receive hinge pins, 3 the starting point for the drill, used to make holes for the hinge pins, lies at the intersection of the diagonals of the end faces of the wall projection. After drilling, the square form is rounded off. 4 rear view of hinge.

with a fine bit, and later enlarge the hole with a heavier one).

A peg or dowel is glued into this drill hole to act as a pin for the hinge, that is, it is glued only to the outside lid tabs, which thus become the pin tabs. The pin should turn easily inside the two tabs left on the box wall. In order to achieve this, it will be necessary to make the pin slightly thinner by sanding it where it projects into the wall tabs. Make the two pin dowels an inch or so longer than actually required. You will have to take them out more than once in the course of the work. This will be easier if they are long enough for you to grab the ends with pliers.

Drilling the hole for the hinge pin is one of the most critical operations of the entire job. If the drill is allowed to slip even slightly, the pin will not lie along the required axis of rotation, and the hinge will jam. For this reason we shall proceed cautiously and refrain from driving the drill holes right into the center tab of the lid, as this would only increase the risk of a sticking hinge. This center tab is only for show. It serves to improve the appearance of the box, but has no practical function.

From a technical point of view, we should bear in mind that when drilling we are boring along the length of the wood. Great care is therefore required to prevent the tab from splitting. Mark the exact starting point for the drill with a pin, use only a very sharp bit and avoid excessive pressure when driving it through the wood. It stands to reason that such difficult designs should not be carried out in very brittle or in very soft wood. But even when working with very dense pearwood or tough maplewood, we should always bear in mind that we are shaping material that is only a fraction of an inch thick.

Even if we get as far as the first test fitting of the hinge pin without an accident, we shall find that the hinge will still not work because the tabs are still square. Anything that has to turn easily must be round. So take the hinge pins out and round the three lid tabs with a chisel, a rasp and fine sandpaper. Care must be taken to preserve the true shape of the back of the lid. Only the hinge tab should be rounded. The best thing to do is to mark the thickness of the lid clearly above the tab by making a clean chisel cut parallel with the edge of the lid. Do not round the tabs—especially in the front—more than is absolutely necessary for the pivoting movement. Otherwise you will unnecessarily weaken the construction.

When the pin tabs have been correctly shaped, the lid can be hung in temporarily, and you can start rounding the wall tabs. The pin tabs will serve as guides for this. When this job has also been completed with the necessary care, it should in theory be possible to open and shut the lid freely. In practice, however, there will still be plenty of places where it rubs and where irregularities occur; these can be removed with very fine sandpaper. In this connection pay attention to the joints between the individual tabs to see whether they are not too tight.

When the hinge has passed the final test, we can glue in the pins. Take care that the ends of the pins are not coated with glue, otherwise they will stick to the sockets in the wall tabs. The hinge will pivot more easily if the ends of the pins—but only the ends—are waxed before the pins are glued. After the glued joints have set, the projecting pin stumps are cleanly removed, and our box is complete.

One would hardly take all this trouble with a cheap, commonplace piece of wood, unless it were for the sake of practice. For a box of this kind, an example of our craftsmanship and skill, a fine wood with a handsome grain is called for. Its surface will be its own ornament. On the other hand, boxes made from a block of wood with a neutral grain, especially those with sliding lids, are very suitable for setting off rich chip carving. But please work only from a well thought out design, and remember the difficulties connected with end grain surfaces when it comes to making fine cuts.

Carving in relief

A wide and very attractive field of activity producing work of great beauty and craftsmanship is ornamental relief carving. There are not many crafts in which, after some practice even the less skilled can achieve things with a real claim to be of lasting value.

The purpose of ornamental relief carving is purely decorative. In practicing this hobby, we are in the field of applied art, and it is no longer sufficient merely to handle the material in a workmanlike way. Careful consideration must be given to the harmonious proportioning of the available surface and to the selection of an appropriate style of ornamentation, in order to avoid a clash between the structure of the object and its decoration.

Formal instructions and cut-and-dried rules will not take you very far in this field. Those seriously interested will be well advised to spend a few hours in a crafts museum, where they can study ancient carved chests, door paneling and chairs, in which the functional and the ornamental are often admirably combined.

In such places you will find endless inspiration. You should by no means, however, engage in mere thoughtless imitation. Avoid slavish copying at all costs—even if your sketching ability is good enough for you to take home in your sketchbook all the details of the ornament on a chair-back you have seen, unless, of course, you have deliberately set yourself this task. Those who study the wealth of forms encountered in museums that exhibit peasant crafts and primitive art will soon find that a whole series of basic motifs keep recurring in the work of the old masters. The same applies to folk songs. They also deal with the impulses and feelings of simple, unspoilt people, and yet they are not monotonous. Nature was the teacher in this type of art, which is deeply rooted in rural life. Certain groups of motifs have been developed from nature's rich store of ornament, and these we keep encountering in endless variation. There is the oak leaf and the maple leaf, the entwined vine and the grape; and from the animal kingdom the sly fox, the peaceful dove, the busy bee and the prophetic woodpecker, who all give an underlying meaning to the ornamental relief. Neither must we overlook ancient symbols expressing spells and charms against evil, which are rooted in mythical prehistoric times and have remained alive up to the present day. A few of these symbols are the witch's broom, the tree of life, runic letters, and also the butterfly, the symbol of perpetual return.

So why not make use of this wealth of ideas and shapes in your own designs. They are timeless, and also there is a genuine inner relationship between our present work and the old folk craft of long ago. By critically observing historic and often very large works, we can learn about far more than the mere application of ornament. We can, as it were, look over the masters' shoulders and learn a lot about the techniques by which they transferred natural objects onto a wooden surface, stylizing the form to harmonize with the structure of the material.

Now we have reached the point where we must put our theoretical knowledge to work.

For this we shall need medium-hard or hard wood, which will clearly reveal the carved contours. Our work should not only look attractive, but should be practical as well; thus the material must be able to stand up to normal wear and tear. Close-grained oak is the right wood.

And now an example: suppose we set out to enliven the four panels of a closet door with ornamental relief. Let us assume that our design has been decided upon and we have chosen a continuous oak-leaf motif, finished off by a flat, not too narrow frame. This design is neatly drawn up to full size in pencil on strong tracing paper (it can be traced from a sketch) and is then transferred to the freshly planed wood surface by tracing over carbon paper. Then the wood bearing the tracing is clamped to the work table with screw clamps in such a way that two edges are lined up with the right-hand front corner of the table. Arranged in this way the work-piece always presents two directions of attack and does not need to be changed around too frequently.

As far as possible try to work only with straight chisels, the carving will remain fresher and more spontaneous. Smooth, slick shapes similar to those found in plaster or stucco should be avoided at all costs. Start by cutting the inner edge of the frame, which should be slightly tapered and not vertical. Therefore the chisel should not

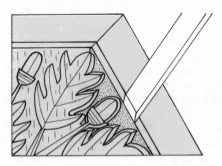

The technique of relief carving. First cuts along the inside edge of the frame and the contours of the ornament with the chisel held in a slightly slanting position.

be held exactly upright. At the same time care must be taken not to cut too deep. In his enthusiasm the beginner often tends to exaggerate the relief. One should always bear in mind that relief work is meant to enliven flat planes and that its character should therefore remain plane-like.

The relief grows downwards from the surface. For this reason, in carrying out the second operation we should remember to maintain this surface everywhere at the same height; this means that we must not go below the level of the frame in which the original thickness of the plank is still contained.

We now have to prick in the outlines of the various ornamental shapes and cut back the wood near their edges until the shapes begin to show up against the plane. Simultaneously we very sparingly cut away the background. This process should be carried only to the point where the shape emerges clearly in three dimensions. Then follows the interesting part, the application of the finishing touches. With a small, keen chisel, sharpened on a leather strap, carve the surface and edges of the leaves and the curves of the acorns; the veins of the leaves are gently scratched in and the filigree of the stalks defined.

Cutting out the background is not too easy. In this case sandpaper, which in other forms of woodwork is our last standby, is of no avail. By using sandpaper we would only blur the contours. Therefore forget about sandpaper and use two bent chisels, one with the cutting edge sloping to the right and one with it sloping to the left. If the background has largish empty spaces, we can make a virtue of necessity and stipple the background with a punch. Narrow spaces can be worked with small punches made from wood screws, by developing the groove in the head into a lattice by filing in additional

Treatment of the background with a punch or matting tool heightens the contrast. The empty spaces run together.

notches. In spaces where there is no room for even the smallest punch, the background is enlivened simply by making a few pricks. A background treated in this way offers a great deal of contrast. The smoothly carved, restful surface of the ornamental motif stands out distinctly against the lively background which enhances the plastic effect. In general, however, arrange your design in such a way that empty spaces in the background are avoided or at least restricted to a bare minimum.

Ornament of this kind can be applied anywhere where large surfaces need to be enlivened by decoration. If you visit a museum where craftwork is exhibited, as previously advised, you will notice that the old masters used relief decoration for adding interest to the broad surfaces of the walls and lids of their chests; that they emphasized the structural principle of a door by decorating the frame, or by fluting the panels; they even raised an ordinary piece of furniture like a chair to the level of a work of art by finely carving the arms and the back.

Those who have already gained some skill in this craft may well venture to add to their home the luxury of one or even several hand-carved chairs, or to raise their coffee table above the mass of factory-produced furniture by adding a relief in keeping with its style, or even to lend some individuality to a wall closet by means of suitable surface ornamentation.

When planning such an ambitious task, give the structure of the piece of furniture precedence over the artistic decoration, and leave the assembling to the very last. Suppose we take a chair as an example: first produce all the individual structural components in accordance with a scale working drawing; then try fitting these together loosely, for testing. If the test is satisfactory, carve the appropriate surfaces. Only then, when all the carving tools have been put away, is the final assembly carried out.

If you intend to attempt to make a chair for the first time in your life, you should try and have a deep discussion with an experienced craftsman concerning the necessary jointing techniques. At all events it is better to

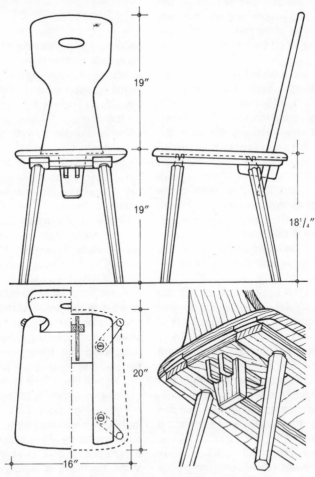

Working drawing for a simple plank chair.

have the different structural components accurately cut in a good workshop according to your design. This is particularly advisable if your own workshop is not yet properly equipped for such extensive work. Even the most magnificent carving does not justify the existence of a wobbly chair that might collapse at any time. In their design for the cross-bracket or a full back rest, some may arrive at constructions involving pierced filigree work. This is traced onto the wood from the drawing and then cut with a fret saw or coping saw, if the dimensions permit. Following this, the work is glued to a backing board with joiner's glue and fixed to the working table with screw clamps. Only those who do not value their table top and who do not mind chipping it to bits when working on the pierced ornament with chisels, need save themselves the trouble of gluing the carving to a backing board. The careful worker, who uses a backing board, should incorporate a sheet of newspaper in the glued joint. If this is not done, the two boards will be inseparable once the carving has been finished. The layer of paper will prevent the boards from sticking firmly and the joint can always be parted again with the help of a knife or a chisel.

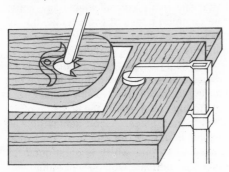

Work involving pierced ornament is temporarily glued to a backing board to avoid damaging the top of the work table.

Those considering ignoring our advice on the sequence of operations should bear in mind that a complete heavy oak armchair is harder to control than one of its arms alone. And apart from this, even the careful may be unlucky and nobody can make a pact with fate, not even wood carvers. It can be very annoying to make a wrong cut or splinter off a fragment of wood from a chair frame which has been assembled and glued and doweled together to last for centuries. In such a large piece of work, not all the parts that are being carved will be of the same quality or have the same properties. If the chair has not yet been assembled and glued together, it is easy to make good any accident by simply replacing the damaged part. So do not throw away your tracing pattern before you are ready to smoke your first leisurely cigarette in your new home-made rocking chair.

Inlaying and Veneering

The technique of decorating wood surfaces by inlay work is different again. This two-dimensional art consists in the decoration of the surfaces of furniture, utensils or whole walls by inserting thin pieces of variously colored woods, tortoise shell or mother-of-pearl, but also of horn, straw and metal. Two methods can be used. Either genuine inlay, where the wood base is appropriately hollowed out to form a bed for the inlaid material, or applied inlay. In this latter technique the entire surface of the base is covered by a veneer which has been put together like a mosaic.

The art of inlaying—or to use the Italian word "intarsia"—rests on a venerable tradition. It came from the Far East in ancient times, reached its peak during the Middle Ages and particularly in Italy during the early Renaissance, and was again employed

Applied veneer

with great success in French furniture of the 18th century, which is famous for its artistic effects. Since that time the craft has declined in importance and nowadays is hardly practiced at all. This is surprising, as modern furniture and interior decoration with their flat, broad surfaces would seem to offer many possibilities for applying inlaid work. Nevertheless, this craft seems practically predestined to serve as a source of decorative exercises in the "do-it-yourself" workshop. Very little material is required, the technique is easily mastered and, apart from good taste, you only need a careful methodical way of working.

So as not to complicate matters, we shall first deal only with wood inlaying, and for the time being ignore true inlaying and occupy ourselves exclusively with the applied technique, which is similar to veneering. Any wooden surface is suitable for this, even a tray, a table top, a wall or the lid of the famous jewel box which most amateur woodworkers produce.

Some of the basic rules for veneer work can be transferred directly to inlaying; after all, covering a surface with a thin veneer consisting of several parallel sheets is nothing more than a primitive type of inlay work. The first rule to be applied is to take into account the direction of the fibres. Solid wood as well as plywood may be used as a base. Solid wood is veneered by making the fibres of the veneer run in the same direction as those of the base. The opposite applies to plywood, where the fibres of the applied veneer should run at right angles to the fibres of the top face veneer of the plywood board. We shall therefore arrange our motif in such a way that as many as possible of its veneer sections are correctly related to the fibre direction of the base. Otherwise there is a risk of the applied layer splitting.

The inlaying technique described here involves covering the entire surface of the base. This produces a one-sided strain which must be counteracted by fixing a false veneer to the opposite side. If the opposite side is not exposed, inferior or waste veneer may be used for this purpose, but in the interest of balanced stress the back veneer should be of the same thickness as that on the front. The fact that the base must be dry, quite even and neatly sanded will be obvious to anyone who has observed the impeccable, mirror-like smoothness of an inlaid surface. Our raw material is veneer, which is available in a rich range of colors from native and foreign woods. The kind of veneer used has, of course, a decisive influence on the effect of the finished work. Inlay is a high-quality surface treatment and therefore, if at all possible, the best of all veneers, namely sawn veneer, should be used. This preserves the natural structure of the wood and its surface is closed, because the wood fiber has not been broken. For this reason it polishes up well, and there is no danger of the glue penetrating, as is the case with knife-cut and peeled veneers. Cut the veneer with a very sharp chip carving tool, a fine fret saw, or better still with a special veneer saw knife. The common edges of two sheets should, wherever possible, be formed with a single cut, thus ensuring an exact fit. If the veneer is cut with a fret saw, it is advisable to stick adhesive tape over the cutting line before starting to saw. This saves the veneer from splintering and prevents the breaking off of small jagged pieces. Good-quality glue is just as important for our work as good veneer. Cold glue, which is quite good for other less intricate work, is not suitable in this particular instance, as it will discolor the joint. It is advisable therefore to use synthetic resin or cellulose adhesives. These also have the advantage that they can be used cold and they prevent the veneers from sliding around during the sticking process. On the other hand, they have the disadvantage that they require a hardening agent and set immediately. Any errors cannot be made good.

One of the best types of glue for inlay work remains the good old-fashioned joiner's glue in its more elegant form of skin-glue. Its adhesive power is excellent and it does not penetrate even thin peeled veneers as easily as ordinary bone glue. It is important, however, that it should be applied quite hot in a warm room using preheated parts; also, after the jointing operation, sufficient time must be allowed for it to set under effective and even surface pressure.

The veneer is brought to the correct temperature for gluing with an ordinary electric iron, the base is easily warmed on the hot plate of a stove. The temperature is right when the surface feels comfortably warm when held against the cheek. In spite of all the inconvenience of using joiner's glue, it nevertheless has the great advantage of not setting within seconds, so that if we work reasonably fast, we can make some adjustments in the fit. Also joiner's glue is cheap. If for any reason thin knife-cut or peeled veneer has to be used, it is advisable to mix a little chalk in with the glue. This makes it harder for the glue to penetrate the pores of the weak material when it is under pressure during the setting operation.

The setting pressure must be uniformly effective over the entire veneered surface. This is best achieved by putting the glued work between two strong, completely even boards that have also been warmed and then clamping the whole together with as many screw clamps as possible. This means that the entire inlaid surface must consist of uniform pieces of veneer of equal thickness.

Example of ornamental veneering. The main motif is inlaid in a continuous veneer background.

However, it will not always be possible to obtain the raw material in such uniform thicknesses as to prevent differences in level from resulting. This condition may be made even more acute by the sometimes inevitable use of mounting or framing strips. This nuisance can be overcome by putting a piece of soft cardboard, for example so-called photogravure cardboard, between the pressure-distributing board and the veneered surface. Do not try to use newspaper. Printing ink comes off on the veneer and can never be removed.

To illustrate this method of applied inlaying, suppose we take the simple example of

91

Assembling a chessboard

a chessboard. Here we are dealing with straight lines, but these are suitable for pointing the way to the successful fitting together of other, more complicated inlay designs.

As a backing we shall take a $1/4''$ thick square of plywood with edges 18 inches long. This might seem rather large, but first of all we want a playing area with good

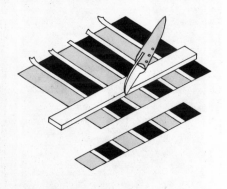

Assembling a chessboard made out of strips of veneer. Cutting the small squares from a series of alternating black and white strips.

visibility, and secondly we do not want to make our work harder in this practical example by using tiny elements that have to be laboriously fitted together. In order to achieve a good contrast between the squares, we shall choose maple veneer as inlay material for the white squares (bird's-eye maple is particularly attractive) and ebony or the slightly warmer black rosewood or jacaranda wood for the black ones. Each of the 64 individual squares measures 2 inches along the side and there are eight in a row. For people who are quick at arithmetic, and who have already spotted that 8 x 2 inches can never add up to the measurement given for the base, we should add that the difference of 2 inches will provide

space for a neutral edge, to be put around the actual playing area.

To return to the practical work. Start by cutting a total of eight strips—four from the white and four from the black veneer—all 2 inches wide. Guide your cut with a steel-edge ruler. For measuring use precision rulers and a magnifying glass. You can't be too accurate. The individual strips are laid next to each other in alternate colors with contact along the fibers, and assembled with adhesive tape to form a single surface. You can buy special veneering tape made of thin, but tough paper with a special adhesive. The adhesive must be free of acid, so as not to discolor the sensitive veneers, and must be fast-setting, yet not too strong. Such tape is obtainable in various widths, the narrower ones being more practical. For assembly work using the cold glue process, regular adhesive tape can also be used.

Always do the sticking on the exposed side. Once the strips have been fitted together, reduce the square to exactly 16 x 16 inches by trimming the edges. The rough playing area thus obtained is now again divided into strips 2 inches wide, but in the other direction. Those who have worked with the necessary accuracy can now fit the

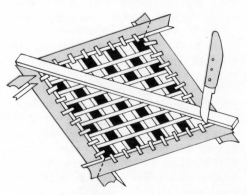

Cutting the corners of the assembled playing surface.

resulting strips together in the regular checkerboard pattern, again using adhesive tape. After the individual squares that project on the right or the left have also been made to fit the large square, the playing area is finished and is now enlarged to the full size of the board by adding a border.

The border should repeat the two-color scheme of the playing area. For this purpose cut strips of white veneer $^3/_{16}$" wide and slightly longer than the edges of the playing square. These are attached to the inner square in such a way that their ends overlap completely at the corners. To this white intermediate strip we now add a second closing strip of dark veneer. The width of this dark outside strip is determined by the width of the free zone still remaining around the edge of the backing board. The outside strip must be wide enough to project at least $^1/_2$" beyond the backing board on all sides. We need this projection in order to glue on four retaining blocks. These blocks will serve as guides when we mount the checkerboard veneer, fitting closely against the edges of the board and preventing the veneer from slipping. For this reason they must be glued with great precision following closely the dimensions of the backing board and parallel to the edges of the veneer and backing.

Before this, however, the corners of the border strips must be neatly mitered. This is best done with a steel straight-edge, cutting through the two overlapping strips in one stroke. If the square has been correctly constructed, the necessary miter cut will lie along the diagonal of the square, extended beyond the corners. To mount the assembled playing surface, complete with guide blocks, simply coat the top of the pre-warmed backing board with a good-quality, warm and easily flowing glue (do not heat the glue to more than 140°F).

Try to make do with as little glue as possible. The less the moisture that penetrates into the wood when gluing, the less the risk of warping. Then quickly apply the veneer, cover it with a sheet of paper, and run a warm iron over the whole surface, pressing hard. The warmth of the iron will reactivate any of the glued areas that may have dried out, and this will tighten up the veneer. Then exchange the sheet of paper you used for ironing for the protective cardboard already mentioned and put the entire work into a press consisting of screw clamps and two flat boards.

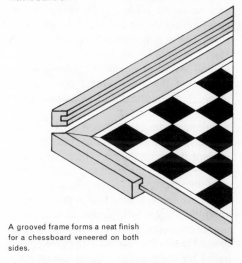

A grooved frame forms a neat finish for a chessboard veneered on both sides.

After letting the work dry for at least 24 hours in a well-heated room, it is time to start cleaning up. First, trim the edges and tidy them up with a smooth plane. Be careful not to go beyond the corners; work inwards from both sides towards the middle of the edge of the board. After soaking off the assembly tape, scratch away what remains with a knife blade. The whole surface is then shaved in the direction of the fibers with a spoke shave and sanded with the finest sandpaper on a sanding block. Those who

Figure compositions

really know how to handle a smooth plane and can grind the iron to a really fine edge, and who also know how to adjust this tool to the finest limits, can use it for cleaning up the playing surface. But with all this finishing be careful not to go right through the edges of the veneer.

After the conclusion of this operation, the width of the joints between the individual components will show with what precision we have worked. Joints as fine as a hair will vanish with subsequent polishing. In the light-colored parts wider joints can be filled with a filler made of chalk and shellac; in the dark parts the chalk can be replaced with very fine brick dust or reddle, or even with soot. These emergency measures, however, can only be applied after putting on several layers of polish, as otherwise the surface of the wood would discolor too much. This is discussed in greater detail in the next chapter.

Before starting to polish, it will be necessary to veneer the back of the chessboard to prevent it from warping. Those who have succeeded with the front will have no difficulty with the back. The procedure is practically the same, except that in this case the complete veneer is mounted in one piece, unless of course, you are ambitious enough to want to use the reverse side of the chessboard for some other counter game. After your experience with the chessboard, it should be fairly easy for you to find a way of doing this.

Finally, when both sides of the board have been veneered, it will be necessary to provide a frame worthy of the job, since the exposed edges of the backing board are anything but beautiful. A light, grooved strip of wood, about $5/_8''$ thick, is attractive and also practical, since then the delicate playing surface will never lie flat against the table. This strip can be made into a square

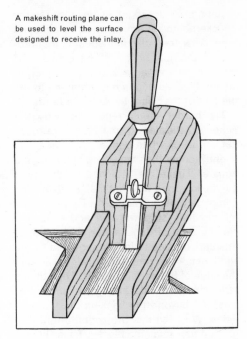

A makeshift routing plane can be used to level the surface designed to receive the inlay.

frame with mitered corners and the board fitted into the grooves. Splines about $1/_8''$ thick can be glued into the corners of the frame to act as reinforcement, but this is a rather delicate job. All this, however, must wait until the board has been polished.

Inlay work becomes much more complicated when the designs are geometrical or involve figures with elaborate outlines. Do not stick to strictly naturalistic forms when developing such picture motifs. To stay true to the material we must endeavor to be creative without going beyond the possibilities offered by the wood itself, which, as we have seen, is a unique material with its own means of expression.

If it is intended to construct a motif by fitting together individual pieces in the manner of a mosaic, which was practically the case with the chessboard, then the work will proceed basically in the same way. However, especially if the design is a fairly large one, we shall no longer use strips of adhesive tape for assembling the pieces but an accurate template; this template is made by tracing from the original design, including all the internal connecting lines. Transparent Japanese paper is suitable, but any other tracing paper can be used, as long as it is strong enough and does not stretch. The paper is dampened slightly with a sponge, left for a few minutes and then— while still damp—stretched tightly over a level surface, such as a drawing board (with the drawing on the back), and taped down. Once this sheet has dried you will have a perfectly smooth surface for assembling the veneer. Working outwards from the center, put your mosaic together out of the variously shaped little plates that you have meanwhile cut from another tracing. To assemble these pieces you can use starch paste or a good rubber cement. This contains no water, the veneer will not swell and can later be easily detached. Therefore corrections are simple to make. Be sure you fix the top surface of the veneer to the paper. When working on a very large job it is advisable to give duplicate serial numbers to the pieces of veneer and the corresponding areas of the design.

Where the parts are to be set in a continuous veneer background, a device similar to the cutters used in making cookies would be an ideal tool for obtaining a correct fit. This method, however, would be too expensive for ordinary use; therefore first cut the inner, i.e. the inlay piece, around a template made of metal foil which can be sufficiently firmly fixed to the veneer with rubber cement. The shape cut out, including the foil template, now serves as a pattern for cutting the background veneer. Only then is the metal foil detached and the two parts can be fitted into each other. This technique approaches genuine inlaying, where a motif is actually "laid into" a given surface. For example, suppose the lid of a chest is to be decorated with an heraldic emblem. This emblem might be a stylized key, a Bourbon lily, an heraldic beast, or some other symbol. Such a figure would also be produced by means of a metal-foil template and would serve as a pattern for marking the surface of the lid.

The rest of the work would mostly consist in removing the corresponding area of the lid, the outlines of which would have been fixed by deep scratches made with an extremely sharp point. This is the finest precision work, measured in hundredths of inch. The basic surface must be completely flat and the depth of the cut must everywhere be the same, as the inlay must have a level bed, or else it will refuse to stick. An excellent auxiliary tool is the routing plane; with a little trouble one can make this oneself out of a wood block, a clip and a narrow-bladed chisel. The illustration shows what this device looks like.

Don't use overly thin veneers for this type of work. They should project a good $1/_{32}$" above the surface after gluing. Differences in thickness are eliminated after the glue has set and before polishing.

Surface treatment of wood

Wood is wood and should remain wood. Once the tool has done its job, the surface should be left alone. This is the creed of all those who believe in respecting their material. It is a very honorable creed, but cannot be strictly applied in practice. Ordinarily wood is exposed to the effects of time and environment, including dirt, humidity and mechanical damage. Wood must be protected against these influences and made resistant to them by suitable surface treatment. Recommended processes include oiling, waxing, varnishing and polishing. All these seal the pores and harden the surface or even provide a protective film. They also serve to increase the natural beauty of the wood.

The finest surface treatment is polishing. At the same time, it is also the most difficult. This, however, should not put us off, because there is no other means of giving an inlaid surface the mirror-like high gloss that sets it off to best effect.

One point must be made quite clear: the true art of inlaying only starts with the polishing. For this we need perseverance, strength, patience, and sensitive finger tips. We also need shellac, very fine pumice powder, and, above all, a polishing pad, which in times gone by used to be a carefully guarded secret of the old polisher-craftsmen. It can be made from a fist-sized lump of raw sheep's wool, around which is wound a piece of linen that has been washed a thousand times. Don't try polishing with cotton wool. The individual cotton wool fibres are too hard. They scratch and will never give a high gloss. By nature wood is not a polishable material. It is too soft, not dense enough, and too porous. Besides, the surface is not stable, since it works in response to changes in humidity. All these obstacles have to be overcome. The basic requirement for a properly polished finish is bone-dry wood and a surface which has been ground microscopically smooth and clean. For this reason allow the chessboard to dry out thoroughly after the veneer surface has been fixed, then, after the last fine sanding and after having removed the very last grain of dust, you can start polishing.

Start by applying a few drops of a thin shellac solution to the polishing pad and rub over the surface with a circular movement. While you are rubbing, spread minute quantities of pumice over the surface. Pumice serves as a filler for the pores, and also as a polishing agent. The same powder is also rubbed into the fine joints between the individual pieces of veneer so that the joint lines gradually vanish. When the pad starts to get dry, more shellac is added in minute doses.

Do not lose patience if after the first few hours of work your rubbing still seems to produce no effect. The saying that nothing good is ever achieved in a hurry must have been invented by a wood polisher. The first thing you will notice is that your polishing pad starts sticking and no longer slides. Now add a drop of shellac to the pad together with a drop of the very finest bone oil. Then very gradually the surface will take on a bright shine, which will develop into a really magnificent gloss as you continue working away. Now forget the filler and continue working with pure shellac, to which you may add a drop of oil only when the polishing pad starts to stick.

The whole procedure takes quite a time. You can reckon that if you work hard and under very clean conditions quite free from dust, it will take you about a week to achieve a decent polished surface (for the front of a 6' by 12' bedroom closet you can safely allow a month). After this the surface will still need some time to harden under dry and undisturbed conditions. By then you will probably have become so attached to your masterpiece that you will be reluctant to part with it.

A very much simpler operation is oiling. This is the treatment given to figure carvings or utensils, especially to those made of soft wood. It consists of impregnating the surface with hot boiled linseed oil, applied several times very thinly with a soft rag.

After the last application is completely dry, sand the surface with very fine sandpaper. By adding a small quantity of artist's oil colors to the oil, you can at the same time stain the wood, but do not use opaque pigment or body color.

Waxing gives a very attractive surface. Unfortunately this is neither scratch- nor water-proof, so the process cannot be applied to utensils destined for regular use. Pure beeswax is dissolved into a paste in turpentine and rubbed energetically into the surface with a rag. When it is dry, polish with a horsehair brush. Floor polish or neutral shoe polish can be used in emergencies.

An attractive mat effect is achieved by dull finishing. Suitable polish can be bought ready-made, or you can make it yourself from a shellac solution to which a little turpentine and wax has been added. This is applied evenly with a soft rag. A brush tends to leave brush marks. Dull-finishing agents with a cellulose base are very durable, but cannot be made at home.

Finally, a wood surface can be varnished. As with all other finishes, the surface must be well cleaned and sanded before the varnish is applied (the last sanding should be only in the direction of the grain). It is advisable to apply one or two coats of mat cellulose polish before laying on the varnish. If two coats are used, the first must have thoroughly dried out before the second is applied. The priming should be carefully brushed with a horsehair brush, dusted off and covered with a coat of clear copal or synthetic-resin varnish.

The varnish must be well-tempered and should be flowed on in a dust-free atmosphere with a soft-hair paint brush. The surface should lie flat, as varnish tends to run and form stripes. A second coat can only be applied when the first one is quite dry, otherwise the latter will be roughened by the brush strokes. Brushes should always be held at an angle, never perpendicular to the surface.

Staining can only be regarded as a surface treatment with certain reservations. It is a process that gives the wood a colored tint without concealing the grain. The simplest and best staining process for an amateur is to paint the surface of the wood with a water or spirit stain, though oil stains produce equally good results. The commonest stain is walnut stain, which is sold in crystal form. This is dissolved in water or in spirit; after the liquid has settled it should be strained through a woollen cloth. Adding a small amount of ammonia will make the color of the stain more pronounced. Traces of iron will discolor the stain; it must therefore not be mixed in tin cans or applied with brushes that have iron collars. This is particularly risky if the collars are rusty.

Having selected a tint, apply the stain —more or less strongly diluted—with a well-loaded brush. Surplus stain can be absorbed with blotting paper. As the moisture will raise the grain of the wood, it must first be soaked and then sanded. End-grain sections are particularly absorbent. In order to prevent these from becoming too dark by greedily soaking up the stain, they should first be wetted with a damp sponge.

Before staining a valuable piece it is most advisable to carry out tests on waste wood of the same type, so that the intensity of the stain can be varied either by diluting the solution or by adding more stain. When the stain is dry, the roughened surface must be carefully sanded. Then the final finish is applied by either oiling, waxing, varnishing or mat-polishing.

A process which is halfway between tinting and surface treatment is wax staining. A wax stain is a water stain to which ammonia, beeswax and potassium carbonate have been added; this mixture can be bought ready-made and is applied thickly and slightly warm. Afterwards it is only necessary to polish lightly with a horsehair brush in order to obtain an attractive eggshell gloss.

Staining with the ordinary water, oil or spirit stains has the disadvantage that the softer parts of the wood absorb more liquid than the hard ones and therefore become darker. This gives a negative image of the structure of the wood. In general, this reversal of values does not matter, but those wishing to avoid it will have to use chemical stains, which are much more difficult to handle. They can, however, be used successfully if the manufacturer's instructions are strictly followed.

Now, as in former times, ornament is still the most popular means of decorating one's surroundings and everyday objects. Ornament was probably the first conscious form of human artistic expression. It is also interesting to observe its universality. We find ornament in Iceland at the time of the sagas as well as among the Assyrians and Babylonians, we find it in Ancient Greece, in the very earliest Mexican cultures, in the jungle sanctuaries of India, and among the Negro tribes of Africa.

Perhaps ornament was originally a primitive sign by means of which the creator of the first earthenware bowl marked it as his property, or a runic charm scratched into the door post to ward off demons. Repetition of these motifs quickly became true ornament, designed to increase the value and beauty of an object.

The formal language of ornament, which we craftsmen can also learn, ranges from the simple abstract geometrical figure to representational designs based on organic forms. We can fall back on the vegetable kingdom with its wealth of patterns, and on the animal kingdom, which even in ancient times contributed a multitude of symbols to the expressive possibilities of ornamentation. The same animals that symbolize strength, courage, wisdom, and so on in heraldry reappear in coded form in ornament, which can often only be interpreted by experts.

The expression "ornament" always indicates decoration, since the word is derived from the Latin "ornare" = to decorate. It may emphasize or articulate the shape of an object, or it may remain quite neutral, or else cover the surface in profusion. The amazing fact is that ornament can adapt itself to all shapes and to any material. Only occasionally, as in wood, must it submit to the technical limitations of the material, but even in this instance it will continue to follow its own laws.

The laws of ornament

When we start designing ornament we must be aware of these laws and must obey them. The first consideration is that ornament consists not only of the motif itself but also of the intervening spaces. These are needed to make the pattern clear. They are completely equal partners in the total design. The nature of ornament is like that of a canon in music, that is, it involves the continuous repetition of a basic theme in strict order and rotation. The shorter and more distinct the theme, the clearer the

Ornament is like a formal dance. The individual figure is repeated in strict order and rotation. The ornamental motif may either be geometric or based on natural forms.

99

whole will be. Hence, our motifs should be used sparingly and clearly separated. Two, or at the most, three motifs in one ornamental sequence are quite sufficient.

The same principle applies to the colors, if you are designing colored ornament. Don't use too many. At the most two contrasting colors are permissible, and a possible colored background already counts as one of these. You should strive for strong contrasts in regard to color, shape and lines. Even a complicated ornament should not look faded, but should stand out clearly.

Those who keep these basic principles firmly in mind will soon become expert in the design of ornament. Practice composing individual "bars," first using simple basic forms. This will help you to master the principles of the material; later these basic forms can be combined to form ornamental friezes or decorative surfaces.

The design is best drawn on paper overprinted with squares, such as that used for school arithmetic books. This grid will be useful not only in laying out the pattern, in maintaining regular spacing and the correct order of repetition, but also in transferring the finished design to a different scale. To do this we simply transpose the drawing onto squared paper of the appropriate size. You can draw up this grid yourself, or you can work right from the start on regular graph paper and just count the number of "boxes" necessary for enlargement or reduction.

The simplest ornamental element is the stroke or line in varying thicknesses. Lines can be sloped to form a zigzag, added to form a cross, from which you can go on to develop a star, or curved to form a wave. The dot and circle supply us with rounded shapes; squares, rectangles, triangles and diamonds enlarge our stock of basic elements to such an extent that there is prac-

tically no limit to what we can design.

When you have mastered the elementary stage of composing patterns with these abstract shapes and are tempted to use forms taken from nature, take care not to get bogged down in strictly naturalistic representation. Nature can only supply the raw material, which must then be refashioned by the artist.

In our context refashioning means simplification and stylization, rendering the concrete in terms of the plane. Remember that ornament is not a pictorial, but a graphic form of expression, even where it takes the form of relief.

To develop abstract decorative forms from a geometrical shape with two symmetrical halves, for instance a flower-like form from a circle, winding leaves from a rectangle or a star from a square, we can use the old folding and scissor-cutting method, so popular with children, to obtain a charming ornamental effect. If, for instance, you fold a square piece of paper twice to a quarter of its original size and cut the open edge into a fanciful shape, you will get some quite striking forms when the paper is unfolded. These are highly suitable as ornamental motifs on account of their perfect symmetry.

To return to our basic principles—we must keep clearly in mind the purpose which our ornament is to serve. Pure graphics, by which we mean the drawing of ornament as an end in itself, is not included in this discussion. Graphics specialists use paper as a base for their drawing, their tools are paints, paint brushes and pens, and their methods the many graphic techniques. By these methods and with these tools and with patience and skill, they can give expression to the most complicated designs, and apply any kind of surface treatment and any thickness of line.

Woodcuts

For us drawing a picture is only a preliminary stage. Our main task is to carve it in wood. This may be for two reasons: either to make a printing block, which will enable us to duplicate our design as often as we wish, or to produce a single original. We have in mind the ornament applied to the surfaces of works of art and objects of the type we learned to carve in Chapter 4. This is what we shall deal with now. For this kind of work we can use two techniques, incised carving or chip carving. Incised carving is the simpler of the two; this merely involves transforming a traced contour into a carved line of very little depth. For this unpretentious art you need nothing but a sharp carving knife. Even a well-ground penknife will do.

The classic technique for cutting ornament is chip carving. Old utensils and craftsman-made furniture offer rich material for research into this technique, which achieves amazing effects by simple means.

In chip carving you either carve the design out of the surface with a knife, or you keep the design intact and cut out the intervening spaces, so that in the end your drawing stands out in relief against a sunken background. You can only do this, however, if the spaces are narrow enough to remove with a single cut. In good chip-carved ornament, there will be a perfect balance between the parts that have remained uncut and the hollowed-out background. The effect depends upon the interrelationship between the background and the relief, the actual motif and the blank spaces. Chip-carved ornament resembles a zebra, of which no one can say whether it is a white pony with black stripes or a black pony with white stripes.

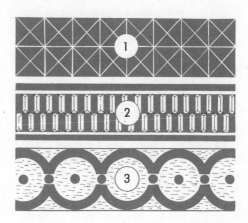

Ways of carving ornament in wood: 1 incised carving, 2 chip carving, 3 flat carving.

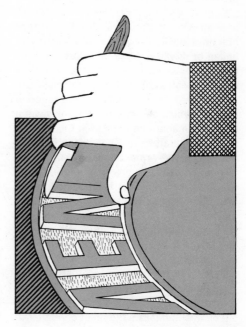

Use of the knife in chip carving: push against the wood with the bent thumb and draw the blade towards you.

101

Chip carving in color

The only tool really necessary for this technique is a single knife: a short, straight blade with a rounded back and a wooden handle. This knife is for cutting, not writing. Therefore do not grip it like a penholder, but grasp it with all the fingers of your right hand, so that the end of the handle peeps out near your little finger. The thumb, slightly bent, is placed firmly against the surface of the wood and the blade is drawn towards it. Be careful, since it is easy to cut your thumb. This grip, however, gives the correct slant necessary for obtaining a cut with sloping sides. Don't make the cuts unnecessarily deep, the carved surface tends to give a pierced impression in any case. This, however, should be avoided, as wood is not a material suitable for filigree treatment. It goes without saying that all the incisions should be the same depth.

Chip-carved work can also be designed in color. One method is to give the surface of a normally light-colored wood—such as linden or maple—a dark or colored tint, so that the incisions reveal the lighter natural wood beneath. Quite strong contrasts can be achieved in this manner. The second method, which permits the use of several colors, can again be studied in the work of the ancient craftsmen. The variegated color of their carved ornament was obtained by filling in the depressions with colored beeswax. Beeswax, however, is not very durable. In our present age of wear and tear it is best replaced with a hard-drying mixture of tempera color and kaurit glue. When quite dry rub over the entire surface with fine sandpaper.

This process, in which greatest restraint must be exercised as regards the choice of colors, so as to avoid a glaring and cheap effect, deemphasizes the relief character of the ornament. We now have an ornament or pattern, all parts of which lie at the same

Chip carving in color. Top: the cuts appear transparent against the tinted surface of the wood. Bottom: the carved areas are picked out with colored pastes.

level in relation to the finished surface. The effect achieved is similar to that of inlay work.

Apart from incised and chip carving, there is also the flat-cut technique. This is characterized mainly by broader raised surfaces, separated by wide spaces. These spaces can no longer be cut by the chip carving method. They are recessed to an even depth with proper carver's tools. In this technique also the design outline is cut with sloping sides, as a vertical cut would make neat carving of the corners very difficult.

Those who wish to take up relief carving in earnest, should start by practicing the chip and flat carving techniques described in this chapter. They will soon find that a direct path leads from these simple exercises to the higher levels of relief ornament.

Lettering as ornament

In craftwork, lettering is very often used as ornamentation and has to be developed in a decorative manner. There are lettering specialists who have created a seemingly inexhaustible treasure of ornamental elements by continuously modifying standard alphabets, which in themselves are already very attractive, such as Gothic or Old English, to mention only two. A wide field opens up before those willing to devote their efforts to this exacting art. We must content ourselves with no more than a fleeting glance at this form of artistic expression, as otherwise we would get lost in its intricacies.

The restraint in the choice of ornamental motifs which wood imposes on us by reason of its obstinate structure becomes even more obvious when we concentrate on carving only letters. For example, it will hardly be possible to add to a bowl carved in close-grained wood a band of Gothic lettering with its sharp, angular strokes. For such a purpose we would be well advised to choose a type of block lettering with a straight-line structure, against which the wood will not put up too much resistance.

These conditions are best fulfilled by Roman lettering, especially if we use only the capital letters. This spare classical style, designed to be chiseled in stone, has an-other advantage besides its beauty: it is comparatively easy to learn—especially in the simplified form of block lettering. Also, Roman capitals are all the same height and thus from the start present the appearance of a self-contained frieze. The forms of the individual letters are developed from the square, the rectangle and the circle. Unskilled carvers will find it easier to base their design of a line of text or a band of lettering on these elementary shapes. The available space is first divided into individual rectangles and squares, the horizontal edges of which are equal to the width of each particular letter, and each rectangle is then transformed into a letter by carving. Practice this a few times with pencil, cardboard and carving knife, and you will soon get the right feeling for the correct spacing between letters. Also bear in mind the basic principle of ornament, and avoid crowding the upright letters. Remember the rule of thumb that rounded or slanting letters should be set closely together, while those with straight vertical contours require somewhat more space. On the whole, the letters in a decorative band around the edge of a plate or bowl can be set quite close together. After all, the main purpose of such lettering is not the easy legibility at great distances required of a packet of detergent in a store window, but rather the creation of

Lettering as ornament: developing block letters out of a succession of squares and rectangles.

a general decorative impression. Those who want to know what the carving says are free to pick up the plate and read it at leisure. This increases the personal appeal of the object and gives it greater intimacy. If a larger space is required in between words to make the inscription more legible, this can be emphasized by means of a recurring symbol, such as a diamond, a cross or a star.

There is a great difference between a straight inscription, such as a frieze around the top of a chest, and an inscription carved around the circular edge of a plate. In the latter instance, the axis of each individual letter has to be aligned radially with the center of the plate. This is best done by drawing lightly with a soft pencil a series of diameters through the middle of the plate. These can then be used to line up the letters. A band of lettering around an oval bowl requires the axes of the letters to be aligned partly perpendicularly and partly radially in relation to the center-line. The correct slope of the axes at the two narrow ends of the bowl can be found by aligning them with the centers of the two circles from which the oval shape was originally developed.

Block printing in wood and linoleum

Some changes will be necessary if we are to carve an ornament or a decorative motif that can be freely duplicated. Our printing process using home-made blocks, is essentially the same as that the newspapers use every day. Only the raised parts of the block, which project above the recessed background, actually print. Thus we must work in a manner exactly opposite to that in which we draw with charcoal on paper. In drawing, the picture is formed by applying

strokes of charcoal to the sheet, but in block cutting the "invisible" becomes the object of our attention. The areas which are to remain blank are cut away from the surface of the block while the actual "drawing" is left intact.

The second point to watch when making a block is the mirror-image effect. In order to obtain a correct impression, we have to cut the block in reverse. With some symmetrical motifs, a back-to-front effect may make no difference, but it can produce surprising results in printing lettering or figures, which suddenly turn out to be left-handed. However, this difficulty is easily overcome. The design is transferred to the block from a tracing. Trace the original onto strong transparent paper and when transferring this copy to the block, simply reverse it so that the back of the sheet is uppermost. Thus a mirror-image of the actual motif is reproduced on the block.

When reproducing complicated designs and, in particular, actual pictures, it is not enough just to transfer the tracing directly. You will find that as soon as the tracing is transferred to the block you will be left with a rather confused and muddled impression. In order to avoid mistakes it is therefore advisable to cover the block with a very thin coat of white tempera color before transferring the design. Before you start cutting, for the sake of durability, the transfer should be inked in black India ink. Your task will be easier if you look at the original in a mirror, because the mirror will show you your design in reverse, as it should appear on the block.

Wood and linoleum can both be used as materials for block printing. It is true that wood is more durable than linoleum, but it has a very distinct structure which has to be considered when cutting fine lines and curves.

The masterpieces of Albrecht Dürer and Hans Holbein are magnificent woodcuts with lines nearly as fine as those on copperplate engravings. There are some types of wood which have such a fine structure that lines of practically any shape and even the most delicate cuts are possible, but the work is not easy. The best material for woodcuts is boxwood which is very hard. Boxwood, however, need only be used where a large number of prints are to be made; for the average amateur craftsman it will be too expensive. On account of its amazingly fine structure boxwood is the material best suited for end-grain blocks.

We shall confine ourselves to the techniques of carving plankwise with the grain. Experienced wood engravers have always valued pearwood, because of its hardness and uniformly tough structure. For our purpose, however, cherrywood will do just as well, as it is not quite as hard and therefore easier to handle. The board you choose must be well-seasoned and dry. It should be quite level and its surface cleanly planed. Knots and other blemishes would make the board quite useless for our purpose. You can buy blocks ready-made, but do not choose anything too weak. The block should not be much less than an inch thick. Our tools will be the same chip-carving knives and narrow gouges and veiners which we have been using up to now. For linocuts in particular, a V-tool will make work easier. For fine incisions a chisel-like knife with a short oblique cutting edge will give good service. For carving purposes, the block is placed on a soft non-slip base—such as a leather cloth folded double—and held with the left hand while the right hand guides the tool. Always remember to keep the holding hand behind the cutting hand—you will save yourself a lot of jabs. In order to get a clear outline, the knives must be very sharp. It is advisable to have an oil stone ready for honing the knives occasionally in the course of the work. Only very big blocks need be clamped down in a screw clamp for carving.

Carving usually begins with the edges of the larger surfaces. When the block has thus been roughly divided, start carving the details and interior shapes. Only right at the end are the large blank background areas cut back.

Linocuts are very much easier to make than woodcuts, as the material is much softer. Apart from the tools which we used for woodcuts and which can also be used for lino, it is possible to buy various tiny little knives which are fitted into a penholder like nibs, or which can be inserted into a special handle. In this way the blades can be interchanged with ease.

The linoleum should have a fine soft structure and should, if possible, be about $1/4''$ thick. If it is too hard or gritty, it will break

Making a linocut. The design is painted on the linoleum in black tempera color.

away when cut and will also blunt the knives. Linoleum only gets really supple when it is well-tempered. Pieces which have been stored in the cold should only be cut after they have reached room temperature. If you find a tempting, soft and "mild" piece of lino, which does not seem to be thick enough to make into a printing block, you can give it more strength by gluing it to a piece of plywood.

Making the print

The difficulties encountered in block cutting—whether in wood or lino—lie not so much in the actual methods as in the artistic aspects of the process. The two techniques have a great deal in common, and the prints obtained are sometimes so similar that laymen find it hard to tell whether they are looking at a woodcut or a linocut.

The nature of the linocut is characterized by its limitations. The soft material cannot give the fine lines that are possible with hard wood. The outlines are not so sharp and look more blurred than in a woodcut. The pictorial element is the surface, whereas with the woodcut it is the line. An expert in woodcuts will be able to distinguish the structure of the wood, which also prints; he may even be able to tell whether the print was taken off an end-grain or a plankwise block.

The inherent structure of the wood is the first hurdle along the path from the artist's conception to the finished print. This hurdle confronts us right at the start, because the design itself is determined by the nature of the wood. By turning to the slightly less rigorous linocut the first hurdle can be avoided, it is true; but even then it will be necessary to respect the laws on which both techniques are based.

Once again we have to consider the principle of the surface, which is the essential element in woodcuts and linocuts, just as it is with ornament and relief. In other words, the three-dimensional effects obtained in other branches of the fine arts are not in keeping with the woodcut, which should not produce the illusion of a third dimension; the tricks of foreshortening and overlapping, used in other techniques to produce an impression of plasticity, are best disregarded by the woodcut or linocut artist.

There is no other graphic process that compels us so to simplify the form, to limit ourselves so completely to essentials and to the extremely sparing use of all our artistic resources. Therefore right from the start the pictorial motif has to be translated into this simple language. The narrow scale of available tonal values makes it impossible to depict a delicate misty landscape with its wide range of grays in the medium of the black-and-white woodcut. The only way of achieving a sort of half-tone effect is to use hatching or shading by means of which an enclosed surface can be defined. Woodcut effects are similar to those revealed by a walk at night through a snowy mountain village when the moon is full. All color is blotted out and the hard light of the moon with its sharp-edged shadows suggests the importance of leaving out unimportant details and concentrating the essential pictorial elements into broad contrasting shapes.

In photography, where the normal tendency is to strive for as wide a range of grays as possible, there is a process known as tone separation. By using two negatives copied one on top of the other in the enlarger, the wide range of grays present in the original can be reduced to two or three tone values between black and white. In this way, all the substance is sucked out of the pictures, and the result is a flattened, poster-like effect.

With the help of transparent paper, zinc white and black distemper, this idea of tone separation or tone concentration can be

A colored linocut impression can be obtained either as a monotype or by means of repeated printing with several color blocks. Monotype means printing once only. These prints are taken from one block, appropriate

A four-block colored linocut. Green is obtained by overprinting blue and yellow.

followed right through to produce a completely transformed photograph, so that practically nothing of the picture originally recorded by the lens remains. This method produces amazing results and leads to transformations of motifs that are particularly suitable for the multicolored linocut on account of their flat appearance. We can also take another hint from photography: woodcuts and linocuts resemble exposures made against the sun.

areas of which are colored with a short bristle brush using various inks. If several blocks are to be used for color printing, a black block is first prepared and from this a separate block is made for each color. Let us assume that we want to make a print using the basic colors blue, red and yellow; we first take three very strong prints from the black block and transfer these to three other white-coated lino blocks. This must be done very quickly, before the ink dries.

The print is laid wet side down on the lino block and the design is impressed with a rubber roller or brayer. Mark these blocks with the color they will later be used to print. This precaution will save you from cutting away the wrong sections. Remember that objects in mixed colors must appear on all the blocks printing their basic colors. If, for example, your design shows a green tree between a blue lake and a yellow cornfield, the tree, the green of which is a mixture of blue and yellow, will have to appear on both your blue "lake" block and the yellow block with the cornfield. The individual blocks must be cut very carefully, so that the differently colored surfaces register correctly. White lines showing between adjacent forms are particularly ugly. Therefore cut the individual blocks too large rather than too small, because a slight overlapping of the colors in the finished print is the lesser evil.

All the trouble you take over accurate cutting will be wasted, however, if an exact fit is not achieved during the printing process. You can provide markers for yourself by leaving on the black block, beyond the edge of the actual picture, two little squares in diagonally opposite corners; these are transferred to and cut out of the color blocks. The small squares on these blocks will also be inked and will reproduce in printing. As long as you use thin transparent paper, you will always be able to get a good register by using these markers. Another method of getting a good color register is to make neat little corner pieces using a template and stick them to the edge of the block, against which the sheet of paper will later be laid for printing. The individual blocks will then have to be slightly larger than the sheet to be printed. Should this not be the case or if the sizes of the blocks vary, you can overcome this difficulty

by surrounding them with identical frames of plywood or stiff cardboard and then fix the corner pieces to these.

For black and white linocuts use black printer's ink dissolved in turpentine or "Japan-Aqua." The latter is a special water color made specially for block printing, and is available not only in black but in many bright colors. However, you can also print with ordinary water colors in tubes, if these have been mixed with a little gum arabic; a drop of glycerin will stop them from drying out too quickly. Roll out the ink evenly on a glass plate or stone slab with a rubber roller, which is then used to apply it to the block. Even better than a rubber roller is a roller made of gelatin. The sheet of printing paper is first dampened in between blotting paper; it is then picked up with both hands by a pair of opposite corners, positioned carefully and rubbed down with a brayer or creaser. You can make yourself a substitute creaser by shaving a tooth brush. Very delicate papers are covered with another sheet of paper and are then rolled on the block with a rubber roller; smaller sizes print well if pressed down with a hand-warm iron. Anybody who still owns an old copying press can make quite wonderful prints with this. The advantage here is that the pressure will be uniform over all parts of the plate; there is also less wear and tear on the paper. If several color blocks are used for printing, after the indispensable first test print, we shall need more than just one impression. An economical method of working is to print the entire quantity required in one color at a time. Start by printing the black block, then continue with the lightest color and finish with the darkest.

The classical paper for hand-printed woodcuts and linocuts is Japanese paper. With thin papers like this we can watch the progress of color absorption from the back, without having to lift up corners of the paper to check. For water colors thicker papers are to be preferred, as they have greater wet strength than thin ones, and because they hold the moisture and therefore retain their power of absorption longer. Smooth, sized papers have to be used with great care. They absorb color unevenly and tend to slide about on the block during printing. Good quality rotogravure paper, however, is eminently suitable.

We can print not only on white paper, but also on colored paper, if this is absorbent and uncalendered. Quite amazing effects can be achieved on gold or silver paper. You can even impress your design on leather, fabrics and raffia.

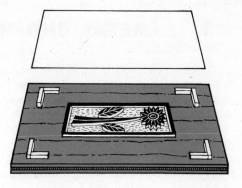

Small linocuts can be framed in cardboard or plywood. Light corner pieces are fixed to this frame to mark the correct position of the printing paper.

109

6 METAL UNDER THE HAMMER

Those accustomed to working in wood will have to change their way of thinking completely when they come to metal. Wood has a natural-cellular texture, whereas metal is crystalline in structure. Wood is shaped primarily by chipping or cutting. By comparison metal is far more versatile. It can not only be shaped by cutting and shaving, it can also be melted and therefore cast. Another of its properties is of even greater interest to us, its ductility. This is the property on which most of the examples of this chapter are based. It enables us to work metal by the process of cold-forming.

For this purpose, we shall require a hammer and an anvil. These will not be as big and heavy as those used by the blacksmith, but we shall need a much larger selection. On page 43 you will find a list of the basic metalworking tools. Even the skilled craftsman will get by with these, but naturally, it is possible to extend this collection by adding some of the more sophisticated hammers, stakes, and chasing tools.

Metalworking is an extremely flexible craft and has many specialized branches. Within the framework of this book it will not be possible to discuss all these branches in detail. Nevertheless, we shall need to add to the tools already mentioned two other simple devices which are of particular importance to the beginner. These are two plain wood blocks, the end-grain surfaces of which are used as anvils. We shall need one with a flat or very slightly hollowed surface and another, somewhat smaller one with a hemispherical head. Since we shall start by working with soft materials, a softer base will be better than a hard one, so basswood will be a suitable choice.

It is possible to make a cheap lead anvil, instead of using a wood block, by saving all sorts of lead waste and melting this down into a compact mass in a large tin can. Lead has the advantage that all sorts of depressions and grooves can be formed in its surface by a few blows with a hammer; it also has its disadvantages, however. Besides, wood is cheaper, and we have already learnt in Chapter 4 how to reshape its surface satisfactorily if required. When in use the wooden block is clamped into the vise.

In view of the cost involved, we shall not consider the two noble metals gold and silver; thus, for hammered work we shall use mainly copper, brass and aluminum. Of these three copper has the highest coefficient of expansion. This is the really classical metal for hammered work, especially as it cannot be cast satisfactorily. Brass, which is harder, also has a rich tradition in the field of cold-forming, and aluminum is a really contemporary material which is constantly gaining wider popularity on account of its fine silvery gleam, its unobtrusiveness and its easy workability. Its greatest advantage is that the craftsman is not hampered by any limitations imposed by the material itself. Anything at all can be done with it.

The raw material for metalwork comes in the form of semi-finished sheet ready for further processing. The thickness of the material will depend on the finished size we have in mind. For small bowls, up to the size of your hand, sheets with a thickness of about $1/32''$ will be adequate but a full-size copper jug will have to be at least $1/16''$ thick. The basic material for brasswork of medium size is normally $3/64''$ thick. To hammer a sheet of brass more than $^1/_{16}''$ thickness requires a considerable amount of strength and a high degree of perseverance. Commercially, the thickness of art metals is usually expressed in thousandths of an inch by means of the Brown and Sharpe, or B & S gage.

When buying sheet metal watch carefully that you are not sold any scratched pieces. A scratch on the surface always remains a scratch. You can try later on, with more or less success, to camouflage it by a well-placed blow with the hammer, but you will never quite get rid of it.

All metal beating and hammering is based on the two techniques made possible by the ductility of the material, namely stretching and upsetting. Even in the process of forming a simple fold, the sheet is stretched on the outside of the bend, whereas it is compressed to quite some extent on the inside.

Another example will illustrate the stretch principle more clearly. If we lay a strip of brass on the anvil and hammer it along the left edge using the peen, the strip will gradually acquire a right-hand curve that gets progressively tighter. This is caused by the stretching of the hammered edge. At the same time you will notice that the material in the stretched zone has become thinner. The opposite principle, upsetting, becomes clear when we place a short length of square bar upright on the anvil and give it a few hefty blows with a sledge hammer. The length of the bar is reduced, but its cross section increases: the material has been upset or compressed.

Quite apart from the natural inherent limits to elongation, which vary considerably in different metals, every metal will sooner or later become hard and brittle under the hammer blows. As soon as you notice that its resistance to the hammer is growing, you can restore its original ductility

by red-heating it. This thorough heating, which is absolutely necessary and which can be done with a soldering torch or a bunsen burner—you have one in any gas stove—does not mean that this process can be called hot-forging.

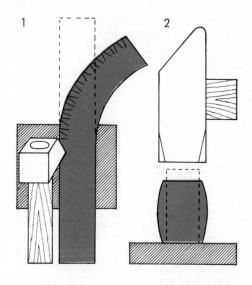

Stretching and upsetting: 1 The lefthand side of the strip is stretched and thinned under the blows of the hammer. 2 Upsetting or compressing makes the cross section thicker.

In order to avoid disappointments, it is necessary to maintain absolute cleanliness during all hammering work. The impact surfaces of the hammers and the faces of stakes and planishing blocks must be polished to a high gloss. Rust marks or even very slight traces of oxidation will cause defects and blemishes in the surface of the finished article. All tools must therefore be treated with great care and must be well looked after.

The working material also has to be kept clean. Before the actual work is started,

The round blank

sheet metal must be pickled in a suitable acid bath (sulfuric or hydrochloric acid, diluted in the proportion 1:10), then thoroughly scoured in clean water and dried. This pickling process must be scrupulously repeated after every heating operation, so as to remove even the smallest trace of scale. Any impurity remaining on the surface will be driven into the surface by the hammer to such an extent that no known trick will remove it. It will remain embedded as a permanent blemish.

Sinking and Raising

In practice the path from your imagination to the finished piece of work starts with the cutting of the blank from the sheet of metal. In making a circular bowl or an ash-tray, the basic round can be laid out with the help of dividers. For asymmetrical shapes, as for instance a shade for a wall-lamp in the form of a distended sail, we first make a paper template, transfer the outlines to the metal sheet, and then cut round these with tinners' snips. When using thick material the cutting operation can be made easier by clamping one lever of the snips between the jaws of a vise so that the snips are lying horizontally: the second, free blade is then pressed down with the left hand, while the right hand guides the material you are cutting. Don't force the snips together completely for each individual cut, but keep feeding the sheet of metal in, otherwise you will get a ragged edge. Cut from the right, that is to say, push the sheet into the snips in a counter-clockwise direction. In the course of the cutting operation a burr will inevitably be formed, and before continuing with the work this will have to be removed with a file or flattened out on a leveling block with the mallet.

In the actual hammering work two different techniques can be used. These are called sinking and raising. Sinking is the more basic of the two, and this is the one the apprentice should use in making his first attempts at forming moderately curved shapes. This, however, does not mean that this method is only suitable for hammering shallow forms. On the contrary, quite definite cup-like shapes can be formed from round blanks, the diameter of which need hardly be much larger than the diameter of the top of the finished cup.

This technique then involves a hammering operation, in which we work outwards from the center; the outer sections of the blank will be stretched very little, if at all, and thus will not yield any extra material; on the other hand, the material for expanding the disc must come from somewhere, and therefore a relatively thick piece of sheet

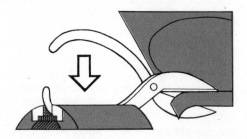

Cutting a round blank from thick sheet metal. The work can be made easier by clamping one lever of the snips in the vise.

metal is required for the sinking technique. If the wall of the cup becomes as thin as paper due to the hammering, it will hardly serve its purpose. It will certainly not stand up to the strain of a boisterous drinking bout.

Start sinking a bowl by placing the round blank on a wooden block and, commencing in the center, hammer along a spiral towards the outside edge. The individual hammer blows will beat out the metal, and the surface of the originally flat disc will stretch and stretch and gradually become concave. As soon as you reach the edge, go back and start working along the spiral all over again, thus gradually deepening the central hollow.

It will simplify the work at the beginning if you make a shallow circular depression in the wooden block that you use for sinking. This is justifiable when you are using a hardwood block, but for various reasons it is preferable to acquire precision in spiral hammering from the start on the flat end-grain surface of a block of softwood. First of all, such a block is soft enough to yield to the metal as it is struck by the hammer; and secondly, the nature and art of hammering sheet metal does not consist in forcing the metal into an existing mold, but rather in shaping the desired profile by varying the intensity of well-directed hammer blows. Thus, the hammering should become less intense when approaching the end of the spiral and the edge of the circular shape. If, on the other hand, you are making a dish or a plate, which has a flat, unstretched edge contrasting with steep or even slightly convex side walls, you will apply somewhat more force to the edge sections, once the bottom has been sufficiently flattened out.

Hammering a punch bowl big enough for twelve persons, for instance, out of brass sheet $^3/_{32}''$ thick is not as quick a job, as, say, baking a cake. For this reason save your strength and don't employ a hammering technique that will tire out your arm after the first ten minutes. Admittedly, this is forging work, but there is no need to swing the hammer from the shoulder. It is not so much a question of a few very hard blows as of a series of taps of uniform or varying intensity following closely one upon the other. Hammer with firm, but springy staccato blows from the wrist. In principle you should always aim at the same place with your hammer, whilst moving and guiding the metal workpiece with your left hand. This is the only way to achieve precision.

The same principles apply to the second working technique, which is used more frequently, namely raising. The difference is that the form is not developed by working outwards from inside, but by hammering the outside of the object. Here the shape is created not so much by stretching the central part of the round blank, as by drawing the edges more and more inwards. Of course, the metal disc is stretched radially, but to an even greater extent it is compressed tangentially. This is where deep raising differs from the process of sinking.

To raise a metal cup or a spherical shape first place the blank over a grooved wooden stake (see figure) and hammer out a series of radial folds broadening from the center towards the edge. It is quite easy to cut out such a stake with a carpenter's chisel. The stake is clamped into a vise and used as a base for hammering. The middle part of the metal blank which, for the time being at least, remains flat, is supported on the stake bottom uppermost. Start hammering at the center and work towards the edges, rotating the blank as you proceed. Use a not too broad raising hammer, starting at the edge of an imaginary inner circle (i.e. the perimeter of the bottom or base) and work outward. Actually you do not work outwards with the hammer, but pull the round metal sheet out from underneath it.

After this first operation the blank will look like a badly pleated shallow lampshade. In this condition the workpiece is heated and pickled, before the second operation is begun. This consists mainly in smoothing out and flattening the corrugations which

Raising

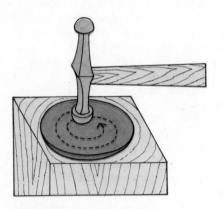

Sinking a bowl over an end-grain block. Hammer along a spiral path from the center to the edge.

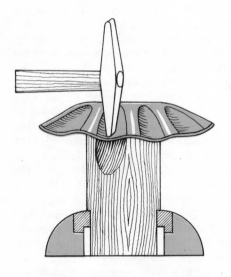

Raising a bowl over a wooden stake. The radial folds are beaten out with a creasing hammer.

you have just hammered in. But—and this is important!—the smoothing is done in a very special way by tangential blows across the direction of the folds. You also do this with a raising hammer, or better still, if you have one, with a creasing hammer. This looks like an elongated cross-peen hammer, but has two peens instead of the usual one peen and one face. In the beginning you can also make do with the peen of a cross-peen hammer. This, however, must be well polished with the very finest emery cloth, and its edges must be rounded off on both sides. The reason for this is that if you chop into the metal by accidentally holding the hammer at an angle, the sharp edges of the peen will leave traces in the surface, which will be more permanent than the impact that Alexander the Great made on the history of the world.

Again working from the middle towards the edges, start flattening out the folds, turning the work over the horizontal arm of a curved stake. If you have not got a metal stake of this type, you can make do with a heavy wooden pin with a rounded end clamped in the vise. The peen of the hammer is held not radially, but tangentially to the metal round and the blows are delivered with a slight outward pull.

When this circular hammering process has brought you to the outside edge, red-heat again and pickle, and then start the same cycle all over again. However, when making the second series of folds, see that where formerly there was a valley there is now a ridge, so that the thickness of the metal remains everywhere the same.

The more often this sequence of creasing and flattening is repeated, the more the wall of the hollow shape will gradually rise. All the time the material near the center is being stretched and that near the edge compressed, so that the cross section of the metal becomes thicker in the direction of the edge. During the last phase of development of a bowl-shaped form, this edge will become the more compressed, the closer we try to approach a spherical shape. Moreover, the bottom, which so far has remained flat, will also have to be rounded. Drawing in the edge is not without its dangers. Take particular care to prevent the metal creeping together and overlapping in folds. When making objects with a strongly expressed profile it is advisable to make a cardboard profile template so that progress can be continuously checked by fitting this template against the outer wall.

When the rough shape has been obtained, there follows the last and most difficult operation—planishing. For this you will need a planishing hammer. The object being worked is guided over the rounded surface of a steel ball stake, the curve of which is adapted to that of the vessel wall. It is this process that gives the characteristic surface finish peculiar to "handwork"; it will be all

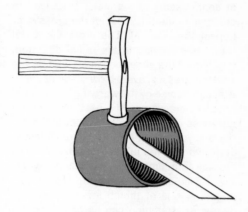

Planishing the walls of a vessel over a planishing stake.

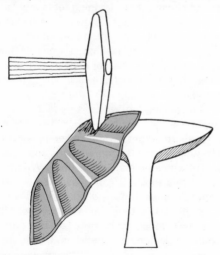

Flattening out the folds over a curved T-stake. Note that the hammer should be held tangentially.

the more attractive, if you avoid exaggeration.

We started learning the technique of raising by forming a series of tapering radial indentations. However, this step is not necessary in all instances. You can often save yourself this work, particularly when hammering a shallow bowl; in this case you can start straightaway with the tangential hammering. In order to do this, however, it will first be necessary to sink the center part of the metal blank. This is not without risk, particularly when using thin sheet, as the tearing strength of the material can very easily be exceeded. Although metal is surprisingly stretchable, we must always bear in mind that pronounced bulges, as well as excessive compression, put a great strain on the material. If you torture the metal too much with your hammer, it will react by breaking suddenly. For this reason avoid trying to achieve soap-bubble effects; also avoid unnatural and violent changes of direction and bulges. Quite apart from the fact that such shapes are very difficult to produce, they also run contrary to the style of hammered metal work.

As we have already seen, any stretching

Polishing

or compressing of the metal must lead to changes in the thickness of the cross section of the material. The more the metal round is stretched in the radial direction, the thinner the sheet becomes, and as the work progresses, every blow of the hammer is accompanied by the worrying question of how far dare we go. The best gage for the thickness of the cross section of the material is at your finger tips, in the truest sense of the word. If you just feel the thickness of the wall from time to time as you are working, it will save you some unpleasant surprises. A rule of thumb for a reasonable degree of stretching can be based on the diameter of the original round blank. If the largest elongation does not exceed one third of the original diameter, conditions may be regarded as being normal.

The last process that the workpiece undergoes is polishing. It is a question of taste whether you polish your metal object to a high gloss, whether you give it a dull finish or whether you are content to leave it with the "natural surface" resulting from the last gentle taps with a planishing hammer.

Nowadays the work is made easy by the use of mechanical buffers and polishing wheels. Typical wheels for these machines are made of muslin rags, cotton, felt, and bristle. Various polishing compounds are available for different purposes.

However, even in the days when there were no electrically powered buffs, it was possible to obtain beautifully polished metal surfaces. So why not revert to the old hand methods and polish with linen or leather rags, with pumice powder and oil, or with commercial buffing sticks and paste. In any case, for small and angular objects this method of working by hand has great advantages. After using some polishing compound, you will have to clean the surface afterwards with a grease solvent, such as benzene or gasoline. Finally, rub it down with a clean woollen cloth.

A dull finish is achieved by working over the surface with fine steel brushes. Those who admire highly polished brassware, but are afraid of always having to clean it, can coat such objects with a very delicate film of clear Zapon varnish, which must be free from dust and blisters. Coats of varnish that have become worn can be removed with acetone.

Chasing

Of all the ornamental techniques that can be applied to a metal surface, chasing is the one most closely related to the hammering techniques we have already discussed and is the easiest method for the hobby craftsman to carry out without any appreciable extra expenditure.

The most important tools for this precision work you can make yourself; they are called chasing and stamping tools and can be made of tool steel, broken files or long wood screws. The attraction of making these profiled or fashioned irons is the opportunity they offer for individual design. Keen chasers collect quite a variety of these in the course of time.

The chasing tool which is used most frequently is the liner or tracer, with more or less sharp edges, which is employed in chasing lines; also important is the pearl punch with a hemispherical head. With the aid of this tool you can chase screen-like patterns consisting of individual dots. Apart from these two tools there is a variety of stamping tools, with more or less pronounced designs and patterns. If soft outlines are required, you can use wooden stamping tools, which you can also cut to the desired shape yourself. For these you will need a hard wood. If you cannot get boxwood, it should be pear or plum. If you have wooden stamping tools you will have to use a softer base than that which you use for steel tools.

The technique of chasing is based on the partial sinking of the surface of your working material by the impact of the chasing tool or punch; this forces the metal into a softer base, forming a raised pattern on the other side. In principle there is no difference whether you want to obtain a linear pattern or a composition involving broad masses. The surface can be worked either from the back, which gives the effect of soft forms and transitions, or from the front, which produces a considerably sharper outline and a more emphatic pattern.

As a base for this type of work use a tightly stuffed sand-bag—or if the pattern is very fine—a bed of chasing pitch.

Chasing pitch is best made from a mixture of pitch and casting sand or brick dust. The necessary flexibility is achieved by the appropriate addition of tallow or wax and turpentine.

When a hollow vessel, say for instance a vase, is to be chased, the above mixture is melted and poured into the vase. Naturally, you can then only work on it from the outside. A wooden handle can be cast into the pitch inside the vase; this handle is then clamped into the vise. The warmer you keep the pitch, the softer the base for chasing will be. The principal rules are: warm, soft pitch for working with wooden punches, and cold hard pitch for finer chasing. Large flat objects, like sheets of metal, can be laid in a bed of pitch. Very soft and quite flat metal sheets can be chased by using a stack of newspapers as a base. This applies in particular to practice work in soft aluminum. However, a very high standard will hardly be reached in this way.

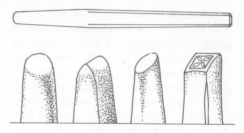

A selection of chasing tools: from left to right, pearl punch, two tracers, and a stamping or matting tool with an individual motif.

How to hold the chasing tool. The workpiece is supported in a bed of putty in an improvised pitch bowl.

117

Chasing tools and punches

The real enthusiast will buy a hollow cast-iron pitch bowl in which to bed the workpiece. To stop this bowl from rolling off the table, but at the same time to make it possible to turn and twist it in all directions, it is stood in a circular collar made of strips of leather sewn together. The hobby craftsman who has to rely on improvisation can make do with a small metal bowl or a cut-down tin can resting on a flat sand-bag. Whether a complete hollow vessel is to be filled or a metal sheet is to be placed in a bed of pitch, you must always make sure that there are no air bubbles and therefore cavities beneath the surface. In the process of chasing the metal is often stretched practically to breaking limit. If it rests over a cavity, accidents might well happen.

The boundaries between chasing proper and embossing are fluid. Chasing really involves the modeling of broader surfaces by raising, the actual impression made by the chasing tool forming only one element of the over-all design; in the more primitive work of embossing the stamping tool or punch produces its own ornamental effect. Continuous repetition, the recurrence of a single motif, is characteristic of embossing.

However, we do not have to worry too much about these more or less academic distinctions. In practice we can learn a great deal by looking at the ring finger of an experienced chaser. The last joint will be bent outward to an appreciable degree. This proves that throughout his professional life the man has always guided the chasing tools in the correct way, and this is what we want to learn from him.

The original chasing tool of the professional chaser is about four or five inches long and its impact surface slopes slightly to the right. When making tools yourself from square tool steel ($^1/_4''$ cross section), try to file it to this shape, which will facilitate your work. The slender tool is held between the thumb and first and middle fingers of the left hand. In doing this, the middle finger must press hard near the nail against the ring finger, the tip of which rests on the metal surface. The tip is kept firmly in touch with the object you are working on, and slides along the line which you want to chase, acting as a brake. This helps to guide the chasing tool smoothly and without skittering. Those who press hard and long enough in this way, will end up with a finger like the professional chaser's.

You can get special chasing hammers with an extra wide face, but you can work quite satisfactorily with a not too heavy cross-peen hammer. Here, too, the individual hammer blows must be delivered with a loose wrist. If space and the shape of the object you are working on allow, you can support your right elbow on the table.

Assembly

Only very few metal objects can be made from one piece. In most cases assembling or joining will be involved. This is even necessary for a very simple ashtray which is to stand on three brass ball feet. But even in making a tall jug or cylindrical can soldered together lengthwise, there will be a question of joining or assembling.

Soldering is a simple, but very important assembly technique, but soft soldering with easy-flowing solder is not really accepted by professional gold-, silver- or coppersmiths, because in their eyes this method is not in keeping with the material. The hobby craftsman, however, will in most instances content himself with this technique, which is described in Chapter 3 under "Soldering."

For hard soldering, alloys of the metal to be soldered and other metals are used, mainly therefore alloys of gold, silver, brass and copper. The difficulty which the hobby craftsman faces is to obtain the high temperatures necessary, as the melting point of these solders lies above 500°C. Such heat can only be obtained by means of a gas-soldering apparatus or an oxygen blowtorch. The goldsmith uses a so-called soldering pistol which is heated by illuminating gas and enables the heat to be accurately directed. A mouth blowpipe or a pair of bellows serves as a blower.

During this process the object you are working on should rest on a soldering bowl filled with charcoal or on a wire grid. It goes without saying that the surfaces to be soldered by the hard soldering process must be quite clean and must have been pickled, so that the bonding alloy can form under exclusion of oxygen. Generally borax is used as both a flux and pickling agent, and is sprinkled onto the surface to be soldered. Larger areas are soldered with stick solder, but for smaller areas the goldsmith uses solder chips, so-called 'paillons'.

The process of hard soldering, durable and 'invisible' as it is when carried out by skilled people, cannot be used in our special field of work for soldering brass objects. A utensil worked in brass would have its temper drawn out if heated to the high temperatures necessary for hard soldering. Thus, it would lose its strength and also the stability which it gained under the hammer.

For copper work we can only use two assembly techniques, namely riveting and seaming. For a long time riveting was regarded as being rather inferior, because it was noticeable that the object was not made out of one piece, but "put together". But its very honesty makes this solid assembly technique attractive, quite apart from the fact that well-placed and nicely shaped rivet heads can be regarded as an ornamental feature. The process of riveting itself is explained in Chapter 3 under "riveting."

A much greater degree of skill and practice is required for seaming and flanging, two processes which are indispensable if, for instance, we have to put a bottom in a copper jug.

A simple seam is made by folding the edges of two sheets of metal, hooking these folds into each other, and hammering the seam down. It is obvious that such a joint is not very durable. At the first opportunity it will spring apart. This can be prevented by locking the seam. To do this, place the seam close to the edge of the anvil, and bend up one of the sheets along the seam. This will effectively prevent the second sheet from coming loose. The process has the added advantage that the surfaces of the two sheets are brought to the same level.

The same procedure as described so far is followed when forming a right-angle seam. This time, however, do not lock the seam, but simply bend the top sheet at right angles over the edge formed by the bottom sheet.

At the start of the operation the width of the seam is marked on both sheets, each sheet is then bent over a seaming stake— you may also use the edge of the anvil—with a wooden mallet; then the fold is completed on a flattening block. To make sure that this fold is not too tight and to prevent the metal from tearing, it is safest to control the operation by inserting a piece of sheet metal of the same thickness as the object you are making between the inside faces of the fold. All these operations are carried out with a wooden mallet or rubber-faced hammer. For all metalwork assembly processes, where a change in the cross section of the metal either by stretching or compressing must be avoided, the same principles apply: soft hammer—hard bed; hard hammer— soft bed.

Folding—seaming

This simple seaming technique is used for inserting a bottom in a copper jug. However, in order to do this, you will have to bend the bottom edge of the cylindrical part of the jug at right angles to the wall, so as to form a flange for the seam. And this is where the difficulties start.

The width of the flange must be marked out along the bottom edge of the jug and the flange itself must be gradually hammered out with a raising hammer or with the peen of a cross-peen hammer. The line marked out on the bottom of the jug is laid exactly against the edge of the anvil, so that the part destined to form the flange lies on the face of the anvil. The jug itself is held in a slightly slanting position with the left hand, i.e. on the left-hand side of the anvil. Constantly turning the jug around the guide line, beat the slightly tilted edge down onto the anvil with rapid hammer blows delivered from the wrist. When carrying out this work or any other hammering process (and also when folding sheet metal over a seaming stake) bear in mind that the hammer always stays put, while the object you are working on is moved past underneath it. When bending over the edge of the jug, remember that the metal has to stretch most on the outside. Therefore the strongest hammer blows must be delivered against the outer sections, becoming gradually more gentle as you work your way inwards, i.e. as you approach the sections which initially are less curved.

When, working accurately and patiently, you have turned the edge over at right angles, place the object on the anvil and flatten the flange with a planishing hammer.

Whereas the top of the jug needs to be flanged, the corresponding edge of the bottom will have to be rimmed. This means that the metal must be compressed. Do not make an arithmetical error when cutting out

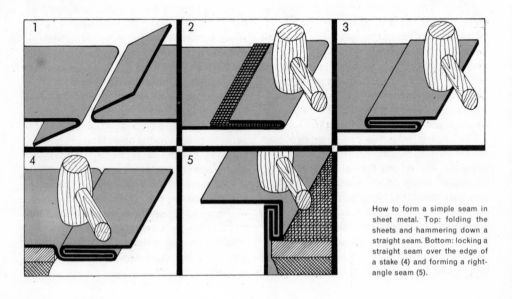

How to form a simple seam in sheet metal. Top: folding the sheets and hammering down a straight seam. Bottom: locking a straight seam over the edge of a stake (4) and forming a right-angle seam (5).

the round blank for the bottom. The radius of the blank is composed of the radius of the top of the jug plus twice the width of the seam including the thickness of the sheet with which you are working.

The width of the seam is also marked out on the bottom blank, parallel to its perimeter. The rim is then formed with a wooden mallet over the rounded surface of a half-moon stake until it stands up at right angles. You should try to obtain a seam with a clean, sharp edge. Again hold the object in your left hand and turn it counter-clockwise under a rain of even hammer blows across the top of the stake. When the rim stands out vertically, both it and the flat bottom are smoothed out on the anvil.

This is followed by the actual process of assembly, namely the joining of the two separate parts to form a seam. The top is fitted into the bottom, and the whole is placed on a sufficiently broad and level surface, and the rim on the bottom is flattened over the flange on the top with a creasing hammer. In doing this, the top must be pushed hard down against the

bottom so that a tight joint results. A more attractive appearance, and at the same time a tighter joint, is obtained, if this simple seam is made into a double seam. For this purpose the jug, which has now become a complete vessel, is placed over a round bar fixed in a vise so that the end of the bar fits snugly against the bottom and side wall of the jug. Then the simple seam, which stands out at right angles to the main body of the vessel, is beaten down tight against the side of the vessel. Seams of this type with rounded edges are not particularly attractive; the seam is therefore given a neat, finished edge with a planishing hammer on the square stake or anvil. Do not hit the edges with too much force, otherwise you will drive the seam apart.

In making a seam we practiced bending edges on sheet metal. If the edge of a single sheet of metal is folded over and hammered down tight against the surface of the sheet (wooden mallet), the result is a single hem, which becomes a double hem if folded over once more. By this process the sharpness of the metal edge is removed and at the same

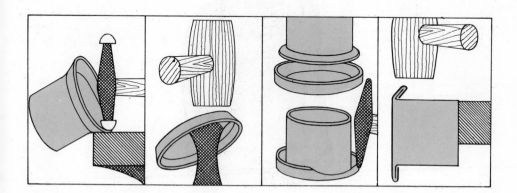

Bottoming a vessel by the seam technique: 1 forming a flange on the walls of the vessel, 2 forming a rim on the bottom, 3 joining the two parts by means of a seam, 4 transforming the simple seam into a double one.

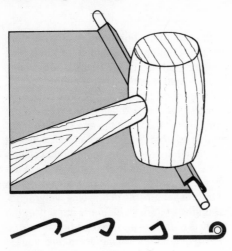

Rounding off and stiffening a free edge by forming a wired hem.

which is determined by the required edge dimensions, presents no difficulties. The width of the strip required for wiring is two and a half times the thickness of the wire. The total width is marked off on the edge of the metal sheet. First bend over a third of this width and then, on a seaming stake, dress over the total width. Insert the wire in the rough groove thus formed; then work the metal to the curvature of the wire on a hard surface using a wooden mallet. Finally, the bend is carefully smoothed with a planishing hammer. You can apply the same process to a round sheet, after having raised a sufficiently high rim. Practice on a straight edge first, however, to avoid spoiling a half-finished job into which a great deal of effort has already gone.

time the edge itself is made a great deal stronger.

This strength can be further improved by inserting an iron wire into the fold. This gives a blunt, soft finish with a pleasing effect. If the metal sheet is straight-edged, the insertion of the wire, the thickness of

Generally speaking, the saying "practice makes perfect" applies to metalwork more than to anything else. This chapter, naturally, could do no more than lead you to the fringe of one of the most exciting and attractive of the crafts. After this introduction the rest is up to you.

Two assembly techniques applied to a single vessel: a copper jug with a seam at the bottom and a riveted handle.

BOOKBINDING 7

The hobbyist who has succeeded in rebinding a tattered book will be capable of coping with any other simpler form of cardboard or paper work. So let us be ambitious and start at the top. When we have mastered this craft, the rest will drop automatically into our lap.

Bookbinding materials need much less attention than the two materials we have discussed so far, that is, wood and metal. All we really need to remember is that paper, like wood, has two directions with different characteristics, namely with and across the "grain." This is a result of the paper-making process and one of its consequences is that moistened paper stretches more in the transverse direction than in the direction of the grain. On drying it shrinks again, developing a considerable pull. A comparatively thin paper stretched over cardboard or even plywood will mercilessly buckle the backing when it dries. Moreover, this tension will last longer than that of a medium-sized steel spring. Even if a piece of cardboard distorted in this way were clamped in a press for as long as a hundred years, it would still be twisted when it was finally released.

This obstinate pull can be counteracted by the method used in veneering, namely by pasting a paper of equal thickness on the opposite side. But even this will only be fully effective if the grain runs in the same direction in both sheets.

This question of directionality has to be taken into account in another important bookbinding material, the cloth used in making the case. Binder's cloth, like all other textiles, is woven from longitudinal warp threads and transverse weft threads, which are readily recognizable. The continuous surface of paper, however, presents us with a different problem. To distinguish one direction from the other, draw one edge of the sheet between the thumb nail and the tip of the index finger of your right hand, squeezing lightly. If this produces corrugations in the paper, the transverse direction stands revealed. It is in this direction that the paper will expand more when moistened and pasted. If the edge stays flat or the corrugations are relatively small, it is the grain of the paper that you have between your fingers.

With binder's board, manufactured from waste paper and rags, this method runs into difficulties. In this instance a bending test on a piece of waste will prove helpful. When

The sewing frame

you try to bend the board, it will break more readily in the transverse direction than in the more elastic grain direction.

In bookbinding, therefore, it is an inflexible rule that the grain of the paper must always run from top to bottom parallel to the back of the book.

Bookbinding Tools

The sewing frame is the most important of the bookbinder's tools. As its name indicates, it is used for sewing together the layers of paper or signatures that form the pages of the finished book. The sewing frame consists of a base board with a threaded steel rod mounted vertically at each end of one of the longer sides. At the top these rods pass through holes drilled in the ends of a wooden crossbar, the vertical position of which can be adjusted by means of pairs of wing nuts. The tapes or strings to which the signatures are sewn are stretched vertically between the base board and the crossbar.

The same simple principle can be used by the hobbyist in making his own sewing frame. The steel rods can be replaced with two sufficiently large wooden C-clamps. These clamps are fitted to each end of a strong, flat board at least 1″ thick, 16″ long, and 9″ wide, so that the rear edge of the board lies snugly against the vertical arms of the clamps. The only part still missing is the crossbar at the top of the frame. This can be cut out of a strong plank the same length as the base board. Its width should be equal to the horizontal arm of the C-clamp less the thickness of its vertical arm. The crossbar is held in place by passing the spindles of the clamps through holes drilled in its ends. The centers and diameters of these two holes must be accurately fixed. As far as possible

the diameter should not be greater than that of the lower tapered part of the clamp handle so that the crossbar will not slip.

Begin assembling the sewing frame by removing the spindles from the two clamps. Then lay the crossbar over the upper arms of the clamps so that the holes coincide, and screw the spindles back again. Now push the base board up against the backs of the clamps and screw down the spindles. The frame is now almost ready for use. All it lacks is a means of stretching the sewing tapes or string. Tapes are fastened simply

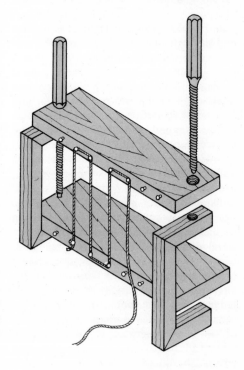

Two wooden C-clamps form the pillars of a home-made sewing frame.

with thumb tacks. String is passed over small nails driven into the front edges of the base board and crossbar. If you bind with string, it is only necessary to use one piece. Using a knot that can be untied, fasten one end of the string to a nail on the right or left of the base board; then lead the other end over the two nails in the crossbar directly above, continuing back and forth until it can be firmly knotted to the last nail. This is the easiest way of obtaining an even tension in all the strings. A sewing frame can also be made from a base board and a permanent wooden frame. This is a cheaper solution. On the other hand, the C-clamp frame has the advantage that when the frame is not in use, the clamps are available for other kinds of work.

For example, the bookbinder frequently needs a clamping press. Generally, he employs a narrow wooden hand press for this purpose. The pressure is applied by means of two spindles on which semi-rounded wooden clamping blocks are threaded. These are tightened with special wooden keys. An improvised clamping press can be made from two strong pieces of hardwood and two sufficiently long threaded bolts. The clamping force is exerted by screwing down a pair of wing nuts.

The actual assembly of the press is a very simple process that is clearly illustrated in the drawing. Clamp the two flat pieces of wood together and drill the four holes for the bolts in a single operation. The bolts should be carriage bolts with a half-round head. Just below the head the shank of these bolts is cut square. If corresponding square recesses are formed in the wood, the bolts will not turn when the wing nuts are screwed tight. These nuts must always be provided with washers; otherwise they would crush the wood. These washers can be screwed down with flush-head wood screws to pre-

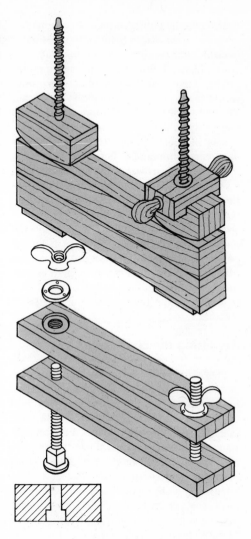

The binder's clamping press. Top: press with clamping blocks and wooden keys. Bottom: home-made press.

vent their being lost.

The book is not clamped directly in the press, however, but is placed between two wooden spreaders to spread the pressure

The signatures

evenly over its entire surface. Accordingly, when fixing the length of the bolts, the thickness of the spreaders must be taken into account. Furthermore, these spreaders must not be made of ordinary lumber, since this would bend or even split under pressure. The fibres of the board must run at right angles to its length. Bone-dry beechwood makes the best spreaders. Where necessary, you can manage simply by clamping the book between two boards with C-clamps. If you have no end-grain boards, insert two heavy crosspieces (if possible edgewise) between the boards and the clamps. It should be noted that the manipulation of such makeshift presses requires a lot of patience. The pages of the book easily get displaced in the process of adjusting the numerous components of the press. This, however, should be avoided at all costs.

Preparing the Signatures

The usual task confronting the amateur bookbinder is that of rebinding a much-read book or a new, but flimsily bound copy. He will start by detaching the pages in layers, that is in signatures, generally consisting of four double leaves folded down the middle and inserted one inside the other. This makes an octavo-size book with signatures containing eight single leaves or 16 pages. In the majority of books the signatures are marked with a collating number at the foot of the first page. Occasionally you will see two numbers, one connected with the title of the book, and another with an asterisk on the following leaf. As a bookbinder, you will be interested in the first of these numbers which indicates the beginning of a fresh signature. These figures are used to collate the book immediately before it is sewn, that is, to make sure that the individual signa-

tures are arranged in the correct order. If this is done negligently, the sequence of the pages will be destroyed, and, for example, page 49 may follow page 32, if signatures 3 and 4 have been carelessly switched. An even greater disaster may occur if the fourth signature is inserted after the third, but upside down. In this case page 32 will be followed by page 48 and all the pages from 33 to 48 will be upside down and in reverse order. These amusing, but frustrating mistakes, can only be put right by taking the whole book to pieces again.

We are now back where we started. The individual signatures must be opened in the middle and the stitches cut. Then they can be detached from the rest of the book. If staples have been used instead of thread, these must be pried open and taken out.

Carefully remove any odd pieces of thread and scraps of glue from the backs of the signatures, and repair them if they are worn through or torn. Use the narrowest possible strips of thin typewriting paper for this purpose, making sure that the grain of the paper is parallel with the long sides of the book. The strips must be narrow—less than $3/8''$ wide—so that they remain as inconspicuous as possible when the book is opened later on. Immediately the paste has dried, the mended double leaves are folded again and replaced in their correct position in the signature. This folding is done with a bone folder, an implement that no bookbinder should ever be without.

If, while taking the book apart, you occasionally come upon separate plates, drawings or maps that are not incorporated in the signature as double leaves, you should study carefully the way they are attached, and try to reproduce it. If you are dealing with heavy art plates, it is safer to attach them with white super-cloth. Super-cloth is a thin, sized cotton material always used in the bookbinding trade wherever superior strength is required. Where it is possible to insert a plate at the beginning or end of a signature, the strip by which it is attached should be carried around the back of the signature, so that it is picked up later on by the sewing thread.

In repairing the back of a tattered signature we find ourselves faced with the problem of choosing the right glue. In bookbinding a single glue will not satisfy every purpose. Sometimes we need a thin glue, sometimes a stiffer one. We also require a paste for sticking paper. Moreover, since we shall use fairly large quantities, we shall naturally tend to prefer the cheapest satisfactory material. Thus, we arrive at the classic bookbinding adhesives: joiner's glue and starch paste. Apart from their remarkable bonding powers, the advantage of these adhesives lies in their high water content. The paper to which they are applied stretches considerably but dries absolutely smooth.

After being allowed to steep in cold water (until fully saturated), joiner's glue is heated in a water-bath, without adding more water, and used in the warm state. Don't heat the glue to more than 140°F, otherwise it will lose its bonding strength. Starch paste is a thick mixture of wheat starch or flour and cold water. After allowing them to soak briefly, mix the starch granules with a little water until the paste is quite smooth and free from lumps. Then, stirring vigorously, add just enough hot water to transform it into a mass with the consistency of a pudding mixture. Don't prepare an excessive quantity, as this paste soon decomposes, giving off evil-smelling vapors. A few drops of formalin will help to prolong its life.

When all the repair strips and the strips for the plates have been coated with paste, the repaired signatures are refolded and put back in order. Then, correctly squared

off, they are clamped in the press between two boards, and left under pressure overnight. In the meantime we can start preparing the end sheets. Every book has two end sheets, one at the front and one at the back. It is no easy matter to cut paper or cardboard exactly to size with only a steel rule and a triangle. Unfortunately, we have little choice, since a proper cutting machine will rarely be available. Paper can be cut by hand with the aid of a sharp knife. The slanting cutting edge of a cobbler's knife is very suitable for this purpose. Cardboard can be cut with an adjustable cutter. Use a hardwood board as a foundation (not cardboard). Thin paper can be cut easily on a glass plate, although this blunts the knife rather quickly. Cutting paper with razor blades invariably leads to trouble. They are far too flexible and always give a crooked cut.

The end sheets are double leaves of tough white or tinted paper. One half is later pasted to the case board, while the other functions as a loose leaf between the case and the book proper. The end sheets are stitched together with the first and last signatures and must therefore be folded in a special way.

Let us take this book as an example. Each trimmed signature is approximately 6″ wide and 9″ high. The end sheets required for these measurements will be 9″ long, and twice the width of a signature plus 3″, that is 15″. When cutting these end sheets be sure that the grain is parallel with the back of the book, otherwise the case will soon work loose.

With the end sheet lying before you on the table—in the case of tinted papers the colored side should be on top, reinforce the back of the right outside edge with a ¹/₂″ wide strip of super-cloth and then fold it inwards until only a strip 3″ wide remains on the left hand side. The folded edge on the right is firmly creased and then the 3" wide strip on the left is similarly folded to the right on top of the double sheet. When the left-hand fold has also been well creased, the whole affair is turned over, so that the narrow flap now lies underneath. Now the end sheet is again folded over about $1/4$" along the edge where it is three layers thick. The first or last signature is inserted into this fold before sewing.

If the paper is particularly thick, the sewing fold of the end sheet should be made slightly wider. It is most important to crease these sewing folds very sharply with the bone folder. Better still, put the end sheets in the press overnight with the rest of the book. This has the further advantage that the title page, the face of the book, is saved from getting soiled in the press. At the same time, the title signature can also be protected by placing it in the press back to front (with the last page on the outside).

Sewing with String and Tape

After all these preparations have been duly completed, we are at last ready to start on the main part of the job, namely sewing the book. There are two possibilities: we can sew either on string or on tape. In either case the sewing should be sufficiently strong to give the book a sturdy backbone. A medium-sized octavo volume should be sewn at four points in the middle and one at each end. The two outermost points should lie $1/2$" from the top and bottom, or "head" and "tail" of the book.

If, for example, a book is to be sewn in three places, a pencil line is drawn across the middle of the back. This fixes the position of the center stitch. A convenient way of making the mark is to place the pile of signatures on the table against the vertical

edge of a triangle. After the center of the back has been found and marked, the two halves thus formed are again divided in two; the actual sewing marks, however, are made

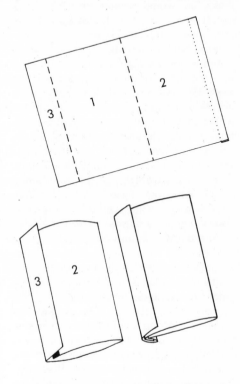

Folding diagram for end sheets. Fold 2 over 1 and 3 over 2.

slightly nearer to the head and tail of the book. Finally, the outermost sewing points are fixed $1/2$" in from the head and tail.

If it is intended to sew on string, the back must now be notched. The book is replaced in the clamping press after removing the two end signatures and replacing them with sheets of cardboard. The back of the book, perfectly aligned, should project $1/4$" above the top of the press. If the pencil marks on the backs of the signatures line up, the signatures have been correctly stacked, at least in the horizontal direction. It is smarter, perhaps, to clamp the book first, and then make the sewing marks on the back with a pencil and try-square. Then there will be no chance of the signatures slipping.

To prevent the strings from forming thick ridges on the back after sewing, they must be recessed. Accordingly, notches are made for them to lie in. This can be done with a fine backsaw, but far more accurately with a small round file. Proceed very cautiously, and make sure that the notches are not cut too deep. Otherwise the book will lack support and its shape will quickly become distorted. Moreover, if the notches are too deep, the strings will be visible inside the book, and this does not improve its appearance. It is better to make the depth of the notches a little less than the thickness of the string. The positions of the two outside stitches are not notched, but incised lightly with a knife. The incisions must not reach the inner double leaves of the signatures.

After the string has been stretched over the sewing frame at the correct intervals, it is time to start sewing, beginning with the last signature. Thus, the book is sewn from back to front. To simplify this part of the work, after the signatures have once more been collated to make sure they are in the right order, the book is placed on the left next to the sewing frame with the title page downward, and the head pointing towards the front edge of the table. The sewing is done with linen thread and a long, but slim darning needle. The softer the paper, the thicker should be the thread, to prevent it from cutting in. If it is waxed, the thread will show less tendency to stick.

Remember that the top and bottom signatures are not notched. Consequently they

need to be sewn in a special way. The reason they are not notched is to prevent the string from being exposed at the end sheets. Do not sew directly on the base board of the

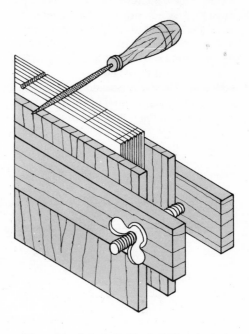

Filing notches in the back of the book. These notches are for the strings to which the signatures are sewn.

sewing frame, but on a piece of wood rather bigger than the book itself. There is a good reason for this. After the book has been sewn and the string cut, we need to have an end at least 1" long to stick down to the end sheet. By raising the first signature off the base board, this piece of wood guarantees us the necessary length of string.

Begin by taking the last signature, including the end sheet, from the top of the pile with the left hand and place it (end sheet undermost) on the sewing frame with the

Sewing on string

head pointing to the left and the notches coinciding with the strings. Insert the index finger into the middle of the signature and hold it open. Guiding the needle and thread with the right hand and working from the inside of the signature, pierce a hole for the thread $\frac{1}{2}''$ in from the tail, draw the needle back and pass it through the hole again from in front. The thread is pulled through the hole, until an end only about two inches long is left on the outside.

Now the needle is passed back through the signature just in front of the first string, carried around the string, and pushed back through the signature at right angles to the back of the book just on the other side. The other two strings are picked up in exactly the same way, until the needle finally reappears $\frac{1}{2}''$ from the outside of the signature at the head. The first (actually the last) signature is now sewn. The thread is pulled tight towards the left, the back of the signature is pressed down firmly between the strings with the bone folder, and the second signature is placed on top. The needle then follows the opposite course, back from left to right, only now there is no need to pierce any holes, since this has already been done

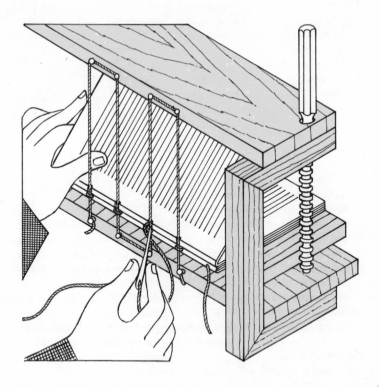

Sewing the first signatures (string binding). Note that the end signature is not notched.

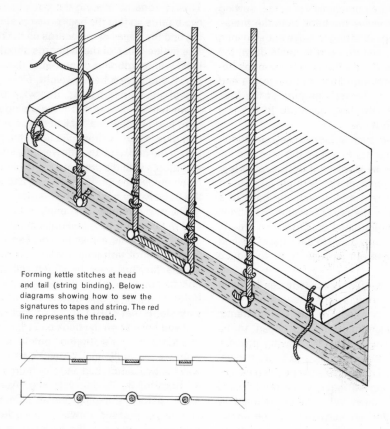

Forming kettle stitches at head and tail (string binding). Below: diagrams showing how to sew the signatures to tapes and string. The red line represents the thread.

by notching. Thus, after circling the string the needle is passed back through the same hole, drawing the string into the notch prepared for it. When the thread appears on the right, it is knotted with the end left hanging from the first signature; the second signature is pressed firmly down, and the third one is added. This time when the thread arrives at the left, it is not run directly into the fourth signature, but is first looped through the thread of the second signature in a so-called "kettle stitch."

Always remember to pull the thread tight after sewing each signature. If one signature is left loose, it will slip later on. The last signature, which together with the second end sheet is placed on top of the pile, is treated in exactly the same way as the first. Thus, a hole must first be pierced from the inside $1/2''$ from the edge, if the thread runs from outside to inside. No thread is endless. If you are obliged to splice it, make sure that the knot lies on the back of the book. Inside the signature it would make an unpleasant bulge.

Knotting the thread after securing the

title signature completes the actual sewing process. Remove the book from the frame, cut the loops of string to leave ends an inch or so long, and proceed to paste down the end sheets. To do this, open the book behind the first signature and paste the end sheet to the second signature at the fold. Then paste the last signature to the last signature but one.

Before all such intermediate operations make it a practice to line up the head and tail of the book by stacking it on the table top. After the ends of the strings have been teased out by rubbing with the back of a knife—this is the next operation—the book is again straightened up. Only then are the teased-out ends glued to the edge of the end sheet, spread out fanwise so as to reduce their bulk.

As already mentioned, tape can be used instead of string. In this case narrow linen tapes are stretched over the sewing frame, and the signatures do not need to be notched. This makes the sewing process somewhat more tedious and troublesome, but the tape method has the decided advantage of being stronger, since none of the paper is cut away. When tapes are used, all the signatures are sewn in the same way as the two end signatures of a book sewn on string. Be careful not to pass the needle through the tape, however. Wherever the needle travels from outside to inside, a hole must first be pierced from the middle of the signature. After sewing, the tapes are simply cut to the correct length and pasted to the edges of the end sheets.

Preparing the Book for the Case

At this point the book is held together only by thread, but the next operation, gluing the back, will strengthen it considerably.

This is done by placing the book between two boards so that the back projects slightly beyond the edges of the boards on the right. The inside faces of these boards should be lined with cardboard or non-absorbent paper. If you have a heavy weight, place it on top of the upper board; otherwise press down hard with your left hand, using your right hand to coat the back of the book with thin glue. Then, without changing the position of the book, rub the still wet glue into the signatures with the peen of a clean hammer. Now remove the cardboard lining and leave the book to dry between the boards.

The next operation, trimming, is best carried out on a printer's guillotine cutter. If no such machine is available, you can either leave the book untrimmed, which is not very satisfactory because the edges will inevitably be soiled, or place the book in the vise between a pair of boards and trim it with a very sharp, flat chisel about an inch wide.

If you have sewn the book on string, draw this to the printer's attention before he puts it under the guillotine. When sewn in this way the two unnotched end signatures have an unfortunate tendency to slip. Accordingly, before trimming these signatures should be pressed forward by vigorously rubbing the edges of the back with a bone folder held on the slant. In trimming the fore-edge of the book—and later on the head and tail—it is best to cut off as little as possible, just enough to make sure that all the pages are caught by the knife.

After the fore-edge has been trimmed, the rectangular back is rounded by hammering. Place the book with the fore-edge in front on the table and, holding it firmly in your left hand, round the back by tapping it gently with the hammer. Hammer slowly along the entire length of the back, paying special attention to the first third of the width. Then turn the book over and treat the other side in precisely the same way, until the back has been evenly rounded off. The fore-edge will then have a concave profile reflecting the curve of the back. This not only looks elegant, but also has the very practical result of making it easy to turn the pages of the book, without having to lick the thumb. The back must be definitely rounded, but at the same time do not go too far and hammer it into a sharp ridge.

After rounding the back, place the book in the clamping press again. For the next operation it must be clamped particularly firmly. In this case, the edges of the spreaders must be as sharp as possible. Arrange the book in the press so that at all points the back projects $^1/_8''$ beyond the edges of the boards. Mark this projection in pencil on the end sheets. You may even moisten the inside edges of the spreaders to prevent the book from slipping out of position.

It is essential to work with the greatest accuracy, since we have now to hammer two folds in the back of the book, the same thickness as the case boards. Thus, if you intend to use especially heavy case boards, the above-mentioned projection may have to be rather more than $^1/_8''$. When the clamping press has been correctly positioned and the maximum pressure applied, place it in front of you on the table with the back uppermost and start flaring out the signatures. This flaring is done with the peen of the hammer, held parallel to the back of the book. Starting in the middle the individual signatures are hammered forwards and backwards (in relation to the bookbinder), until the edges of the first and last signatures form an acute angle with the edges of the boards. The final shape of the back is shown in the accompanying drawing.

The back is then generously coated with paste. Again the paste is rubbed in with the peen of the hammer and left for a while to give the glue underneath time to soften. The whole back is now rubbed down with a ball of paper crumpled in the hand. Finally, a strip the same width as the back of the book is cut from a piece of soft, but strong paper. If the book is sewn on tapes, the strip is divided into lengths that will fit exactly in

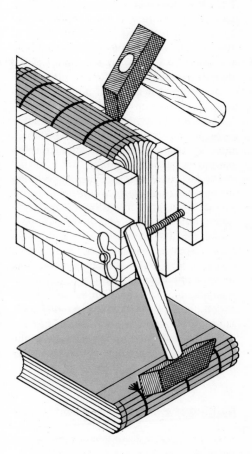

Flaring out the back with the peen and rounding it with the flat of the hammer.

between the tapes. These are saturated with paste and stuck firmly in place on the back of the book, which has previously been brushed over with a thin glue. The backs of very heavy books are stiffened with a second full-length strip. Books sewn on string with notched signatures are also reinforced with a continuous strip running the full length of the back.

Since the unavoidable heavy pasting allows a lot of moisture to penetrate into the back, the book must be left to dry out at least overnight, before the head and tail are trimmed. In trimming, the flared edges of the back of the book must be protected from the pressure exerted by the clamp of the guillotine cutter. This is done by placing the book between two pieces of cardboard, thick enough to make up the difference between the back and the body of the book. Place the book on the machine so that the sloping guillotine blade cuts in the direction from the back towards the fore-edge.

The last job in the process of preparing the book for casing-in is to glue on the headbands, the purpose of which is not merely to adorn, but also to prevent dust from penetrating into the back of the book. You can make your own headbands out of a suitable piece of cloth, but it is much simpler, less tedious and more economical to buy a pair ready-made. The headbands are strips exactly the same width as the rounded back, and one is pasted at each end. They are correctly positioned if the thickness of the colored burr just projects beyond the head and tail.

Making the Case

We can now proceed to make the case of the book, consisting of the back lining, the two boards and the actual binding. The back lining is a strip of tough paper, such as the cover of a Manila folder, exactly the same width as the back of the book, but $1/_4''$ longer (not including the burr of the headband). The two case boards are cut out at the same time as the back lining. The best material for this purpose is special binder's board. Ordinary brown cardboard is not tough enough and breaks too easily. The case boards and the back lining should be the same length. The exact width will be determined later. For the time being we shall make it $1/_2''$ more than the width of the signatures, measured from back to fore-edge. Watch the direction of the grain and cut the corners exactly at right angles, insofar as this is not taken care of automatically by the cutting machine.

Now let us return to the back lining. The strip of Manila folder is glued to a piece of wrapping paper the same length as the lining, but about $1^1/_4''$ wider on both sides. The grain direction of both pieces must be parallel to the back of the book. In this instance use glue rather than paste so that the lining becomes quite stiff on drying out. Only the lining is coated, not the paper.

The projecting flaps are now folded twice:

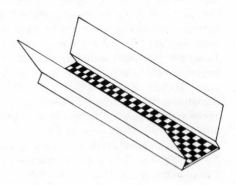

Folding the back lining. The distance between the folds should be such that the lining fits snugly against the back of the book.

once inwards along the edges of the lining, and once outwards parallel to and about $\frac{1}{4}''$ in from these edges. This dimension of $\frac{1}{4}''$ is not inflexible. The distance between the two folds should be equal to the flaring of the back.

To obtain a binding of high quality it is essential for the lining to fit the back like a glove. Accordingly, the freshly glued lining must be drawn sharply across the table edge until it is sufficiently rounded to fit the back snugly at all points. When trying out the lining, give the back a last careful check. It should be perfectly smooth. Even the tiny bumps formed by gluing on the headbands should be smoothed away before the lining is attached.

The lining is attached as follows: The two flaps of paper are coated with glue as far as the first fold. Then the back of the book is lowered vertically from above onto the lining, taking care that the latter projects the same distance beyond the headband at both top and bottom. When properly adjusted, the two glued flaps are stuck down over the corresponding flaps of the end sheets. The paper should be drawn tightly over the edges of the book so that the lining fits snugly against the back.

Immediately afterwards the two boards are attached. Don't make the strip of glue along the back edges of the boards unnecessarily wide—an inch is more than enough. Place the boards on the end sheets, over which the flaps of the back lining have been glued, in such a way that they fit snugly against the hinge. You may need to make some adjustments at this point, but in any case the edges of the case boards at the head and tail should lie exactly in the same vertical plane.

When the glued joints have been allowed to dry out for a time in the press, only a few finishing touches remain before the actual

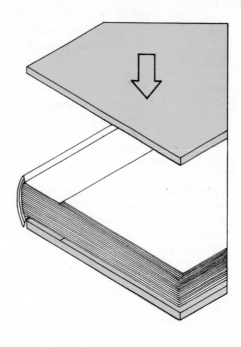

Attaching the case boards to the flaps of the end sheets, over which the back lining has previously been pasted.

binding is applied. First, the front edges of the case boards have to be trimmed to the correct size. These edges should project at least as far beyond the fore-edge as the top and bottom edges project beyond the head and tail. Mark off this projection on the boards with a pencil, and cut off the surplus material with a knife guided by a steel ruler, working from the inside. For this job you will need an assistant to lift the pages slightly and hold the book while you cut. The clamping arm of a guillotine cutter performs the same function.

If you look at a bound book, you will see

that the binding, whether paper or cloth, is tucked in not only over the edges of the boards, but also at the back. At first sight, it would seem impossible to do this with the type of back construction we have described, since the boards are glued directly to the back lining leaving no gap for tucking in the binding. This is soon remedied with a pair of scissors. Open out the case boards and hold the book vertically in your left hand, raising it slightly off the table. Now insert the scissors carefully between the flap of the back lining and the fold of the end sheet (cut only the end sheet) and make a notch about an inch deep. Later on the binding will be tucked into these notches.

Take this opportunity to check whether the entire width of the end sheet fold is glued to the boards. For the most part this will not be so, since we deliberately refrained from coating the boards with glue over the full width of the end sheet folds. In fact, this is not at all necessary. Where the glue ends, score the paper with a knife and rip the loose parts out.

Now the book lies before us clad, as it were, in its underclothing, and we can proceed to measure it up for a suit or binding. The easiest form of binding for a beginner is a half-binding. In this case only the back and the corners are bound with cloth, with the back cloth extending about a quarter of the way across the boards. Binder's cloth, sometimes called art linen, is not a linen, but a cotton fabric sized on one side so that it can be glued. In addition to this mat cloth, obtainable in various colors, there is also calico, a very strong material finished on both sides, which is used for strengthening edges and corners.

The cloth for the back is cut to the desired width, but an inch or so too long, taking care to make the warp threads run parallel to the length of the back. Brush the sized side of the cloth with thin glue, place it on the table, and press the back of the book down from above exactly in the center, leaving an equal width of cloth projecting at head and tail for tucking in. As soon as the cloth sticks, pick up the book and place it on the table so that the back projects over the table edge on the right. Now rub the cloth down firmly on the back only, lifting the strip of cloth that overlaps the upper board slightly with your left hand. When the back binding has been smoothed down, take the bone folder and neatly press the cloth down into the hinge between back and board. Only now is the strip that overlaps the board rubbed down. During all this time the strip of cloth intended for the other board is allowed to hang limply over the edge of the table.

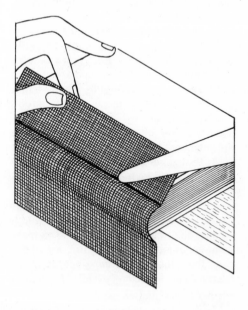

The quarter-binding: gluing on the cloth back. Before the cloth is glued to the board, it is pressed down into the hinge.

For the time being the projecting edges of the binding are also disregarded; they are not tucked in until the cloth has been glued to the second board in the same way as it was glued to the first. To do this, of course, it is first necessary to turn the book over. When the cloth has been firmly glued to the back of both boards, the book is placed back down on the table with the boards opened out flat. Then take hold of the pages in the left hand so close to the table top that the thumb and index finger press against the boards from the inside, while with the other fingers the signatures are pulled slightly away from the back. This pinches together the notches in the end sheet folds, providing sufficient space to tuck in the binding over the headband. This must be done carefully and coolly so that the tuck is smooth and free of creases. Then shut the book and touch up the headband with the bone folder, while the glue is still wet. Now it is the turn of the four cloth corners. These are cut out of a strip of cloth in the shape of four trapezoids of equal size. The width of this strip depends on the size of corner desired. Smaller corners generally look better than larger ones.

The corner strips are brushed with glue and laid over the corners of the boards so that the shorter side of the trapezoid projects beyond the corner a distance equal to the thickness of the board. Turn down the upper edge of the corner, and tuck in the small projecting piece of cloth before turning the rest of the corner strip down over the front edge of the board. In this way the corner is solidly sealed off. Moreover, there is no harm in rubbing down over-sharp corners with sandpaper before applying the corner cloth. However, beware of carrying this sandpapering too far.

The final size of the corners is determined by turning down the corners of the paper binding that covers the remaining surface

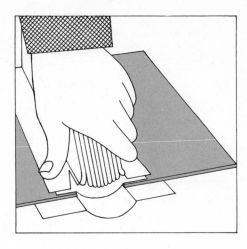

Two notches in the flaps of the end sheets make it possible to turn the cloth back down over the boards.

of the boards. The same applies to the width of the strip of cloth overlapping the boards from the back. This width is marked off on both sides with a hard pencil to provide a guide line for the edge of the binding paper. This paper should be cut big enough to project about an inch beyond the other three edges of the board. The size of the cloth corners is determined by turning over and cutting off the corners of the binding paper.

After cutting out the two binding papers, brush them with glue, and place them over the boards with equal overlaps at head and tail and with the back edge coinciding with the pencilled guide line. All that then remains is to rub them down firmly with the ball of the thumb, fold over the edges, and rub them down again on the inside of the boards. Press the paper down firmly around

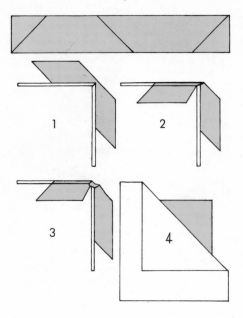

Cutting and pasting down cloth corners (1-3). The final size of the corners is determined by turning down the binding paper (4).

binding paper and corners all overlap the edges by different amounts, and this would show through the end sheets. All must be cut to an even width with a knife and a steel rule and the excess strips ripped off. During this operation place a block of wood under the boards so that they are supported horizontally and do not crack under the pressure of the knife.

Now one of the sheets of wax paper is placed under the front end sheet, which is then pasted with even strokes of the brush, working from the back of the book in the direction of the fore-edge. If the end sheet starts to curl up, hold it down with one of the fingers of your left hand. Then quickly pull out the wax paper, run your finger around the edges of the end sheet to wipe away the paste there, and shut the book. Then repeat the same procedure on the rear end sheet, trying to beat the record you have just established with the front one. After you have shut the book from the back, again without allowing the wet end sheet to curl up, press down vigorously a few times on the cover with both palms. Then place a sheet of wax paper over each of the two unpasted end pages and clamp the book between two pieces of cardboard in the clamping press. The spreaders and cardboard must, of course, be properly aligned, the edges of the press coinciding with the edges of the case boards. The back of the book should remain outside the press. Next morning the book is removed from the press, and the work of rebinding is complete.

Should you wish to give your book a full cloth binding, the cloth should be cut and pasted in a single piece, together with the necessary overlaps. This time don't start with the back, as with a half-binding, but place the whole of one board solidly down on the prepared cloth. Then proceed in the same way as with a half-binding. Turn

the edges of the boards, either with your thumb nail or with a bone folder, to prevent pockets of glue forming in these critical zones. Otherwise, once the glue has dried and hardened, these spots will quickly wear through.

We are now rapidly approaching the final stage of the binding process. This must be completed quickly, so make sure that all you need is placed within handy reach before you start. This will include a few sheets of wax paper, slightly larger than the book, two spreaders, the clamping press, and a pot of paste. All these are needed to paste down the end sheets.

First, however, we must tidy up the inside faces of the boards, since the back cloth,

the book around, hold up the still unpasted part of the binding in your left hand, rub in the first hinge, then work on the back, and finally on the second board. If you have chosen an open-textured, unsized cloth, glue not the cloth, but the boards and back. This will reduce the risk of the glue seeping through. In this instance the projecting edges of the binding are tucked in separately later on.

The procedure is much the same for a simple paper binding, which, however, is only simple if the word is not applied to the actual working process. Here, too, the binding paper is cut in one piece, but great care is required in pasting down and tucking in the edges, since in this case we are dealing with paper. After pasting, the entire surface has the stability of a wet sock and easily wrinkles and creases. Take particular care when rubbing the paper into the hinges, since at these points it is especially liable to tear. The hinges should be taken care of before the paper is stuck down to the boards. Do not cut the paper at the corners until you are ready to tuck in the edges of the binding. Cut off just enough for the corners still to close. These corners, like the back, can be reinforced with strips of calico before being bound, as they will suffer most wear and tear.

Binding paper is available in many qualities and shades, both in solid colors and in patterns. Previously the bookbinder prepared his own binding and end papers, and those who do not care for the commercial designs can do the same today. Unfortunately we have not the space to describe the details of this process. Nevertheless, the binding paper does a great deal to determine the quality of the finished book and you would be fully justified in making a well-considered choice. Don't accept inferior quality, because apart from having a smart appearance, the binding paper should also be tough and strong, otherwise it will soon look shabby and threadbare.

Album Binding

The amateur bookbinder is not always faced with the problem of a binding a set of folded double leaves. He may often be handed a stack of loose sheets and requested to bind them in the proper order. This is a very different situation from that we have considered so far, since it leaves us without any proper signatures that can be sewn on string or tape.

The civil servant solves the problem with a paper punch and a loose-leaf file, but this process produces dossiers, not books. Nevertheless, we can adapt the same principle to our own purposes. Its application is illustrated in the photo album, which almost always consists not of folded signatures, but of a stack of single sheets of cardboard.

If we can master the various operations involved in making a photo album, we shall at the same time equip ourselves with a very useful method of binding other collections of family documents as well. For example, a series of childrens' drawings can be mounted on cardboard and bound into souvenir volumes in exactly the same way. The photo album technique can also be used to bind travel diaries, and by a simple trick an album can be transformed into a handy file to hold your various documents. This trick consists in binding not just plain sheets of cardboard, but a series of wallets with the left-hand edges glued to broad strips of super-cloth. In this type of construction the strips of cloth are gathered together at the back and the separate wallets form the "leaves." If you make the wallets out of transparent plastic film, you will have

The photo album

an album for your record collection.

Assuming, then, that we begin with a simple photo album, the first step is to cut the pages of the album out of cardboard sold in sheets. These sheets should be cut so as to reduce the waste to a minimum. Whether you choose white, beige, or brown cardboard is entirely a matter of personal taste and has no effect on the work itself.

To prevent our practice piece from developing into an unwieldy tome, we shall content ourselves with thirty leaves, measuring say 10″ by 14″. It is both customary and practical to make thick-leaved photo albums with the short side forming the back. In our example, therefore, the back of the book will measure 10″. Remember this when cutting the leaves from the sheets of cardboard, since the grain of the cardboard must again run in the same direction as the book.

A good photo album will be interleaved with sheets of tissue-paper to protect the photographs. These are cut from strong material, equal in size and number to the album leaves, and set aside ready for use. This is also a good time to cut out the two case boards. These should be about $^3/_8$″ wider than the album leaves, but equal in length. The additional $^3/_8$″ is needed for the protection of the head and tail of the volume. Similar protection will later be obtained at the fore-edge by other means.

The cutting out does not end with the boards, however. The idea of a photo album is to keep adding pictures of varying size which, of course, makes the album grow gradually thicker. We must provide for this growth in advance by "padding" the back, so that when full the album will still close flat. This is done with inch-wide strips of the same cardboard as that used for the leaves of the album. These strips are inserted between the leaves, or rather after every second leaf, since the cardboard is thicker

than even a double layer of ordinary photographic paper. Since our album has 30 leaves, 15 inserts 10″ long will be enough. Naturally, if you are binding a series of wallets or a record album, the inserts will have to be much thicker, since the contents of the individual pockets are then much more bulky.

When all these parts have been prepared, the backs of the individual leaves are folded so that later on it will be possible to turn the pages. This fold is actually a double fold, and is best made over a metal straight edge. If a suitable piece of metal is not available it is possible to use the sharply planed edge of a wooden board, over which the cardboard is folded with the aid of a bone folder.

To ensure that all the leaves are folded in the same place, clamp a steel ruler to the board to the left of the edge over which you intend to do your folding. This will serve as a stop for the individual leaves. The edge of the ruler (which can be replaced with a straight piece of wood) should run parallel to the folding edge of the board, a distance of $12^1/_2$″ away. The front edges of the leaves of the album are pushed one at a time against the stop, so that the other end projects $1^1/_2$″ beyond the board on the right. With the aid of a second ruler, press the leaf down hard with the left hand, while forming the crease with the bone folder held at a slant in the right. After all the leaves have been given a first fold, the ruler forming the stop is advanced $^3/_{16}$″ towards the "folding" edge, and the second crease is formed in a similar manner. In each case the front of the leaf must face downwards and the back upwards. Thus both creases are made in the direction of the front of the leaf.

After this process is complete, the leaves are stacked and laid on the table front side up with the fore-edge pointing towards the binder. They are now ready for the insertion

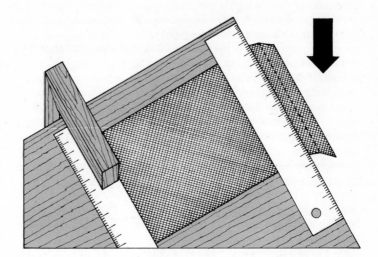

Album binding. The back is formed by making a double fold in each leaf over a sharp edge. The clamped ruler on the left serves as a stop, ensuring that the folds are all made in the same place.

of the sheets of tissue-paper.

These are arranged in a single pile with the narrow right-hand edges overlapping, shingle style, to leave about $^1/_8''$ of each sheet exposed. Place a piece of wax paper over the topmost sheet of tissue-paper, again leaving $^1/_8''$ or so at the edge. The whole of the exposed "clinker" surface is then coated with paste, so that each sheet is neatly provided with a narrow adhesive edging. Then one by one the sheets of tissue-paper are lifted off the pile and attached to the front faces of the cardboard with the edges accurately aligned, so that the leaves are just covered. The work must proceed rapidly so that the narrow strips of paste on the sheets of tissue paper do not have time to dry. All that now remains is to insert the strips used to pad out the back, and the album is ready for binding. To prevent the strips from coming loose, stick them to the corresponding leaves of the

album with a couple of blobs of paste.

The back of the album will not be properly held, until it has been firmly bound between the case boards, and making these is our next task. We have two possibilities from which to choose: an open back, with the binding consisting virtually of only the two case boards, or a closed binding. In either case, the leaves of the album and its binding are laced together with silk or leather cord.

It is clear that a closed binding makes a far more durable album than an open back. Accordingly, let us attempt a closed binding, and at the same time acquaint ourselves with the principles used in making albums of every kind.

Just like the leaves, the two case boards must be provided with a hinge at the back. Since the board is so thick, however, simple folding will not be enough. Remember that the leaves of the album were folded $1^1/_2''$ from the edge. The breadth of the back of

The closed binding

the album should be a little less than this, so that later on the pages of the album will still turn easily. This means that we must cut a strip $1^1/_4''$ wide off one of the narrow sides of each case board. To these two strips we add a third cut from the same cardboard to serve as a back lining. The length of the lining must be equal to the width of the boards, and its width equal to the total thickness of the leaves plus twice the thickness of the caseboard.

All these separate elements are now joined in a continuous case by means of a broad strip of cloth. This strip should be the same width as the boards plus $1^1/_2''$ for tucking in at head and tail. In estimating the length, start with twice 3" for the overlap onto the two boards and add the widths of the three strips forming the back and the four gaps.

Just as in binding the back of a book, this piece of cloth is coated with glue and laid flat on the table. First the back lining is placed exactly in the center. Then follow the two $1^1/_4''$ wide hinge strips at a distance corresponding to the thickness of the cardboard, and finally the two case boards. Here a slightly larger gap must be left, since this represents the hinge about which the case boards turn. For a cloth back it should be about $3/_{16}''$ wide. These gaps also cause the boards to project beyond the fore-edge of the photo album.

After the cloth has been rubbed hard down, the edges are turned over and pressed as far as possible into the hinges with a bone folder. Be careful to avoid wrinkling the cloth. These hinges must be reinforced on the inside by means of an additional strip of cloth. This is cut from the same material as that employed for the binding, but super-cloth or calico will do just as well. The strip should be just long enough to fit into the clear gap between the edges of the turned down binding and should overlap about $1/_2''$ onto the adjacent cardboard surfaces on the right and left. Thus, the strip should be about $1^1/_2''$ wide, since it must also be pressed firmly down into the hinges.

The rough case is now complete. After the glue has dried in the press, the cloth corners are added and the boards are covered with binding paper. These operations are exactly the same as for a book with half-binding. Nor is there any difference between making a cloth-bound album and a cloth-bound book. A wholly paper binding, however, is hardly advisable for albums. At least, the hinges should be reinforced with super-cloth, otherwise they will quickly give way.

In any case, the inside surfaces of the boards should be covered with neatly pasted end sheets. Take a sheet of cardboard of the same material and the same width as the album leaves. The length of this sheet should be such that the inner edge falls $3/_{16}''$ short of the hinge.

After the finished case has thoroughly dried out in the press, the back is pierced for lacing. Three holes will be enough for a closed binding. These holes are punched through the top of the case only. Then the leaves are inserted and the whole album is clamped to a wooden board with the back firmly supported. If you have a high-speed power drill and a very sharp bit of the right size you will now be able to bore the holes in a single operation. If such equipment is lacking, you will have to use a cardboard template as a guide and punch boards and leaves individually. This method calls for great precision, if the album is to close neatly. The manner in which the cord is laced through the holes will be obvious from the drawing.

In the case of an album with an open back, the process is somewhat simpler. You can

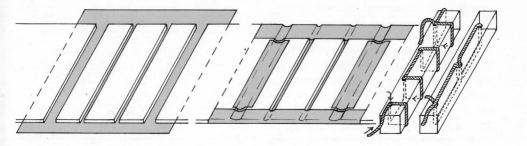

The closed binding. The individual pieces of cardboard are mounted on the cloth back. The hinges are reinforced on the inside with additional strips of cloth. On the right: method of lacing open and closed backs.

now dispense with the strip for the back lining. The back consists only of the two strips cut from the case boards and a piece of cloth. For this purpose cut out a strip of cloth about 3″ wide and just long enough to be folded over at the head and tail. Now draw a pencil line down the middle of the strip in the long direction. After coating it with glue, stick down the hinge strip along this boundary line. Then attach the board alongside it, leaving $^3/_{16}$″ for the hinge. Before folding the cloth over at top and bottom, cut off a strip the same width as the tuck from the free half of the cloth. The meeting cuts from above and below should slant away from the board and should be made about $^1/_8$″ in front of the edge of the hinge strip. The cloth still left projecting above the board is now turned down and the free half is folded over. Thus the cloth covers the hinge from the inside too, giving it additional strength, provided that it is firmly rubbed down into the open space. All the other work on the two boards is carried out in the same way as for a closed binding. In view of the relative weakness of an open back, however, it is better to pass the binding cord several times around the outside of the album. In this case use a fairly thin cord, since it must pass three times through each hole. It is a good idea to reinforce the holes with brass tubular rivets. These not merely protect the walls of the hole but at the same time give the whole binding a smart finish.

Passe-Partout

Passe-partout makes a neat and effective frame for water-colors, photographs, and prints. White, light-tinted or black cardboard about $^1/_{16}$″ thick is best suited for this purpose. Two pieces of equal size will be required, one for the frame proper and the other for the backing. Starting from the center-line lightly trace the outline of the picture opening on the exposed side of the framing sheet. A ratio of $3^1/_2$:3:5 for the top, sides and bottom of the frame is generally considered harmonious. In order to get the oblique cut typical of passe-partout, place a steel ruler with a beveled edge a short dis-

143

The open back—passe-partout

tance away from the pencilled outline of the picture opening so that a cutter (with a strong blade sharpened on both sides), inclined at an angle of 60°, can be drawn accurately along the line in a single movement under strong pressure. When these cuts have been made on all four sides, the waste piece of cardboard in the center can easily be knocked out of the frame from behind. Rough corners are carefully cleaned up with a razor blade. The upper edges of the two pieces of cardboard are then joined with a strip of adhesive tape. Similarly, after its correct position has been lightly indicated in pencil, the original is attached to the backing by the upper edge only. A slim border in gilt, color or India ink will further enhance the effect of passe-partout.

Cross section through a passe-partout frame. From top to bottom: frame proper and picture opening, original, backing. Below: the picture opening is cut out.

A DASH OF COLOR—PRINTED AND WOVEN FABRICS 8

Man's need to adorn himself and decorate his surroundings is well satisfied by textile fabrics which can be dyed in innumerable ways. Thus, almost everything woven now has a two-fold purpose. This is most obvious in clothing which is so much influenced by fashion trends, but even cushions are seldom used solely to pillow the head. They effectively perform the no less important function of adding color accents to the interiors of our homes. Similarly, we do not curtain a window merely for the sake of privacy or to keep out the sun. The colorful folds of draperies are an important device of the interior decorator. Indeed, their original practical functions are now often secondary to their ornamental effect.

The remarkable ability of textile fabrics to introduce color and beauty into the human environment can produce the most fruitful results in the field of hobbies, affording boundless possibilities of developing the imagination and the decorative sense.

Batik

A most exciting, but easily mastered method of decorating delicate fabrics, this ancient Javanese dyeing technique is particularly suitable for scarfs and shoulder wraps, graceful shawls, fancy handkerchiefs, and silk ties. Fabric lampshades and even expensive book bindings and table cloths are given a distinct individuality by a batik design or border.

The principle of batik work consists in protecting selected parts of the material to be dyed with wax, so that the dye is prevented from penetrating the waxed areas.

When the wax (which can be applied in the form of a pattern, ornament or figure) is removed, after the fabric has dried, the areas it covered show up clearly against the dyed background.

Thin silks and batistes are suitable materials for batik, but so are pure cotton and linen. Whatever material is used, however, it must be completely free of size if satisfactory results are to be achieved. The size —generally a chalk-starch filler in which the material is soaked—prevents the wax from sticking so that it splits off during dyeing. Moreover, size also takes dye. Washing in warm water, however, dissolves out the size, and with it the dye. Thus, a not inconsiderable part of the batik design is left floating about in the washing machine. What remains is a washed-out and no longer decorative rag.

Sized fabrics must therefore be completely freed from size before the decorative work is begun. The fabric should be wrung out vigorously in a hot solution of washing soda and then rinsed several times in clean, warm water.

For waxing use only pure, unstained beeswax. Crude beeswax from an apiary is not clean enough for our purposes. If such wax is heated long enough—but not boiled—in a wide, open vessel, the lighter impurities will rise to the surface and can then be scooped off. The heavier impurities will settle to the bottom. After the wax has cooled, it can be taken out in a solid block and the bottom scraped off with a knife. This process might have to be repeated if the wax is particularly dirty. Prepared beeswax and special batiking waxes can, of course, be obtained from all artists' supply stores.

Before it can be used, the wax must be melted and kept warm in an old tin can or preferably a porcelain crucible over a spirit flame. Again the wax must on no account be allowed to boil. If you work on a stove, you can melt the wax in a water bath which retains the heat even better than the thick walls of a porcelain crucible. Wax kept in a water bath remains brushable longer.

The molten wax is applied to the material with a bristle brush. Only when drawing fine lines, which should generally be avoided, should hair brushes be used. The batik artist employs broad masses of color rather than thin lines.

If you are still hesitant about how to proceed, sketch out a few simple designs in transparent colors on water-color paper. These will serve as a guide during the gradual completion of the actual work. The more experienced will achieve fresher impressions by working quite freely, after first fixing their ideas with just a few lines pencilled on the material itself.

The fabric should always be stretched before the wax is applied. Since the brush, dipped in hot wax, is drawn over the fabric without applying pressure, it is best to stretch the material over a wooden frame using thumb tacks to keep it tight. To protect the edges of the delicate batik fabric, tack through a strip of stronger material. If you have no wooden frame, the fabric can be stretched over the edge of a bowl. In this arrangement the surface to be painted is again suspended freely. Finally, you may stretch the fabric over several layers of blotting paper previously pinned flat to a drawing board. This method has the disadvantage that the hot wax seeps through the fabric, which then adheres to the paper base. If you are obliged to resort to this make-shift solution, pull the material off the paper base with great care when waxing is complete. If necessary, you can first warm the paper lightly from the back with an electric iron.

If the colors are to be clearly separated on

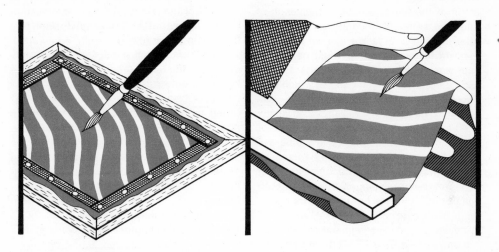

Working in batik. While the wax is being applied, the fabric is stretched flat over a wooden frame. For the purpose of rewaxing small areas, it is enough to weight down one end of the fabric and drape the other end over the left hand.

both sides, it is imperative that the fabric be thoroughly penetrated by the hot wax, so that the individual threads are completely protected from the dye. Check the finished wax coating, and in case of doubt supplement it from the back.

As wax begins to flow at 140°F, only cold dyeing processes can be used. Prepare the dye in accordance with the maker's instructions in a vessel large enough for the fabric to be introduced with a minimum of folds. If the fabric is creased or crumpled the wax film may crack, whereupon the dye will penetrate into the material beneath.

The fracturing of the wax coating produces the "crackling" so characteristic of batik. We have no intention of ignoring this

exciting effect, but prefer to postpone it until the final dye bath, when the fabric is gently crumpled to produce the necessary cracks.

In dyeing multi-colored designs always start with the lightest and finish with the darkest colors. The individual dyeing times vary with the color and the material between a few minutes and half an hour or more. Do not be nervous but wait patiently until the desired effect is obtained. Rinsing in cold vinegar water between dips is advisable to prevent undesirable running of the colors, although even this will not give sharp color separation. The flowing together of adjacent areas of color is a characteristic of batik. After each dip the fabric must be hung up flat and free of folds and allowed to dry

147

Hand printing

thoroughly before a new coat of wax is applied. Do not dry over radiators or in the sun.

When working out your designs and also when waxing, always remember that the effect of the finished batik is the result of adding a series of separate colors. Thus, after dipping in a yellow dye, all the parts that are to remain yellow must be coated with wax. A delicate situation arises when two colors, the intermingling of which produces a third, utterly different color, lie side by side. This applies, for example, to yellow and blue. A cloth dyed yellow will turn not blue, but green when dipped in a blue dye bath. Bleaches must therefore be used, or else the parts intended to become blue must be waxed before dyeing in the yellow bath and the wax removed before transfering the fabric to the blue bath. This must be decided in advance when working out the design.

If only small areas of a multi-colored batik require rewaxing, the work can be simplified by dispensing with a second stretching over the wooden frame. Instead just place the fabric on the table, lay a weight at one end, and then proceed to wax holding the opposite end of the fabric off the table with the left hand. Take particular care not to damage the existing layer of wax.

After the fabric has passed through all the dye baths, the wax is removed. The bulk of it is sucked out by ironing the fabric between sheets of clean blotting paper. This is followed by washing in gasoline and a final rinsing in luke-warm water. Gasoline is inflammable and highly explosive. It is preferable to use carbon tetrachloride instead. This smells like gasoline, but is so incombustible that it is even used to put out fires.

The drying and ironing of the fabric completes the batiking process.

Block Printing

A more rigid technique of decorating light-colored fabrics, lacking the freedom of batik, is the now rarely used method of hand printing. This is really nothing more than a refined type of dyeing on the batik principle. Here too, the fabric is printed with a water-repellent paste and then dyed some deep shade, often blue. When the fabric has dried, the paste—like the wax in batik—is removed, leaving the design standing out clearly against the darker background.

Much more interesting than this negative process is the positive technique using colored printing blocks. The printing itself should present no difficulties once the procedures described in Chapter 5 have been mastered. In particular, it would be well to recall everything said there concerning the use of ornament, especially the

A design hand-printed by a technique similar to batik. The pale lines stand out against the darker color of the background.

advice concerning the interaction between motif and background, which also determines the success of printed fabrics.

Linoleum blocks are not very suitable for this printing process, as they are attacked by the dye and soon become useless. During printing the block has to withstand some rough treatment, since it will transfer the design to the fabric only if given a heavy blow with a hammer or otherwise heavily compressed. The printing blocks must therefore be made of hard wood, the contours of which still print sharply even after long use (pear or cherry). Furthermore, the block must not be too thin. A thickness of $1^1/_2''$, however, will be good enough for most purposes.

The choice of dye has a decisive influence on both the quality and durability of the print. Many makes of dye are available, but the "fastest" are undoubtedly those based on synthetic resins. While most dyes do not call for any aftertreatment, fabrics printed with synthetic resin dyes must be thoroughly ironed. The iron must be quite hot, since heat is required to transform the originally water-soluble synthetic resin into an insoluble mass that binds the dye firmly to the fabric in the form of a thin film.

As with ordinary woodcuts and linocuts, the colors are rubbed down on a glass plate or stone slab and then transferred to the printing block by means of a rubber roller. Printing colors are plasticized by adding a few drops of turpentine.

Both linens and cottons lend themselves very well to printing. New materials should be given preference over those that have been repeatedly washed. On the former the colors will be clearer and not so blotchy. Remember to remove all the sizing from the fabric before printing.

Printing is best done on a soft, pliable base. Use a bed of newspaper or a thick

piece of felt laid flat on a sufficiently large table top. Place a large sheet of blotting paper over the base to soak up any color that

Positive printing with the aid of an inked block. Correct spacing between the individual elements of the design is ensured by laying out a square grid on the surface of the fabric.

may seep through. The fabric to be printed is stretched tightly over the base with thumb tacks and moistened slightly with a sponge just before the printing block is first applied. This increases its absorbing power. In order to make a regular pattern the printing surface is divided by a series of thin charcoal lines into a network of squares, the areas of which correspond to the size of the printing block. If several motifs are printed in an ornamental sequence, all the blocks employed should be equal in size.

The printing itself should proceed swiftly and surely. So do not start until all the preparations have been carefully made.

After the printing block has been inked with the roller, it is set down on the fabric vertically from above. It must be in the right position from the start—this, in fact, is half the art—since the slightest movement of the block results in blurred outlines. The beginner will discover that, at first, hitting each square plumb in the middle is somewhat difficult. Confidence can be gained by making a few trial prints on small remnants of the same material. In any event these trial prints are necessary to determine the exact amount of color required for inking the block. If the layer of ink is too thick, the print will be blotchy and blurred, if it is too thin, the print will be too faint.

When the block is actually in place on the material, it is held firmly with one hand, and made to print by striking it with a wooden mallet. The outlines will be sharper, if the block is given just a single blow. Whether one blow is sufficient can only be determined by making a trial print. If the block has been printed correctly, it is lifted off vertically with the same sureness as used in setting it down.

You may consider the print successful if the dye adheres evenly to the threads of the fabric. Apart from the fact that bare patches can be made good with a bristle brush, we need not feel concerned about minor irregularities. On the contrary, they enhance the value of the article, for they are the unmistakable characteristic of a hand-made print. The dye will need a little time to dry. Only when it has dried, should it be exposed to a hot iron, assuming that a synthetic resin emulsion was used. A large and expensive piece of hand-woven linen will be irretrievably ruined by a single misprint. The careful printer will therefore thoroughly test a complicated surface composition employing several motifs—such as might be used for a wall hanging—on a good, absorbent paper, before proceeding to print the actual linen. This will not merely enable him to make technical adjustments, but will afford him a final opportunity of subjecting the design as a whole to a critical reexamination.

Apart from the laws of ornament, another rule must be observed, that of texture, which is derived from the fact that a piece of cloth is a woven article. Not only should the printed motif not become an end in itself (that is, the fabric should not be reduced to serving as a mere vehicle for the design) but the printing should respect, rather than overwhelm the textile surface formed by warp and weft. It is much truer to the material to weave in or embroider a colored pattern. Both techniques—weaving and embroidering—necessarily follow the directions imposed by the weave. Accordingly, you should design your printing blocks to conform with the woven structure of the fabric. In this way you will do justice to the material and master the secrets of the discrete, yet expressive language of fabric printing.

Screen Printing

Screen printing is both artistic and rational. Like batik, this process, by means of which large areas can be rapidly printed, also requires a wooden printing frame. This should be made of fairly thick material mortised and tenoned at the corners. The finished frame is covered with pure, fine-mesh silk or organdy. The best screen materials, however, are copper and bronze gauze, but these extremely fine wire meshes are very expensive and break uncommonly easily. They should be handled most carefully, since even the slightest kink will show up later on as a printing flaw. However, if they can be stretched successfully, the metallic gauzes are much more durable than any textile screen. Therefore, if you intend to engage in the "mass-production" of prints, you would be well advised to purchase the more expensive material. The gauze is drawn tight over the bottom of the frame and fixed with thumb tacks to its outer vertical edges. Inserting strips of thin cardboard between the tacks and the gauze will help to maintain the tension.

The positive-negative effect of screen printing is achieved by partially masking out the surface of the screen with lacquer, that is, all the areas of the screen that are not to print are brushed with lacquer to prevent the paint from penetrating the mesh at these points.

The transparency of the gauze makes the preparation of the screen much easier. If the gauze is laid over a previously prepared design, the drawing will show through clearly enough for you to trace off the outlines on the gauze with a pencil. As soon as the drawing has been transferred, raise the gauze off the table by inserting two narrow pieces of wood beneath the frame, one on each side. Then replace the original design with a sheet of packing paper. This serves only to protect the table top during the masking out process which now follows.

Don't lose your patience at this stage. A single coat of lacquer is not enough to give a reliable seal, so the process must be repeated several times and on both sides. If you work with enamel lacquer, let the first coat dry before applying the second. This takes time. Asphalt lacquer thinned with turpentine dries much faster but is harder to apply with the necessary neatness. Moreover, it can be washed out of the fabric again with gasoline or carbon tetrachloride. To prevent paint from seeping between the wood of the frame and the screen during printing, the crack in the angle between the screen and the vertical inside face of the frame is covered with strong strips of gummed paper.

In preparing the frame, leave a broad band (at least 2") on each of the narrow sides of the screen between the actual design and the wooden surround. This should be completely blocked out with lacquer. Provide a total of 4" for these bands when measuring up the frame. During the printing process this space serves as a paint reservoir. The paints—use the same materials as in block printing—are distributed over these areas and, after the frame has been set up, are brushed over the printing surface onto the fabric with a broad, hard rubber squeegee. Apply a fair amount of pressure so that the paint penetrates freely and evenly through the mesh of the gauze staining the fibres of the material underneath. The success of the printing process can be checked by raising the frame on one side and, if need be, applying a second coat of paint.

The preliminary treatment and mounting of the material for screen printing are the same as in working with printing blocks. The only problem is how to match the material and the design. The gauze is pierced with a needle at four inconspicuous points in the blocked out area, as close as possible to the corners of the screen. When the paint is applied, these holes appear as tiny dots on the material beneath. When the screen is set up again, pins (with the heads snipped off) are stuck into these guide marks, and the corresponding perforations in the screen are slipped over the pins, thus ensuring very accurate alignment.

The whole alignment problem can be much simplified by using a screen large enough to make room for several repetitions of the basic motif. The ultimate refinement lies in making a screen equal in size to the material to be printed. Should you wish to

In view of the difficulty of removing fabric colors, once they have been applied, hand painting constitutes a rather risky under-

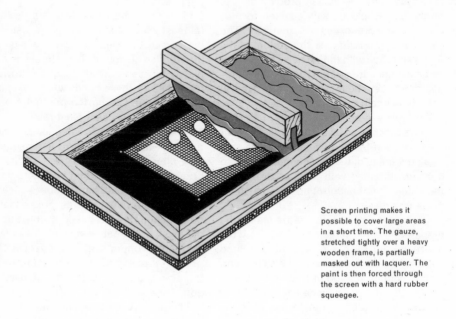

Screen printing makes it possible to cover large areas in a short time. The gauze, stretched tightly over a heavy wooden frame, is partially masked out with lacquer. The paint is then forced through the screen with a hard rubber squeegee.

print in several colors using a full-size screen, simply mask the non-printing parts of the screen with cellophane.

Hand-Painted Fabrics

When we undertake to paint a picture on the blank surface of a bright piece of silk using only a brush, we cast off all previous material limitations. Freed from the necessity of manipulating a printing block or screen, there is only the brush between our artistic visions and their practical realization.

taking for the beginner. He can best overcome the fears inspired by a stretch of blank fabric by first sketching his proposed design on drawing paper. This will differ considerably from the preliminary designs used in block printing and batik, since hand painting is concerned less with colored surfaces than with delicate linework, the drawing being subordinated to the character of the fabric, usually a smooth, finely woven material. The luminosity of the colors is especially effective on bright silks, artificial silk, and nylon, but also on fine linens and cottons.

Although it is usual to paint such delicate fabrics only in transparent colors, opaque and even relief paints are available for darker materials. Painting with liquid colors is the most common technique, although many specialists prefer to work with colored crayons. The technical difference between these two styles consists mainly in that liquid colors are applied with a fine hair brush (squirrel hair) to the dry fabric, whereas in working with crayons it is necessary to moisten the fabric with a sponge. Here again the preparation of the fabric is confined to washing out all the size. As in waxing batik materials, the fabric must be tightly stretched. The familiar wooden frame, or possibly a convenient old picture frame, will serve as a stretcher. A double embroidery ring, in which the material can be clamped, is another convenient device. A rectangular frame is better, however, since it permits the more careful tautening of the material. It is important that the natural run of the threads be preserved, that is, the weave must not be distorted. Start by laying the material loosely over the frame with the threads running vertically and fasten it at top and bottom in the middle of the cross members of the frame. From these first two fixed points work evenly to right and left, making sure that the threads always run parallel. Only when the material has been firmly fastened to the two longer sides of the frame, should you turn to the shorter ones. Again work from the center towards the corners of the frame. The warp threads should always run parallel to the longer side of the frame.

The transfer of the design from paper to stretched fabric is made easier by the transparency of the latter. Stitch the design to the back of the material with a few tacking stitches, and under it place a sheet of smooth cardboard. Then trace it through in thin, just recognizable pencil lines. During this process the cardboard is braced with

the left hand. If the fabric is too thick to see through, try using the "window pane" trick. This consists in pressing both design and frame up against the window pane. When the sun shines through the material from the other side, its transparency is much increased. This trick will only work, of course, if you have not painted your design on opaque packing paper. In this case you must stretch the material over the frame in such a way that the front, that is, the side on which you intend to paint, faces inwards so that the thickness of the frame does not get in the way when the fabric is applied to the window pane.

If even the sun's rays fail to give the desired degree of transparency, the only thing to do is to trace the design from above. If possible, avoid using ordinary office carbon paper, since the marks it leaves are conspicuous and difficult to remove. The best solution is to rub the rougher side of a sheet of typewriter copy paper vigorously with graphite powder or a soft lead pencil. Of course, tracing with paper prepared in this way demands the utmost care and a

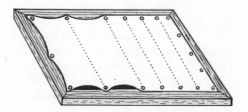

Fabric for hand painting must be carefully stretched over a painting frame. The material is laid loosely over the frame and tacked down in the middle of the longer sides. Tacking then continues evenly to left and right, the natural lie of the threads being scrupulously preserved.

relaxed hand, if the pure white of the fabric is not to be hopelessly smeared. The risk of such a catastrophe can be reduced by placing a sheet of thin paper under those parts of the design you are not in the process of tracing.

When you start painting, remember that textile fibres avidly absorb any form of moisture. The more absorptive the material, the drier your brush should be, if you are to avoid blurring the outlines of your design. Accordingly, do not dip your brush deeply into the paint pot, but transfer a few drops of paint to a porcelain palette or an old saucer, and wet the brush cautiously. Remember, however, that these paints dry out quickly. Therefore, always take from the paint pot only as much as you can handle.

Many paints are available for this type of work. A variety of thinners and other "doctoring" agents is also obtainable. Some of these make the paint slightly more viscous when exposed to the air. In this condition the paint does not blur so easily as when used in the pure form. Transparent colors are, of course, not suitable for dark materials. By mixing it is possible to obtain new shades, and clever exploitation of this fact enables one to manage with a relatively small stock of different colors.

Certain liquid paints, which are mixed with water, can be sprayed as well as applied with a brush. Since they dry very quickly, they are much less likely to blur. In view of all these advantages these paints are perhaps the best choice for the less experienced. They, too, can be freely mixed, or brightened by adding permanent white. The addition of white, however, gives these paints more "hiding power." On the other hand, mixing with "permanent colorless" increases their transparency. After being ironed on the back with the hottest possible iron, textiles treated with these dyes will be proof against washing, boiling, and the weather. This process is not suitable for nylon and other synthetics, however. If these are pressed with a hot iron, nothing remains but a tacky paste. Like the fabrics themselves, the paints cannot stand rough treatment.

Weaving

As long as we decorate our material by painting it, the material itself remains a more or less neutral background upon which the design leads an independent existence of its own, that is, it is bound neither by the run of the threads nor by the structure of the fabric. It is quite true that in working out a design we try to avoid a conflict with the nature of the woven surface, but this effort ceases to be very meaningful when the weave itself is so fine that the texture becomes practically invisible. For example, it would be ridiculous to try to allow for the structure in painting a flimsy batiste.

However, the circumstances will certainly be very different, if we try to build up a colored design using only the threads themselves. This art, known as weaving, makes use of the thickness of the spun fibre to build up a mesh-like surface consisting of interwoven threads. The sorely tried bachelor applies the same principle in darning the gaping holes in his socks, first running the warp threads along the length of the hole, and then shuttling back and forth with the weft.

It is clear, of course, that this rigid process imposes severe limitations on the resulting design. We have just learned about the various printing techniques which constitute one of the earliest and simplest methods of overcoming these limitations. At the same time, the desire to achieve results doing fuller justice to the nature of the materials, by using only dyed threads, has led to the development of more refined procedures, by means of which it is possible to play quite startling variations on the rigid simplicity of the basic weave.

A close study of all these interesting possibilities is beyond the scope of this book. We shall confine ourselves to a description of a technique offering a solid opportunity for making wall hangings of great beauty and charm. This is the age-old method of carpet knotting which has been brought to such a high level in the Near East. Strictly speaking, this process is a combination of weaving and knotting. The carpet foundation is woven, while the actual pattern is knotted into the mesh with strands of colored wool.

The sock-darning principle can easily be applied to a larger surface by making use of a long, flat box the narrow sides of which are raised about 4 or 5 inches with the aid of two boards nailed on edgewise. At intervals of about $1/_8$" warp threads are strung across the neatly trimmed end-grain faces of the two boards. Nails, or better slots, cut to the same depth with a fine-toothed saw, will serve to hold the threads in place. As in darning, you can now carry the transverse threads over and under between the warp threads with a needle to obtain a woven surface. Actually, this simple process, known as plain or tabby weaving, closely resembles sock darning. Nevertheless, it can be used to produce smaller articles and lengths of woven fabric in a variety of colored patterns.

If you wish to weave a full-sized wall hanging, however, this primitive device will clearly be inadequate. You will need a regular loom. The width of the article to be woven will still be limited, but there will be no restrictions on its length.

Such looms, of course, can be bought in

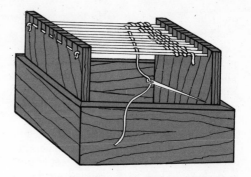

Plain weaving, in which the weft is passed alternately under and over the warp, is very similar to darning.

every size and with all sorts of technical refinements. The enthusiast, however, will want to build his own. A handy carpenter will not find this difficult, since the basic components of such machines are all the same and essentially quite simple.

The principle of a frame with the warp threads running along its length will be preserved in our design, as it is in every loom. If you also bear in mind that a length of string occupies the least space when wound on a stick, the design principle will become as clear as day. We shall construct a frame the sides of which consist of two strong, rigidly jointed pieces of wood supporting rotatable cross members known as "beams." First the warp is wound around the warp beam. Then during weaving the finished cloth is wound onto the cloth beam at the other end of the frame, in order to provide more weaving space between the two beams, as the woven surface continues to grow.

As the finished material is wound on, the cloth beam increases in thickness. This growth is determined, firstly, by the thickness of the cloth, secondly, by the industry of the weaver, and, lastly, by the length of the article being woven. Thus, the frame must be designed so as to leave enough room for the cloth beam to expand.

The construction of a small, but efficient loom is illustrated in the drawing. You should not, however, look upon the general arrangement or even the details as fixed, but vary them to suit your own needs and preferences.

A loom designed for broad widths of material is a rather clumsy piece of apparatus that occupies space even when not in use. It should therefore be assembled with easily dismantled wedged joints. In any case the two beams should be removable. Special attention should be given to the means of attaching the warp to the beams. This can be done by drilling holes at right angles to the beam axis and about $1/_8''$ apart. In this arrangement the warp thread is doubled and passed through two adjacent holes in the warp beam; then the two ends are threaded through corresponding holes in the cloth beam, where they are knotted.

Instead of drilling holes in the warp beam, we can form a slot running parallel to its axis, in which a narrow strip of wood can be inserted. The loops of the warp are hung over this strip, after which it is replaced in its slot and fastened at each end with cord or rubber bands. In this way the warp threads are held firmly to the beam.

The construction of the mechanism controlling the rotation of the two beams calls for a certain degree of mechanical skill. The bearings are drilled in the sides of the frame with a suitably sized center bit. The beam journals that turn in these bearings are formed simply by reducing the diameter of the beam by $3/_8''$ at each end. (Rub down the journals with rasp and sandpaper). An alternative, though more primitive type of bearing is shown in the inset in the top left-hand corner of the drawing. It has the advantage of making it possible to remove the

beams without having to dismantle the whole frame.

The quickest way of making the beams is to cut them out of a thick broom handle or the roller of a broken spring blind. However, the beams do not have to be circular in cross section. Eight-sided beams planed down from a square piece of wood are equally acceptable. All that matters is that the journals that rest in the bearings be perfectly round. The length of the left journal should be equal to the thickness, and that of the right journal to double the thickness of the sides of the frame. On the right side the end of the journal is again squared off to receive the ratchet wheel which has a corresponding square opening in the middle. A wooden pin through the end of the shaft will be enough to hold the ratchet wheel in place. The latter, the teeth of which should be curved in a direction opposite to that in which the warp threads are stretched, can be sawn out of a thick piece of plywood or laminated plastic with a fret saw. The pawls, which turn about the shank of a wood screw can be fashioned out of the same material.

Another type of locking device can be made by replacing the ratchet wheel with two wooden pins pushed crosswise through holes drilled in the projecting journals. These perform the function of the teeth of the ratchet. A ring of small holes, concentric with the bearing, is drilled in the side of the frame and in these a wooden peg is inserted at a point determined by the required position of the beam. This peg serves the same purpose as the pawl in the ratchet mechanism.

This contraption, however, only becomes an effective loom when the all-important heddle frame is added. This is a comb-like element, the teeth of which are drilled through in the middle. Unlike an ordinary comb, however, the heddle frame is closed

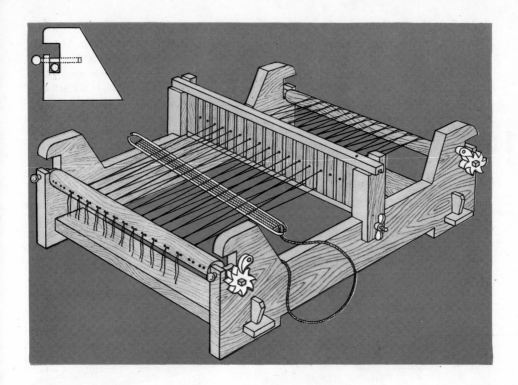

Home-made loom with heddle frame and heddle-frame supports, stick shuttle, removable beams, and pawl and ratchet locking mechanism. For the sake of clarity the warp is not shown wound onto the warp beam.

on both sides. It can be made from a strip of plastic about an eighth of an inch thick and four or five inches wide. The length of the strip should be about $^3/_4''$ less than the clear width of the loom frame. Notches are cut in one of the long sides of the strip with a fine-toothed saw. These should be just wide enough to allow the warp threads to run through them freely. The same applies to the diameter of the neat hole drilled through the middle of each tooth. The heddle frame is strengthened on both its longer sides by gluing on grooved wooden bars. The upper bar should project about a

hand's breadth beyond the face of the loom on each side. Another way of making a heddle frame is to glue a series of individual "teeth" between the two grooved cross bars.

The chief object of the heddle frame is to form "sheds," a device for accelerating and simplifying the weaving process. This is done as follows: the heddle frame is placed between the two beams in such a way that the warp threads pass alternately between the teeth and through the holes drilled in the middle of each tooth. If the heddle frame is now raised, half the threads are lifted out of

157

Heddle frame

the plane of the warp forming a pocket or "shed," through which the shuttle with the weft wound around it can easily be passed. Before the shuttle returns, the heddle frame is lowered sufficiently far below the plane of the warp to form another "shed," this time underneath.

The length of the heddle frame is determined by the number of warp threads in a given width of material. Thus, a weave consisting of very thin, closely packed threads calls for a finer heddle frame than a loose one with bigger spaces between the warp threads. For a coarse weave, in rug making, for example, or in weaving with thick wool, you should generally count on five threads per inch. As the weave becomes finer, this figure rises to 10, 15 and even 20 warp threads per inch of material. The making of

such fine heddle frames borders on precision engineering and demands patience, accuracy and the greatest care. One way of obtaining greater accuracy is to paste strips of paper marked off in tenths of an inch over the length of the frame.

The only thing still needed to complete our loom is a heddle frame support. This is a device for bracing the heddle frame against the pull of the warp when a shed is formed. It is made of two pieces of wood of the same thickness as the other parts of the frame. These pieces are notched, in opposite directions, at top and bottom and held tightly against the sides of the frame by means of wing nuts. Normally the heddle frame is placed approximately halfway between the warp and cloth beams.

The loom is now ready for use, and we

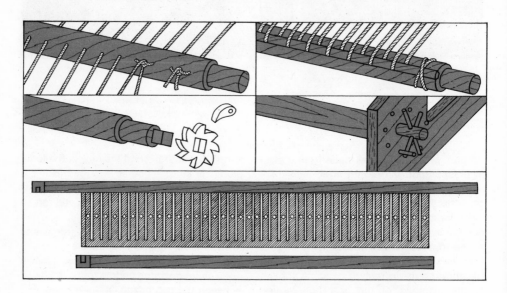

Details of the home-made loom. Top: fastening the warp to the beams either by knotting through holes drilled in the beam or with the aid of a strip of wood lashed into a groove in the beam. Center: two ways of locking the beams—ratchet and pawl or hole and peg. Bottom: the slot and hole heddle frame with hanging and reinforcing bars.

could start weaving at once, if the warp had been "beamed." This warp beaming is an art in itself, in which the possibility of hopeless confusion increases in direct proportion to the length of the warp. The warp must be at least 20" longer than the rug we propose to weave. To this must be added 10% of the rug length, which is taken up in the process of weaving as a result of the crisscrossing of the threads. The number of warp threads is theoretically determined by the width of the material and in practice by the number of holes and slots in a corresponding width of the heddle frame. The sideways contraction must also be compensated by adding 5% of the number of warp threads.

Winding a warp of medium length (up to six feet) presents no special problems. A pair of screw clamps fixed to the table edge with the handles on top at a distance apart corresponding to the length of the warp thread, provides two points between which the warp yarn can be measured off by running it around the clamp handles. That done, the yarn is tied at one end, while the opposite loop is hung over the left thumb. The so-called "stretching" of longer warps is described below.

First, the heddle frame is laid flat on the table with half its width projecting over the front edge. To prevent it from toppling over it is fastened firmly to the table top with a small clamp. In a handy position, to the left of the heddle frame, lies the strip of wood that fits into the groove in the warp beam. The weaver now sits down at the table, lifts the warp loops off his thumb, and starting from the left passes them from below through the slots of the heddle frame. A crochet hook will prove very useful at this point. In order to prevent the loops from dropping back, they are slipped over the strip of wood that fits into the warp beam, which is now slowly pushed forward over

the heddle frame from left to right. When all the loops have been secured this strip of wood is bound in place, the warp beam mounted on the frame and the heddle frame on the heddle frame supports. The free ends of the warp then lie loosely over the cloth beam and hang down over the table edge.

We now come to the actual winding of the warp threads onto the warp beam. For convenient winding it is possible to devise a hand crank which can be attached to the squared end of the warp beam instead of the ratchet wheel. It is important that the warp be distributed evenly over the length of the beam and tightly wound. In this case an assistant is needed to hold and steady the loose ends of the warp threads on the other side of the heddle frame.

When the warp has been wound until the ends of the threads are within an inch or two of the cloth beam, it is cut at the point where it was tied. The warp now ends in a bunch of individual threads which run through the slots of the heddle frame in pairs. Now, from the warp beam side, one thread of each pair is pulled through the slot, passed through the adjacent hole, led back to the front of the loom and threaded through the corresponding hole in the cloth beam. Behind the latter each hole thread is knotted tightly to the adjacent slot thread. After this has been done all along the beam, the beaming of the warp is complete. The threads must all be knotted at the same point, so that the warp is evenly tensioned over its entire width. The warp tension can be checked by pressing on it lightly with the flat of the hand. If you find that one of the threads is too slack, it may be tightened by placing a folded strip of paper underneath it on the warp beam. The even tensioning of the warp threads is of the utmost importance for a good, smooth weave. Slack threads result in flaws in the

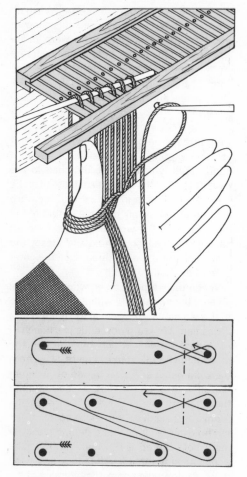

The stretched warp is led through the heddle frame and looped over the strip of wood that will later be slotted into the warp beam. Bottom: diagram showing how warps of different lengths are stretched over turning posts. The loop formed by crossing the thread is slipped over the left thumb when the warp is beamed.

ately by inserting an additional piece of yarn, using the special "weaver's knot" devised expressly for this purpose.

If the warp is not wide enough to take up the full width of the loom, it must be centered on the beams, so as to avoid imposing a one-sided strain on the frame.

In our examples illustrating warp beaming we assumed that the threads were fastened to the warp beam with a strip of wood. Where this is not the case and the beam merely has a series of holes, after having been threaded through the slots of the heddle frame, the loops of thread must be hung directly over the warp beam. They are then cut separately and reknotted after one end has been passed through the hole in the beam. This is practically the same as tying the warp threads to the cloth beam.

Measuring off the warp thread is called "stretching." Stretching becomes a problem of space when handling very long warps. However, we must be quite clear about the procedure, since weaving a piece of cloth four to six yards long on our homemade loom is only a matter of patience and industry.

A characteristic of the stretched warp is the cross or lease illustrated in our sketch. It must lie near a turning post and is formed by crossing the thread between two screw clamps. If there is room enough, you can measure off another length over a turning post suitably located. It is more practical, however, to run the entire length in a zig-zag path between the legs of two upturned chairs. In the case of broad warps made up of fine threads the task of counting the separate threads can be lightened by marking every twentieth or thirtieth thread with a small piece of wool. In beaming, the small loop formed by crossing the threads is hung over the left thumb. As far as possible the warp should be left on the chair legs until

cloth which cannot be removed. The same tightening procedure is employed if a thread slackens off during weaving. Conversely, if a warp thread breaks because it is overstrained, it must be joined up again immedi-

the ends of the threads have been safely fastened to the warp beam. Alternatively, the whole warp, starting at the end, can be wound onto a warp stick.

The actual weaving is the simplest part of the whole process. The knack consists in forming sheds with the heddle frame and passing through the weft with a shuttle. The weft is packed or "beaten" against the edge of the "web," or material already woven, with the heddle frame. After a short spell of practice, the even rhythm of: shuttle from the right—change shed—beat—shuttle from the left—change shed—beat will become part of your flesh and blood to such an extent that it will even monopolize your dreams.

The stick shuttle is a long, narrow piece of wood with curved ends along the length of which the weft threads are wound. Do not pass the weft thread through the warp in a straight line, but in a broad curve. Only after the shed has been changed is the weft pulled taut against the edge of the web. This is the only way to avoid the horrible distortion of the edges, caused by the pulling in of the outside warp threads as a result of the weft threads being drawn too tight. No less ugly are open loops at the edges due to the weft threads being too slack. The weft thread must be looped carefully at the edges so that it passes smoothly, but freely around the outside warp thread. The edge of the cloth will be neater if the outside warp threads are doubled.

When the shuttle is empty, don't leave the end of the weft thread at the edge of the warp, but cut it so that it hangs down underneath the web somewhere near the middle. The new weft thread is not knotted, but passed through the same shed together with the old thread over a matter of 20 to 30 warp threads. Finally, the ends of the threads are simply cut off. Do not pack the

individual weft threads too tight, since the idea is to weave a fabric that will fall in soft folds, not hang as stiffly as a board. This remark applies equally to rug weaving.

In plain weaving warp and weft appear to contribute equally to the finished texture. If the weft threads are packed so closely together that the warp threads are completely concealed, the result is known as a weft-face fabric. In a warp-face fabric, on the other hand, the weft threads disappear beneath the very closely set warp.

With the aid of these weaves and by utilizing different colors for warp and weft, a wide range of different patterns can be devised. The task we actually set ourselves, however, was to weave a knotted rug, in which the pattern is formed by a series of tufts of thick, bright-colored wool.

The warp is a tough, thin rug yarn, spun

Making a knotted rug is a combined weaving and knotting process. The pattern is formed by tufts of colored wool arranged in rows. The drawing shows how Smyrna knots are formed around pairs of warp threads.

Weaving and knotting

especially for such work. Owing to the thickness of the knotting wool, which forms both knots and weft, the warp threads should not be set too close. Take a heddle frame that will keep them about $^1/_8''$ or so apart.

The actual design is built up from a large number of individual dots, like a newspaper photograph, except that in this case the dots are tufts of colored wool knotted into the warp. We shall work with the ancient, well-tried Smyrna knot, which is formed around pairs of warp threads, using a bone or wooden carpet needle or crochet hook. A homemade hardwood (plum wood) shuttle will serve the same purpose.

As already mentioned the technique is a combination of weaving and knotting. Thus, for example, the design may provide for a neutral border in a weft-face weave. As soon as you reach the patterned part of the design, which is reproduced in strips running from bottom to top, begin tying the rows of Smyrna knots, cutting off the thread ends about $^5/_8''$ above the warp. The individual knots should be tied quite firmly. A Smyrna knotting stick will prove very helpful at this stage. This is a flat wooden stick with a slot running the full length of one side, over which the individual knots are looped. The thread is changed only when changing color. When the whole length of the stick has been looped, a knife is run through the slot cutting the entire row of knots and freeing the stick for further use.

Every finished row of knots is anchored to the web with a weft thread passed in front of it. If you wish to keep the colored pattern particularly loose, two weft threads are used instead of one. Do not forget to pack the weft thread against the web with the heddle frame. Before winding the web or finished part of the rug onto the cloth beam, it is neatly and evenly clipped. Do not attempt to do this with a small pair of sewing scissors. Since one cannot always be carting one's loom off to the barber's, it is best to purchase a very sharp pair of shears for this purpose.

When the rug has been woven, the warp threads are knotted in pairs at both ends and left as a fringe of any desired length. They can also be cut off after knotting and a wool fringe worked into the bottom edge of the rug. The upper ends of the warp threads are then knotted into loops, through which a bamboo pole is threaded for hanging the rug. Another method of rug hanging is to tie rings into the warp loops.

The indispensable guide to the colored maze of the woven pattern is a full-scale drawing of the rug design, which is best transferred to squared paper and stretched under the weaving frame. If during weaving you make sure that the edge of the web always lies directly above the corresponding point in the design, as the work progresses the pattern you have drawn will gradually be transferred to the woven surface.

The knotting technique can also be applied to a ready-made foundation consisting of canvas or burlap stretched over a rectangular frame. It is then known as hooking and the product as a hooked rug.

The Gobelin technique offers the greatest freedom in the use of color. It employs a weft-face weave and very tightly stretched, thin warp threads. Remember that in this weave only the weft threads are visible on the surface. There is no tying of individual knots. A separate shuttle is needed for each color, unless carpet or pack needles are used, since in this case every patch of color is woven separately in the manner of a mosaic.

The critical zones lie where the patches of color meet. If two adjacent warp threads are taken as boundary marks and the direction of the colored threads reversed when these threads are reached from left or right, the result will be a clear, sharp separation of the colors, but also a split in the fabric the same length as the vertical boundary. This type of weave is known as a Kilim weave. The slits can be avoided, if the different-colored weft threads, approaching the boundary from opposite sides, are interlocked. For the sake of increased strength, the weft threads should also pick up the warp thread lying at the boundary, provided this does not make an ugly lump in the fabric. The interlocking weft gives those very soft color transitions so characteristic of Gobelin tapestries.

Rug weaving is an activity very much like fishing. It requires patience, calm and an easy mind. Where these qualities are lacking, weaving and knotting will breed them.

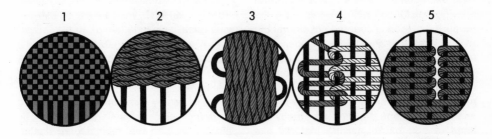

Some common weaves: 1 plain or tabby, 2 weft-face, 3 warp-face, 4 Gobelin technique, 5 Kilim technique.

No great skill is required to recognize the relationship between weaving and basketry. We have already observed that weaving is a very old craft indeed. However, basketry is even older. It is considered one of the so-called primitive techniques and must surely have been one of the very first really useful activities of human beings—that is, if the procuring of food is counted not among the useful, but rather among the indispensable human occupations.

Like weaving, basketry is based on the crosswise interpenetration of strands of material. The boundary between weaving and basketry cannot always be strictly defined; a soft basket-making material like raffia or rushes (esparto) can be handled as weft without difficulty on a loom. Similar material, in theory at least, could also be used as warp; in practice, however, this will not happen very often on account of its poor wearing qualities. It is also arguable whether the circular braiding of, for instance, a raffia mat is not really a kind of circular weaving on the darning system. From the point of view of materials, too, there is no real difference. It is true that textile yarns are regarded as weaving materials, and plant fibres as basketry materials, but many textile yarns have their origin in the vegetable kingdom, just like the fibres used in basketry. As far as synthetic materials are concerned, the dividing line is even harder to draw; the synthetics industry not only supplies nylon and rayon for weaving purposes, but synthetic bast or raffia in all colors for braiding.

The warp in weaving is the stake in basketry. For instance, the vertical ribs of a waste basket are called stakes. The weft in weaving is called the weaver in basketry, and can be varied in many ways to produce different effects.

We shall start by describing not how to make a complete basket, but how to braid a simple' plait with three or more strands. Work with a flexible material such as rushes or bast. If you wish, you can also use strong twine (sisal or manila hemp). In the following, however, we shall disregard twine, as it is machine-made and can not therefore strictly be counted among the natural vegetable fibres.

The necessary materials can be obtained simply by filling out an order form or by paying a visit to the nearest craft dealer. On the other hand, if you wish to enjoy the subtle pleasure of searching out your raw materials at the source, you can obtain the greater part of your basket-making supplies directly from nature's own storehouse, and cut out the middle-men. There is a special charm and satisfaction in such a return to natural origins, in the rediscovery of half-forgotten sources, and in the search for a practical natural product.

Of all the various types of easily located rush grass the well known bulrush and the finer-fibred woodland sedge grass are particularly well suited for our purpose. Those who want to collect the bulrushes themselves should do so in the first half of June, if possible. At that time the fully grown rushes bloom. Immediately after they have bloomed the stalk becomes woody—slowly at first, but more rapidly later on. This process deprives the rushes of just those properties for which we want them. After cutting, the rushes will have to dry out in the sun for a few days, before work can begin. If you work with fresh green rushes you will eventually notice an unpleasant shrinkage in your basketwork. The dried rushes must be slightly dampened before starting to weave. Then stretch them for half an hour so that they become flexible and elastic again. Braided rush plaits are very hard-wearing.

parison with that of the bulrushes. However, even with this material you can obtain yard-long plaits, if you fold each leaf lengthwise and then, while plaiting, keep pushing a small section of the next leaf into the fold of the one just braided. Always start by pushing in the tip of the leaf, even if the broad leaves—as is usually the case—have been cut into three narrower strips. Dried corn

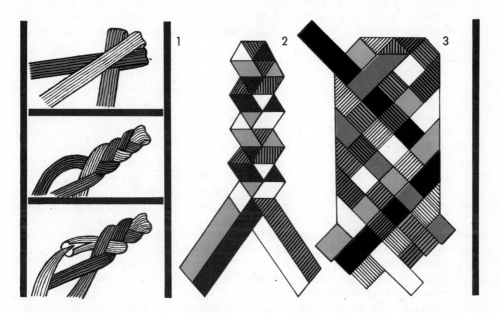

Plaiting: 1 plait with three strands, 2 flat straw plait with four strands, 3 straight-edged plait using seven strands.

The thin corn leaves found wrapped around the cob are well suited for fine braiding work. These small leaves have an attractive pale yellow shade and only drop off after the cobs have been dried. The outer greeny-brown leaves, which are considerably tougher, are also suitable and these can be collected even during the corn harvest. Corn leaves are broad, it is true, but their average length of 8 inches is short in com-

leaves will also have to be made flexible by dipping them in warm water. Your stock of raw material required for the job in hand should be wrapped in damp cloths. Over longer periods, however, all vegetable basketry materials have to be stored, well dried, in an airy place, as otherwise they will develop spots of mildew or may even rot away.

Straw is a strong and noble weaving material, and the most attractive of all the different types is rye straw. It is advisable to gather straw for basket making during the harvest, straight from the field. Once it has been threshed it is too crumpled and cannot be used. Naturally, the straw must also be quite dry. Dampen only small quantities for immediate use. Straw stalks are rarely used in their full length, as they taper away too much. Cut the stalks you have collected into top and bottom ends and sort them into various thicknesses; in this way you can get straw all of the same thickness for the same job. Before you start work, compress the moistened straw, i.e. put it through the wringer to flatten it.

When braiding straw the stalks are given a sharp edge in order to obtain a plait with smooth sides. New stalks are joined by the thicker end. Allow these to stick out about $1/2''$ from the braid; later, when the plait has dried out, cut these ends off cleanly.

Bast from the ordinary plants found locally is not suitable where basket work with a reasonably attractive appearance is desired. What in practice is called bast or raffia usually comes from the raffia palm, and is imported in large quantities, either bleached or dyed, from Madagascar. If individual special color shades are required, raffia may be dyed like linen in a strong dye bath with textile dyes. The raffia must be allowed to soak in the dye bath for about an hour. Avoid vigorous stirring, otherwise what you remove from the bath will be a tangle impossible to straighten out, instead of individual strands. The different widths of raffia strand should be sorted out carefully, or wide ones will have to be split for delicate work. When making thick plaits, several strands will have to be combined into a single compound strand. Raffia is a flexible, but at the same time a very tough and durable material. However, the plait must be braided firmly. This means that the individual strands will

have to be twisted at right angles, while the left thumb holds the edge of the plait. Raffia can also be manipulated in the dry state, but the work will be easier, if it is kept wrapped in a moist cloth.

Braided Mats and Coiled Baskets

The braided plait is really only the raw material from which the final article is made. Regarding the plait as a whole as a single strand, a two-dimensional surface can be obtained by folding the plait and sewing the parts together. This can be done by setting them on edge or laying them flat one next to the other. The sewing is done with raffia or fine hemp yarn, and in any case as invisibly as possible. The necessary use of needle and thread brings this work into the area of typical feminine activities. This is not meant as a criticism, but as a suggestion. By coiling a plait in a tight spiral about a central point, we obtain a circular surface. If, on the other hand, the innermost strand is laid in a straight line as long as your finger, then bent back sharply and carried in the opposite direction beyond the point where the plait began, the resulting surface will have an oval shape. A square surface results, if, starting with a short end, you guide the plait in a meander pattern, bending it at right angles at each corner. A rectangle is developed from the square in the same way that an oval is developed from the circle. However, you can also obtain a rectangle by laying the plait in a zigzag or hairpin pattern. This is done very simply by knocking two rows of nails into a board at a distance apart equal to the required edge length; the plait is then laid backwards and forwards between these turning points. By this method a large number of squares of the same size can be braided, and then joined together to form a large mat. The squares can be made in different colors and the direction of the plait in the individual squares can be alternated when sewing them together; this will give some interesting checkered patterns.

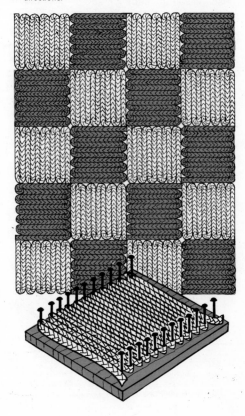

Square, rectangular and round mats can be made by coiling plaits at different angles and sewing the coils together.

The basic forms obtained from these plait combinations are useful as rugs, table mats and protective surfaces of all kinds. If fine braiding material has been used, they can also be worked into bags and covers. The originally geometrical shape can be transformed into quite irregular outlines by introducing odd lengths of plait, and it is even possible to form shoe soles. A very durable material for such purposes consists of very tightly braided rush plaits sewn together edgewise.

With some skill it is possible to take a flat plait and make it into a three-dimensional form. For instance, you can coil a flat braided straw plait spirally, like a snail's shell, so that instead of lying in a plane the edges overlap slightly, as in clinker construction, as a result of being slightly drawn in; you will then find that with every turn, the work will bulge further out to form a steep or gently sloping wall, depending on the amount

Mat made by sewing together individual squares consisting of plaits laid in zigzag fashion. Alternate squares in different colors have the plaits running in opposite directions.

Coiled baskets

you draw in or gather. A good example of this technique is the ordinary straw beach hat.

It goes without saying that such objects are not particularly strong. In order to produce baskets that are reasonably stiff, a different method is used. Consider the difference between a flat watch spring and a cylindrical coil spring and you will immediately understand the mechanical principle of a round waste basket.

In making such a useful receptacle, the braided plait, which we have been using so far, is replaced by a rope, about as thick as a finger, consisting of a straw core wrapped around with raffia. Instead of straw you can also use long reeds or sedge grass. The thinner the individual fibres of the core, the more solid the finished rope. By cleverly overlapping the stalks forming the core you will not only obtain a rope of a uniform thickness, you will also be able to make it as long as a three-volume novel.

The base of the basket is a circular surface in the form of a spiral coil. The first inch or two of rope is wrapped a little thinner, in order to make the starting loop nice and tight. This difference in thickness can be evened out by using thicker raffia when sewing the base together. The end of the last length of rope must also be tapered, by cutting back or pulling out some of the center stalks; the final round will then fit flush and will not form a step.

The wall is built up on the same principle, by laying the rope in circles, starting with a thinned down end at the base. This time, however, do not lay the coils side by side but exactly one on top of the other, until a basket of the desired height has taken shape. The end of the top coil is gently tapered, to give an even finish.

For a beginner it is not easy to build up the walls uniformly and vertically working freehand, as the rope will twist in all directions. It is much easier to keep to the right dimensions and shape, if the basket is worked over a last, similar to that used by a shoemaker. Even professional basket makers take advantage of this when they want to produce several baskets of exactly the same size, using softwood forms for the purpose. The amateur can use large cans or glass jars. Small baskets with sloping walls can be built up over flower pots.

There are innumerable possibilities of giving your basket a lively effect by working in different patterns; these are obtained by varying the coiling technique and the method of sewing up the rounds. The simplest way is to wrap the entire length of the rope tightly with raffia of the same color, so that nothing of the core can be seen; then sew up the rope as you go along with very thin hemp yarn to make the stitches quite invis-

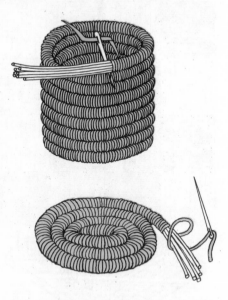

Making a coiled basket. The flat bottom and cylindrical walls of a waste basket can both be made by coiling a rope consisting of a straw core wrapped with raffia.

Some examples of coiled baskets of varying design.

ible. You can also vary the color or shade of the raffia wrapping at regular or irregular intervals and thus obtain a more or less pronounced stepped pattern. Another variation: use coils all the same color with the emphasis on a different colored, decorative raffia stitch for sewing them up; by carrying the stitch straight up the sides of the basket you can emphasize its vertical lines. It is equally attractive, if instead of wrapping the core continuously with raffia, you allow parts of it to remain exposed to form a checkered or irregular pattern. Of course, this method will only be effective if you use a core with a good appearance, such as fine straw. It is all the more attractive, because it is "honest." Quite apart from this, the unique gloss and natural color of the sun-bleached straw cannot be equalled by any artificial means.

Building a waste basket will be simplified, if you prepare all the rope you expect to need in advance. However, it is also possible to carry out the two operations of wrapping and sewing up the coils simultaneously. In doing this, thread the raffia into a pack needle and use it both as your sewing and as your wrapping material. You can then either stitch through into the existing coils after each loop, always pushing the needle between the wrapping strands; or you can make several loops around the rope you are working on and then stitch the wrapped section to the existing coils. The first method results in a considerably stronger wall.

The technique of coiling a rope with a straw or rush core—the core being either invisible or exposed—can be used to make a fruit bowl. In this instance the bottom coils are gradually gathered in and stitched together to form gently sloping walls. This is the method which beekeepers once used to make their beautifully rounded straw bee hives.

169

Table mats—coasters

Weave and Circular Braiding

Weave braiding, which starts with a double cross of flat strands and results in a surface with a linen-like texture, has probably been practiced by all of us with colored strips of paper when we were very young. By substituting selected raffia strands or rushes for colored paper, we can obtain fine-meshed mats that really resemble woven material. These can be used as table mats, pads for flower pots and vases, and coasters for liquor glasses or anything else that might harm polished furniture.

Such articles are easy to start, but it is not so easy to finish them off, as it is not quite clear how to fix the edges. You can either turn the ends of the strands back and push them into the completed weave, or you can stitch around the edge with a sewing machine and then cut off the strands neatly about $1/4''$ behind the stitching. If very soft raffia has been used, pairs of adjoining strands can be knotted together to form a short fringe.

Those anxious to make circular shapes by laying flat braided straw plaits in a circle will have to learn to braid a plait from 5, 7 or even more strands. Such plaits, when stitched together flat, adapt themselves well to the rounded shape, like tapered strips of material, and do not bulge.

Smaller, fine-woven circular shapes, coasters, for example, are better produced by the method of circular braiding. The effect here, as compared with weave braiding, where warp and weft alternate regularly, is more like a real braid; seeking an analogy with weaving we could call the resulting texture a weft rep or weft-filling structure. In circular braiding the framework of widely spaced, tightly drawn warp threads is replaced by a series of spokes radiating from the center.

These spokes consist of the same soft fibres as the actual braiding strands. For this reason we must give them some sort of temporary reinforcement, and a piece of strong cardboard serves this purpose very well. Draw a circle with the same diameter as the required mat on this piece of cardboard. Along the circumference of the circle pierce holes spaced about $1/2''$ apart. Then sew through these holes with a strong yarn, using a backing stitch. Into the resulting loops fix the spokes, which should pass radially through the center of the circle. Be careful always to have an uneven number of these radial spokes, as otherwise the strands will not go alternately over and under when braiding. If you have an even number, you will have to braid with two strands. The areas between the spokes are then filled in by moving steadily around the wheel with a pack or darning needle. By changing the color of the weaver, a concentric striped design can be achieved. When the last round has been woven, the fixing

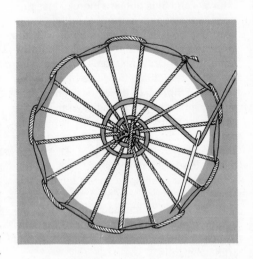

Circular braiding is a technique suitable for small round mats.

loops are cut, and the end of the radial strands are tucked down against the edge of the circle and neatly sewn in with thin raffia. This produces an attractive and distinctive finish. A different way of finishing is to darn each end into the weave as far as the next loose end with a darning needle. If the cardboard base gets in your way while working, you can use a wooden ring instead for setting up the "wheel." You will have noticed that in this hobby there is hardly any operation that could not in some way or other be varied or modified. For this reason braiding, which at first sight may have seemed to be rather limited in scope, is really a hobby offering many opportunities to the imaginative.

Baskets made of Reeds and Wicker

A direct path leads from simple braiding processes to basket making proper. The most suitable materials for this are peeled rattan and willow twigs or wicker. For some purposes split hazel twigs may be used.

Rattan, which is marketed as reeds of various thicknesses both round and flat, is extraordinarily flexible and is therefore very easy to work. It only has to be soaked for a very short time before use. However, it breaks easily if bent too sharply. It is an ideal material for the learner, but its outward appearance is not very attractive. It has a dull, nondescript surface and attracts dirt. Even when they are given a coat of paint or varnish, reed articles do not have a very pleasing effect.

The most pleasing basket work is done with willow twigs, not only on account of the texture, particularly if only thin, clean withes of even thickness are used, but also on account of the warm, silky sheen of the peeled twigs.

Willows are widely cultivated and can be used in the round or split form. Willow twigs, which are cut in early summer and in August, have to be processed in several working operations and with special tools before they are ready to be used for basket work. The round twig is first split into thirds or quarters with a special splitting tool; it is then drawn through a wicker plane and planed into flat pieces, which are finally reduced to uniform size by another special cutting tool.

We shall not discuss all these processes here, as they would require an additional outlay for special tools, and wickerwork materials can be bought pre-cut and ready for use. Of all the different types of wicker available commercially, American willow is the one most widely used. Take care to buy material with a fine pith. The wood is then especially tough and does not break so easily as that of wicker with a coarse pith. Soaking for at least an hour is important; after that it is just as important to let the canes rest and absorb the moisture for another hour. Material which has been soaked, but which is not to be used, should be dried immediately in the open air. The peeled twigs do not respond well to being soaked several times. They become unattractive and develop mildew and mold spots. It is therefore advisable never to soak more material at any one time than you will be able to use.

Some Common Weaves

Before starting to try our skill on a waste or ornamental basket, it will be as well to find out what methods can be used. For the sake of simplicity the various possibilities have been presented in the form of a drawing; if you study this drawing for a few minutes, the basic principles will soon become clear. All these weaves with one exception are worked like fencing or hurdles, the basis of all wickerwork. The principle is most obvious in simple randing or over-and-under weave, where one weaver is worked around the row of stakes in an even rhythm. This is the most usual type, the "bread and butter" style, so to speak.

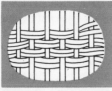

Some common wicker weaves

Simple randing with a single weaver or over-and-under weave

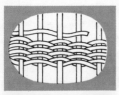

Double over-and-under weave with two weavers

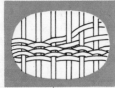

Randing with an even number of stakes and two weavers

The pairing weave

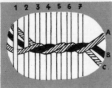

The three-ply coil weave

A more restful impression is achieved, if the weaver is doubled, but otherwise the procedure will be the same as in simple randing.

For both these methods an uneven number of stakes is essential, otherwise you will not be able to change stakes after the first round. If for some reason you are forced to work with an even number of stakes, two weavers will have to be used alternately. The end effect of this method is the same wall texture as that given by simple randing.

A different type of weaving with two weavers is the pairing weave, where it does not matter whether an even or uneven number of stakes is used. In ordinary randing with two weavers, each weaver stays on the same level, so that you can first thread the lower one and then follow on with the top one; in the pairing weave, however, the two weavers cross each other between stakes. They alternate between top and bottom, and thus form a very solid structure with the stakes. This means that both weavers must be worked simultaneously.

If during this threading operation you come to the end of one weaver, you will have to insert a new one; this operation, called piecing, is done by crossing the end of the old weaver and the beginning of the new one behind the same stake. The natural tensile force inherent in willow twigs will hold the new weaver quite firmly in the basket wall. When the basket has been completed and has been left to dry out, all the projecting ends are cut away. The skilled basket worker uses a reed cutter or diagonal cutter to snip off the ends. They can also be cut off obliquely with a sharp chisel. However, take care not to cut the ends too short, otherwise they may creep out from behind the stake.

A completely different type of basket weave is the three-ply coil weave. This is particularly strong and should be used in sections of the basket which have to stand up to strain or wear and tear, for instance, when starting to weave it should be used for the first round or a couple of rounds near the edge of the base, and also at the top before the ends of the stakes are bent down.

The three-ply coil weave employs three (or even four) weavers. The process is clear from the drawing, where for simplicity's sake we have given the stakes consecutive numbers while the three weavers are marked A, B and C. To commence, weaver A, coming from behind stake 1, passes in front of stakes 2 and 3, goes around the back of stake 4 and again appears in front. Leave it there, until weaver B, starting at the back of stake 2, is passed in front of stakes 3 and 4 and completes the same cycle by going around the back of stake 5. Then weaver C appears from behind stake 3, passes in front of 4 and 5, circles around the back of stake 6, and appears again in front of stake 7. This completes a full cycle of the three weavers. Then start again with weaver A, which passes in front of stakes 5 and 6, is taken around the back of stake 7, and emerges in front of stake 8. Weavers B and C follow in the same way, always one stake behind, and very soon the nature of the weave becomes apparent; the effect is somewhat like a twisted rope. The whole thing might seem rather confusing at first, but it really is no more complicated than dancing a waltz. Both are in three-four time: one - two - three . . . one - two - three! Only in weaving count not the steps, but the stakes. Thus for each weaver: once behind and twice in front, once behind and twice in front, and so on.

The individual weavers are laid starting with the thin end, that means you work with the thick end from left to right. When a weaver has been used up, insert a new one below the projecting tip of the old one, again starting with the thin end.

The three-ply coil weave with its "twisted" strands is more striking than the "one plain, one purl" pattern of simple wickerwork. It also increases the strength of the structure. Thus, apart from reasons of usefulness and variety, alternating a three-ply weave with simple randing will enliven fairly high basket walls and break up the monotony of the surface.

Making a Basket

The foundation of a basket is the base and we shall start by making a base on the principle of circular braiding. In this case, however, the skeleton no longer consists of thin strands of bast, but of strong reeds, which cannot be laid down at random at the point where they intersect. We must therefore start with a simple cross and the number of reeds used will depend on the diameter of the base. For the base of a medium-sized waste basket, approximately 10″ in diameter, we shall need eight reeds; after the basic cross has been splayed out, these will form 16 spokes radiating from the center. If a smaller number of reeds were used, the weave would become too loose near the edge of the base. The reeds should be of an even thickness. Half of them, in our case four, are slit over a length of an inch or so in the middle with a pointed knife. The other, slightly sharpened reeds are inserted through these slits, so that we obtain a cross with four equal arms, each consisting of four reeds. In the event of a very fine weave being required, with reeds too fine to be slit, there is no alternative but to lay the arms of the cross one on top of the other. This, however, makes the next step, binding, considerably more troublesome. For this purpose select a very long, flexible and well soaked winding reed, double it over to form

The circular base

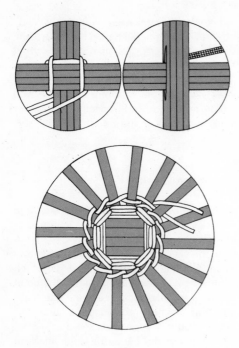

Setting up the spokes for the bottom of a waste basket. Top: the basic cross. Bottom: splaying the cross and the first rounds.

adjacent arms of the cross is bisected. Fasten them in this position with two pairing rounds; then the cross, which now consists only of pairs of reeds, is divided once more to form a circle of regularly radiating spokes, which are again secured with two rounds in a pairing weave.

We now have our basic wheel. If the angles between the individual spokes are not perfectly equal, this need not be a cause for undue concern. Reeds can be far more stubborn than a pencil mark on paper. Anybody who handles them will soon find this out. Irregular spaces between the spokes can soon be evened out in weaving.

The entire base can be worked in a pairing weave, but ordinary randing or over-and-under weave will be quicker. In this case, however, it will be necessary to use two weavers, as we are working with an even number of stakes. Insert strand A behind spoke 1, strand B behind spoke 2. Keep the thin end on the left and continue working with the thick end. Start a new strand with the thin end also.

Wickerwork using full, i.e. not split or cut down willow twigs, is called "beaten" work, because the woven rounds are beaten together with a mallet in order to make them as dense as possible. For finer work, however, it will be enough to press the rows together now and then. Nevertheless, this at least should not be forgotten when making wicker baskets.

Those who prefer not to work with two weavers over an even number of spokes can avoid this by means of a simple trick. Next to the four reeds that are passed through the split reeds insert an extra reed half the length of the others, so that one arm of the basic cross will consist of five reeds rather than four. Then, when splaying out the cross, extra space can be made for this fifth member by adjusting the individual

ends of unequal length, and hang the loop around one of the quadruple arms of the cross. The ends of the first reed must be unequal in length, so that the following weavers can be staggered, instead of being always inserted in the same place. With these two ends work two rounds in a pairing weave around the point of intersection of the arms of the cross, drawing them up as tightly as possible and thus fixing the arms in position. Unless you are left-handed, work from left to right, as always in weaving. When working around a base, therefore, you always travel in a clockwise direction. Now start splaying out the cross, that is, carefully bend apart the individual reeds. First bend the two reeds on the outside of each arm in such a way that the right angle between the

spokes. This will give you a base with an uneven number of spokes and you can then work straightforwardly with one weaver only.

The question whether and how to finish off the woven base need not concern us until we know what happens next. Even if the spokes of the base were long enough to bend upwards in a right angle, they would be too few to form a sufficiently firm support for the walls of the basket. Therefore cut the spokes off after the last round of weaving has been completed. One way in which we can now continue the work is by pushing the pointed ends of the wall stakes into the weave, to the left and right of each radial spoke. Here an awl will be helpful, or even a screwdriver pushed into the weave and turned edgewise. Once inserted, the stakes are bent upwards close to the edge of the base. The place where the bend is to be made must be well soaked in water, even hot water, otherwise the stake will not bend, but break, and be ruined. It will then have to be replaced with a fresh stake. In order to avoid such accidents, holding the awl in the right hand, press the handle firmly against the back of the stake and use your left thumb to force the stake into an upright position. Avoid creating a giant spider when inserting the stakes; instead deal with them individually. Always proceed from one stake to the stake exactly opposite. When the first six stakes have been bent up, tie their top ends together and continue working by repeatedly tying in the new ends.

After the first two rounds of weaving, using the three-ply coil weave, the vertical framework of the basket will be firm enough for the top to be untied. Work then continues with either single or double weavers, with three-ply rounds inserted at intervals, depending on the appearance desired, until the correct height has been reached. The

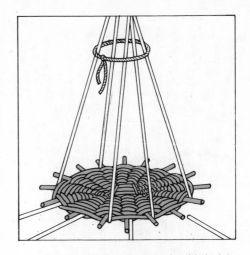

Inserting the wall stakes next to the spokes of the basket bottom. To simplify the work the stakes that have been bent upwards are temporarily tied together.

final round should again be in three-ply coil weave.

The whole process of weaving the walls can be made a lot easier by driving an awl through the center of the base into the work table. The basket can then be turned around this spike, which will form a simple pivot.

For the beginner the work will hardly go as smoothly as it sounds. The first basket will probably be a rather funny, distorted object. The second one, however, will no doubt have reasonably taut and neatly sloping sides, and by the time you make the third one you will have mastered the trick of achieving a nicely rounded wall by carefully bending the stakes, or by varying the tension in the weavers. The work will be much easier if you use a ring gage. This is a simple device consisting of a circle made from a willow rod which is tied around the top of the stakes parallel to the base. Its diameter, which is larger than that of the base, determines the angle of slope of the wall in relation to the base.

175

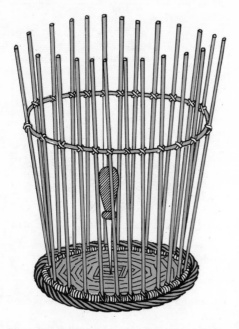

A ring gage, tied to the top of the wall stakes fixes the slope of the walls. Before starting to work on the walls, drive an awl through the center of the base into the work table to act as a pivot.

Another means of making the transition from the base to the wall of the basket consists in inserting the wall stakes vertically into the edge of the base, from above, instead of pushing them in from the sides and bending them up, as before. In this case, however, it is essential to provide the base with a firm edge or border.

A good and simple method of obtaining such a border is to wrap a winding reed, that is a reed split in half, around the outside of the base. Both ends of the winding reed must be well tapered so that the overlap forms a smooth joint.

At the same time as the edge is bound, the wall stakes are passed through the edge of the base from above with the aid of an awl, allowing the stem ends to project on the underside. These projecting ends must be well soaked. They are then bent sharply to the right and woven into a round of three-ply coil. This not only firmly anchors the stakes, but raises the basket off the floor.

The first method, namely inserting the stakes radially from the sides and then bending them up, does not provide material for such a rim, but no self-respecting basket should be without one. If we employ the first type of construction therefore, we have no choice but to insert shorter stakes 8″ to 10″ long (possibly some waste left over after completing the top edge of the basket) through the base of the basket into the wall, next to the wall stakes. Those who have used three-ply coil weave for the first rounds of the wall, as recommended above, will find it rather hard to insert these short stakes, because they must project at least 2″ into the wall. But with a lot of patience and the help of an awl or a screwdriver and, if necessary, by rubbing the stakes with a little soap, it can be done. Once the stakes have been

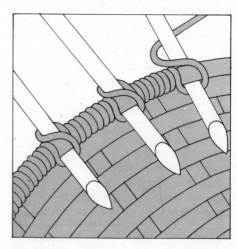

Transition from the base to the wall of the basket by means of wall stakes inserted vertically into the edge of the base. The edge is strengthened by wrapping it with a winding reed.

inserted, they are woven into a round of three-ply coil.

In basket work, as distinct from life, the last steps are the hardest. Having neatly completed the last round of weaving at the top of the basket, we can afford to be proud of the skill we have acquired. However, the ends of the stakes are still sticking up in the air and remain to be transformed into an attractive border. The simplest way of doing this is to cut each stake down to a suitable length, point the ends and carry the stake in an elegant arc back into the wall, crossing over the stake next to it.

Somewhat more complicated, but far stronger, is the simple woven border. Stake 1 is bent behind stake 2, and passed at an angle in front of stake 3, where it can be left for the time being sticking outwards. Do the same thing with stake 2, only this time pass behind stake 3 and end in front of stake 4. When all the stakes are pointing nose down, each end is woven together with the three ends to the right of it, under, over and under, until the last stake in the round has been woven in. Then all the ends are tightened up and allowed to dry out thoroughly, before being tidied up. If desired, the individual ends can be woven over six neighboring stakes, instead of only three. But even this type of border will be more notable for its beauty than its strength.

The only really genuine border is the so-called closed border. It is practically impossible to describe this operation clearly in words, so once more we have fallen back on a drawing.

The procedure is quite simple for the first three stakes. Stake 1 is passed behind stakes 2 and 3 and pointed downwards in front of stake 4. Then take stake 2, which is threaded behind stakes 3 and 4 and left hanging in front of stake 5. Finally, stake 3 is dealt with in the same manner in relation

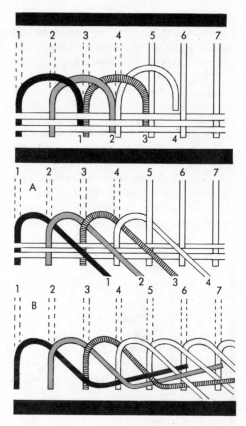

Reed borders. Top: wall stakes bent back into wall of basket. Bottom: two stages in the weaving of a simple border.

to stakes 4, 5 and 6. For the second stage we return to stake 1. This is passed in front of stakes 4 and 5, behind stake 6, and comes to rest in front of stake 7. Then stake 4, which has so far been left standing upright, is bent, threaded behind stakes 5 and 6, and also passed in front of stake 7, so that the ends of stakes 1 and 4 are lying next to each other in front of stake 7. Then, as section C of the drawing shows, we go back to stake 2. This is passed in front of stakes 5 and 6,

The closed border

then behind stake 7, and left in front of stake 8. Stake 5, which has so far remained upright, is threaded behind stakes 6 and 7, and left beside stake 2. Now take stake 3, pass it in front of stakes 6 and 7 and behind stake 8, and leave it in front of stake 9; once stake 6 has been passed around the back of stakes 7 and 8, we will have three pairs of stakes. We have now reached a stage where we are obliged to think up something new, in order to be able to carry the work further.

The new development consists in picking up stake 4, one of the first pair of stakes, and passing it in front of stakes 7 and 8 and behind stake 9. Stake 1, the other member of this pair, is left permanently in its place. However, the next upright stake, namely stake 7, is bent to the right and passed behind stakes 8 and 9, and now forms a new pair together with the end of stake 4. Next, treat stake 5 and the upright stake 8 in the same way, and continue working by this method until the end of the round. The end means the place where we started from and here we meet with another difficulty because there are no more upright stakes. Some must therefore be inserted at the beginning of the round. Admittedly, this is not easy. First, we have to stop and think for a moment where the last stakes should go. However, if

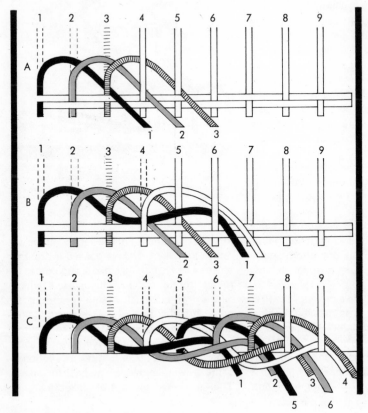

The closed border is the strongest and the most usual way of finishing the edge of a basket. The drawing illustrates the three steps involved in making such a border.

you look once more at drawing A, the whole thing will become clear. Secondly, the weave will be so tight that it will only be possible to insert the ends with the help of an awl. Thirdly, the ends are so stiff, that they will not lend themselves very willingly to these contortions. The best thing is to dip the whole fringe of top stakes into hot water for half an hour before you start weaving. The end stakes will also become slightly more manageable if you flex them a few times between your finger and thumb.

After the last stake has been tied in, the whole basket must be allowed to dry out, before it can be cleaned up. If this final stage is rushed, it may well happen that the ends of the weavers and the stakes will slip out in the course of further drying, forming holes.

In completing this basket we have learnt to handle one type of basket work, the basic one. The basic principle can be varied in an infinite number of ways, however. Discovering them is one of the chief attractions of the craft.

10　CLAY IN THE POTTER'S HAND

The molding and firing of clay was the first really creative craft to be practiced by man, for clay was the material used to make the first bricks, and never are we more keenly aware of the magic of the creative act than when watching the transformation of a shapeless lump of clay into a handsome vessel under the skilled hands of the potter.

Watching a pot being shaped on the wheel is always a fascinating adventure and to want to imitate the craftsman is an understandable desire. The fact, however, that formerly a potter had to serve a seven-year apprenticeship and took weeks just to learn how to place the lump of clay correctly in the center of the wheel rather damps one's enthusiasm, as does the fantastic amount of dirt which pottery involves. You just cannot sit down in your city clothes in the evening after work and start throwing pots on your potter's wheel. This wheel should be kept in a room where water and clay can safely spread over all and everything, except the potter's stool. This at least should remain clean.

The potter will also require a kiln, where the clay can be fired. This process gives pottery its beauty and durability. The durability or life of fired pottery surpasses that of most other materials and is only equalled by that of natural stone. It suffers neither from moths nor rust, nor any other form of decay. It can lie buried in the ground for thousands of years and when dug out of the soil, it will be as beautiful and fresh as on the day it was made.

Slab-built pottery

Nevertheless, it is possible to do without the potter's wheel, since by using the well known technique of slab-built pottery, we can produce results of equal validity and beauty.

Clay is found more or less everywhere in the world. Theoretically it is possible to pick up a bucket and spade, dig some clay and work this in the state in which it comes from the ground, just as the potters did in olden days. This, however, will inevitably lead to disappointments. To be suitable for our purposes the clay must first undergo a rather lengthy and complicated process of preparation. Thus, it is simpler to buy the clay ready for use from a pottery, which will save a great deal of time, or from a special supplier or craft store in the form of dry clay powder.

However, it is impossible to escape the preparatory work entirely. Dry clay powder has to be soaked in water, in the same way as plaster. Put the water into a pot or vessel and pour in as much clay powder as the water will absorb. Allow the mixture to soak for one day, and then spread the paste over an absorbent base (a block of plaster or unglazed tiles or bricks). When the clay can be easily lifted off, shape it into a block, cut it in half with a wire and slam one half against the other with great force. The purpose of this exercise, called wedging, is to make the clay uniformly plastic and to expel any air bubbles that may be trapped in it. If this were not done, the air bubbles could have the effect of an explosive charge during firing. The process of slamming and kneading is continued until the clay is workable. You will soon get the right feeling for this. When a wire can be drawn through the clay smoothly and evenly, as through a lump of butter, the material is of the correct consistency.

Fat clays, which, however, do not contain any fats in the sense of butter or lard, are more pliable and have a smoother consistency than lean ones. They are therefore particularly suitable for free shaping or modeling. On the other hand, they crack easily when drying. Thus it is preferable to work with a lean clay, which can be dried and fired with less risk. Materials that can be added to make the clay leaner are clean, sharp and absorbent sand (quartz sand), brick dust, whitening (Spanish white), and chamotte (or dead-burned fireclay). Once prepared, the clay is stored in a zinc bin or bucket, over which a damp sack is laid to keep it moist and fresh.

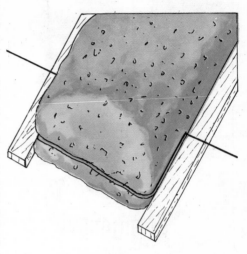

Dividing the wedged clay into slabs and strips with a cutting wire and two pieces of wood.

The expression slab-built pottery is a good description of this comparatively simple craft. Here the work of shaping goes hand in hand with building. The requirements of architecture and plastic art become one. This is mainly because the clay which is rather unstable in its plastic state must be provided not only with an attractive shape but with structural strength as well. In other words, the work must be self-supporting, since the clay shape is not compatible with internal supports or bracing. As building blocks we can use square, rectangular or circular slabs and clay coils. Anyone who is not sure how to handle these should observe how pretzels are baked. The clay is kneaded and rolled in the same way as pretzel dough. However, the clay should always be squeezed flat from the side, to avoid air being kneaded into the mass. A good working surface is formed by medium-

Construction techniques

The building blocks used in slab-built ceramics are the clay slab and the clay coil. A modeling stand will prove helpful in shaping the walls.

should use the piece of wood as a straight-edge. Then with a few rolling movements, using the palm of the hand or a flat board, the edges are removed and the strips rounded. This method is preferable to rolling coils directly from the slab, as there is less chance of making coils with hollow centers.

Now cast your mind back to the method we employed to build a round waste basket using coils of raffia or straw. We can build a clay vessel with a round or oval base in exactly the same way. Whether you prefer to cut the bottom out of a clay slab or build it up in spiral coils, like the walls, is up to you. It is also up to you whether you construct the wall of the vessel from a strand of clay a yard long, or whether you use a number of short strands, the lengths of which correspond to the diameter at that level. The latter method is simpler and the wall is built up by staggering the joints between the different coils.

Alternatively, you can build the vessel with clay slabs, just as the Eskimos build their igloos from blocks of snow. But this assumes that you have already acquired a certain knowledge of the secrets of working in clay. The unskilled would be well advised to stick to the coil method for a start. However, if you prefer to try something more difficult, start with an elementary form, such as a square or a rectangle, and make, for instance, a cigarette case or a butter dish; such box shapes can be built up with simple slabs. A round vessel with vertical walls can also be made with rectangular slabs; these are laid cylindrically around the base and welded together. Such joints, which are quite frequent in this type of ceramics, deserve special attention. The obvious solution of softening the clay in the joints with water and thus "pasting" the slabs together is one of the original sins of slab-built ceramics, because uneven moistening of

thick plywood, which is preferable to a heavy block of plaster, since the latter breaks easily and absorbs too much moisture. It is undesirable for dried-out clay crumbs to get kneaded into the fresh clay, and therefore the working surface must be kept scrupulously clean.

Coils of even thickness can be made more easily if a brick-like shape is formed and laid on the table, the two long sides wedged between narrow pieces of wood of equal thickness. By drawing a wire horizontally across this brick at the same level as the top of the wood, we obtain a clay slab of uniform thickness. This slab is then easily divided into strips with a rectangular cross section, using the thickness of the wood as a guide. This means that when cutting the strips, you

the clay must be avoided at all costs in the interests of successful drying and firing.

Thus, the clay should be of the right consistency. Unfortunately, no formulas for this can be given. The consistency is good when the clay does not stick to your fingers; it is too dry if the coil breaks when sharply bent. Between these two extremes there is a whole range of different grades of pliability, and in practice everybody will soon find out which one is the most suitable for his own fingers. The right synthesis between strength and plasticity must be found. The clay must not be so soft that it sags under its own weight like butter in the sun. On the other hand, it must be plastic enough to be easily and smoothly pointed and joined.

A very practical aid in making slab-built pots is the modeling stand. This looks like a small, one-legged table with a revolving top, which you can set up on your work table and rotate slowly while you are working. Thus it is really a potter's wheel for the amateur. You turn the stand and at the same time carry up the coils using both hands. At regular intervals a new end is pressed firmly into the coil beneath. The angle at which the new coil is added determines the shape of the wall, whether it will bulge or neck.

When using very lean clay, or clay of rather sluggish consistency, it will be as well to roughen slightly the parts of the coils that come in contact, either by crosswise nicks made with a knife or by slight pressure with the blade of a large rasp. As soon as a coil has been laid, it must immediately be joined with the coil beneath by smoothing the clay into the intervening grooves. If this is not done immediately, there will not be enough room left for the hand to move freely inside the vessel. This smoothing is best done with the finger or with a flat modeling tool which you can make for yourself from hardwood boiled in linseed oil.

Surface treatment

Given a certain amount of imagination, hardly any other material offers such a variety of different and lively ways of surface treatment as clay. The coiled structure in itself makes an attractive finish or texture, which shows clearly how the pot was made. However, the surface can also be beaten quite smooth with a spoon or a flat piece of wood, after the outside has slightly dried. An even denser, shiny surface can be obtained by rubbing the clay with a damp cloth after it has acquired a leather-like consistency. This stage is reached when the pot is nearly dry, but has not yet lost all its plasticity. A roller can also be used to rub down a leather-hard, slightly moistened surface. If a less perfect finish is desired, the outside can be scraped with a knife. Decoration in the form of incised linear patterns can be added to the vessel with a wooden graver or stylus, again while the clay is still leathery. Avoid overloading the vessel with exaggerated ornament, since ceramic articles should get most of their effect by virtue of their shape alone.

When all the molding has been done, the pot must be left to dry out completely. Before being put in the kiln it must be bone dry. Never put the vessel near the central heating or in the sun, since the drying process must be carried out slowly, preferably in a damp room, so as to avoid the risk of cracking. No definite figure can be given for the length of time required for drying. This depends on the humidity, as well as on the size of the vessel and the thickness of the walls, and varies from one week to a month. During this time the vessel will have to be turned and twisted several times, to allow it to dry out uniformly, starting from the base. Otherwise it will get distorted.

If a pot cracks during the drying process

—and this will be all the more likely the fatter the clay—it is unfortunate. If, on the other hand, it shrinks, this is natural and has to be accepted, and this fact should be borne in mind during the modeling process. Depending on its composition, the clay will shrink to a lesser or greater extent during both drying and firing. Therefore it will only be possible to work exactly to scale if the degree of shrinkage of the clay has been determined beforehand in the laboratory. For the purpose of a hobby-craft, however, the shrinkage factor can be determined with an adequate degree of accuracy by measuring the sides of a clay slab in the fresh state and again when it is bone dry; the difference is then expressed as a percentage, which is borne in mind when determining the size of the object at the start of the work. In general, however, such precision is not required.

Clearly, firing is the most difficult operation for the hobby-craftsman. The heat of a kitchen stove is not great enough for this purpose. To build a kiln oneself is complicated and involves a great deal of work. Buying a small kiln, fired by electricity, or gas, is the best solution, though it would be less expensive to make use of the facilities of a neighboring pottery or ceramics studio.

Ceramic glazes

There are at least two aspects to work in ceramics. It is true that we have just emphasized that shape is the most important property of a clay pot. It cannot be denied, however, that a beautiful glaze will enhance the effect of even the noblest shape. There are even people who only find ceramics interesting when they get to the glazing stage. They look upon the wall of a clay vase, a dish, or a jug merely as the ground for a decorative coating and only really start using their imagination after the work of modeling and firing, or at least the first firing or bisque, has been carried out. These people go to a craft supply merchant, buy bisque-fired pots and then paint and glaze them in their own studios, before sending them for final firing to a pottery, regardless of how far away this may be. This is quite feasible, because bisque-fired pottery, if well packed, can stand up to the strain of transportation quite well.

The original object of glazing was not to make a pot more beautiful, but rather to waterproof it. Once-fired pottery, such as the ordinary flower pot, for instance, is bisque-fired at a temperature around 950°C and the surface then turns yellow or brick-red, according to the composition of the clay; this surface will be very porous and permeable. By the application of a glass-like coating—hence the name glazing—the pores are sealed and the pot becomes impermeable.

The preparation of glazes is a science in itself. We do not have to bother with this, because for simplicity's sake, we will buy transparent and colored glazes ready for use. These will usually be so-called fritted glazes, the components of which have been fired in a special frit kiln and then ground into the finest powder. Adding certain metallic oxides turns transparent glazes into colored ones. In accordance with the instructions usually provided they are mixed with water to a soup-like consistency and then applied to the pot. During a second or maturing firing, the glaze, which in its dry state consists virtually of powdered glass, flows and forms a hard, continuous skin. Each type of glaze has its own flow temperature, which must be reached during the second firing. For ready-mixed glazes this temperature is always given. It is usually between 900 and 1100°C.

Engobe is a decorative technique that can be used in many ways. Different effects can be obtained by wiping or scratching the slip away and by using a slip tracer.

Glazes to which an adhesive (dextrin) has been added can be applied directly to the leather-hard surface of unfired ceramic ware, and the pot can then be fired in a single firing. But care must be taken, since even the adhesive sometimes fails to prevent the glaze from flaking off. If a clay vessel is to keep its natural finish on the outside and be glazed only on the inside, fill a ladle with some well-stirred "glaze soup," pour this into the vessel, swirl the liquid round inside, and then pour out the surplus liquid while the vessel is being constantly rotated. This operation must be carried out fairly quickly, as the porous pot will absorb the water in the glaze like a sponge. When the water has evaporated, the glaze will remain on the pot in the form of an evenly distributed layer of powder. Great care must be taken, because this powder is easily wiped off.

Small objects are glazed by dipping. The pot is dipped into the liquid glaze practically up to the top edge. Those who work slowly will get a very thick coating of glaze, which when fired will give the not always desirable impression of having run. Such an object should only be dipped for a longer time when a clay that fires rather dark is being coated with a light-colored glaze.

For larger objects this dipping process would require too deep a glaze bath, which is uneconomical. Therefore it is best to glaze them by the ladle method, that is, hold the pot over the basin containing the glaze and pour the glaze over the pot with a ladle starting at the top. At the same time turn the vessel slowly, so that the glaze spreads evenly over the entire surface. Surplus glaze forming drips on the base can be dabbed off with the finger tips. Unavoidably, small islands will be formed by the fingers of

Pouring glaze over a bisque-fired pot.

your left hand which holds the pot, and these must be carefully painted over with glaze, after the vessel has been set down. The best method is to allow a small amount of

glaze to drip onto these areas from the tips of your fingers.

A most important point is to see that the base of the vessel remains free of glaze, otherwise it will stick to the shelf during firing. This must be watched especially carefully when using the dip process. Any raw glaze must be scraped off with a spatula and the bottom of the pot wiped with a damp sponge.

Greasy hands holding the pot will unavoidably cause defects in the glaze, as traces of grease on the pot will repel the watery glazing liquid. Another thing: always keep stirring your liquid glaze. Glazes are not solutions, but mixtures. The fritted, glass-like particles float in the water, but rapidly fall to the bottom under their own weight. There are some glazes with so-called floating agents, which retard the settling action, but even when using these types, continuous stirring will be necessary to ensure an evenly thick coat of glaze.

By using not only transparent but also colored glazes, we can enliven the surface of our pottery with color effects. For example, we can dip the vessel into a colored glaze at an angle, or pour one glaze on top of another with a ladle, or else we can apply the glaze with free strokes using a soft paint brush.

All these methods are frequently used in order to obtain color effects, but they are usually impossible to control and rather haphazard. A more disciplined coloring technique is engobe or slip glazing. The medium is engobe or clay slip to which have been added metallic oxides or minerals that change color when they are fired.

Engobe is sold ready for use in the form of a fine, colored powder. All you have to do is to mix this with water to the consistency and smoothness of custard. Lumps and crumbs are just as unwelcome in engobe as in a custard pie. It is therefore advisable to strain engobes through a fine sieve before use.

Unlike glaze, which is applied to the pot after the first firing, engobe is flowed onto the raw, leather-hard clay and is allowed to dry out at the same time as the clay, before the pot is fired. It is therefore imperative that the engobe slip, which consists mainly of clay, should have roughly the same shrinkage coefficient as the principal material, that is, as the wall of the pot to which the engobe is applied. This must be borne in mind when selecting and matching the raw materials. Otherwise, the painted ornament will flake away from the wall during drying and firing.

There are many possibilities of decorating pots in color using the engobe technique. We can pour the clay slip either over the entire surface of the pot or over only part of it, employing the same technique as described in connection with glazing. The vessel will then be evenly coated. It is also possible to pour engobe in different colored, separate or partly overlapping streams.

Another technique, which can be better controlled, is the "wiping" method. Cover the vessel with engobe and then remove part of the slip in a striped pattern with your finger, while the surface is still damp. The color pattern thus consists of alternate stripes the color of the basic clay material and of the engobe which has not been wiped away. From here it is only a short step to scratching out whole surfaces, linear patterns, or figure compositions in the dried-on layer of engobe. This is best done with a steel tool, preferably a knife. With this technique, in addition to flat patterns, we can also produce a relief-like effect by scratching away not only the slip but also the top layer of leathery clay.

The greatest artistic freedom, however, is offered by engobe painting which can be

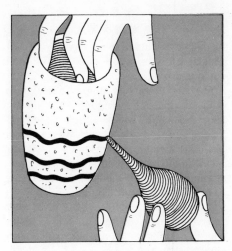

Engobe painting can be done with the old-fashioned painting horn, a rubber bulb (illustrated), or a slip tracer.

done either directly on the outside of the clay pot or over a previous coating of engobe. There are some inherent limitations to this method due to the thick consistency of the slip and the impossibility of correcting errors, but this gives it an original simplicity which is very attractive. It is possible to apply engobe with a paint brush, but this is difficult as the clay slip is rather stiff and thick. For this reason the old engobe artists thought up the painting horn, from which the creamy paste is dripped onto the clay surface. The painting horn looks somewhat like a small watering can with a narrow spout, and works roughly in the same way. A rubber bulb or the handy slip tracer will serve the same purpose. Engobe painting with any of these tools requires the nerve of a high-diver and a very steady hand. Just as it is impossible to wipe away any of the color, once it has been applied, it is also impossible to correct any line that is too thin by adding more engobe. Have a good look at examples of engobe painting before you tackle it yourself. You will notice that the main elements of this type of decoration consist of dots, short curves and rapid squiggles.

The safest way of painting a hollow vessel is to slip the pot over your left hand and apply the engobe with your right hand holding the surface horizontal. However, before you start it would be advisable to try your skill with the painting horn on a small piece of waste material. If you have no waste clay, you can use thick packing paper. Continue shaking up the contents of the horn while you paint, even if you have previously tested it for the right consistency: this will ensure an even flow and will prevent the clay slip setting in a thick sludge on the bottom. The more paste-like the application, the more plastic and modeled the finished surface.

After firing, engobe will look dull and chalky, because it is really a clay slurry. The surface will look somewhat like a raw earthenware pot. The colors will only acquire their full brilliance after the whole surface has been given a coat of transparent glaze and the pot fired for the second time.

Majolica or Faience

All this means that the engobe technique is a type of underglaze painting, a process which can also be carried out in other ways with the special underglaze paints now commercially available. These paints, supplied in an ordinary paint box, are similar to watercolors, and like these are dissolved with a damp paint brush before being applied to the bisque-fired clay pot.

Quite different from these techniques is majolica or faience, where the real art of painting with a paint brush plays the most important part. Both names are used to describe the same process. The name "majolica" comes from Majorca, the Mediterranean island where this type of ware with its magnificent designs was introduced by the Moors in the ninth century A.D. The technique itself, however, is very much older. Genuine faience work is found in the tiled walls of Persian palaces dating from 500 B.C. The art spread from Majorca to Italy and reached its climax there during the fifteenth century. The famous workshops in the town of Faenza gave the technique its French name of "faience." Later Delft faience achieved worldwide fame, after the technique was imported to Holland from China during the seventeenth century.

The distinguishing mark of genuine faience is the stannic oxide content of the opaque white foundation glaze over which the special non-running colors are applied. During the firing process the colors and the glaze blend and merge, and this process gives the colors their final brilliancy and purity.

The foundation glaze is applied to the bisque-fired clay in the form of a white, powdery coating, only when the pot is quite dry. It is on this powdery layer, which greedily absorbs any moisture in the paint brush with unbelievable speed, that we must paint. An added difficulty is the fact that majolica paints, which may be bought in a wide variety of different colors, are really nothing but extremely finely ground glass suspended in water, like the glazes already mentioned. A little dextrin is usually added, but even this does not make them much smoother.

This intractibility of the paint, and of the flour-like base, can only be overcome by working very rapidly with light strokes of the brush. It is quite impossible to sketch in the design with a pencil. From this stems the fresh impromptu character of faience painting.

Examples of the ancient and delicate art of majolica or faience painting.

The learner will have to practice with a paint brush and majolica paint on paper or a piece of waste clay, in order to prevent his enthusiasm being dashed by too many obvious failures. There is a trick, which removes nearly 80 percent of all the technical difficulties, but this the genuine majolica painter will refuse to use as being unworthy of the art.

This trick consists in firing the foundation glaze at a moderate kiln temperature, which makes the surface much easier to paint on. A beginner might make use of this method; however, when he has mastered the art, he will himself want to take the more difficult path of the powdery unfired glaze.

189

LAMPS

There is no life without light, and without attractive lamps no cosiness in the home. No wonder then that after acquiring a knowledge of some common materials and elementary techniques, we should experience an urge to make ourselves a lamp. Let us content ourselves first of all with making a floor or table lamp. To go on from there to wall and ceiling fixtures will not be difficult, once we have mastered the basic principles of construction.

A typical floor or table lamp consists of a lamp stand, a light source, and a shade, which does more than anything else to give the lamp its decorative effect. The most obvious materials for the lamp stand are wood and metal, but we can also utilize ceramics and even glass. The lamp stand is built in two stages, since for constructional purposes at least we must separate the stem from the base.

The base can be round or square. The choice of wood is a matter for individual taste. Any hard or medium-hard wood with a distinctive surface is suitable. This applies to both base and stem.

The simplest and quickest way to make a round base is on a turning lathe. If one is not available, we must carefully apply the techniques learned in carving a circular bowl (Chapter 4).

Once the rough block has been rounded

off, the base, like the bowl, must be hollowed out, but only enough to form a space on the underside, sufficient to house the electrical wiring and the switch, and a rim for the lamp to stand on. Unnecessary weakening of the base must be avoided, so that most of its weight is retained. The heavier the base, the more firmly the lamp will stand.

Stability does not depend on weight alone, however, but also on the nature of the contact with table or floor. The smaller the area in contact the better. Accordingly, we should leave a solid rim no more than about $^5/_8''$ wide, the entire center part of the base being recessed some $^1/_4''$.

It is a fact that a three-legged table will not wobble, even on an uneven floor, and we can make use of this fact in designing our lamp stand, if instead of using the whole rim as a bearing surface we support the lamp at three points only. One of several ways of doing this is to dowel three small wooden balls to the rim at equal intervals. This method of construction makes it possible to run the leads into the base from below. It is more elegant, however, to drill a channel radially from the outer rim to the center of the base, after first hollowing out a small chamber in its underside. The mouth of the channel can be plugged with a brass or plastic bushing to protect the cable.

Next, using the largest possible center

bit, drill a hole from above through the center of the base into the chamber below. Into this the stem will fit. It is preferable to widen the upper part of this hole to the exact width of the stem so that the stem can be recessed about $^1/_4''$ into the base. With smaller models, in which the diameter of the stem is not larger than that of the largest available drill, the base is drilled to a depth of $^1/_4''$ with the large drill and the drilling continued with a smaller one. This also gives us the necessary shoulder. The simplest, fastest and most accurate way of carrying out all these operations, since they are all centrally symmetric, is on the turning lathe.

a glance. If the model is as large as a floor lamp, the switch should be mounted on the stem, unless one is satisfied with a switch incorporated in the lamp socket. This possibility, of course, also holds good for the table lamp, making the work on the base somewhat easier. If the beginner finds it difficult to recess the base in the manner described, perhaps through lack of suitable tools, he should simply drill a hole straight through the base with a diameter about $^1/_2''$ less than that of the stem. In this case, the shoulder is formed not in the wall of the opening but only in the end of the stem, so that, instead of being recessed into the base

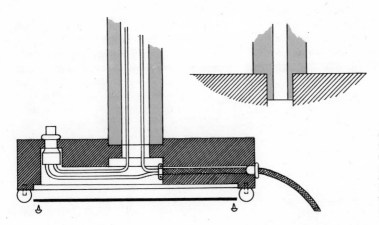

Cross section through a wooden lamp base with recessed stem, showing push-button switch and arrangement of lamp cord. Inset: an alternative form of the joint between stem and base.

The recess for the switch, however, must be made by hand, even by the owner of a lathe. In table lamps the switch should sit at the edge of the base opposite the mouth of the channel through which the lamp cord enters. The switch is mounted by means of a threaded component supplied by the manufacturer. The method of assembly is clear at

in its full thickness, the stem merely sits on top of it.

The final shaping and decoration of the base, of course, must wait until the construction work is over. There is no reason, however, why the base should remain as flat as a board. It can equally well be given a curved or hemispherical surface, if the

Stem and fixture

veining of the wood invites this treatment. The temptation to "enliven" the base by gluing on wooden dogs, owls or life buoys should be resisted. Nor should you burden it with built-in clocks, ashtrays, or barometers.

The problem of the stem lies mainly in piercing a central channel for the leads to the lamp socket. Drilling is out of the question, since even if bits as long as the normal lamp stem existed, the attempt would literally go awry. Instead we shall assemble the stem from two prefabricated parts. The rough square length of wood, which will later be fashioned into a round stem, is first cut in two lengthwise. The next step is to form a long groove in each of the newly cut surfaces, deep enough to house comfortably half the thickness of the cord. This is done with a gouge, leaving the same edge distance on each of the two halves of the stem (marking gage). The width of the groove should be the same as the width of

the gouge so that only one cut is needed. Once the grooves have been made, the two halves are glued together again. Before this, the surfaces must be very carefully trued, and after the glue has been applied the two parts must be held together under pressure by means of several screw clamps, for the joint should not only hold but also remain unseen.

One more thing. The two grooves which form the channel for the cord in the glued stem should not run right to the top. Leave the last $1^1/_2''$ at the top of the stem closed, and drill through this piece from above only after the parts have been glued. The hole should be drilled where the diagonals of the square end face intersect. The object of this will soon be clear.

At this stage of the work switch over from wood to metal and complete the top of the lamp with a fitting for mounting the shade support and the lamp socket. Use a piece of

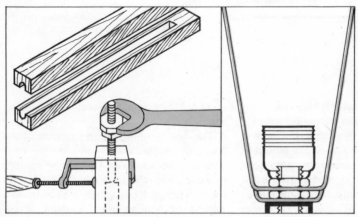

Construction of a hollow lamp stem. The square stem is cut in two and semicircular channels for the lamp cord are chiseled out of the inside face of each half. Screwing in the threaded brass tubing. Shade support assembly.

192

threaded brass tubing, of the type that can be purchased for a few cents, together with the corresponding nuts, from any electrical store, where you will also find the right switches, bushings, couplings, terminals, lamp cord, and anything else you may require for the installation work.

When the threaded tubing has been firmly screwed into the hole (it should be slightly larger) previously drilled in the top of the stem, we are ready for the next stage. Of course, we cannot screw the tubing to the depth required with our bare hands. A medium large pair of pliers is called for. So that the jaws of the pliers do not crush the thread, lock two nuts tightly together on the tubing, and then screw the whole assembly into the hole. Instead of pliers you can use a suitable wrench, to save damaging the nuts. The tighter the tubing is screwed into the wood, the more stable the connection. But at the same time there is a danger that the pressure of the screw will split open the glued joint. For safety's sake it is wise to balance the pressure from the inside with a screw clamp applied to the outside, thus rendering it harmless.

The threaded tubing is screwed in at this stage, that is, while the stem is still in its rough state, so that the screw clamp will not spoil the finished surface. The tubing must stand perfectly straight so that later the shade and lamp socket will be exactly upright.

Now we have to finish the stem. By planing off the corners, the square shape is made eight-sided. The edges are then rounded off with coarse and fine sandpaper. Finally, the bottom of the stem is shaped to fit the hole drilled in the base and glued in place. We can now concentrate on mounting the lampshade and the lamp itself. If the top of the stem offers a sufficiently wide perch for the shade support, this is simply slipped

over the threaded tubing and secured with a nut. Otherwise the support can rest on a shallow cup or bent washer similarly secured. A standard lamp socket is then screwed to the end of the brass tubing.

Wiring the lamp

The lamp is now complete except for the wiring. It is necessary to make it clear from the outset that handling electrical apparatus carrying high-voltage current always involves a certain risk. Faulty appliances can cause outbreaks of fire as a result of short circuits and even death from electric shock. These are risks which must not be dismissed lightly.

The prudent hobbyist will therefore have his lamp wired by a qualified electrician in accordance with the local code. Those who have sufficient experience in dealing with electric wiring and lighting fixtures and are prepared to accept the consequences of their actions should now take the lamp cord and insert it from the side through the channel drilled in the base, having first unscrewed the cap of the lamp socket and removed the terminal block. They should then pull through a length of cord equal to the length of the stem plus twice the radius of the base. An insulated clip attached to the cord or a simple knot will prevent it from being pulled back through the channel. This arrangement is important because it takes the stress off the terminals when the lamp is in use.

On the inside of the clip the braiding is cut away from the cord to allow the two wires, still protected by their insulation, to run separately. One wire is now carried up the stem directly to the lamp socket, while the second is connected across the switch before the free end is also carried up through the stem. When connecting both the switch and the lamp socket take care that no more of the insulation is cut away than is absolutely necessary. After the wires have been secured to the terminals, the end of the insulation must penetrate at least $^1/_{16}$" into the switch housing. Before being clamped, the numerous thin strands of wire should be tightly twisted together. Even better, they should be joined with a drop of solder to form a semi-rigid pin which should be scraped bright before being inserted.

After the switch has been screwed into the base, the wire ends which are sticking up through the cap of the lamp socket are cut to the right length and joined to the corresponding terminals. Then the socket is replaced in the cap, and screwed up, and the installation is complete. It only remains now to close off the base of the lamp by screwing a plastic disc into the recess formed specially for this purpose. If iron or even better lead is used instead of plastic, the base will be heavier and the lamp, which is now ready for use, more stable.

Lamps in Metal, Glass and Clay

Metal is perhaps a more "modern" material than wood. For example, a lamp consisting of a wooden base combined with a brass stem is not only tasteful but relatively easy to make. The brass stem has the advantage that it can be bought in the form of an already hollow tube of almost any length and thickness. There are objections, however, to mounting it in the base with joiner's glue. We must screw the tube into the base from underneath. Cutting the necessary thread at the bottom of the stem is easy if you own a threading tool or can borrow one. There are workshops, however, that will do this sort of job for a small sum, and also supply

you with a suitable nut and washer. But neither of these will be of any use, if there is no counter pressure acting on the other, that is the upper, side of the joint. This is provided by a sleeve soldered to the stem a distance equal to the thickness of the wooden plate above the thread. If a ready-made sleeve of this sort is not available, take a sufficiently thick brass ring and file it down on the inside until it fits over the outside of the stem.

A decorative sleeve is also a suitable termination for the upper end of the stem. It will even be indispensable if the wall of the stem is not thick enough to make a reliable soldered joint. Again we are faced with the problem of reducing the wide stem to the much smaller diameter of the threaded mounting for the lamp socket. The problem can be solved by filing out a round brass cover plate at least $^1/_{16}$" thick and equal in diameter to the outside diameter of the stem or reinforcing sleeve. In the center of this plate a hole is drilled through which the socket mounting is passed with a nut threaded onto it. Nut, socket mounting, and brass plate are then soldered together to form a single unit.

A second disc—a simple washer will do— just small enough to fit inside the stem is secured firmly between two nuts on the lower part of the threaded mounting. The length of thread projecting above the brass disc depends on the type of lamp and the size of the proposed shade support. This head assembly is now pushed down from above until the cover plate sits firmly on the top of the stem, where it is soldered in position. The strength of this joint depends essentially on the quality of the contact between the top of the stem and the cover plate and on the tight fit of the lower bracing disc inside the stem. The function of the latter is to brace the soldered joint between cover plate and stem, but especially that between cover plate, socket mounting and nut, against a leverage load acting from the side.

Providing the lamp with a brass base introduces further complications. In fabricating such a base we shall have to make use of the metalworking techniques described in Chapter 6. We can either form a flange on a disc of thick sheet brass to get a round base with a flat top, or we can make a dome-shaped base by means of the method used to sink metal bowls.

In the case of small, light models, the brass alone will be stiff enough to carry the weight of the lamp. At the same time, a tall lamp designed to stand on the floor will be considerably more stable if its weight is carried by a separate frame, the sober practicality of which is concealed beneath an elegant skin of beaten brass. Also in the interests of stability, the center of gravity of the lamp should be brought as low as possible, that is to say into the base, by adding extra weight. A $^1/_2''$ thick iron plate is surprisingly heavy. Lead is even heavier. In addition, it is easier to work. A plate of this kind will take over the functions of the lamp base and as long as its thickness and diameter are carefully chosen to match the inside dimensions of the brass dome, it will remain completely unseen. When the lamp is assembled, its underside should be flush with the lower edge of the decorative dome, though it is better that it should project slightly beyond this edge than fall short of it. To assemble, use a threaded connection, similar to that for the combination lamp with a metal stem and a wooden base. First, the brass dome is screwed to the tube forming the stem, to which a collar has been soldered to act as a stop. Then the lower end of the stem is passed through a hole drilled in the center of the iron or lead plate and secured with a lock nut against a second nut previously threaded onto the stem just above the plate. The lower nut must be recessed into the base. Since in most cases the base plate will have to be cut to size by a commercial workshop, ask them, while they are about it, to form a recess in the bottom big enough to receive the lock nut when the lamp is assembled.

The size of the cavity formed between the brass dome and the base plate will depend on the thickness of the threaded connection. The lamp cord is introduced into the base

Reducing the diameter of a metal lamp stem to that of the threaded socket-mounting. A washer of the same width as the inside of the stem protects the soldered joint at the top from lateral forces.

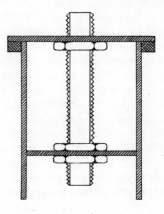

Lampshades

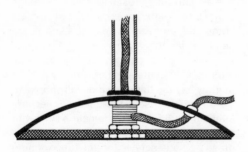

Section through a metal lamp base showing threaded stem, lock nuts, brass dome, and iron base plate.

bottle. The stability of the lamp can be further increased by filling the bottle with sand. Beads or lead shot will produce the same result.

Installing the lamp socket in the bottle neck is not easy. The only practical way of doing this is to use a long cork with a hole bored through the middle and a brass cap. Naturally, exaggerated demands cannot be made on a connection of this kind. It would be unwise to overload it with a top-heavy or wide-brimmed shade.

through a hole drilled in the brass dome and enters the stem through another hole drilled in the part of the stem lying between the two nuts clamping the base plate from above and the dome from below.

Rough iron and lead base plates are not popular with housewives since they scratch furniture and floors. It is best to glue a thin felt pad to the underside of the base and so avoid all trouble from the start.

Straw-covered Chianti bottles make attractive table lamps. So do ceramic jars and pitchers. Potters who make their own lamp bases have the advantage over the Chianti fans of being able to make a hole near the bottom of the vessel through which the lamp cord can be discreetly introduced. This is not possible with a Chianti bottle. If a glass base is used, the cord will have to be passed through a hole bored directly beneath the shade holder in the threaded lamp socket. The best switch for such lamps is a push-button inserted in the cord. Another reliable and elegant solution is a socket with a built-in switch. So that the pull of the cord is not transmitted to the top of the lamp, which could only too easily upset it, the cord is bound with straw to the neck and body of the

Lampshades

As far as the total effect is concerned, the shade is more important than the stand. The shade is the most conspicuous part of the lamp and also determines the quality of the light.

The support for the shade has already been mentioned in connection with the stand. Such supports can be obtained in various sizes and styles from any electrical dealer. At the top they have a small plate with a threaded nipple to which the shade is fixed with a washer and cap nut. Shade frames can also be purchased ready for use in every conceivable shape and size. Purists will solder up their own in galvanized iron or brass wire. A sufficiently large iron or brass washer will serve as central support and suspension point. The really creative work, governed purely by individual taste, begins with the choice of covering fabric for the shade. Don't forget, however, that, apart from its decorative aspect, a lampshade also has a very practical function. It must soften the harsh light of the bulb and distribute it pleasantly, but at the same time it must never act as a barrier to the light. The lampshade's purpose will not be fulfilled if the proper utilization of the light is forgotten in

196

the search for decorative effect. This lies at the back of all the rules governing the choice of materials. These rules apply with equal validity to paper, plastics, parchment and textiles and depend on the particular requirements with respect to quantity and quality of light.

Easiest to deal with is the simple pleated paper shade, for which a strong, fibrous or embossed paper should be chosen. All we need is a strip of paper fully twice as long as the lower circumference of the shade and a small piece of silk cord. The width of the paper should be equal to the distance between the top and bottom rings of the frame plus an additional 2″ at top and bottom.

In pleating the shade we are faced with the problem of dividing a given length of paper into folds of equal width. This is most conveniently done in two stages. First, fold in the ridges pointing upwards, and then the ridges pointing downwards. Begin by dividing the whole length of the paper in two with a vertical fold down the center. By folding in each end to meet the center fold, you can divide the paper into quarters, and by folding in the new edges into eighths. In this manner seven folds have been formed in the paper. Now, in the next step, fold in the left hand edge to meet folds 1, 3, 5, and 7 in turn. Then do the same with the right hand edge, i.e. fold it in to meet folds 7, 5, 3, and 1. Continue this game of folding in from each edge, aligning the edge with alternate existing folds, until the whole length is divided into strips about $3/_4$″ wide. Then turn the paper over and make the counterfolds. Once again, the correct positions are found by aligning the edge with folds produced during the first stage, omitting alternate folds. Practice this on a piece of wrapping paper. See page 198.

After these preliminaries, the folds are bunched together concertina-wise and a hole is punched about 3″ from the top;

through this is passed the silk cord for drawing in the top of the shade. Finally, punch a semicircular notch in the inside edge of the folds about $3/_4$″ from the top. This notch is intended for the upper rim of the frame. Then the end pleats are glued together to form a cylinder, the silk cord is drawn tight, and the shade is complete.

Lampshades in silk or crepe de Chine in the shape of a truncated cone are made from two lengths of fabric, one for the sides and the other for the top. The width of the fabric for the sides is calculated from the height of the shade plus $1^1/_4$″ each for a narrow hem at top and bottom. The length is calculated according to the amount of gathering or pleating desired. But it should not be less than twice the length of the bottom rim of the frame.

A gathered shade is easier to make than a pleated one, for whereas pleats have to be fastened individually to the linen binding around the wire frame, while simultaneously balancing out the difference between the circumferences of the upper and lower rings, gathering is as simple as fixing a curtain between two cords. These cords are passed through the hems formed at the top and bottom of the shade and the fabric is gathered together on them as closely as required. The fabric is then fastened to the frame.

It all depends on the size of the shade whether we cut the full length of fabric from one piece, or take several lengths the width of the bale and bring them together at the selvages. With skilful gathering, we need not actually sew them together. Instead we can conceal the joins in the folds, without any gaps appearing in the shade.

The way in which we cover the top also depends on the size of the shade. With small shades, it is sufficient to cut a round piece of fabric of the desired size using a

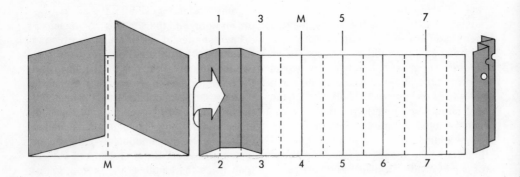

How to pleat a paper lampshade. Note the position of the holes punched for the draw-string and the upper rim of the frame.

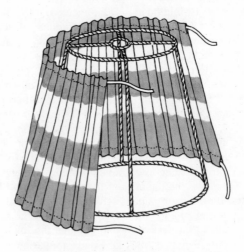

Attaching the pleated shade to the frame. The frame has previously been wrapped with linen tape.

paper pattern. Larger sizes need up to four trapezoidal sections which are joined together. The necessary reduction in area in the direction of the center is obtained by means of radial folds.

Generally speaking, delicate silk fabrics should not be brought into direct contact with the wire frame, but should be lined with white or cream art silk. Firstly, however, it is necessary to bind the whole frame with linen tape. This is not only to protect the fabric, but also to provide a surface to which the lining and the silk can be stitched.

In contrast to the outer fabric, the lining is stretched tightly over the frame, and this is done from the inside. It is essential to divide both sides and top into sections, using paper patterns, and to cut the fabric accordingly.

Once the lining is smoothly in place, cover first the top and the sides with the outer fabric. Finally, cover the gathered hems or the pleated edges with a suitable colored border.

Using the brown paper pattern method, it is also easy to find the shapes of sections from which to build a shade in parchment, cellophane, oiled paper, or similar semi-stiff materials. Only very small shades of this type can be made in one piece. More pretentious shades have to be assembled from several parts. Do not try and conceal this method of construction by gluing the joints —glued joints will be visible in any case—but draw attention to them with honest-to-goodness seams. Sew with silk cord, straw, leather thongs, or other contrasting materials, butting, rather than overlapping, the edges of adjoining sections. The needle holes are made before sewing. Suitable stitches are the cross-stitch or the extremely attractive "sailor's" stitch.

When the individual parts have been joined to form a bucket shape, this is fitted

over the frame and the bottom edge is fastened to the bottom ring of the frame with a binding stitch.

Some very attractive lampshades can be constructed by covering the frame with natural or colored bast and straw. It is a matter of personal taste whether you first cover the frame with cambric or artificial

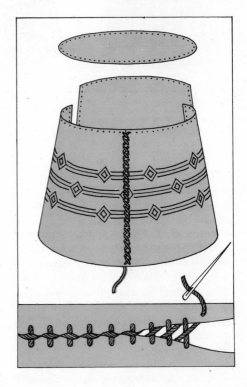

Making lampshades out of several pieces of stiff material. Below: the so-called "sailor's stitch."

silk. In either case, the wires of the frame must be wrapped with straw.

The simplest way of making a straw shade is to run a continuous strand up and down between the top and bottom rings until you have formed a dense wall of closely packed

Straw shades

Straw lampshades. Interesting and lively effects can be obtained by dividing the shade horizontally or vertically into bands of different color. If an openwork technique is adopted, the shade should be lined.

loops. If more than one strand has to be used the knots should be arranged to coincide with the rings. They are later hidden by adding a plaited border.

Another type of straw shade is obtained by dividing the shade into several horizontal bands by means of three or four straw plaits (depending on the size of the shade). These bands are then filled in with differently colored straw, to form a zigzag, criss-cross or parallel pattern. Such a shade, which may have many gaps in its straw covering, should certainly be lined.

Anyone who has become reasonably proficient in basket making can weave himself a lampshade entirely out of rattan. This technique is especially suitable for making self-supporting shades, in which the functions of frame and covering are combined.

As in basket making, begin by weaving a base around an odd number of intersecting reeds. A useful aid is a very thick cardboard ring with an outside diameter of about 2″ for a lamp of medium size. The necessary number of evenly spaced holes is drilled in the side of the ring and the spokes pushed through until they cross in the center. This not only temporarily stiffens the base, but ensures a correct start. The length and the number of the spokes depend on the size of the shade desired.

Begin weaving the base close to the outside edge of the cardboard ring, starting with at least one pairing round for the sake of greater stiffness (for the various weaves see Chapter 9). Continue with simple randing until the base has grown to the required size. On reaching the transition zone between wall and base, the stakes are freshly soaked so that they can be made to "turn the corner" easily. The curve of the sides is controlled solely by the relative tautness of the weavers.

Be sure that the stakes remain stretched even when the weavers are pulled tight, and always start new weavers from the inside of the shade.

Unnecessarily heavy borders should be

avoided in such a lightweight article as a lampshade. After finishing weaving, form the edge by trimming and sharpening each stake and bending it back in a gentle curve into the wall close to the next stake but one. An awl or a small screwdriver, or failing these a knitting needle, will open a path for these ends.

Finally, the starting point of the woven shade is finished off in similar fashion. The temporary cardboard support is carefully cut out and the stakes are again tucked into

the weave close to the next stake but one. This is a rather intricate process in view of the narrow space available and the stubborn resistance of the ends. It is advisable to soften up the stakes in hot water and form the bends over an awl handle.

Our "self supporting" shade is now ready and can be mounted, either hanging or standing, without the use of a separate frame. It is held by the usual screw cap which can be bought together with the bulb fitting.

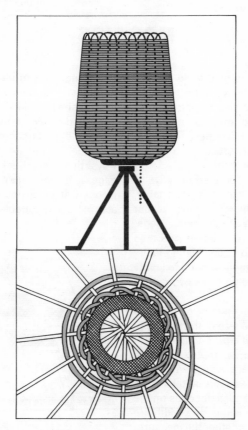

The self-supporting woven shade. Below: spokes inserted through cardboard ring. Start weaving with at least one pairing round.

12 MOSAICS

The popularity of the tiled table is thoroughly understandable. No other table top provides such an effective combination of utility and resistance to wear and tear. Moreover, it is indisputable that a tiled table will add a very personal touch and a certain air of refinement to any home.

Our interest will be centered on ways of constructing the surface of such a table, since the actual frame will simply be put together from ready-made parts (legs, brackets, rough top). Of course it is also possible to tile the top of an existing table, if it is attractive and stable enough to justify the expense, and if the tiles can be made to fit in both directions.

Since the fixed dimensions of the tiles determine the ultimate size of the table top, we would normally cut a base to the necessary measurements and complete the table by attaching ready-made legs. Heavy fibreboard or plywood makes a very suitable base for a tile top. The thickness depends on the size of the table. The length and width are calculated by adding together the measurements of the tiles in each direction plus the width of the joints.

The regularity of the joints makes an important contribution to the general effect of the finished surface and should not be neglected. Even if the table is relatively small, the joints can comfortably be made $^1/_8''$ wide. To ensure that the joints are always the same thickness, use two joint gages in the form of a pair of carefully planed wooden slats. Strips of waste plastic are also extremely suitable. These are laid in the

Making a tiled table top. Two slats of equal thickness ensure that the joints are all the same width.

The tiled table

joints at right angles while each row of tiles is cemented in place, after which they are removed.

The tiled surface will only be level, if the base is absolutely flat and clean. The tiles are fixed one at a time with a special cement obtainable from the tile supplier. Remember that this cement hardens very rapidly. The tile must be placed correctly from the start, since later on changes will be difficult to make and will certainly have an adverse effect on the durability of the table. The cement-coated tile is first stood on one edge and then lowered onto the base. Edge tiles should be flush with the edge of the base.

When all the tiles have been cemented, finish off the edge of the table neatly with a mitered molding the same thickness as the tiles. Instead of a wooden rim we can use an adhesive-backed plastic or brass strip. The latter is screwed to the table edge and the joint covered with a special clip.

Lastly, the empty joints are filled with a white cement grout (1 part cement to 2 parts sand). The sand must be clean and very fine grained. Best of all is the sand used by masons for fine plasterwork. The grout must not be too thick, but should fill the joints smoothly. After the joints have been filled, the whole surface is at once carefully cleaned. Splashes of grout that are allowed to dry on the tile surface are extremely difficult to remove. Before any weight is placed on the tiled table, enough time must pass for the grout to set.

Much greater freedom in the choice of colors, designs, and size is possible with the smaller mosaic tile. Miniature mosaics in ceramics, colored glass or plastics have the advantage of being adaptable to almost any shape. Consequently, they can be used to decorate not only rectangular tables, but also round and even irregular ones. Window seats, the surrounds of mirrors, walls, and

even whole floors can all be embellished with this versatile material. The construction of a mosaic is more than a mere game with colorful stones, it is a plastic art with its own laws. Although the finished mosaic should indeed be carefree in character, the size and shape of the individual stones are by no means unimportant. In addition, the contribution of the joints to the total effect is much greater than in the case of tiled surfaces.

Mosaic stones are sold as glass mosaic and as ceramic chips with a sintered surface in a wide range of lustrous or pastel colors. They can be used as sold, but your work will have greater individuality if they are broken into different shapes and sizes with a pair of pliers. You can also gather and shape your own raw material in the form of fragments of colored tile and colored or stained glass. Rough edges can be smoothed down with a file and sandpaper.

There are two methods of laying a mosaic, the positive and the negative process. Of the two the positive method is simpler and for this reason is to be recommended to the beginner anxious to gain experience with this material. With this method, however, an even surface can only be obtained by using stones of the same thickness.

As with the tile table, a smooth sheet of thick plywood or fibreboard will serve as a base. On this we can sketch out a rough plan, or we can lay the colored stones in a free pattern. Once again use a special cement to fix the individual stones, and make quite sure that sufficient space is left between them. They must never stick together! After laying the stones, finish off the edge with a wooden molding, plastic strip or metal border, and fill the joints with a very thin white cement grout rubbed in by hand. Surplus grout is scraped off immediately with a spatula. When the grout has begun to harden, the whole surface is cleaned with a weak solution of hydrochloric acid and rubbed with a clean cloth damped in clean water. Not until the joints have thoroughly dried out, which will take a couple of days, is the surface of the mosaic polished with a thin coating of wax.

A variation of the positive technique consists in laying the stones in a self-supporting cement bed. This method is always employed when the base for the mosaic is brickwork or wall plaster.

But even on plywood the stones can be laid directly in cement or a plaster of Paris compound. In this case, the molding is placed round the edge of the base right at the start to prevent the cement from spilling over the sides and to stabilize the process. The cement bed is prepared as a stiff mix of Portland cement and sharp quartz sand and is spread over the base with a trowel in an even layer about $^1/_2$" thick. The stones are then pressed into the bed of cement, but not so far that the cement squeezed up between them completely fills the joints. Where this

occurs, the cement must be scraped out, since the beauty of the joints depends on their being capped with a white grout after the cement bed has had half a day in which to set. Scratching out the most important outlines in the smooth wet cement is a great help in ensuring the correct construction of the picture. Moreover, because the cement sets slowly, changes can be made. Small mosaic surfaces can be laid in a single step. If, on the other hand, you propose to cover larger areas, it is advisable to lay the cement bed and insert the stones in stages.

If the completed mosaic is eventually to be removed from the assembly board, the edging is not screwed or glued in place, but forms a loose frame around the base. In this case the plywood is coated with form oil to prevent the cement from sticking. The same applies to the smooth inner surface of the edging strips.

In making a negative mosaic we proceed in a completely different manner. The design is laid out full-size on paper in water colors, but in reverse, so as to form a mirror image.

Laying mosaics: the positive technique. The stones are laid in a bed of cement on a plywood base corresponding to the size of the finished mosaic. If a larger base is used, the edges of the mosaic can be defined by a special casting frame.

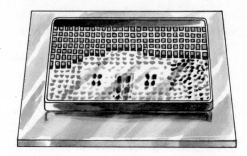

Laying mosaics: the negative technique. The stones are laid face down on a sheet of plate glass. Below: section through the finished mosaic. The permanent metal frame is anchored to the cement grout by means of a wire cross.

The paper is then placed under a sheet of plate glass, the upper surface of which is rubbed over with a light soap solution. The mosaic is assembled face down on this casting base, the stones being arranged according to the design beneath and fixed with a water-soluble adhesive. Once the mosaic has been correctly assembled, a casting frame is added. This may be either a temporary arrangement of smoothly planed and oiled slats or a well-made permanent edging. A very durable frame can be made by anchoring a metal strip in the cement base by means of a soldered wire cross, but a few long nails soldered by their heads to the inside face of the strip will serve the same purpose.

After the frame has been set up on the sheet of plate glass, a thin white cement grout is poured over the back of the mosaic until all the joints have been filled and the stones covered by a layer about $1/4''$ thick. Because of the necessarily high water content, this grout should be made from equal parts of cement and sand. It will take longer to harden it is true, but it will set all the more firmly.

The moisture in the grout loosens the adhesive holding the stones to the glass, so that when the grout has set, the mosaic can be removed in one piece. In case of difficulty you may have to let water seep between the glass and the mosaic and wait patiently until the adhesive has softened sufficiently to release its hold.

When the cement is completely hard and dry, the mosaic will be a self-contained solid unit ready, after its surface has been cleaned, to be mounted on any suitable base. If the mosaic is to serve as a table top, it should have been framed from the start in a molding designed to serve as the table rim. The sides of the frame must be high enough for a wooden backing board to be applied after the grout has been poured. This board should fit exactly inside the frame, but must not be applied until the grout has thoroughly dried out. This takes some time. If the chemical drying process is accelerated, the grout will crack. For the first day of drying it is best to cover the back of the mosaic with damp cloths.

Before mounting the backing board, rub the grout smooth with pumice stone or a brick to remove any hollows. Then glue in the backing board with a synthetic adhesive and fix it with brass screws driven through the frame.

Self-supporting mosaics

If a large enough sheet of glass is not available as a casting base, the mosaic can be glued to a sheet of strong tracing paper previously mounted on a plywood board with strips of glue. If we lay out the design on the tracing paper and then turn it over, we shall see its mirror image on the back. When the grout has set, pull off the paper from the face of the mosaic.

A final word about laying out the design. The design should not consist of systematic rows of squares filled out in water color. Improvise with short brush strokes boldly and freely applied. Each stroke corresponds to a piece of the mosaic, and the spaces between indicate the importance of the joints. In this way you will best achieve the uninhibited yet stylish freshness which constitutes the unique charm of mosaic surfaces.

Women and children are adepts at ornament, and they understand it thoroughly. Games and play provide plenty of work for a child's imagination, and its quick, innocent eye can see designs of real beauty and true utility in seemingly shapeless materials that to its elders are little better than trash. This simple pleasure in natural forms and colors has been basic to the arts of decoration since the primitive days of the cave artist and the Stone Age potter, and it can still produce many an enchanting trinket.

The cheapest materials for elementary lessons on the principles of personal ornament are supplied by Nature herself. Every Fall yields an abundance of fruit stones, pumpkin seeds and hazelnuts, which children make up into simple necklaces and bracelets. Insects may have already opened a path for the thread, and all you have to do is use the hole to start a fine drill on its way through the nut. Fruit stones must be thoroughly dry and perfectly clean before you start work on them. Dry them and drill them. Then coat them with zapon varnish. Next hand your "pearls" on a thin knitting needle, spacing them well apart, and paint them with a fine camelhair brush. Support the needle on two hooks (or over the angle of a drawer) in a clean atmosphere, until the paint is quite dry.

Wooden beads of various shapes and sizes can be bought in the stores, and these can be painted in the same way. They may also be patterned by branding them with a hot iron, or they may be colored in "harlequin" sets from an endless range of tints.

Pumice and shellac will bring up a very attractive high polish on the surface of hazelnuts, adding a warm glow to the natural soft color of the shell. Fragments of coconut shell make a very interesting raw material for necklaces in great variety, because of their rich, dark brown color, and their suggestion of the mysterious fascination of tropical places. Work on these pieces requires a great deal of patience: the surface of the shell is not quite flat, and so it has to be worked over repeatedly with a flexible file and sandpaper of various grades, until it is smooth enough to take a priming coat as a ground for decorative work. The best procedure is to do the preparatory smoothing on large fragments, and then to cut these fragments into small, irregular pieces with a fret saw. When painted, these smaller pieces can be trimmed and polished around the edges, and they will then present the attractive appearance of real gipsy-style ornaments.

The fine, careful drilling of polished nuts and shells calls for considerable skill in the use of boring tools on a very small scale. The occupation is a highly rewarding one, producing ornaments of original design which add a colorful touch to outdoor clothes.

Simple necklaces and bracelets

The craft of working metals into decorative articles should always begin with wire, which is the most practical and versatile material to use for necklaces and armbands.

For ornaments intended for personal wear we shall need a supply of good brass wire of various gages. When we have become proficient in working this material, we may graduate to silver wire, a considerably more difficult, expensive medium.

made from a piece of round steel bar. For very narrow and tight coils we can even snip the head off a round nail and use the shank.

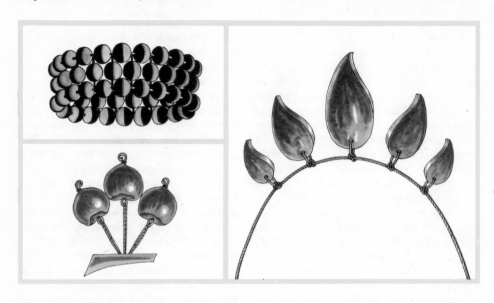

Examples of the use of natural materials in making simple ornaments: 1 necklace made of pieces of coconut shell, 2 brooch made of polished hazelnuts, 3 bracelet made of wooden beads painted in two different colors.

We shall need a few additional tools and appliances: some rods or mandrels and a variety of pliers for holding and shaping work. A small needle file will be needed for filing down the rough ends of the wire, and a jeweler's saw for piercing sheet-metal ornaments, and for cutting out small parts that cannot be removed with a file. For more durable work, or work exposed to more wear and tear, we shall, of course, need a soldering iron with interchangeable bits.

We can make satisfactory mandrels for ourselves by whittling down cylinders of wood to the diameter required and forming across one end of the cylinder a saw cut of the same thickness as our wire and about $1/4$" deep. A more durable mandrel can be

These mandrels are exceedingly useful because they guarantee that all our chain links will be of uniform size. Simple as this device is, it facilitates the "mass-production" of bracelets and finger rings. The mandrel is used as follows: Secure one end of the wire in the transverse slot at the end of the mandrel; bend over the free end at right-angles; wind the free end around the mandrel in a close, uniform, and fairly tight spiral. When the whole length of the mandrel has been wrapped with wire, place it in a vise, and cut the coil lengthwise with a metal saw, thus obtaining a quantity of uniform rings. Join them in a chain, and bring the ends of each link together with flat-nose pliers, then solder.

Having mastered this basic operation, we can obtain an almost unlimited variety of shapes for our wire jewelry by making a number of mandrels to produce rings of different sizes. To the jeweler a "ring" is not necessarily a circular object; the mandrel might be oval or rectangular, square or heart-shaped, or based on some free form.

To make a figure-of-eight link we shall need to employ a simple auxiliary device for bending the material. Cut a length of $^3/_8''$ round steel bar into two short sections. Secure these in a vise, spaced about $1^1/_2''$ apart. These dimensions apply to $^1/_{16}''$ brass wire, and should be varied according to the actual size of wire you intend to use. Coil the wire around the two upright bars in a figure-of-eight, as though you were making a skein of wool, taking care to maintain an even pressure and to keep the loops close together. When the skein is complete, take a pair of round-nose pliers, and squeeze the

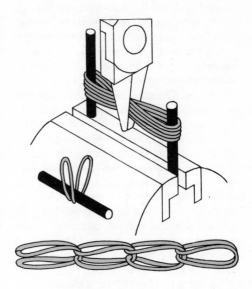

Bending and joining heavy figure-of-eight links.

opposite sides together at a point exactly half-way between the upright bars, until the wires meet. To do this it is necessary to release one of the upright bars. Do not withdraw it from the coil, however, or the loops may lose their shape: rest the end of the bar on the vise, as in the illustration. Next, release the second bar, and remove it from the coil. Use the first bar as a sawing block to cut the coil of wire into links as previously described.

Now file the ends of the rough links flat and squeeze them together into the same plane. Then take one of the links and bend it around the bar previously used as a sawing block until the ends touch.

The first link is now complete, and we proceed in the same way with the remainder until we have enough for a chain. Assembling the chain presents no problems.

If the material is strong and thick enough, it will not be necessary to use solder at the

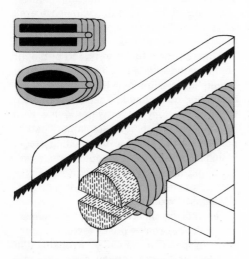

Forming numbers of uniform wire links over mandrels of different shapes. The coil of wire is divided into links by making a saw cut along the length of the mandrel.

contact surfaces, because the tensile forces can be satisfactorily resisted by the closed end of the loop alone. But where the material is thin and brittle, soldering will usually be necessary, as the links will not be able to withstand ordinary use, unless they are reinforced. The soldering of thin wire can sometimes be avoided by doubling or trebling the wire strands in each link. The technique of shaping the wire, by coiling it round a mandrel, is the same as for single strands of thick wire, but the cutting procedure is different: do not saw through the whole of the coil, but take the snips and cut through single strands at regular intervals according to the number of turns of wire required in the finished link. Then join up the links by easing them into one another as though they were key-rings.

It is not at all essential for a chain to consist of a series of identical and uniform links. Though wire has substance, weight and other physical properties, its main characteristic for the craftsman is its linearity. Its strongest effect depends on contrast. Thus the design of a chain may be varied by alternating single-strand circular links with multistrand flattened ovals, a combination which gives a most attractive linear pattern. The use of links of different sizes has many advantages, giving the designer almost unlimited scope. For example, lengths of wire can be wound tightly into fairly large flat spirals; the outermost loop pulled out at the same point on either side to form projecting eyes; and flat rings passed through these eyes to link the spirals, forming an attractive chain-type necklace. This design depends upon the careful balancing of circular elements of two different types and sizes. A slender necklace consisting of elongated links connected by flat rings is another example of the same principle. Such a necklace can be made even more attractive by

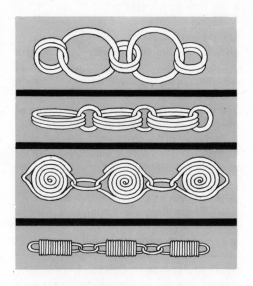

Examples of chains the effect of which depends on the alternation of links of different sizes with different numbers of turns.

closely wrapping thinner wire around the elongated ovals, which should then be the same thickness as the connecting rings. At either end of the coil of thin wire leave eyes large enough for the connecting rings to pass and still have room to move.

If brass wire is found to be too brittle for cold working with pliers, it can be heated to a dull red in a bunsen burner or a blowtorch, and quenched in a pickling solution. Clean it carefully under water with a wire brush. This will remove any impurities deposited on the metal in the heating stage. Finish by polishing to a smooth surface with a lapping abrasive, and apply a protective coating of clear zapon varnish as a protection against oxidation.

The making of fasteners for necklaces, bracelets and chains poses technical problems of peculiar difficulty. Probably the simplest and most popular method is still the "hook-and-eye" device; another slightly more elaborate type of fastening consists of a flat coil of thin wire on the key-ring principle. Making these fasteners requires great care and experience, with a high degree of accuracy in cutting and matching the parts. If you have made a successful wire bracelet or necklace, you will probably not wish to rely on a home-made fastener. It would be more prudent to buy a good one ready-made.

Earrings, Lockets and Pendants

The ornamental wire chains we have just described are works of art requiring no further adornment. On them charms and pendants would be quite out of place. Conversely, a chain made to carry a pendant should remain decently in the background.

On turning to the study of pendants we leave the domain of wire for that of sheet metal, and it will be necessary to know something about designing on metal surfaces. To our stock of materials we must now add thick sheets of medium-hard brass and copper, and for fine work a small supply of silver foil and gold leaf. At first, it is best to stick to simple operations that are well within the range of the amateur craftsman's equipment and skill.

Our first project is a two-dimensional operation, making pierced ornaments out of flat sheet metal, and our principal tool will be the jeweler's saw. If we bear in mind the principles of silhouette cutting, we shall have an excellent foundation for the work in hand, because in each case the same rules apply. We must remember, however, that we are now working in metal and not in paper, and we must therefore avoid elaborate interior shapes and large intricate flourishes of a kind which a saw blade could not easily follow. Take care that no detail anywhere in the pattern is structurally isolated, and that the points at which the pattern is attached

to and supported in the outer frame are not too slender and weak, or else the vibration of the saw blade will tear the pattern out of the frame in the very act of cutting it, something we must learn to avoid. Each element in the design must be linked with some other element, and the details must all bolster and support each other. It is a fundamental law of design that the pictorial elements and the empty spaces must balance, positive and negative being equally distributed over the field of the design. The practical work of piercing the pattern will offer no difficulties to any workman who knows how to handle a saw frame. The design is transferred to the metal with a sharp pencil and a sheet of carbon paper, and then (since the carbon tracing is easily erased) incised with a sharp

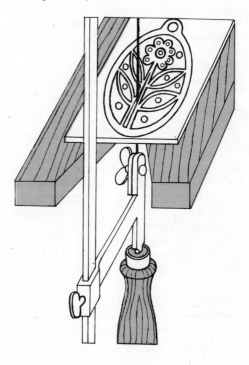

Piercing an earring with a jeweler's saw.

211

scriber. Next, in each of the surfaces to be removed, that is, in each piece of waste, drill a hole sufficiently large to admit the blade of the saw.

Saw blades of all sizes are available for piercing flat metal; some are exceedingly fine and are used for cutting out tiny angles and other awkward parts that cannot be removed by small files. The saw frame should be light and strong and should preferably have a round back, as this pattern can be made to turn a sharp curve. Get the best saw frame you can afford: the quality of the work you can do with it will justify the outlay.

First of all, pierce all the open work in the middle of the design, as this leaves the piece still fairly strong, and finishing is not made troublesome by weak spots at the edges. Do not attempt to saw along the outside contours (whatever their shape), or pierce a hole for the hook or link, until this preliminary work has been done. Always keep the saw upright, so that the side of the saw cut is clean, true and vertical, and so that the saw blade does not snap in the cut.

Do not worry too much if your saw cuts are not quite up to standard: a final, careful trim with a needle file will correct most of the imperfections. The life of needle files is, very understandably, rather short, but they are very cheap, and may be economically bought in sets of half-a-dozen assorted shapes and sizes.

It now only remains to finish off by buffing and then polishing the work. We shall then have an attractive personal ornament. Be careful not to spoil the delicate details by converting sharp edges into round ones, or by rubbing thin parts into holes. Carefully remove all tool marks, and polish the surface to a brilliant finish with a little moistened rouge on a calico mop.

The metal-piercing technique we have described can be used to make pendants and brooches, buckles and clasps for belts, rings, bracelets and personal ornaments in great variety. The possibilities are not exhausted by ornament, since we can go on to make gadgets of every description: key tags, briefcase clasps, handles and clips for vanity bags, name plates for walking-sticks and umbrellas, luggage labels, and napkin rings, to name but a few.

Ceramic Ornaments

A pendant of a very different kind can be made using clay as the raw material. Suppose we want to make a simple pendant for a necklace, with a natural motif, such as an animal, a leaf or a flower, in bas-relief. We shall first have to make a plaster mold, which, however, will simplify mass production of the ornament. In this process the secret of success lies in making a good full-size model of the pendant in wax or oiled clay. The relief must be kept free of undercuts, that is the edges of all the raised surfaces must slope outwards, like the sides of a hill.

Prepare a roll of clay by spreading it on an oiled slab of marble or slate. The oil is intended to prevent the clay from sticking to the work top. This clay will be required to make a dike or wall to contain the liquid plaster as it is poured.

Now lay your wax model, face upwards, on a flat wooden work top, and build the clay dike around it. The dike must be at least an inch higher than the highest point on the model, and there should be a clear margin all around the model, forming a space of about 2″ between the edge of the model and the surrounding wall. The clay dike should be buttressed all around with pillars, also of clay, or auxiliary walls may be made of

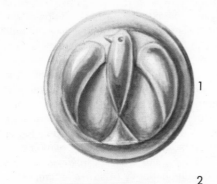

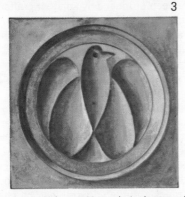

Making a mold for ceramic pendants: 1 wax model, 2 model covered with plaster on the bottom of the casting box, 3 the finished mold (plaster surface colored).

work top remains exposed between the model and the dike. Brush this over with clay-water to prevent the plaster from sticking to the work top. Now prepare the plaster.

Do not worry if your first mix is not successful, as experience is necessary before the consistency of the plaster can be accurately gaged. First add a large pinch of alum to your bucket of clean water; then sprinkle in the plaster at a uniform rate, very gently, and not too quickly, so as to avoid bubbles. Do not allow any lumps to fall in. Sprinkle in a circular motion to obtain an even spread. Remember, avoid bubbles. When the plaster is level with the surface of the water, stop pouring it in. Wait until all movement ceases. Then stir the mix very gently from the bottom of the bucket, for a short time only. Now pour the mix very slowly into the tank from one side, to reduce the risk of introducing air at the same time. Allow the plaster to set for at least one hour. When it is quite hard and dry, you can remove the dike. Now turn the mold over and withdraw the model. A good impression of it will remain in the mold, complete in every detail. The alum added to the water at the start of the process has the effect of increasing the hardness of the plaster. Finish by sharpening all the contours with a small knife or broken razor blade. Firing the clay in the kiln is a simple matter, provided the material contains no air bubbles. The plastic clay body must be carefully kneaded before it is pressed into the mold. While still soft, clean off surplus material and smooth the back with a straight edge, then remove from the mold. Before the mass hardens, pierce the eye for the chain. Leave the piece to dry out thoroughly in the air, and when it is bone-dry, put it in the kiln for firing.

Methods of glazing ceramic articles and decorating them with engobe are described in Chapter 10.

pieces of wood, firmly bound with string, to give the necessary stability. No other structure will have the strength to stand up against the weight of the liquid plaster. Cardboard is not a suitable material for making the outer retaining walls.

We now have a rudimentary tank in which the model lies face upwards. An area of the

Decorative pins—enameling

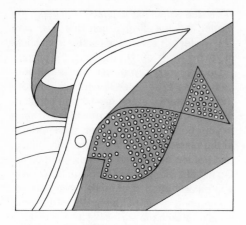

A decorative pin. The form is outlined with the punch, then cut out with snips.

The same process of obtaining a cast from a mold prepared from a wax model can be used for making wall plaques and badges of every description.

Brooches and scarf pins

The list of personal ornaments we can produce in our craft workshop is still not exhausted. In addition to pierced buckles and pendants, wire chains and bracelets, we can also turn out brooches and scarf pins made of sheet metal. Our experiments with the jeweler's saw have already indicated one of the means by which such ornaments can be made. If we wish our pierced brooches to arch in the manner of a shield or breastplate, we must first hollow out the metal from the back, employing the method described in Chapter 6. Be careful not to get the metal too thin. First, trace the design with carbon paper, as described above, and fix the outlines with a sharp scriber, working on the back of the metal to avoid difficulties when piercing. The curved brooch will not saw well unless it is held

upside-down, that is, with the bulge downwards. The saw blade must always be held perpendicular to the work, which is best sawn over a V-block or bench pin.

In the chapter on "Metals under the Hammer," we discussed the techniques of stamping and chasing. The skilled and resourceful brooch-maker can combine both these processes with saw-piercing to achieve some very interesting results.

Stamping and chasing, however, can be used independently of saw-piercing, starting with either a flat or a curved blank. Geometrical patterns, figures, and foliage can all be reproduced with chasing tools. A butterfly, beetle or lizard makes a simple, but striking design. The figure thus outlined can then be cut out with the snips.

This is not a difficult process, and some very satisfactory examples of chased work have been produced by amateur craftsmen. It should be borne in mind that hard, thin sheet metal is only good for low relief. Stamping and chasing require thick, soft metal with a high coefficient of expansion, since such material will tolerate a high degree of deformation.

The simplest and safest method of attaching a brooch to clothing is by means of a pin soldered to the back of the ornament. When designing a pierced brooch, be careful to leave sufficient metal on the back for soldering on the joint and catch. Brooches are quickly rendered worthless by clumsy joints, poor catches, and weak pins. These details deserve as much attention as the ornament itself.

Enameling

The desire to enrich the coloring of our ornaments brings us to one of the most ancient of all the decorative arts: enameling. This craft calls for a combination of artistry in metals, graphic skill and a keen sense of color.

Enameling has certain features in common with the glazing of pottery, since it consists in the application of vitreous glazes to a metal surface by fusion.

For our present purposes the most suitable metallic bases for our enamels will be silver or a red brass (copper base zinc alloy containing not more than 10 percent zinc) or, best of all, pure copper. Yellow brass makes a poor base for enamels. Although we are chiefly interested in making small pieces, such as brooches, clasps, buckles, scarf pins, rings and cuff links, we should not be misled into using excessively thin metal. Metal to be enameled on one side only must as a rule be at least $1/_{32}$" thick. If for some good reason thinner metal has to be enameled, a protective counter enamel must first be fused over the back of the material to prevent it from warping.

All metal surfaces intended for enameling must undergo a thorough preliminary surface treatment. Copper must be lightly annealed, then vigorously scoured under water with a wire brush. It should then be pickled in a 10 percent solution of sulfuric acid, boiled in clean water, and dried in sawdust. The greatest care must be taken to remove every trace of oil or grease before firing, otherwise a firing flaw will result. Even a fingerprint will ruin the surface. Absolute cleanliness is the "golden rule" of enameling, which in other respects seems to depend upon almost magical skills, especially at that breathtaking moment when the brilliant colors spring into life during firing.

Alloys of silver—refined silver does not tolerate enamel—must be annealed, then boiled in a 10 percent solution of sulfuric acid. The boiling must be done in a well-covered glass vessel or enameled crucible

in a room with good ventilation, as the vapors are not exactly healthy.

The basic constituent of vitreous enamels is a colorless flux consisting of quartz, feldspar, and borax. Enamels are classified as transparent, translucent or opaque. The beautiful color effects and opacity are obtained by adding various metallic oxides and opacifiers. Enamel is supplied in solid sticks, which must be wrapped in a piece of linen and broken up with a mallet. The

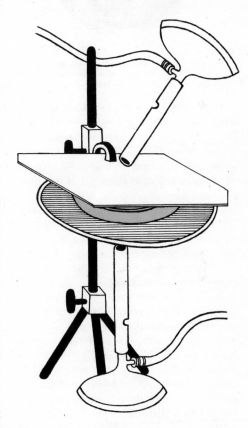

Firing enamels between open flames. Two bunsen burners will supply the necessary heat. The enamel is protected from the direct action of the upper bunsen flame by means of a metal sheet.

Typical of surface enameling is the interpenetration of the individual colors during firing. A sharp dividing line between adjacent colors is not possible.

obtained by continuous experiment. Research into the many problems associated with enamel colors can be both fascinating and rewarding, but it is necessarily laborious and risky and is best left to craftsmen with some experience in enameling techniques.

The beginner should concentrate upon opaque enamels which are easier to handle. More of the transparent enamels react with the metallic surface when fired, a process by which they are more or less radically changed. In such cases it is necessary to apply and fire a base of colorless enamel or flux before the actual colors are laid on. Silver, which is ideal for transparent enamels thanks to its bright surface, is particularly prone to color changes as a result of chemical reactions. Silver must therefore be given a special protective coating of silver flux or "fondant" before the colors are applied.

The flux must be ground with the greatest possible care into the finest possible powder. It is then dusted through a close-meshed sieve directly onto the surface of the

chips must then be ground down to a fine paste: place them in a mortar, add water, and grind the mix to a paste with a porcelain pestle. When the paste has been ground sufficiently fine and smooth, wash it very carefully by repeated rinsing until it is quite clear and free from dirt. Finish the cleansing process with two washes in distilled water. Then, take a glass spatula and carefully transfer the paste to a small flat dish. Each color must be kept in a separate dish.

The wet enamel may be flowed onto the prepared metal surface in a thin, uniform coat, using a short, flat brush or a special applicator. By this method bands of various colors can be laid on side by side. Another enameling technique is to produce a speckled appearance by applying a fine-grained ground and spraying this lightly with a coarser enamel. On firing, the coarser grains fuse into the finer ground and stand out as tiny islands of brilliant color.

There is no simple way of mixing enamel colors. Intermediate tones are obtained by repeatedly fusing one glaze on top of another, and the necessary skill is only

Cloisonné work combines the pictorial element of color with the graphic element of cellular structure.

metal. Colored enamels can only be dusted onto fairly large, flat surfaces. Always brush the metal with tragacanth solution or quince mucilage to bind the powder. This is also advisable when the enamel is applied wet, particularly on any steeply sloping surface. If no binder is applied, there will always be a risk that when the powder dries it will chip at the edges and flake away. Do not attempt to lighten your work by mixing the enamel powder with the binder. After applying wet enamel, tap the edges of the work gently. The powder will then settle, and the moisture will rise to the surface where it can be removed with strips of filter paper.

When the enamel is perfectly dry, it can be fired. Move the pieces only with the greatest care and without the slightest vibration, since the enamel is still in the form of a dust-dry powder, unless, of course, a coating of binder has been applied.

The article is fired quickly at a high temperature (950°), preferably in an electric muffle furnace. If no such furnace is available, the open flames of two bunsen burners will give the intense heat required. One burner, placed under a tripod, supplies heat from below, while the other, held in the hand, is directed at the top of the work, which rests on an asbestos mat and is shielded from the direct flame of the upper burner by a square of sheet metal, mounted in a clamp. If a shield of this kind is not provided, the work will be scorched by the flame and the colors spoiled. If an enamel is, also used on the back, the piece can be supported on a sheet of mica which is easily detached from the enamel after firing and leaves few traces on the work.

When the work glows a bright red and the enamel appears to have a mirror polish, the firing process is complete. Turn off the bunsen burners and allow the work to cool, slowly and naturally.

This method of firing between open flames has the great advantage that the entire process can be closely observed, so that we can see the featureless enamel powder fuse and become completely transformed into a brilliantly colored flux. It is even possible to improve the surface of the work by using a small steel rod to smooth over any faulty patches or to remove surplus enamel. Extraordinary color effects can also be achieved at this stage by dropping minute particles of enamel on to the hot, plastic surface of the melt.

A perfectly satisfactory surface may well be obtained after only one firing, but it is also possible to add a second coat of glass-clear, colorless flux, and fire the work again, but at a lower temperature, so that the new enamel is not baked into the colored ground beneath. It is not advisable to fire too often —four firings are permissible, but there is a risk of damaging the work. It is better to obtain a fine surface by polishing—a somewhat troublesome job, but a rewarding one. First, grind down the surface with water and carborundum of different grades, starting with a coarse stone and finishing with a fine one. Grinding dulls the surface, but a pleasing mat finish can be restored by working with hot wax and tissue paper. If you require a mirror surface, continue with pumice and a block of moist lindenwood, and finish with a colorless polish applied on a chammy leather. These, however, are refinements; they are rather troublesome, and not everyone will wish to undertake them.

One highly specialized branch of enameling is called cloisonné. When handled with taste, this technique produces the most exquisite ornamental work. In a simplified form, this highly refined craft can be practiced even by the amateur, though he should not attempt it until he has acquired some dexterity and practical experience.

Cloisonné enameling

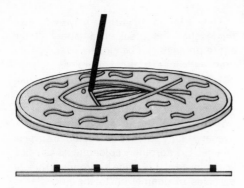

Preparation of the base to receive the enamel. The pieces of wire, stuck on with tragacanth, are pressed into the flux while it is still soft and then the work is refired.

When enamels are simply painted over a metal surface the bands of color merge and blend; there is no sharp line of demarcation between the different zones. In the case of cloisonnè enamels, however, the areas of color are completely separated by walls of rectangular wire, soldered to a base of the same metal. The variously shaped cells thus formed are carefully filled with colored enamels as required by the design. The piece is then fired in the usual way.

Geometrical patterns and mythological or natural figures can all be formed in wire. The best cloisonné enameling combines the advantages of beautiful color effects with those of strong, simple drawing.

Modern enamelers sometimes build up a cloisonné design not by soldering to the metal surface, but on a bed of flux, to which the cell walls are fixed with tragacanth. As soon as the flux begins to soften in the muffle furnace, the wire walls sink into the melt. The work is quickly withdrawn, and the wire is tapped down into the flux with an iron rod, until it rests firmly on the metal at all points. When the work has cooled, the cells are filled with enamel, and the object is returned to the furnace for the final firing.

At this stage it is more important than ever that the surface be carefully protected

Typical of cloisonné work is the rigid separation of the colors by means of pieces of rectangular wire. The wet enamel is introduced into the cells with a short flat brush or a spatula.

from dust and dirt, since the slightest impurity will ruin the enamel. If such an accident should occur, remove the spoilt enamel, fill the cell with new paste, and start again.

Firing is the really creative part of the enameling process. It is in firing that the enameler gives his work colors of a purity and brilliance that can scarcely be approached by any other art. Not every firing is satisfactory, but every attempt is an adventure that may lead to a most gratifying success.

Damascene work

We conclude this section on hand-made jewelry with a description of damascening, in which metal is inlaid in much the same way as wood. Damascene work is a form of decoration in which practical use is made of the fact that one metal differs from another in color and hardness. The object is to decorate the surface of a sheet of hard metal by incising a linear design, chiseling out the lines, and hammering a softer metal into the resulting grooves. Thus, silver wire or narrow strips of aluminum foil may be beaten into grooves formed in a plate of steel or brass to create a predetermined pattern flush with the surface of the darker metal.

Admittedly, this is not a craft that can be quickly mastered, but its demands are not higher than those of other crafts in which a reasonably skilful worker can turn out some

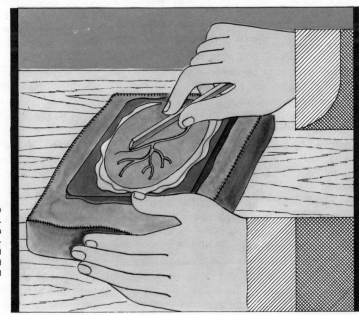

Damascening. Engraving the metal base with a scorper. The work is cemented to a block of steel which is supported on a leather bag filled with sand. This bag is rotated with the left hand to control the direction of the cut.

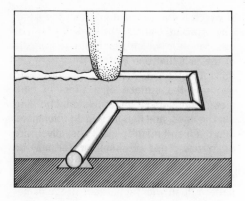

Damascening. The inlay wire is driven into a dovetailed groove cut in the base.

over the lines with a scriber. Now take a scorper, or broad graving tool, and cut a groove in the plate, still following the design, to receive the inlay wire. The graving tool must be carefully ground and sharpened. Do not try to remove the full depth with your first cut: cut away the metal in small chips and deepen the groove very gradually. If you possess a multi-purpose power tool with metal-cutting attachments, it will greatly lighten the preliminary work. Be careful to obtain a groove with clean edges, since this will determine the sharpness of the finished design.

The inlay is bonded to the base by mechanical means: if the bottom of the groove is made wider than the top, the soft metal, once driven home, will not spring loose. Patience and concentration are necessary to obtain a neat dovetail.

astonishingly good work. If you have some experience with a graving tool or scorper, you will be able, with patience, to develop a technique capable of yielding some very acceptable examples of damascened work on buckles and badges. The field will widen as you acquire more skill in the art.

The metal of the base must always be harder than that which is inlaid. It should also be as dark in color as possible, so that the sharpest possible contrast can be obtained. Steel, bronze, brass and copper are all suitable in this respect. It is possible, though not essential, to darken the base artificially. Iron in particular, is greatly improved by being darkened: the metal is coated with oil, which is then burnt away, the process being repeated till the desired tone is obtained. The inlay metal may be soft aluminum or silver wire. After mastering the technique you may also use the more expensive gold. Gold looks especially handsome against a background of dark iron.

Let us take as an example an elaborately flourished capital letter or monogram. First, draw the design on the metal in pencil, working with great accuracy, and then go

One of the problems facing the beginner is to choose a suitable support on which to work. This support has to be very stable, yet it must also be movable, because the direction of the cut is changed by moving the work, not by altering the direction of the tool. A large leather bag filled with sand makes an ideal support, as it can be effectively steadied and turned with the left hand, while holding the tool in the right. Small, intricate work can be cemented to a handy block of steel.

To hammer in the inlay wire, lay the work on a block of end-grain wood. Take a flat-nosed punch, and drive the wire, a section at a time, into the groove, until it is firmly wedged in place. This hammering must be done carefully so as to avoid stresses and spring forces that might cause the wire to jump out of its bed. The holding power of the groove can be improved by roughening the bottom with oblique chisel cuts, which bite into the soft metal inlay. When the hammering is finished, remove any surplus metal with a scraper or file, until the soft metal is flush with the main surface. Now grind and polish, and your work is done.

Damascening is a typical old-fashioned craft in the sense that it is anything but rational. The technical problems are of a kind that a skilful craftsman can master reasonably quickly. The materials are cheap and easily obtained. But time, patience and application are required in unusual abundance. Is the effort worth while? Yes, because any piece of work undertaken for its own sake, and not merely for material gain, brings its own reward: the satisfaction derived from a job that is thought out with care, executed with patience, and completed according to plan.

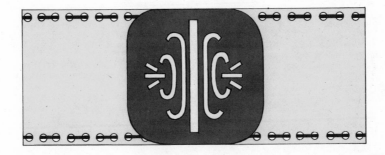

In this belt buckle, which illustrates the possibilities of damascene work, the silver inlay stands out brightly against the darkened iron background.

MORE SCOPE FOR PLAY

A profound meaning lies behind the games of children. This, it is true, is a platitude, and over the years many wise and searching books have been devoted to tracking this meaning down. The experts still tend to differ, but they are almost all agreed on one point, that amongst other things the purpose of games is to prepare the child for the more serious pursuits of later life.

The jay, from some purely unconscious urge, busily buries acorns in the earth and through this "senseless" activity makes possible the thoroughly useful growth of whole

223

forests. Just as the jay is completely unaware of the usefulness of his actions, the child too fails to recognize the purpose of his playing. He never stops for a moment to inquire whether what he is doing has a goal or is in any way useful, but is only interested in whether it brings pleasure and fun. For this is the only important thing for the child.

And yet play serves a purpose beyond his childish interests. Just like the acorn-burying of the jay. But this may not be recognized until much later, when he has grown into a man and been lured away from the playfulness of his youth by the mistaken doctrine that only those things which are won with sweat and tears are worth while. One day, however, perhaps only when he is very old, he will realize that in spite of all his material successes his life has remained basically desolate and empty. Perhaps he will even recognize the reason why his life did not satisfy him: because he did not leave any room in his busy existence for "frivolous" distractions and "idle" pleasures.

Like many others who have been taught in early youth to regard games as a useless waste of time, this man has missed one of the essential elements of a full life. The following chapters, devoted to play and playthings, aim at giving greater scope to the spirit of gaiety and fun.

THE DOLL'S HOUSE ARCHITECT 14

There is no getting away from it: there is a serious housing shortage in the world of dolls. To the doll family, too, a home of one's own means more than life in a cardboard box. So it is a really worth while task to launch out as a small-scale building contractor and, say at Christmas time, build a three-room luxury doll's house. The tools we already have, and the materials are inexpensive. The cost bears no relation to the pleasure which the work will bring us and the pride of possession which the shining new house will arouse.

All house construction begins with a plan. Before the masons and carpenters are sent to the site, we must assume the role of an architect, make a rough sketch of the project, and then prepare our working drawings. These will show the building in plan and elevation, as well as all the principal dimensions. Drawings of this kind are best made on graph paper. After the plans have been drawn, prepare a complete list of materials, so that everything will be there when the foundations are chiseled out and there will be no delays.

Being up-to-date people, we shall erect our doll's house from prefabricated plywood components using "stressed-skin" construction. Hardboard is an alternative, but more expensive material. The methods remain the same, except that the toughness of hardboard makes the work more difficult to carry out.

The client wants a single-story, three-room ranch house with entrance hall, hip roof, and removable front wall. The roof should also be removable, for this house should be no mere ornament that is only pretty to look at—the mother of the dolls will want to be able to supervise the proceedings. Consequently, there must be easy access for the hands, and the front wall must remain open during the game so that we can watch what is happening inside.

Naturally the dimensions and sizes which follow are in no way binding. They are intended primarily as a practical example and can be altered according to the wishes of the individual, and, in particular, according to the space available in the home. But to one thing the doll's house architect must

Drawings and materials

pay particular attention, namely always to maintain harmonious proportions.

Our model house has a ground plan of 24″ x 15″ with a wall height of $7\frac{1}{2}″$. The height of the roof from the eaves to the ridge is 5″, the length of the ridge 13″. The outer walls are built of plywood $\frac{1}{4}″$ thick, while $\frac{3}{16}″$ is sufficient for the interior partitions. An unnecessarily heavy roof should be avoided; $\frac{1}{8}″$ plywood is sufficient. Window and door frames are made of the same material. To brace the free-spanning roof we shall need stiffeners measuring 1″ x $1\frac{1}{4}″$. Only the ridge beam requires a heavier cross section, namely $\frac{7}{8}″$ x $2\frac{1}{2}″$.

A very important part of the structure is the foundation, for which we shall use a $\frac{3}{8}″$ thick baseboard measuring 26″ x 17″. For this, too, simple plywood would be sufficient. However, since we are building a luxury home with a superior "parquet floor," we shall plump for a sheet of fine hardboard. The final item in our list of materials is a length of half-inch molding which will serve to decorate the base of the walls and the eaves. Both upper and lower moldings will run all around the house, a total distance of 78″. At the corners the molding is mitered; this means that we must add twice the thickness of the molding on each side. The total length of molding required will thus be $(2 \times 78) + (2 \times 2) = 160″$, and we can give our materials supplier quite a respectable order. The molding need not necessarily be a fancy one; a simple quarter round will do.

To the end of our list of materials we should add a few sheets of tile paper and imitation brickwork. If stucco is preferred a bag of plaster and some joiner's glue will be required. Finally, we shall need a quantity of small $\frac{3}{8}″$ and $\frac{3}{4}″$ flush-head wood screws, thin wire nails, and glue. The majority of these items will be a permanent part of our workshop supplies. For assembling the parts use a quick-setting cold glue instead of the less practical joiner's glue. Since we are general contractors for the entire project, we will also have to provide window glass and a few scraps of wallpaper.

On the Site

When all our materials have been assembled, we can give some thought to the specifications. Measurements should be accurate and tools sharp. Nails should only be used where the material is too thin for wood screws. All building components should be rubbed smooth with fine sandpaper before being assembled. All surfaces to be glued should be carefully planed. Glue is not cement, and rough joints will not hold. The combined use of screws and glue at points of special stress is not a sign of pessimism. With these admonitions in mind we can set to work.

Begin by drawing an accurate plan of the building, showing the various wall thicknesses and all the door openings, directly on the foundation board. Give all the different building components reference numbers. The foundation board is designed to extend one inch beyond the "brickwork" on all sides, thus leaving sufficient room for the base molding.

The windows and doors of our model house should have the following dimensions: inside doors 3″ x 5″, front door $3\frac{1}{4}″$ x $5\frac{1}{4}″$. Inside dimensions of window openings in the living rooms 3″ x $5\frac{1}{2}″$, in the kitchen 2″ x 3″. Width of door frame $\frac{1}{4}″$. Width of window frame $\frac{3}{16}″$.

Begin construction by cutting out all the walls in plywood. At the same time cut the molding into the required lengths. Use a handsaw, not a fret saw. The latter will not be needed until we have to cut out the win-

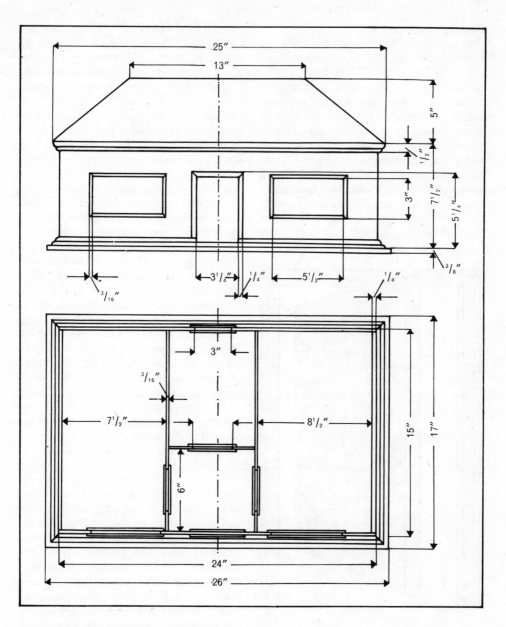

The working drawings for a doll's house include a plan and an elevation showing all the necessary dimensions.

dow and door openings.

In cutting out the outside walls, allow, on the one hand, for the corner joints and, on the other, for the removable front wall, in accordance with the original plan. For the corners a simple butt joint is generally sufficient, the front and back walls overlapping the ends of the side walls. Only in this way can we achieve a simple solution to the problem of constructing a removable façade. A simple butt joint with the front walls overlapping the sides calls for a reduction in the side wall dimensions equal to twice the thickness of the material. In the finished building the side wall is 15" long.

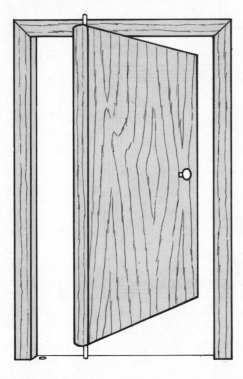

Swing door with socket hinges. The pins in the door engage in corresponding holes drilled in the door frame and the foundation board.

Given $1/4$" thick material, the length required comes to $14^1/_2$". Those who feel that merely butting the walls at the corners is too clumsy, can dovetail them. However, in this case they will have to cut the side walls $1/4$" longer. The original length of 15" is not required, since in any case the front wall can not be dovetailed. Those who have not yet completely mastered the art of dovetailing should not tackle the full length of $7^1/_2$" at their first attempt.

All the building components are now marked with their respective reference numbers, corresponding to the numbers on the foundation board, before the openings in the walls are sawn out. On account of the sharp angles it will be necessary to work with a fret saw. Special care must be taken with the doorways, since we shall not throw the pieces away but convert them into doors.

The doors are all designed as swing doors, since the hinges can then be made very simply on the socket principle. So that the door can swing easily in its frame, round off its inside edge with a rasp and sandpaper. At the center of the corresponding circle hammer a thin round-shanked wire nail into the top and bottom edges of the door. Nip off the nail to leave a stub $3/_{16}$" long and file the end perfectly smooth. It is on these nails that the door will pivot. Corresponding sockets are bored in the door frame above and in the foundation board below. The correct position for the drill is marked by lightly pressing the ends of the nails into the wood. However, it is extremely difficult to get at the top of the door frame with a drill. Instead we must burn in the socket with a hot nail. But there is scarcely enough room even for a slim nail unless the shank is bent at right angles. It is a mistake to suppose that a sharp nail burns better than a blunt one. The fine point loses heat much too quickly, and in conse-

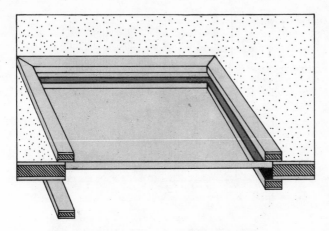

Two window frames glued to the wall hold the window pane in place. The difference in thickness between the glass and the wall is made up with putty or strips of cardboard.

quence the nail does not penetrate deeply, but tends to burn an unnecessarily large hole. Therefore, nip off the point of the nail before burning the socket.

Because of the miniature scale we must give up the idea of a proper door latch. We shall merely add false door knobs in the form of small round-headed brass nails, leaving the door free to swing on both sides.

Continue the carpentry work by cutting out the door and window frames. Of course it is easier to saw these parts in one piece from $1/8''$ plywood than to glue them together from separate strips, but, naturally, this will use up much more material. If you do decide to build the frames from separate parts, miter the corners. It looks better.

The number of door and window frames should be double the number of wall openings, since each door and window requires both an inside and an outside frame. Between these two frames the glazier will later install the window pane. To form the necessary glazing rabbet, make the inside dimensions of the frame, both horizontally and

vertically, $3/16''$ less than the dimensions of the wall openings. This will provide a narrow stop when the frames are glued on.

Glaze with ordinary window glass, normally about $1/10''$ thick. This should be cut accurately to the size of the wall openings and inserted against the stop formed by the outside frame. Later the pane will be held in position by both the inside and the outside frames acting together. Unfortunately, since the outside wall is built of $1/4''$ plywood, there will be a certain gap between the pane and the frames. This must be filled. The realist will feel obliged to do this with putty; a more inventive solution is to fill the gap with glued-in strips of cardboard, and so stop the panes from rattling. But one way or the other, the packing should always be done from the inside of the house.

Unlike the full-scale builder, we must start thinking about the interior decoration of the dolls' house even at this stage. Thus the glazing must be preceded by the paper-hanging and painting. Doors and door and window frames should be painted with at

Walls

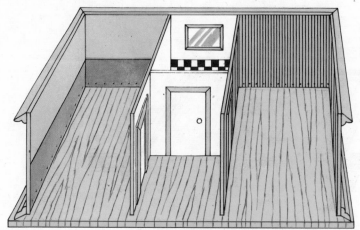

Erecting the prefabricated outside walls and partitions on the foundation board. The front wall of the house is not a permanent part of the structure.

least two coats of white enamel. But never paint surfaces that will later be glued. The moldings can also be given a coat of enamel, either white or gray. While the paint is drying, paper the walls, as far as possible with a continuous strip of wallpaper. After papering, the wall openings can be cut out individually with a sharp knife. Any good paste which does not dry too quickly is suitable. It is important to wet the strips of wallpaper sufficiently before applying them. Paper all the inside walls immediately on both sides, so that they do not warp. The outer walls are also in danger of warping, but the thicker material enables us to wait until the house is assembled before gluing on the outer skin. However, this only holds true if construction moves ahead quickly. Should the work be left for a few days for any reason, we must apply a counter stress to the outside walls by immediately gluing on thin wrapping paper.

When the paperhanger has completed his work, it is time for the glazier to put in the window panes, and for the carpenter to glue the door and window frames to the walls. Now at last the walls are ready for assembling. All the joints should be glued and then screwed. To ensure quality and durability, make use of thin wire nails only in the joints between inside partitions and between partitions and foundation board. And if you must use nails, do not use unnecessarily long ones. A nail is always long enough if two-thirds of the shank goes through into the second piece of wood.

Construction of the house begins with the erection of the outside walls and the simultaneous joining of the corners. The front wall should remain loose; fasten it provisionally to the edges of the side walls with two thin nails. Before putting in the interior partitions, install the base molding, since the partitions would obstruct the nailing. The molding sits against the outside wall, but besides being glued it is given an additional nailing from the inside. Then it is screwed to the foundation board with wood screws. This molding, which runs all around the house, is not mere ornamentation, but serves primarily to stabilize the walls.

As we have said, the base molding must be secured, before the partitions are erected. Before the molding is attached, however, we must give the outside walls their final appearance. If the client has asked for a brick veneer, we shall glue on imitation brickwork with a paper backing. A careful builder will first cover the corners of the house with strips of linen. This will help to prevent the brickwork paper from fraying. If the client has specified a stucco finish, the walls should have been covered during the paperhanging process with a light wrapping paper to which the stucco is now applied. The glue, prepared in advance, is heated

(not boiled!) in a water-bath and diluted to a thin paste. Sprinkle the dry plaster slowly over the surface of the paste and stir well. As soon as the mix has reached the consistency of thick cream, our stucco is ready. Dab it onto the walls with a short, hardbristle brush. The more often the application is repeated the rougher the plaster becomes. Once it is well dried, it can even be painted over, if a colored surface is desired. Through all this, the parts of the wall to which the molding is to be fixed are left unplastered.

At the front door, the base molding is cut back to leave a $^3/_{16}$" high doorstep. Saw it from above to the width of the doorway with

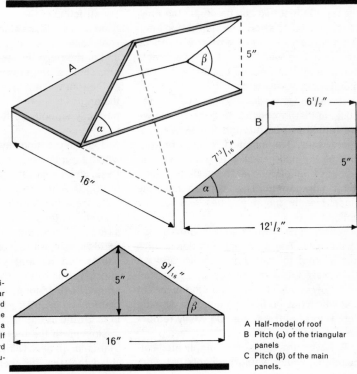

Roof construction. The dimensions of the triangular panels of the hipped roof and the angle they form with the base can be taken from a reduced-scale model of half the roof made of cardboard or determined from an accurate drawing.

A Half-model of roof
B Pitch (α) of the triangular panels
C Pitch (β) of the main panels.

a fine saw and remove the superfluous wood with a chisel. This will provide a stop for the door, which opens inwards, and by attaching a small catch over the door frame we can give it a thiefproof lock before putting on the roof. Like the base molding, the eaves molding is fastened to the outside walls with the upper edges flush. The only exception is the front wall. Here we must take great care to obtain very solid corner joints between front and side molding, since these alone support the weight of the front molding, which serves to hold the front wall in position when the house is closed. At the bottom the front wall is held by the base molding. To remove the front wall, push it up far enough to clear the base molding, and then pull it downwards to release it from the molding at the top. So that this can be done smoothly, the side molding should be slightly too long. A small space between the front wall and the front molding will not hurt. A very stable corner joint is a mitered corner with a thin glued-in plywood spline.

The attentive reader will not have failed to observe that in constructing the house we are forced to nail through the already papered walls. The simplest method of concealing the nail heads is to glue matching pieces of wallpaper over them. Do the same thing in the corners. This is quite acceptable since cleanly glued patches will not be noticed.

We can now move on to the construction of the roof. The architect has designed a hipped roof for our doll's house, and we shall make this a self-supporting structure in $1/8''$ plywood. The roof is an independent unit which has no fixed connection with the "brickwork" since it must be easily removable at all times.

To save ourselves some complicated calculations, which would probably not work out anyway, we can make a cardboard model

of half the roof, cut in two lengthways, to a scale of 1:2. From this we can take all the measurements needed to build the actual roof. A substitute for a cardboard model is an accurate scale drawing. From this we can work out not only the slope of the roof surfaces, but also the width of the two main panels and the gables. The top edge of the trapezoidal main panels is the same length as the ridge (13″). The lengths of the lower edges of the roof panels depend on the dimensions of the base over which the roof is constructed. These are equal to the dimensions of the floor plan plus the width of the molding, in our case 25″ x 16″. When the house is closed, this base also forms the ceiling.

As far as possible avoid using nails in the construction of the roof. The joints are best fixed with a reliable glue. The joints between roof panels and the base, along the hips, and at the ridge are reinforced with stiffeners. These stiffeners must be accurately cut or the roof will not be stable. Not only must the angles be correct but the faces must be perfectly smooth so that the joints can be firmly glued.

Begin by erecting the two main roof panels which form an angle of 32 degrees with the base, and meet at an angle of 116 degrees at the ridge. This means that our ridge beam will have to measure $2^1/_2''$ x $^7/_8''$, to enable us to form a satisfactory joint. The plan shows a ridge 13″ long, but if you cut a ridge beam of this length, without taking the slope of the gables into account, you will find it is too short. In its rough state the ridge beam should be $13^7/_8''$ long, so that there is enough material on each side to form sloping bearings for the triangular gable ends.

Closing off the roof structure with these triangular panels will be no problem, provided that the stiffeners at eaves and hip have been correctly shaped and firmly glued to the section already completed.

The joint at the ridge requires some care. Simply allowing the $1/8''$ panels to lean against each other at an acute angle is not a satisfactory solution. It is necessary to sand a bevel equal to half the ridge angle on the abutting edges of the two panels. Similarly, the bottom edges of the roof panels, which rest on the horizontal base, must be sanded down to an angle equal to the full pitch of the roof. This can be done very simply by placing the roof on a sheet of sandpaper and rubbing until the correct angle is automatically obtained. The gable triangles can be laid flat against the open ends of the hipped roof. Any slight unevenness is smoothed away with rasp and sandpaper after gluing.

In preparing the individual roof panels, we must not forget that they will later be subjected to a pull exerted by the tile paper glued on the outside. We can counteract the one-sided tension by sticking an equally strong paper to the inside of the panels. In doing so, however, remember not to paper the edges to which the stiffeners are glued. For the sake of greater stability, glue $3/4''$ strips of linen over the ridge and hip-joints, before covering the roof surfaces with imitation tiling.

The roof is now complete, except that it still lacks something to give it a firm seat on the "masonry" walls. A few scraps of the material used for the outer walls will certainly be left over, at least the material from the window openings. This will be sufficient to make four blocks $1/4''$ thick in the shape of right-angled triangles. These are glued to the base of the roof in such a way that when the roof is placed in position they fit tightly inside the four corners of the house and so prevent the roof from slipping sideways. If your measurements have been accurate, the correct position of the corner blocks will lie at the points of intersection of four lines

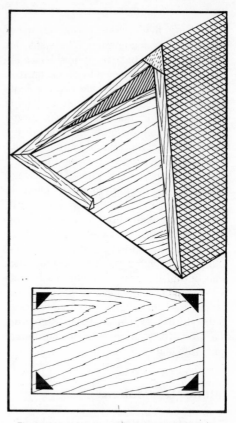

The joints between the roof panels and the base (or ceiling) are reinforced by gluing in stiffeners. Below: position of the corner blocks on the underside of the base. They prevent the roof from slipping sideways.

drawn parallel to the edges of the base and $3/4''$ in (= thickness of wall + width of molding).

If the construction of this luxury doll's house seems too complicated, it is possible to arrive at a simpler structure by replacing the pitched roof with a flat one, in the form of a $1/4''$ thick plywood panel. A flat roof of this kind can be attached to the rear wall of the house with piano hinges, so that when not in use the doll's house will perform the prosaic, but very practical function of a toy box.

Doll's furniture

Finishing the interior leaves plenty of scope for the imagination. The walls, for example, have no base moldings. This state of affairs can be remedied by gluing narrow, ready painted strips of wood into the angle between walls and floor. A mitered joint is only required in the rear corners of the rooms. The connection at the ends of the removable front wall should be a simple butt joint. The windows also offer the skilful decorator many opportunities. The plywood valances, like the curtains, are glued in place. Sewing the curtains is woman's work. Finally, a hardboard floor may not be colorful enough. If so, a gaily patterned vinyl floor can be assembled from odd pieces of tile. Cut the tiles with a fret saw, and lay them with one of the special adhesives for use with plastic tile. The base strips, of course, are not fixed until after the tile floor has been laid. If you decide in favor of a vinyl floor from the start, you can replace the hardboard base with simple plywood.

Interior Decoration

In most people the construction of a doll's house starts a chain reaction of further ambitions. This is understandable, for what is the use of a beautiful home without furniture? Accordingly, we shall now move from the building site to the furniture workshop.

This is an easy move, since the materials with which we work are the same, plywood and plastic. For doll's house furniture thicknesses of $1/8$" and $3/16$" will be sufficient. In addition, we shall need some strips of solid wood (cigar-box wood), upholstery material in the form of wadding, cotton wool and remnants, and for contemporary "hygienic" furniture, a few sheets of colored contact paper in suitable (small) patterns. A good all-purpose glue will solve all our joining problems.

This is not the place to give lessons on style or a comprehensive review of furniture from the Baroque to the present day. In order not to get out of our depth we must limit ourselves to dealing with the fundamental principles of furniture construction. The discovery of form and new designs must be left to the imagination and taste of the individual. Since the technical side of building dolls' furniture presents absolutely no problems, the great charm of this pastime lies principally in the free expression of the powers of invention and in the development of original designs. The fact that the objects are so small permits us the luxury of being able to work from full-scale drawings. In the case of difficult pieces, for example, wardrobes or elegant dressing tables with swivel mirrors and several drawers, and especially furniture which is to be "mass-produced," a working drawing is indispensable. But it only serves a purpose if all the dimensions are included. It would, on the other hand, be overdoing things to make a detailed drawing of a simple kitchen table, of which only one was required.

Among the important working rules, which we shall briefly recapitulate, belongs the careful trueing of all glued surfaces. This will ease the burden on our repair facilities, since a glued joint which does not fit tight will not hold.

Components of the same size are produced as far as possible in a single operation. This is not intended to promote laziness, but to ensure a closer fit. For example, to saw several panels or shelves of equal size, glue the necessary number of boards together with temporary joints. Then saw through the whole "layer cake" with a single cut. A temporary joint which can easily be broken is made by gluing a sheet

Model of a single-story doll's house. Its construction is discussed in detail in this chapter.

The construction of simple dolls' furniture. 1 Table legs are sawn out of plywood in pairs. 2 Legs reinforced by means of parallel strips at the top. 3 Three-legged table with a sawn out frame. 4 Frame of bench table with tie. 5 Simple chair, sides all in one piece. 6 Shelf stand with sloping side panels.

of paper between the pieces. A water-soluble glue must be used so that the parts can afterwards be cleaned without difficulty.

When sawing thin plywood and veneers, there is a risk of splintering along the edges of the saw cut, especially when the teeth of the saw are no longer quite sharp. This can be counteracted by sticking a strip of transparent tape over the line of the cut, sawing through the tape, and removing the remains from the finished article.

The safest way to transfer a full-scale drawing to the workpiece is by tracing. If the drawing will not be needed again, glue it directly to the wood and saw along the lines. If possible, the painting, varnishing, staining or veneering of furniture should be carried out before the parts are assembled. Keep the gluing surfaces free of paint! Painting should precede not only assembly, but also upholstering. Glued cotton wool, cut to the size of the upholstered area, serves as padding. Suitable covering fabric will be found in the sewing basket. It is drawn tightly over the padding and glued to the bottom edge of the upholstered surface. Unnecessarily thick fabrics are to be avoided. They merely spoil the shape of the furniture. In upholstering, glue first the long and then the short sides. To keep the upholstery perfectly smooth, take care not to pull the threads of the fabric out of their normal rectangular alignment.

Wobbly furniture is annoying on a miniature, as well as on a human scale. Cure the wobble of dolls' furniture by standing the finished piece on a flat sheet of sandpaper and smoothing all four legs equally with careful circular movements, careful because the legs should not break off under their first load.

In furniture-making it is the legs that give most trouble. This appears most clearly in the case of the table, which in other respects

is the easiest piece of furniture to make. It usually consists of a top, which can be round, square or irregular, and four legs. To attach each leg separately would soon become tiresome. Consequently they are sawn in pairs joined by a common crosspiece for gluing on the top. Even for fairly large tables $^3/_{16}''$ material is sufficient. If the legs are not to stand vertically but to slope outwards, the top of the crosspiece must be beveled. The slope of the legs must be taken into account even in the sawing-out stage. Sloping legs must also have sloping feet, that is, the surfaces on which they stand should be parallel to the table top. First, cut out the pieces with a fret saw, then rub them smooth on a flat sheet of sandpaper. Rough table legs, and other pieces which are subsequently to be finished with file and sandpaper, should not be cut out of wood that is too weak. In the case of very light tables it is sufficient simply to glue the pairs of legs directly to the table top. With larger tables it is advisable to add narrow strips of wood glued on either side of the crosspieces. These strips must be joined to both the top and the legs of the table. This will considerably increase its stability. In the case of three-legged tables, which have the additional advantage that they never wobble, the third leg is also sawn out with a crosspiece. This runs lengthwise under the table and forms a T with the crosspiece joining the other two legs.

Long bench tables have a tie at the bottom mortised into solid legs at each end. Ties of this kind are better made not from plywood, but from pine or cigar-box wood.

In building chairs, again try to follow the construction principle of cutting the legs in pairs out of a single piece of wood, together with the chair back. The seat and back rest are made separately and glued between the two frames. The stability of larger chairs can be improved by gluing wooden strips under the seat on either side.

Shelf stands are carpentered in the same way. Here again the feet are cut out of the side panels. The shelves are supported on ledges.

The bed stands on feet which likewise sprout from the head and foot boards. The base, an $1/8''$ piece of plywood, lies loosely on two ledges glued either to the sides or to the head and foot of the bed. For the frame of the bed use plywood at least $3/16''$ thick. The glued joints between the parts of the frame can be strengthened with thin wire nails. After nailing, the heads of the nails are nipped off so that they do not show. In dimensioning the base remember that it has to be upholstered to form a mattress. Accordingly, sufficient room must be left on all sides, since the upholstery will take up a certain amount of space.

The bed can be turned into a simple couch by making one of the two sides higher to form a low back, and bringing the head and foot boards to the same height. The feet are shortened and the front is carried down to foot level. If a whole club set is to be made with a couch and several armchairs, attention must be paid to the relative proportions of the individual pieces. Normally, a couch should be $2^1/_4$ to $2^1/_2$ times as long as the armchair that goes with it. The upholstery, like that of the mattress, is made in a single piece and placed in the couch frame on two supporting ledges running its full length. The back and sides should be upholstered, if at all, only on the inside; that is to say, only on the inside should the covering fabric be backed with thin padding. On the outside the fabric should be drawn tight and glued to the underside of the base.

This form of couch upholstery is an exception to the rule that upholstering should be done before a piece of furniture is assembled. In this case only the seat can be upholstered beforehand. Before the seat is placed in the couch frame, the covering fabric for back and sides is glued to the corresponding parts of the frame with the edge turned inwards. We then insert the upholstered seat and finish upholstering the other parts. On account of the smallness of the furniture this is a rather tricky job, since it is difficult to avoid creases in the fabric. In covering the edges and outside surfaces it will be necessary to glue the fabric at intermediate points.

A somewhat sturdier couch can be made from $3/16''$ plywood. Saw out two solid side pieces with legs. Cut the seat and back out of the same material and upholster them individually. The seat covering is not carried over the narrow side edges but drawn from the back to the front in the exact width of the seat with ample tucks on each side. The padding is pushed into the pockets thus formed. The covering is then pulled over the front edge of the seat and glued to the underside. In this way the side edges of the seat remain free of upholstery, and can be firmly glued to the sides of the couch. For the sake of comfort, the seat is made to slope slightly towards the rear. The back must be fully upholstered, that is, the fabric must cover the back and sides as well as the front, although again only the inside surface is actually padded. Only the $3/16''$ wide bottom edge of the back is available for securing the fabric. The strength of this joint can be increased by stapling. The back of the couch, again with a slight slope, is now placed between the sides so as to rest firmly on the seat, flush with its rear edge. The covering fabric, which is drawn over the edges of the back, does not give a good gluing surface. We are therefore obliged to take the strain off the glue by driving two thin headless wire nails through each side.

Upholstered furniture for the doll's house. Top: a bed frame can be developed into a simple box couch. Bottom: a semi-upholstered couch and a Swedish couch with webbing and loose cushions.

A more exciting project is a "Swedish" couch made of $^3/_{16}$" plywood and wooden ties. The legs and arms once again form a single unit. Take care to carry the legs far enough to the rear to avoid too rigid an appearance. The front and back legs are connected by round wooden ties about $^1/_8$" in diameter. So as to give the seat a gentle slope to the rear, the rear tie should lie about $^1/_4$" lower than the front one. A third tie of the same thickness runs between the arm rests (fix by means of drilled socket or wire nail). The frame is completed with narrow strips of linen, strung between the ties.

The seat and back rest are moderately padded. Both parts lie loosely in the frame, the back rest standing on the seat upholstery.

To go from couch to upholstered armchair we literally take a "short cut" by simply reducing the width of the seat. The method of building a couch applies equally to the armchair with the single exception that the seat is only made wide enough for one.

When constructing cabinets we must think solely in terms of the surface and the box-shaped space it encloses. If we do this, the problems will solve themselves. The variety of cabinet furniture comes solely from changes in the dimensions and proportions of the box. We have already made a simple set of shelves. If we close off the back, add a cover on top, and hang a door in front, we have a cabinet ready made. This principle remains always the same, whether we are dealing with a long hi-fi cabinet, a cube-shaped night table, or a tall, roomy wardrobe.

The walls of cabinets always rest on the bottom, that is, on the floor of the cabinet. Likewise the top of the cabinet does not fit inside, but lies on top of the wall panels, even if it is made without a projecting rim. The side walls overlap the back wall, covering its usually not very handsome edges. Inside partitions are always made from material considerably thinner than the case itself. The same applies to shelves, which in the bigger models are carried on ledges. The feet of a cupboard may take the form either of square blocks, continuous cross-pieces or a solid, set-back slatted pedestal.

Only the construction of the door requires further thought. We have to choose between one or two-hinged doors and sliding doors. The door hinges are again based on the socket principle. Sockets are formed in the bottom and top of the cabinet. This means that the doors must be mounted before the top is glued on. If this is forgotten, it will be impossible to get the doors into the cupboard. It is clear from the narrowness of the space inside the cupboard that partitions and shelves must be put in before the doors and top are added. These parts are best built into the side walls while the back of the cabinet is also open.

To prevent the doors from swinging inwards when they are closed, glue small stops to the top and bottom of the cabinet. Single doors have a stop on the inside of the left hand wall panel, since they normally open to the right. The night table standing to the left of the bed is an exception. Similar to the single door is the horizontally swinging flap. This has a stop at the top, but also has a linen tape attached to the inside wall on the left or the right to hold the open flap in a horizontal position.

In view of the smallness of our dolls' furniture, we must do without real door catches, and be satisfied with imitation catches, or rather with handles for opening and closing the doors. If the material is thin, these handles will take the form of glued wooden blocks, or, if it is strong enough, small ornamental nails.

In the case of sliding-door cabinets, the

problem of the lock solves itself. This construction is only used for long, low living-room cabinets. Cabinets of this kind require a really deep frame, since the two offset doors, together with the necessary guide rails, take up a lot of room. The two sliding doors must be made wide enough to overlap about $^1/_4$" in the middle when the cabinet is closed. To make the doors slide smoothly, sand the top and bottom edges very carefully and rub them with a candle stump.

The guide rails are two smooth, thin strips of cigar-box wood. Two of these strips are glued, the thickness of the doors apart, to the bottom and two to the top of the cabinet, before it is assembled. The distance between the front strips and the edge of the cabinet is also equal to the thickness of the doors. Do not measure too skimpily, otherwise the doors will later stick. The rear door panel is placed in its groove when the top of the cabinet is glued on. Then lay the cabinet on its back, insert the front door panel and prevent it from falling out by gluing a wooden strip with mitered corners to the front edge of the cabinet frame. This strip, also made of cigar-box wood or a thick veneer, must be slightly wider than the thickness of the frame so that the groove for the door is deep enough. At the same time it helps to emphasize the frame construction of the furniture. Wooden blocks glued to the sliding doors serve as handles: these must be located as far to the right and left as possible, so that they do not interfere with the free movement of the doors.

In conclusion, a word about drawers. It is advisable to mount them only between full side panels, to which the rails can be properly glued. To improve the sliding action, use solid wood rather than plywood for the rails, preferably pine. The drawers themselves are glued together in the form of boxes open at the top, the sides overlapping

the edges of the back. The front, on the other hand, should conceal the edges of the sides to give a better appearance. Glued-on

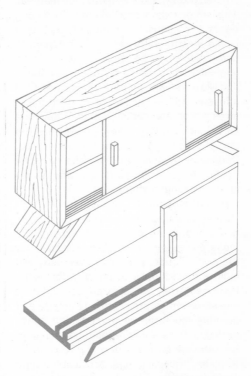

Sliding-door cabinets. Below: arrangement of bottom guide rails. The outside strip is applied to the front edge of the cabinet frame.

wooden blocks make better handles than decorative nails, since the thin wood does not provide enough hold for nails, the projecting ends of which must be cut off on the inside of the drawer.

All the furniture we have described is chiefly made of plywood. No one, however, will seriously claim that a plywood surface is particularly beautiful. If we wish our furniture to be attractive, therefore, we must provide it with a more pleasing finish. This can be done with paint or possibly with contact paper. We can save ourselves all this finishing work by using smooth, brightly colored plastic as our construction material. This is not always possible, but for sliding doors, large panels, and bright table tops it is the ideal material, bringing cleanliness and color into the dolls' home. Plastic laminates can be sawn, chiseled, and drilled just like wood. For gluing, however, a special adhesive will be needed. Many such adhesives are on the market, but all of them are very quick-setting. They grip almost as abruptly as a magnet, and never let go. Consequently, the parts must be correctly positioned from the start; it is impossible to make changes afterwards.

In our account of the methods of constructing dolls' furniture we have deliberately avoided giving precise dimensions. All these pieces of furniture are intended for the doll's house, but since everybody will build a doll's house of the size that suits them best, they will also choose different measurements for the furniture. In size and quantity the furniture must fit the space available. If we superimpose the outline of the furniture on the plan of the room to be furnished, we will quickly arrive at the right measurements.

Miniature Stores

Another interesting construction project, and a thoroughly welcome toy, is the miniature store. The experience gathered in constructing a doll's house will come in handy in this new enterprise, for much that we have learned there can be usefully applied here.

The first glance at the plan has a reassuring effect. We are no longer dealing with a cellular structure, but only with a single room, and even this is only roughly indicated by the walls. All this makes things much simpler.

The base is only slightly larger than the floor space required for the store. In this case a sheet of $^1/_4"$ hardboard measuring 12" x 17" will be quite sufficient. A second sheet of the same thickness measuring $9^5/_8"$ x 17" forms the rear wall. The side wall and shelf on the right and the narrow wall closing off the shelving on the left are made of $^1/_4"$ pine. The shelves and framing on the rear wall are also made of pine of the same thickness. The right hand ends of the shelves, the ends of the low boundary wall on the right and of the shelf attached to it are rounded off to give a more attractive finish. The top corners of the rear wall and the front corners of the base are also rounded.

The actual construction work begins with the preparation of the base. The two long edges are reinforced by gluing on two strips of wood measuring $^3/_8"$ x 1". These serve as feet and increase the stability of the structure. The two front corners of the base are not rounded until the strips have been added. To make the corners the same, cut them around a paper template, the shape of which will also determine the rounding of the top corners of the rear wall.

The rear wall is not placed on top of the base; instead it is glued from behind against the broad surface formed by the base and the reinforcing strip combined. The latter also gives enough depth for the rear wall to be screwed as well. Assembled in this manner, the rear wall forms a screen 9" high at the back of the store.

Before erecting the rear wall, fit it with its set of shelves, since taken in this order the work is much easier. After being cut out, the three long shelves are clamped together, rounded off in a single step, and trimmed to the exact size. The eight identical partitions for the drawers must also be ready before

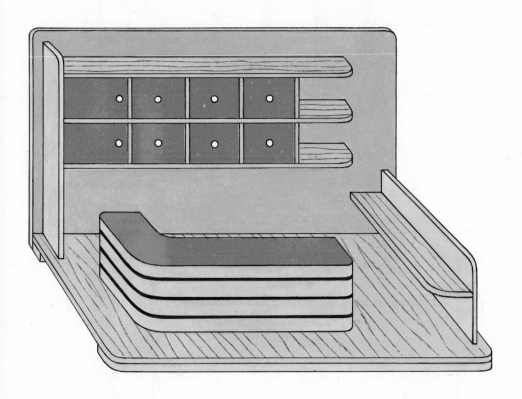

The finished store with freestanding counter. This design is just one of many interesting possibilities.

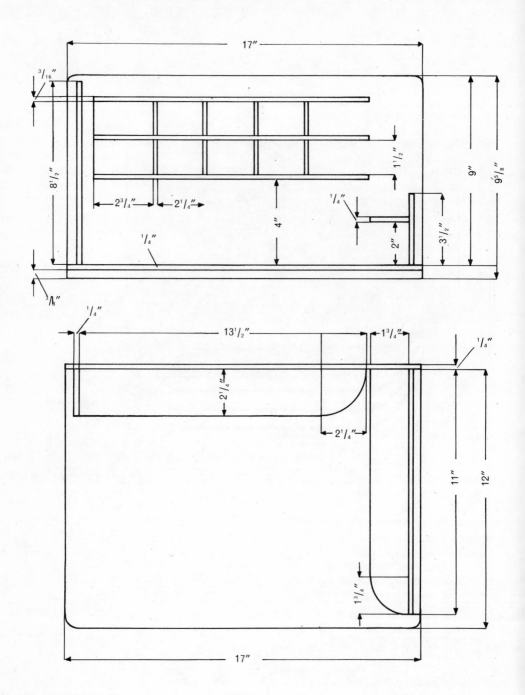

Working drawings for a miniature store. Plan and elevation showing all the necessary dimensions and thicknesses.

we can begin to assemble the frame. The drawers are made slightly narrower and shallower than the clear space between partitions to allow for the necessary freedom of movement within the individual compartments. The two doors, which open to the left, must also be made ready in advance, together with their hinges. The doors are cut out of $\frac{1}{8}''$ plywood. After rounding off the back of each door and driving in the hinge pins, mark off and drill out the corresponding sockets in the shelves.

Now stack the shelves on top of each other again and mark off the exact distances between the eight partition walls on the front edge. Carry these marks across the top faces of the shelves with a try-square. Then fix doorstops $\frac{1}{8}''$ from the front edge of two of the partitions on the left hand side. The assembly of the rear wall can now begin. The shelving starts $\frac{3}{4}''$ in from the left hand edge of the wall. There is 4″ clearance between the bottom shelf and the base, hence it must be glued $4\frac{5}{8}''$ from the bottom edge of the wall panel. Start by fixing this bottom shelf to the wall, and continue by erecting the partitions for the lower row of drawers. Then mount the door in the left hand compartment and close off the lower row with the middle shelf. The upper row of drawers is assembled in precisely the same manner. The large number of glued joints between the shelving and the wall will guarantee a stable structure, provided that the glued surfaces have been properly smoothed. Accordingly, we can spare ourselves the trouble of nailing with a clear conscience. As soon as the shelving is finished, erect the rear wall and close off the doored compartments on the left with the narrow side wall, after rounding off the top edge.

With the erection of the right hand side wall the limits of the floor space are completely defined. Just like the left hand wall, it stands $\frac{1}{2}''$ in from the side of the base and ends one inch short of the front. The joint between this side wall and the rear wall can be strengthened by driving in two flush-head wood screws from the back.

When the $1\frac{3}{4}''$ wide shelf has been glued in the corner between the rear wall and the right hand side wall 2″ above the base, the only part of the wall fittings still missing is the six drawers. Glue these together in accordance with the instructions given earlier in this chapter, using $\frac{1}{8}''$ plywood, and perhaps plastic for the front panel.

We are now left with the most important of the interior fixtures: the counter. A 10″ long, $2\frac{1}{2}''$ wide, and 3″ high counter, with a top projecting $\frac{1}{4}''$ on all sides beyond the enclosing walls, would fully satisfy ordinary requirements. It could be glued together without difficulty and without any special drawings in $\frac{3}{16}''$ plywood, although a brighter effect is obtained by making the top in glossy red or blue plastic instead of in plain wood. If we use the same material and the same color for the counter top and the fronts of the drawers, the whole store will look very stylish.

A simple straight counter might not satisfy the fastidious taste of our future customers. Therefore, we shall give it a somewhat more interesting L-shape with strongly rounded corners. This will harmonize well with the general architecture of the store. This counter, too, should be 3″ high and have an enclosed front and sides, but the top will not project. The long arm of the counter will be 10″ in length, the short arm $5\frac{1}{2}''$. The width of the counter will again be $2\frac{1}{2}''$.

The sides of the counter should be in $\frac{3}{16}''$ material. The plastic top should be cut from a piece measuring $5\frac{1}{2}''$ x 10″. The piece left over can be used to make the fronts of the drawers. A plain plywood top should be $\frac{1}{8}''$

The sales counter

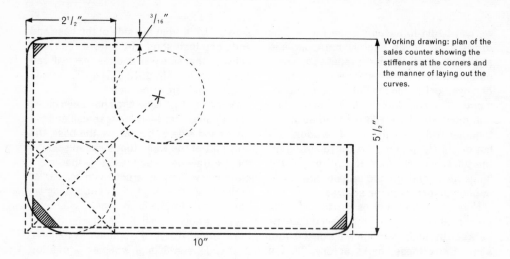

2¹/₂″   ³/₁₆″   5¹/₂″   10″

Working drawing: plan of the sales counter showing the stiffeners at the corners and the manner of laying out the curves.

thick. We shall also need three triangular pieces of wood 3″ long to reinforce the front corners of the counter. $^3/_{16}$″ material is not thick enough for us to form the sharp curves necessary to give the counter its elegant appearance. Two of these reinforcing strips must have sides at least $^1/_2$″ long, the third must have a minimum side length of $^3/_4$″.

The use of these strips will be clear from the drawing. This also shows how we find the correct radius for rounding the outside and inside corners. The circle that determines this curve is inscribed in the square with sides 2$^1/_2$″ long formed at the intersection of the two arms of the counter. The center of the inscribed circle lies at the point of intersection of the diagonals. If we produce one of the diagonals backwards by an amount equal to half its length, we get the center of an identical circle defining the inside curve of the counter. The curves at each end of the counter can be judged by eye. Start building the counter by very carefully joining the two front walls at right angles, at the same time gluing in the reinforcing strip. As soon as the glue has set,

mark out the two main curves with the aid of a paper template. In the case of the vertical curve in front, the greater part of the surplus wood is removed by sawing at a tangent to the curve. The job is then finished with rasp and sandpaper. The same goes for the curve on the front of the plastic top. The concave curve at the back of the counter is cut out with a fret saw and finished off with a round file.

Next join the two short end walls to the front of the counter and glue in the corresponding reinforcing strips. Once again mark off the curves on the edges of the wall, on the one hand, and on the corresponding · edges of the counter top, on the other, and shape them cleanly with saw, file and sandpaper.

If we were now to glue walls and top together and give the edges of the top a final polish, our counter would be practically finished. When the walls had been painted, it would be ready for delivery. But there are possibilities of improving this model still further. If, for example, you find the open construction at the back disturbing, you can enclose the rear of the counter, before attaching the top, with a wall set back about $^1/_4''$ from the edge. Moreover, you can also face the entire front of the counter in colored plastic. This too should be done before the top is glued on.

Certain plastics can be molded when hot. Consequently, they are called thermoplastic. To mold a strip which has been cut to fit the counter front, soak it for a few minutes in hot water, dry it quickly, and while still hot clamp it to the counter wall. On cooling it will keep its shape and can be glued securely to the smooth wooden surface.

Plastics can be glued with the synthetic adhesives mentioned above. Apply a continuous, but thin coat to both surfaces, leave for about 10-15 minutes, then stick together. The surfaces must fit accurately from the start. If you propose to mold and glue plastic, experiment first with a piece of waste. If, after a trial run, you have succeeded in gluing a neat facing to the wall, smooth the edges with a file (work always in the direction of the wood) before gluing on the counter top. If you intend to face the counter with plastic, you must increase the size of the top by the thickness of the plastic facing.

The rough construction is now over. When the painters have done their job and the wholesalers have delivered the merchandise, we can place an advertisement in the paper to inform the public that we are now open for business.

15   HAND PUPPETS, MARIONETTES AND TIN FIGURES

The world and those who inhabit it, good and bad, heroes and rogues, and the parts that they act out, can all be captured for our own entertainment and pleasure in the lively mirror of a home puppet theater. Moreover, the puppeteer can prove to those hardened sceptics who will not admit the existence of devils and witches, or gnomes and water-nymphs, and who scoff at the idea of fairy godmothers and glass slippers, that more things go on between the wings of a puppet theater than they would ever dream of. The puppeteer is master of the whole surrealistic world of fairy-tale. His only limits are the bounds of the individual imagination.

Punch and Judy Theater

The earliest and clearest example of puppetry is found in the Punch and Judy theater, or more correctly, the hand puppet theater. A stage for these performances can be improvised from the simplest materials. All that is needed is to place one table on top of another slightly larger one, with its top facing the audience. This forms a screened-off area for the puppeteers. If we then drape the front and sides of the table with pieces of cloth, we have a completely enclosed space in which all the backstage paraphernalia can remain hidden from view.

A doorway between two rooms will provide a proscenium arch, separating backstage from audience and at the same time enabling simple backdrops to be used. A curtain is suspended at the appropriate height in the room where the spectators sit. A second curtain covers the upper part of the doorway on the other side forming a backdrop. The depth of the frame provides a gap wide enough for the figures to be displayed and manipulated.

A real Punch and Judy theater, with interchangeable backdrops, wings and movable scenery, can be built in the form of a three-part hinged frame that can be folded up and stowed away after each performance.

The construction of such a frame is clearly illustrated in the drawing. The dimensions will depend on the size of theater desired. Exaggerated dimensions should be avoided.

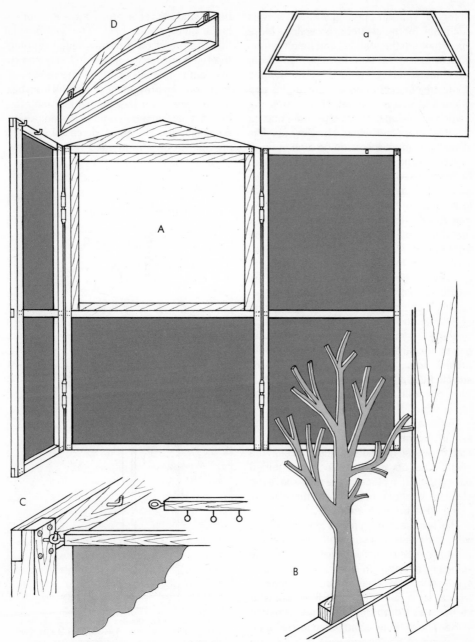

The hand puppet stage. A—the three-part hinged frame with fabric covering and proscenium arch (a—plan view of the frame with side pieces extended and locked in position). B—plywood prop supported on front ledge (clamp not shown). C—the rails for backdrop and scenery are connected to the side pieces of the frame by means of hooks and eyes. D—plywood footlight housing.

249

Theater curtain

A theater with an opening 24″–28″ wide is adequate for most kinds of action. More important are the stability and height of the structure. It must therefore be made from reasonably heavy material. The lapped joints are cut accurately at right angles and glued and screwed together. In fixing the height of the stage, it should be remembered that the puppeteer works standing up. The lower edge must therefore be high enough to avoid the possibility of the top of his head being exposed to view, destroying the illusion and rendering the performance ridiculous. Better a few inches too high than too low. Short puppet masters can stand on a footstool. (By losing their balance at the right moment they can even simulate thunder!) When the frame has been built, the two side sections and the bottom half of the middle section are covered with a heavy fabric. Then a surround consisting of strips of $^1/_8$″ plywood is screwed around the stage opening. In more ambitious projects the part of the surround above the stage should project some 3″ outwards and be constructed like a box closed at top and sides. This box will serve as a housing for the top lighting.

The side pieces are attached to the middle section by means of loose-pin butt hinges that can easily be dismantled. When the stage is set up, the side pieces are folded back and held in place by the rails above the stage at an angle that ensures the stability of the structure as a whole.

The rearmost rail carries the backdrop, while the scenery is suspended further forward. A row of screw eyes will provide sufficient support. In the interest of quick scene changes, it is worth while making several such rails and fitting them out with the necessary drops before the performance starts. The rails can be attached to the frame by means of hooks and eyes. Foreground decor and movable props have a wooden block glued to the back. This will enable them to stand on a narrow ledge running the full width of the stage and screwed to the center member of the middle section of the frame. To prevent these objects from being knocked over by Punch's high-spirited antics, they can be secured to the ledge with small clamps. The actual pieces of scenery are cut out of thin plywood with a fret saw

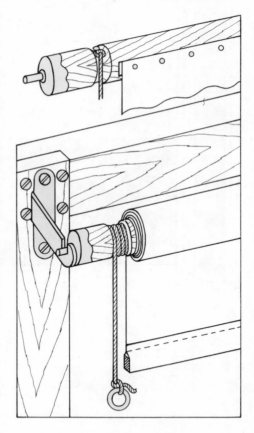

The stage curtain showing roller, draw-string and supporting bracket. The curtain should be weighted at the bottom.

250

and painted in striking colors. The flatter and simpler they are, the more effective they will be.

A proper Punch and Judy theater must naturally have a curtain, and this must run really close to the inside face of the frame if it is to perform its function properly. A rolled curtain is more effective for the puppet theater than a curtain in two parts drawn across from either side, and it is no more difficult to arrange. A piece of broom handle with capped ends will serve as a roller. Pins driven through the hole in the center of each cap act as bearings. Caps, pegs, and the necessary supporting brackets can be obtained from any hardware store. The brackets are screwed to the back of the upper cross member of the middle section so that the roller is absolutely horizontal; otherwise the curtain will not unroll straight. It will also run askew if the curtain material is not cut exactly at right angles and hemmed, or if the upper edge of the material is not nailed to the roller in a straight line. At the bottom of the curtain sew a hem and into it insert a narrow strip of something heavy. The heavier it is, the more smoothly and more quickly the curtain will descend. If necessary, a strip of lead can be used.

On the left or the right, depending on which side the curtain is to be worked from, file an inch-wide groove in the roller to receive the draw-string. This is tacked firmly into the groove and wound around the roller with the curtain hanging down. The roller is then mounted between the brackets. When we pull on the string, it unwinds and causes the roller to revolve; this in turn raises the curtain. When we release the string, the weight pulls down on the curtain, which descends, rewinding the string as it does so. We therefore need a hook, screwed into the frame at stage level, to which we can attach the string when the curtain is raised.

The question of lighting is an independent technical problem, at least in the case of larger theaters. The top lighting can be supplemented with footlights housed in a curved plywood box. The top and bottom of the box should be $3/_{16}$" plywood, the curved wall $1/_8$" plywood or strong cardboard. The inside of the box should be lined with tinfoil. The finished box is hung from the middle section of the frame by means of hooks and eyes. The power line is plugged into a socket below the stage. The entire lighting system works on low-voltage current. Information about the installation of low-voltage lighting systems will be found in Chapter 16. Smaller puppet theaters, which do not justify so elaborate a system, can be illuminated by means of a standard lamp —or better a photo floodlight on a tripod— placed behind and above the audience.

Puppet Heads

A handsome stage and a comprehensive stock of scenery are in no way to be despised in a Punch and Judy theater; much pleasure can be had from the construction of such items. Nevertheless, it is the figure of the star, Punch himself, that remains the most important part of the show, and he should be constructed with loving care. In the real Punch and Judy theater, all the characters are strongly typed. They represent either good or evil, and either belong to the band charged with keeping order in the world or stem from the eerie realm of the beyond. It is the latter, including devils, sorcerers, witches, ghosts, and crocodiles, who time and again tangle the threads of logical action and create dramatic moments of surprise and excitement. Punch, who fights on the side of the good, is often faced with serious opposition from this group. However, the deceitful tricks of the world of spirits are no match for the wit of this eternal rascal and joker who takes the field to champion the cheerfulness of life in the face of death and the devil. Both Punch's grandmother and his wife are also members of the good world, and they do their utmost to keep their beloved mischiefmaker under control, not always an easy task, for Punch is afraid of nothing on this earth, neither the nightwatchman, nor the police, nor the king and all his officers, who are nevertheless responsible for order in the land. Only in the sweet presence of the beautiful princess is his mockery silenced.

The nature of the individual characters and the world they represent must be recognizable at first glance. Only then will the puppets be really effective. Whether a character has a good or an evil nature is shown most clearly in his face. With Punch himself, then, the head is most important. Here there should be no question of a naturalistic portrayal or a caricature of a living person; the heads must be fashioned so as to be effective at a distance. We can therefore confidently ignore all the laws of anatomy and strongly exaggerate the features. Trivial details can be suppressed in the interests of the general effect. The heads should be unmistakable, meaningful and boldly conceived. They must make a direct impression on the spectator.

Apart from these artistic considerations, we must bear in mind two technical requirements: puppet heads should be kept light in weight to avoid tiring the operator's hand, and they must have a hole in the neck that fits firmly over his index finger.

Puppet heads that are light, strong, durable and cheap can be modeled quite simply in papiermâchè. Torn newspaper soaked in a very hot soda solution provides the modeling material; torn up beer mats are also ideal

for this purpose. The soaked paper is whisked into a soft, uniform pulp, and the surplus water strained off through a sieve. The remaining pulp is squeezed as dry as possible by hand and then kneaded, adding paste and a little plaster of Paris, into a plastic mass ready for use. Instructions for making paste will be found in the chapter on bookbinding. Instead of this starch paste, ready-made products can also be used.

Model the head over a round piece of wood about 8″ long and $^3/_4$″ in diameter supported in a bench vise or in a clamp laid on its side. The upper two-thirds of the rod is filed into a conical shape so that the diameter of the tip is reduced to about $^3/_8$″. Using this wooden core, the lining of the finger hole is formed from a strip of firm cardboard; this is first rounded by pulling it sharply across a table edge, then glued over the wooden core, and finally covered with a few layers of newspaper pasted one on top of the other. This conical tube provides a firm grip for thin and thick fingers alike.

A normal hand puppet head is 3″ to 4″ high from chin to crown. To keep the weight of the head down, do not use the valuable papiermâché from the start but first form a rough, egg-shaped base out of dry newspaper wound firmly around the tube. The final papiermâché features, with nose, mouth and eyes, are modeled on top of this. Hair-pins, a paper-knife, and plastic wood will all come in useful in the process. It is important to remember to form a broad lip at the base of the neck, over which the puppet's costume will later be fastened.

The finished head is removed from the modeling stick and left to dry out for a few days. In the course of drying it will shrink a little, and any cracks which appear should be filled with thin papiermâché or with a cement made from French chalk and joiner's glue. Once the head is quite dry it can be

Modeling a puppet head
in papiermâché over a
wooden core.

smoothed with sandpaper. Finally, it is pasted over with a layer of thin white paper, torn, not cut, into strips. The whole is then ready for painting in tempera or poster colors. Puppet heads should be painted by artificial light, for it is under such conditions that they will later be displayed. When dry, the paint should be given a protective coat of zapon varnish.

A devil's head modeled in papiermâché has to be able to withstand Punch's violent blows and other rough treatment. A very much more robust and at the same time lighter head can be made by pasting thin layers of paper, like the skins of an onion, over a head modeled in clay.

While the clay head is still damp, a round piece of wood wound with cloth is pushed in from below. The actual neck, with a lip for attaching the costume is then formed, and,

when dry, coated with shellac. The next job is pasting on layers of thin wrapping paper torn into small pieces. These are thoroughly softened beforehand in warm water. Eight layers are needed altogether. The first layer should on no account be glued, it should simply be pressed damp onto the clay head. The second layer and all the rest are pasted on with joiner's glue that has been thoroughly mixed until it is quite liquid. It can be kept hot in a double saucepan. After each layer of paper has been applied, the head is coated with glue. Likewise, after each layer, the shape of the head must be touched up with a moist modeling tool to prevent the features from becoming blurred as the skin is slowly reinforced. After putting on four layers, pause to allow them to dry thoroughly. Work with paper of two different colors, used alternately, to help keep a check on the

253

Carved heads

number of layers you have applied.

After the seventh layer has been pasted on and has dried, the modeling stick is pulled out and the dry clay core chipped out of the paper covering with a knife, gimlet or screwdriver. This can take some time. A quicker method is to saw off a piece at the back of the head and work from there too. Once empty, the inside of the head is brushed with glue to make it stronger and more durable. To replace the back of the head, paste a circular piece of cardboard inside the skull, and glue the sawn-off piece to it.

We now come to the fitting of the finger tube, which is made in the manner already described. The neck opening is stuffed with newspaper until it is narrow enough for the finger tube to be squeezed in tightly and glued in place.

The basic shape is now finished. The entire head is covered with an eighth and final layer of flesh-colored paper and can then be painted, bewigged, or even graced with a beard.

The higher art of hand puppet making begins when you carve a head in wood. This is the ambition of every enthusiastic puppeteer, and anyone who has the least gift for drawing and has also had some practice in the use of a carving knife and gouge (see Chapter 4) should be able to accomplish this satisfying task. Modeling heads in papiermâché and clay is a good preparatory exercise. The woodcarver, too, should model a full-size head before beginning work. This will help him to control the shape and proportions of the features.

Heads can be modeled in plasticine as well as in clay. Moreover, hobby stores stock special modeling compositions which are highly suitable for the job.

Carve the heads from a block of basswood, since this is the easiest wood to work. The block should consist of two pieces temporarily glued together, since the two halves of the head will later be separated and hollowed out to lessen the weight. Begin by sawing out the neck and chiseling away the lower parts of the block. The re-

When building a puppet head by pasting layers of paper over a clay model use two different colors alternately. In this way you can keep track of the number of layers that have been applied.

The Punch and Judy theater is a theater of types. The allegiance of each character, whether to good or to evil, should be written clearly in his face.

sulting rough peg can be used to clamp the block in the vise. First, however, the finger hole is bored with a $^3/_8''$ drill. If we were to do this later, the hollow head would be crushed in the vise.

Next cut the rough egg shape of the head, fashion the back of the head, and shape both halves of the face from the plane of the nose to the ears. Then the eyes, nose, mouth and chin are roughed out and finally shaped into bold and exaggerated features. Do not spend too much time on individual parts of the head, but keep modeling it as a whole. The beginner is prone to concentrate too

much on details, but this must be avoided at all costs. Finally, the neck and costume lip are shaped. When the outside of the head has been covered, carefully break open the temporary joint and hollow out the two halves until the walls are only a fraction of an inch thick. At the same time, widen both sides of the narrow finger hole conically from the base. When this has also been done, clean the edges of the two halves and glue them together. The head is now ready and can be handed over to the make-up man to be painted and provided with hair and possibly a beard.

255

Marionettes

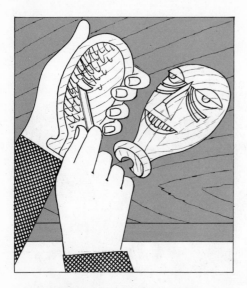

The two halves of the carved puppet head should be hollowed out in order to reduce its weight to a minimum.

The Marionette Theater

Very much more demanding than the earthy humor of Punch's world is the world of marionettes. Whereas the Punch and Judy theater obtains its effects primarily through strong contrasts, the marionette theater moves more in the realm of the fairytale. It inhabits the fringe world of the fantastic and the impossible, where the spoken word is secondary.

Movement is the language of marionettes. Therein lie the technical and artistic difficulties which the theater manager has to overcome. Quite apart from the fact that there is scarcely anyone who, at the first attempt, will succeed in guiding a marionette on its strings across the stage in the relaxed kind of dance of which they are capable, there is also the question of artistic understanding and technical inventiveness in the construction of the marionette and the stage on which it performs. But all this will come when we have once ventured into the mysterious world of dancing strings, where nothing seems impossible.

Hair, wigs and beards are made from pieces of fur, wool and tow. Hands can be fashioned from papiermâche and tissue paper modeled over wire frames. They are better carved from wood and glued at the wrist to a cardboard cuff sewn to the puppet's costume. Those skilled enough can also sew hands in cloth or thin leather, like gloves. After sewing, these are turned inside out and stuffed with cotton wool. Shoes can be made in a similar manner.

The puppets' costumes should also be strongly stylized, like the heads. They should be cut and proportioned to fit the spread of the operator's hand. Preferably in the kimono style, they should be roomy and not too short so that they fall far enough over the arm. All costumes must be made so that they can be tied quickly around the lip formed in the puppet's neck.

Figures and Controllers

As with Punch, the head is again the most important item. Again it is constructed regardless of the strict laws of anatomy, and in this case the characteristic features should stand out clearly not only in a full-face view, but also in profile. Marionette heads are made by the same methods as those used for Punch. The head should also be exaggerated in relation to the body; it should be about one sixth the length of the whole figure. It is also important to ensure that the front half of the head is heavier than the back. Otherwise, instead of nodding graciously to grant the wish of the beautiful princess, the majestic head of the king will tilt backwards as though his majesty were offering his chin to the court barber to be shaved. Such unexpected reactions generally spark off an outburst of unwelcome laughter among the audience. We can avoid embarrassment by placing a small piece of lead in the nose or forehead of our marionettes. In contrast to the hand puppet head, the marionette head has no finger hole. Heads modeled on a stick must be finished off with a piece of rounded wood glued into the neck. A screw eye is screwed into this rounded filler to form the neck joint. Above the ears—and if possible hidden by the hair—two more small screw eyes are screwed into the head for attaching the manipulating strings.

The body of the marionette is a skeleton built of square sticks, preferably pine. For arms and legs, and especially for larger figures, round beech rods have proved their worth. The thickness of the wood depends on the size of the figure, and this is something we must be clear about from the start. For a figure 18″ high, as in our example, wood $^3/_4$″ thick will be strong enough. Unnecessarily heavy figures should be avoided.

Working methodically make a full-size drawing of the marionette skeleton, showing all the bone sizes and body proportions. For a normally proportioned marionette, we can divide the drawing into six sections. Assuming that our model is 18″ high, the top sixth, corresponding to the head, will measure three inches. At the very center, between the crown of the head and the soles of the feet, lies the pelvis. Like the head, the hands and feet are also exaggerated in size; they should be about the same length as the head. With the arms hanging at the sides, the finger tips rest two-thirds of the way down the figure, or some 6″ from the soles of the feet. The wrist is level with the pelvis. The upper arms are somewhat longer than the lower arms; the same goes for the thigh and the lower leg. The neck

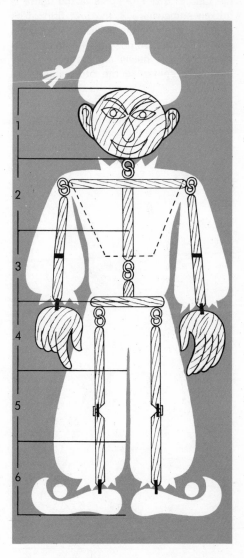

The marionette skeleton can conveniently be divided into six equal parts. Note the positions of the various swivel and hinged joints.

Swivel and hinged joints

joint between the chin and the collar bone is made of two interlinked screw eyes. The lengths of the collar bone and pelvis are in the ratio of 3:2. The spine of the figure is broken somewhere in the first fifth of its length, just above the pelvis, to form a hip joint. The skeleton has rigid joints only between hip and pelvis and between collar bone and spine; all the other joints are flexible.

Before the joints are formed, a trapezoidal breast-plate, easily fashioned from thin plywood, is glued to the skeleton. This is later padded with cotton wool and linen to give

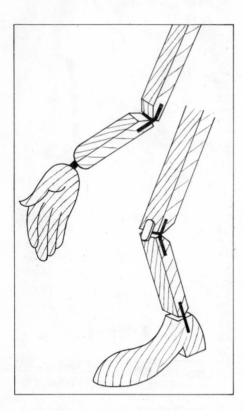

The hinged joints of the arms and legs are made with strips of soft leather.

the figure body. The hunchbacked jester at the king's court also has a similar plate glued to his back.

In the construction of the marionette body two kinds of joints are used: swivel joints and hinged joints. Swivel joints are used at the neck, shoulders and hips. These consist of pairs of screw eyes linked together and screwed into the rounded ends of their respective wooden "bones." The hinged joints of the arms and legs are most easily made by gluing strips of soft leather into notches sawn in the ends of the parts to be joined. A stronger method is to use thin brass hinges fitted in the same way and held by means of small wood screws. As bought, however, these hinges are not flexible enough for our marionettes. The hinge pin must be removed and replaced by a thinner piece of wire, otherwise the figure will move as if it had rheumatism.

The elbow joint is made to bend forwards, like a natural joint. The axis of rotation must lie towards the rear of the pieces joined, while the front corners should be cut away to give maximum freedom of movement. At the knee joint, which bends backwards, the procedure is exactly the opposite. A small, rounded wooden "kneecap," half-glued to the thigh will increase the stability of the figure; it also helps to prevent the marionette's costume from being pinched in the joint during manipulation.

Be careful when attaching the hand; it should be made to flap not in the same direction as the elbow joint, but at right angles to it. For the hand it is important to use the thinnest possible strips of soft leather, so that the joint will turn easily. At the wrists both arms and hands should be thoroughly rounded. The foot joint is formed in the middle of the end of the shin bone which is not rounded but beveled on both sides of the hinge to facilitate foot movements,

downwards movements being the more frequent.

Ideally, the hands and feet of marionettes should be carved in wood. In the case of the shoes, the job is a simple one if we begin carving from the side; with the hands, do not carve each individual finger, but treat the fingers as a continuous whole. If necessary, however, they can be sewn in leather or cloth from a paper pattern. The resulting "gloves" are filled with sand or sawdust. The feet should not be too light so that they return to the ground quickly when released. It is a good idea to fix lead plates to the soles of the shoes.

The secret of the marionette's effortless movements lies in the manipulation of the wooden controller, the individual parts of which are joined to the corresponding limbs by means of strings. The controller is constructed quite simply from $^3/_8''$ square material, as shown in the drawing. Crossbar D is at the front. The size of the controller depends on the size of the marionette, since its separate arms work like levers. Crossbar B, to which the shoulder strings are attached, must be some $^3/_4''$ longer than the collar bone of the figure. Crossbar C is the same length as B, and controls the movement of the hands and arms. Crossbar D must again be some $^3/_4''$ longer than B and C; it controls the walking movements of the marionette. Crossbar D is fixed independently to the controller so that the figure can be made to walk without all the other parts of the body moving up and down in time with the feet. In contrast to B and C, which are firmly glued and screwed to A in a lapped joint, crossbar D is attached to the front end of A by means of a simple pivot. This is done by drilling a hole in the middle of D through which it is screwed into the end of A. Make sure you drill straight and in the center otherwise the Good Fairy will

How to string the marionette. The strings are knotted to eyes in the various crossbars of the controller.

walk with a limp. Hanging from crossbar B and attached to it by two lengths of rubber is a round and rather thinner wooden rod, to the ends of which the two head strings are fastened. As in the case of B and C, this rod is $^3/_4''$ wider than the marionette's head. The piece marked A, to which the three crossbars are attached at more or less equal intervals, should be $7^1/_2''$ in length for a marionette 18″ tall. When eyes have been screwed into the ends of all the arms, the "brain" of the figure is ready to be connected with strings to the various "muscles" it controls.

The stringing of the marionette must be carried out carefully and delicately. The first question is: what kind of strings and how long should they be? Choose a thin nylon thread that is both inconspicuous and extremely strong. A well-waxed, strong hemp yarn is an economical substitute. The length depends on the height of the stage.

It is important that the controller be exactly horizontal while stringing; a well-tried method of ensuring this is to place the controller on a narrow board laid across the two open doors of a cabinet. The floor then serves as the stage—if the distance is too great, a bench or a table can be used to raise the stage level.

The strings are first tied loosely to the screw eyes of the marionette skeleton and then to the respective arms of the controller, leaving some string to spare. Both fastenings are only provisional: firstly, so that they can be adjusted, and, secondly, because the strings must be untied to allow the marionette to be dressed. The weight of the figure is borne entirely by the shoulder strings, and these are installed first. Then follow the two head strings, tied to the rod suspended from B. The third stage in the process of animating the figure is stringing the legs. At the lower end of the thigh, just

above the knee, a small hole is drilled, through which the strings are threaded and secured by a knot at the back; the other ends are tied to crossbar D.

Our marionette is quite lively now, but it still cannot sit or bow. This can be arranged by running a string from the middle of the pelvis to the free rear end of the main bar A. Now all that remains is to attach the strings for the arms. Beginners are usually content to drill a hole in the palm of each hand and thread them with knotted strings attached to the ends of crossbar C. However, they soon realize, that such an arrangement only permits the most clumsy movements of hand and arm; there can be no question of eloquent gestures, because the arm always follows in the wake of the hand, having no independent movement of its own. This can be remedied by introducing a second string somewhere near the middle of the lower arm and attaching this string also to crossbar C of the controller. To prevent confusion between the two strings, the lower arm string can be identified with a small colored flag. Again, to facilitate manipulation further a small strut can be used to separate the two strings an inch or so from the point at which they are fastened to C.

After trying out our marionette to see that all the joints work perfectly, we must untie all the strings again for the purpose of clothing the figure. First, though, the chest has to be padded, and the back too, if necessary. In any event, the pelvis is fitted with a narrow rectangular pad, a little longer than itself. Be sure that the movement of the legs is not restricted, however.

The sewing of the costumes should be entrusted to the hands of an experienced puppet wardrobe mistress, used to handling a needle and thread. Here there are no limits to the imagination, save that too much detail should be avoided since the costumes must be effective at a distance. When dressing the marionettes, the various strings must be threaded on a darning needle and passed through the fabric at the exact spot where the costume should fall on the figure. The ends can then be re-tied to the controller. One further detail remains before the marionette is ready for the stage, and that is to fix a strong screw eye in the top of the controller exactly at the center of gravity of the whole assembly. This is so that the marionette can be attached to a cross wire above the stage and left motionless during or between scenes.

The Marionette Stage

As in the case of the Punch and Judy theater, we can improvise a marionette theater inside a door frame or with a makeshift arrangement of tables and drapes. However, the care we have bestowed on the construction of our marionettes surely justifies the construction of a proper marionette stage.

The basic functions of such a stage naturally require that it be of fairly considerable size. Firstly, the operators, actors and musicians, must be out of the audience's sight. Secondly, the operators must stand relatively high. Thirdly, the dimensions and perspective of the stage area must be in proportion to the size of the marionettes.

Taking our 18″ tall marionette as a standard, we shall need a stage opening measuring 64″ x 34″. The stage itself must be 38″ deep. This will necessitate a framework with the considerable overall dimensions of 8′-0″ high, 8′-0″ wide, and 38″ deep. Obviously, such a structure cannot be made in the form of a permanent piece of equipment without provoking a premature display of

theatrical temperament in the puppeteer's wife. At the same time, the whole framework must be made from strong, smoothly planed 3″ x 1″ material. All this calls for an easily demountable structure with the parts connected by bolts and wing nuts. Where two walls meet at a corner, they are connected by means of angle butt straps.

The basic stage, which can be varied according to individual preferences, is shown in the drawing. Points to note are the slight slope of the stage floor towards the spectator, and the solid seating of the strut running right across the top of the stage, which serves to counteract the tension in the wires that constitute the stage rigging. From one of these wires, which are more practical than wooden bars, pieces of scenery are hung; the other supports the sliding hangers for the marionettes themselves. These hangers, made of flexible wire, have a sliding ring at the top and a hook at the bottom from which the eye on the controller can be suspended.

At one end the horizontal rigging wires are fixed by means of a loop and a screw eye to the upper cross member of the side frame. At the other end, they are fastened to an eye bolt long enough to pass through a hole drilled in the opposite cross member and held in place with a wing nut and washer. In this way the tension of the wires can be adjusted whenever necessary. Be sure, however, that you have the same tension in both wires, otherwise the whole assembly will creak and groan. The center strut, which rests at both ends in a simple shoe, will also serve to support scenery if fitted with a row of screw eyes on the underside.

The decoration of the stage framework is a question of personal taste, but the surface should not be fussy, and subdued colors should be used so that the audience's attention is not distracted. A suitable loose fabric

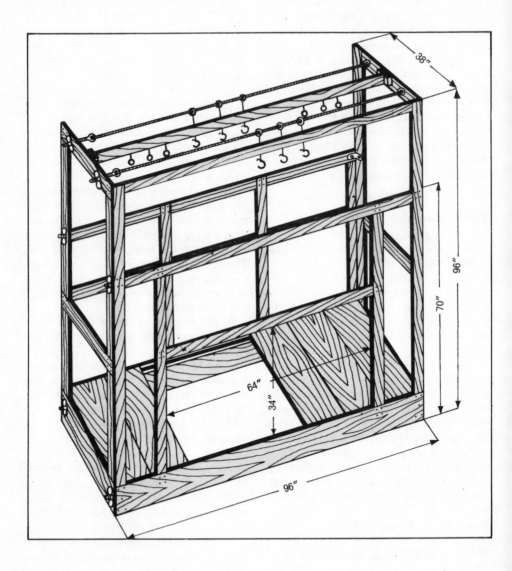

The demountable framework of a large marionette stage (the fabric covering of the front wall is not shown). The walls are made as separate frames which are assembled and held together with bolts and angle butt straps.

covering is better than plywood, since it requires less storage space when the stage is dismantled. The curtain will be no problem after the experience gained in the construction of a Punch and Judy theater.

Stage lighting for a marionette theater can offer a virtually inexhaustible field for experiment. Toplights and footlights can be built on the same lines as those used in the Punch and Judy theater. These two sources of light, however, are not enough for full dramatic illumination. They must be supplemented with two side lights, fixed halfway up, one on each side of the stage. Instead of a front spotlight, which normally lights up the full depth of the stage, we can make do with a strong lamp placed among the audience. To get really sophisticated lighting you should mix blue, yellow and red lights among the white. You can color the bulbs yourself with lamp paint. When rows of mixed lights are connected in series, the most exciting effects can be obtained, from the paleness of moonlight to the shadows of evening. And with a dimmer it will even be possible to simulate the rising or the setting of the sun (see Chapter 16), to say nothing of the backgrounds that can be projected from behind onto a transparent horizon with the aid of a magic lantern. There are many exciting possibilities, provided that the position of the operators does not obstruct the projector. Once one has experimented in this fascinating wonderland, it is difficult to tear oneself away from it, for new ideas are always suggesting themselves.

The Parade of the Tin Soldiers

Making and collecting tin figures is a very special kind of hobby. Its devotees are specialists in the history of art and war, in tactics, strategy, anatomy and historical costume. Specialization is essential, since the variety of possible themes is overwhelming. For almost anything can be reconstructed with the aid of tin figures, from the first Stone Age mammoth hunt to the blasting off of the first space rocket. For young people, especially, there is scarcely a more vivid or graphic way of awakening interest in the history of races and peoples. Lifeless theory becomes charged with colorful actuality: replicas of Caesar and Hannibal, the Persians in their flowing robes, the Greeks at Troy, heavily armed Roman legionaries, and wild Gallic hordes, all bring history to life. Armies of crusaders and migrating nations march past. Cortez strides through Mexico with his Spanish adventurers, robber barons hold up portly merchants, Prince Eugene rides against the Turks, Apaches swarm across the prairie, and explorers penetrate primeval forests or cross the Arctic floes. The passion for collecting and artistic and scientific interests all meet in this original and fascinating hobby. Playing with tin figures is applied history, visible tradition.

Casting Tin Figures

How can the beginner obtain tin figures? Firstly, he can buy them. Anyone seeing a manufacturer's catalog for the first time will be astounded at the variety offered. There are such things as Indian chieftains in large feather head-dresses, an English general from the year 1740, Washington on horseback and Burgoyne on foot, Carthaginian war elephants on the rampage, pioneers and rustlers, Sitting Bull carrying away his wounded brother, entire brass bands with tubas and majorettes, Napoleonic generals,

Plaster molds

artillerymen, pack-mules, culverins, covered wagons, Caesar and Cleopatra together with their slaves, and the complete Judgment of Paris with Aphrodite and the olive branch. The whole history of the world is offered virtually intact.

Secondly, collections of tin figures can be built up by swapping. Most countries have collectors associations that publish journals advertising their members' wants, in addition to interesting articles on the subject. Finally, the handy hobbyist can cast his figures himself. There are few who will be so ambitious as to begin by cutting an original mold in slate. One must be an artist for that. It is quite another matter to make a plaster of Paris mold from an already existing model; in this case the requirements are fairly simple.

First of all, make a frame out of thin, smoothly planed pieces of wood, quite similar to that used in making mosaics (see Chapter 10). The frame must measure $5^1/_2$" x $3^1/_2$" x 2" high. It is mounted on a piece of glass that has first been rubbed with liquid soap or vaseline; it is then filled slightly less than half-full with a fairly thick paste of plaster of Paris. To make the plaster harder, add a pinch of alum or some waterglass. Use cold water for mixing; warm plaster hardens too quickly. After the paste has been thoroughly smoothed with a spatula, wait two minutes until the plaster has started to dry and press the model, sideways on, halfway into the plaster, having previously coated it thinly with vaseline or salad oil. Be careful not to coat the fine detail too thickly, otherwise this detail will be missing from the mold. Make sure the model is pressed in only as far as the half-way mark so as to get no undercut forms in either half of the mold. Bits of plaster forced up around the edges or into the hollow parts of the model as it is pressed in, must be carefully

scraped away with a small knife, after the plaster has hardened.

At the same time as the model is introduced, a piece of doweling is pressed into the plaster to form a pouring channel leading to the mold. This should run obliquely from the top of the frame to the base of the figure so that the mouth of the channel lies as low as possible. A second, thinner piece of doweling should run vertically upwards from the head of the figure. Later, during casting, air will be able to escape through this outlet. These two pieces of doweling must also be coated with grease so that the plaster does not stick to them. Before the plaster has completely dried, make four conical holes in the surface of the half-mold with a blunt pencil. When these are quite dry, carefully rub them smooth with a pumice stone.

The lower half of the mold is now complete. Its surface and the four holes are brushed with graphite or wiped with vaseline to separate them from the plaster of the upper half. For the latter, we use much thinner plaster which should be poured on gently from the side and allowed to cover the model slowly and gradually. Be careful to prevent the smallest air bubble from forming in the plaster. Once the model is covered with a thin layer of plaster, stop pouring for a moment and then fill the frame to the top.

Let the whole thing stand overnight so that the plaster can set properly, remove the surrounding frame, and separate the two halves of the mold, making careful use of a knife blade to remove the pieces of doweling. It is now clear why we made the four conical holes in the lower half of the mold. The upper half has pegs which fit into these holes and ensure the exact matching of the two halves. After taking out the model, remove any surplus plaster from the mold, clean out the mouths of the two channels, and develop the upper opening of the pouring channel into a funnel shape.

After a week of drying, the mold is ready for use. It is sufficient to smear it lightly with soot before casting and to press both halves firmly together while pouring in the molten metal, which is heated, but not overheated, in a cast-iron ladle. The mold may break at the first or second casting because of cavities due to small air bubbles just beneath the surface, the walls of which are burst by the hot metal. However, a carefully made mold can give some 25 castings before the edges begin to crumble, rendering the mold unusable.

While it is very fascinating and rewarding to reproduce a given model in this way, for one's own use or for swapping purposes, the process can also be used to make quite new figures, if pieces from different figures are combined. All kinds of curious shapes can be built up from bent and straight arms, torsos, halves of horses, bare and trousered legs, like an anatomical jigsaw puzzle. It is just this subtle kind of creative casting that is of most interest to the keen tin figure collector. Naturally, the more extensive the arsenal of components, the greater the possibilities of invention.

Like the complete model, the individual members are bedded in the plaster, paying special attention to the joints. Begin with the base and work upwards. The mold produced by this process must, of course, be very neatly retouched. Cleaning away the burrs and ridges of metal from the casting also requires more care than in the case of a complete model.

A soldering iron will come in useful for changing a head or moving the position of an arm. In view of the smallness of the figures this is decidedly fine work. So that the individual parts do not slip under the soldering iron, first stick them temporarily together with glue and bed them in thick plaster, just as in making a mold. When the plaster has dried, remove the figure, sep-

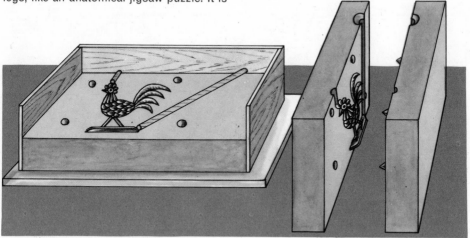

Making molds for tin figures. The model is embedded in the lower half of the plaster mold and the upper half poured on top. The pieces of doweling form casting channels in the soft plaster. On the right: a finished mold.

arate the glued parts, clean them, and apply flux for soldering. Then lay them in position in the mold and solder. By such tricks an Austrian infantryman of 1813 without a greatcoat can be transformed into a Bavarian rifleman of 1871.

Painting the Figures

Only paint can take away the stiffness of the metal and give the figure life and movement. Spirit varnishes, water colors, or oil paints can be used. While the first two require an undercoat of thin poster paint and zapon varnish, oil paints can be applied direct to the shiny surface of the well-cleaned metal. They also have the advantage of durability. What can be inconvenient is the fact that oil paints dry slowly. The addition of a drier hastens the drying, but makes the paint rather too brittle.

For coloring tin figures artist's oils have proved their worth. A white porcelain palette will serve for spreading, mixing and thinning the paints with linseed oil or turpentine—remember the latter makes the colors dull. Only first-class brushes give pleasing results. Dig into your pocket-book and buy quality brushes made from badger or marten hair, which keep a good point.

In painting larger surfaces such as groups of trees, wagon coverings, or even the base plates on which the figures stand, it is more practical to use a less delicate, short, flat brush.

Since the small figures require only very little paint, do not buy unnecessarily large quantities. At the same time, to avoid acquiring a vast arsenal of paint tubes, learn to mix colors from the least possible number of different paints. This is a science in itself, which we cannot go into here, but even after a little practice with the three primary colors, blue, yellow and red, it will be found that one can manage with relatively few tubes. It will

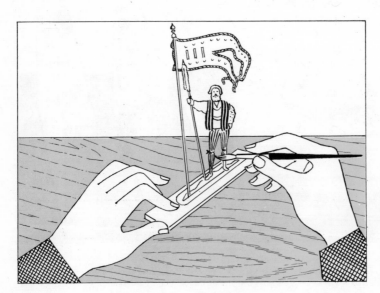

Tin figures are painted with fine badger or marten hair brushes. Before being painted the figures are mounted on a strip of wood which can easily be controlled with the left hand. This makes it unnecessary to touch the figure and perhaps smear the wet paint.

also be found that white plays a similar role among oil paints to that of water in water-colors. Only one effect cannot be obtained by blending oil paints, and that is the metal-lic glitter of gold and silver. And it is just this splendor of gold braid and silver cords, shining buttons and sword hilts, that our tin soldiers cannot do without. This we can supply by mixing bronze powder with a drier or mastic until a brushable liquid is obtained. This must only be applied when the under-coat of oil paint is completely dry.

Artist's oil paints are not enamels. They are thinned with linseed oil or turpentine, and the more of the latter one adds, the duller the final surface will be. Moreover, once dry, these paints attract dirt easily and eventually wear off. It is therefore advisable to give the figure a final protective coat of mat varnish when all is dry.

Before beginning to paint, glue the figure on its stand to a piece of board—not too short—which can be controlled with the left hand. The order of painting depends on the individual. One person may begin with the lightest color and progress to the darkest;

another may start with the broad surfaces and then move on to the details and high-lights, finishing up with the shadows. With figures on horseback, it is best to begin with the horse, continue with the harness and saddle-cloth, and finish with the rider him-self.

The problem of producing a finished fig-ure that will stand up to criticism lies not so much in the technique of applying the paint as in the reproduction of what the collector calls historical accuracy. The real experts know for example, that the coats of a 200-year-old regiment had double buttons, and that in one unit they were overlapping while in another they sat side by side. They know too that since 1851 the Württemberg regi-mental colors have borne the "W" on the right side and the arms on the left, whereas previously they had been the other way around. Anyone neglecting such details is guilty of a serious historical blunder. The costume expert will also recognize a figure of the Egyptian Queen Nefertiti clothed in green as an anachronism, since this color was unknown in her time.

The hobbyist who takes historical accuracy seriously will therefore have to obtain his own authentic information from old prints, historical paintings, or illustrated history books.

Collections and dioramas

Once we have decided upon a special period, and know whether we are going to concentrate on, say, military subjects or folk lore, we encounter the problem of where to keep the figures.

It is relatively simple to keep the whole collection in flat compartmented cardboard boxes, lined with velvet, so that the figures can easily be viewed and displayed, like a stamp collection. This method is good enough for the collector of "types," since he is content to possess just one fine specimen of each kind. Things are quite different when the figures are displayed either permanently or temporarily in the form of a so-called diorama. This takes up a lot of room and makes additional work for the hobbyist, calling for great skill and imagination. Besides being historically accurate, it must also be naturalistic. Hills and mountains, rocks, sand, roads, woods and single trees, villages, and even complete towns, must all be constructed as a setting for the chosen scene.

A plywood tray with edges $1^1/_2''$ high will provide the foundation. On this the terrain can be modeled from pieces of cigar-box wood, bits of turf, and lumps of plaster and putty; all this is covered with colored muslin or brushed with glue and sprinkled with colored sawdust. Natural stones look surprisingly unrealistic as rocks, and these are best represented by decorative cork, of the kind sold in pet stores. Glued papiermâché can also be used to simulate various types of landscape, and poster paint completes the illusion.

All our concern for naturalism will be defeated if in the finished diorama the base plates of the tin figures remain showing. This problem can easily be solved by smearing glue over the plate and sprinkling it with sawdust of the appropriate color.

Plastic trees can be bought ready-made from a toy store. Individual tree shapes can also be represented by tufts of heather or painted loofah. Dry fir and spruce cones, glued to a round piece of wood representing the trunk and then painted, provide very naturalistic tree forms. Whenever it is a question of making larger areas of foliage or a background of dense woods, simply paint them on poster board to give the proper effect of light and shade. It is best to mark in the outlines of such a landscape before painting.

Representing water courses and ponds is more of a problem. For rivers and streams, the simplest method is to cut them out in strong cartridge paper, paint them the color of the sky backdrop, and glue crinkled cellophane on top. The surfaces of lakes and fish ponds can be imitated with pieces of window glass painted on the underside with the tempera color that predominates in the sky. The banks require special care; they can be fashioned from putty or from a paste consisting of sawdust, chalk and size. As this begins to solidify, it is painted with poster colors and sprinkled with colored sawdust.

The need for historical accuracy again arises when we come to reproduce villages, single buildings or whole towns belonging to the past. Large pieces of scenery forming the background are painted on plywood and then cut out with a fret saw. Single buildings or villages in the foreground, which have to be portrayed in three dimensions, must be carefully glued together from matchboxes, cardboard or plywood and painted to appear historically correct. Windows can be made from glued pieces of cellophane. Shingles and thatched roofs, hedges, and all kinds of fences offer many a challenge to the powers of invention.

Essential to the general effectiveness of the diorama is the circular horizon or backdrop. This is made from strong cartridge paper on which an appropriate scene (sky, town, range of mountains, foliage, etc.) is painted in mat colors—poster-tempera perhaps. To help soften the sudden transition from the three-dimensional effect of the actual terrain to the flatness of the background, it is a good idea to imitate the stage designer and place some free-standing decor just in front of the horizon.

However much we labor over our diorama, utilizing every possible aerial and linear perspective, we will not succeed in creating a scene that is equally effective when viewed from every angle. Thus, there are diorama builders who insist that the spectator stand in a certain position, as though he were viewing something on a stage. The beginner, at least, should try to arrange his scene from a single fixed viewpoint. To enhance the illusion, remember the old hint about avoiding right angles in a picture. That is, no plane or line in the picture should run parallel to its surface. With that reminder we can sound the call for the parade of the tin soldiers.

16 UNDER THE CHRISTMAS TREE

At the center of the Christmas festival is the birth of the Saviour in the stable at Bethlehem. ". . . and she wrapped Him in swaddling clothes and laid Him in a manger, because there was no room for them in the inn." From this manger the joyful Christmas message spread throughout the world, and the manger itself has become in the course of the centuries a symbol of the miracle of Christmas. Again and again this miracle has moved not only artists, but also innumerable, nameless, ordinary folk, inspiring them to render in pictorial form the events of the pious legend of Bethlehem. Certainly no scene in human history has been so often reproduced by lay hands as that moment when the shepherds knelt before the manger with the Christ-child and offered Him their gifts. And here something entirely unexpected and miraculous occurs, namely that, however primitive, even clumsy, the means whereby this scene is reproduced, nothing can destroy the peculiar magic that surrounds these simple groups. Rather does it appear as if the evocative power of the figures at the manger is the greater, the more naive and unintellectual the manner in which they are depicted. This should encourage even those craftsmen not lavishly endowed with artistic ability, for, where the Christmas manger, or crib, is concerned, the artistic element counts little, if at all.

The Christmas Creche

In planning the construction of a Christmas creche, we must distinguish between the scenic background, against which the story is enacted, and the representation by means of figures of the incident itself. The group of figures involved in the action is always in the foreground. These figures remain the central reality, while the stable structure merely provides a suitable background to the scene. Before setting to work on the construction of a creche, we should make up our minds about the setting for the action of our Christmas story. Bethlehem, the City of David, was in Asia Minor. Anyone, therefore, who is concerned with the realism of his representation, will seek for oriental prototypes. Nevertheless, the whole concept of the "Holy Night" will have greater appeal if we transplant it into our homeland and transform the stable of Bethlehem into a poor cabin in some mountain region, or a fisherman's hut on the sea-shore. For, where the Christmas creche is concerned, it is a question not of correctness of setting, historical accuracy, or purity of style, but rather of depicting an event which is "above all reason." All we need is a small familiar grouping, pervaded by peace and reverence, to be appreciated by the family and its friends.

The forms that may be taken by the stable structure, ranging from a simple affair of wooden boards to a pretentious Gothic chapel, are well-nigh unlimited. To give binding directions for the construction of a particular model would be to turn this one concept into a "dead" stereotype, and restrict the power of the imagination, which is precisely what should be avoided. The simple sheep-pen illustrated should therefore be regarded, at the most, as a suggestion. However, it will serve as a concrete model against which to set off a few characteristic details.

The size of the structure as a whole will depend on the space available and, like everything else, on personal taste. In order not to vacillate helplessly between wish and reality, we should first draw a sketch containing all the essential features of the scene, and then prepare a ground plan of the creche on a plywood platform which will serve as a foundation for the whole composition.

The erection of plywood walls and roofs has already been described in connection with the building of a doll's house (Chapter 12). It is not necessary, however, to fix the creche, which is not intended to take any particular strain, firmly to the platform. A structure left standing loose has the advantage that after the Christmas festival it can be dismantled and easily packed away. In the case of a building which can be taken to pieces in this way, however, we shall have to strengthen the walls by gluing triangular stiffeners in the corners.

Our sheep-pen will have a thatched roof rather than a tiled one. Cut out the roof panels not from plywood, but from gray pasteboard, and before mounting them on the walls, cover them with straw, beginning at the bottom. Small bundles of straw are sewn onto the roof panels in layers with

Suggested background for a rustic Christmas creche.

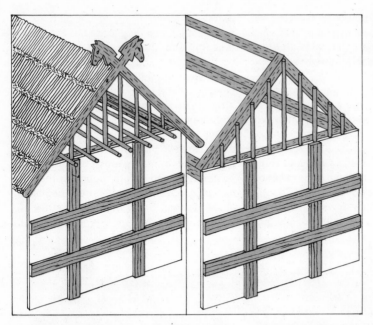

Thatched roof and light framing for the Christmas creche. The gable ends and loft floor are made of thin, round sticks. Half-timbered construction is imitated by gluing strips of veneer to the wall panels.

strong thread. Before the roof is set in place, the projecting edges are strengthened with a narrow piece of pine edging or a strip of plywood. At the ridge the roof is tied in with a sufficiently broad ridge beam that matches the slope of the roof, while at the eaves it is carried on triangular bearers glued to the walls. Such a bearer must be provided even where one of the walls is left out.

The way the roof is secured to the gables will depend on the construction of the gable walls. If these are solid "half-timbered" surfaces on a plywood base, it will be possible for the roof to sit directly on the sloping edges. The work will be slightly more difficult if the gable ends are treated, as in the illustration, not as part of the main wall but as a series of posts. In this case a triangular frame must be provided for each gable. The bottom of each frame must be glued from the inside to the top edge of the main wall, thus providing structural support for the roof. When the roof has been erected, glue a pair of barge boards to each gable. The ends of these boards, which intersect at the ridge, can be carved into the shape of horses' heads. The barge boards can be made "hoary with age" by applying a coat of tempera color. The posts forming the triangular sections of the gable walls are glued on from the outside, after the hayloft beams have been laid across the bottom members of the triangular end frames.

We can achieve a very good imitation of half-timbered construction by gluing narrow strips of dark-stained veneer to the plywood walls and filling in the panels with the plaster described in Chapter 13. Once the plaster is dry it can be made to look like an old mud wall by coating it with tempera color (yellow ochre). Even isolated blocks of stone used to patch up the "tumble-down" wall can be imitated by means of skilfully applied tempera color.

Above all, it is necessary to give the creche an air of poverty overlain by evidence of venerable age. Accordingly, make the gables not out of brand-new doweling, straight as a die, but out of dry twigs gathered in the woods. Use the same material for the log fence, which goes part way around the structure. The corner posts of the sections of the fence should have their longer ends resting in suitable holes drilled in the base platform. Thus they can easily be taken out and packed away.

The posts supporting the projecting portion of the roof must also look old and rough-hewn. Cut them out of round pieces of solid timber, and merely suggest the square dressing by means of a pocket-knife. Special care is also required in order to give the thatched roof an ancient appearance. The silver-gray shade of weather-beaten thatched roofs is obtained by painting the straw with tempera and poster colors. At places where the thatched roof has been patched, the original color of the straw is left. Real moss can be used to get a natural effect.

The inside arrangements of the creche should be modest in the extreme. On the floor of the loft there will be a thin layer of hay, visible from below and through the gable ends. It may also be allowed to hang somewhat untidily between the ceiling beams. Inside, a ladder leads up to the hayloft, otherwise the fixtures are restricted to a few fodder troughs and racks on the walls. These can be roughly glued together out of bits of stained plywood and filled with hay. The floor should be coated with glue and strewn with sawdust.

A great deal of skill can be devoted to the shaping of the landscape, insofar as the size of the platform and the style of the creche as a whole justify such refinements. Anyone who is not satisfied with covering the platform with green-colored sawdust, held in place by a layer of glue, can create a hilly landscape out of fine wire-netting supported on small blocks of wood. The wire foundation should be covered with successive layers of glued newspaper, topped with a thin coating of gypsum. When this is dry it will be possible to paint in pathways and patches of grass in tempera colors. The transitions between the dummy hills and the plywood platform can be smoothed out by means of spackling or a putty made of gypsum and size.

Nevertheless, too much trouble should not be taken with the modeling of the landscape. When the space available for natural scenery is limited, it is only too easy to exaggerate the scale. In any event, make sure that sufficient flat space is available for setting up the figures around the crib.

As we mentioned at the outset, it is the figures—the focus of the action—that constitute the essence of the scene. Naturally, it is an advantage if whoever undertakes the modeling of the figures possesses some talent for sculpture, together with a feeling for form. Nevertheless a person not so gifted need by no means shrink from undertaking the task. Too obvious a striving for perfection is more likely to destroy than to

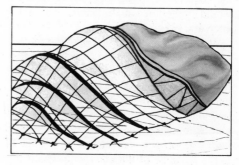

Fine wire netting and bits of wood form the supporting structure for a hilly landscape. The irregular surface is modeled in plaster.

Clay figures

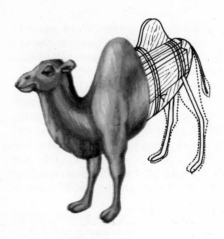

Larger clay figures are modeled over a light framework to reduce their weight.

emphasize the atmosphere of reverence. It is better if the last word remains unsaid.

For this reason, we shall not choose the most convenient way of making a creche figure. This involves buying a pretty, bright-colored sheet of suitable illustrations, cutting out the figures and sticking them onto plywood, and again cutting them out, this time with a fret saw. All that remains then is to glue a supporting block to the back and stand them up. Flat figures of this kind would not fit harmoniously into our landscape, which is built in three dimensions. Moreover, their crude and obtrusive realism would shatter the Christmas mood of reverence and peace.

We shall furnish our solidly constructed creche with fully rounded figures. For this we have available the twin techniques of modeling, in the sense of building up forms, and carving out of the solid block. The inexperienced will prefer the alternative of modeling, using one of the several plastic materials on the market, or clay. This is partly because of the ease with which the material can be shaped, but mainly because mistakes can be corrected by adding mate-

rial as well as by taking it away.

Whether people or animals are to be modeled, always start with the basic mass of the body, forming the limbs by adding rolls of clay—insofar as the work is done in clay which is both a cheap and a durable material. As soon as the basic form has been molded, the finer details are put in. At this stage modeling tools can be of great help to the skilled modeler. Nevertheless, one should always aim at applying the final touches by hand. Technical aids tend to make the modeler lose himself in detail, or else induce him to attempt refinements for which he has not yet got the necessary skill. The results of such efforts cannot fail to be unsatisfactory. As we have already pointed out, it is by no means necessary to strive after finality. For all its simplicity a suggestive form or a gesture broadly depicted may have a stronger effect than a face modeled to the last wrinkle.

More important than any detail is the effort to arrive at approximately the right proportions for the whole. The beginner will therefore do well to develop his figures, whether sitting, kneeling or walking, from the standing form. The clay is soft and the figures can be pressed into any attitude.

Larger figures, which threaten to collapse under the weight of the damp clay, must be molded over a wire armature, which will serve them, so to speak, as a skeleton. Such armatures can be twisted into shape out of fairly soft wire, using flat or round-nose pliers. The form can be built out with pieces of wood, tied to the armature with florists' wire, or with fine wire gauze, since the smaller the amount of clay used in making the figure, the lighter the figure will be, and the less the risk of cracking during the drying process. Fat clays should not be used for modeling, since these are by nature more liable to crack than lean ones.

served where the painting of the creche figures is concerned. Glaring colors should be avoided. Subdued, indeterminate tones should be used, and the colors of the individual figures forming the group should harmonize. Details that have not actually been modeled should not be simulated by doubtful tricks of coloring.

In carving creche figures from the block, use basswood, which cuts easily in any direction. A model made of plasticine or clay will serve as a useful guide. At any rate

Figures carved in wood can be primed and painted.

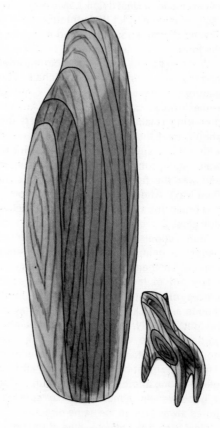

Preferably, the clay figures should be baked. Nevertheless, "bone-dry" figures are also very durable. In this condition they can be painted in tempera colors and, after the color is dry, dipped in liquid wax or, failing this, in stearin. This not only gives the figures an attractive finish, but makes them more rugged.

The suggestions made in connection with modeling should also be scrupulously ob-

Laminated figures made by gluing strips of hardwood together. The forms should be broad and flowing.

275

make several sketches of the proposed figure, from various angles, before beginning to carve the wood. Even while carving, the pencil should be used before the knife. The outlines of the front and side views should be drawn on the corresponding faces of the block, and then the rough profile cut out with a saw. After the edges have been removed, the general form will gradually emerge from the originally square block, after which it is possible to attempt the final surface using finer tools. With the wooden as with the clay figure, the modeling should not extend to the last detail. Leave excessive realism aside and let the contours run in a flowing rhythm about the broad masses of the form.

Wooden figures can also be colored, after priming with poster white and chalk. The featureless basswood, at least, requires some form of surface treatment. Anyone preferring a plain wooden to a colored figure should treat the smooth, clean basswood with a thinly applied, ochre-tinted spirit or water stain, rub this down with horsehair, and wax the figure in clean beeswax (or floor wax). After a final polish with a horsehair brush, the surface will have an attractive dull gloss.

More sophisticated figures, either of people or animals, whose effect depends entirely on their natural surfaces, can be made out of laminated wood. Use small pieces of differently colored, fine hardwoods and thick veneers, such as may be bought cheaply, as waste, from lumber yards. Suitable woods include teak, mahogany, walnut, cherry, oak, and maple. The pieces must be absolutely flat, and are glued to one another under pressure using a good veneer adhesive. Make sure the fibres always run in the same direction.

Next sketch the main outline of the figure on the largest, central piece of wood, and saw it out. Then cut out the smaller pieces and stick them on either side of the central piece. After the whole is dry, proceed with the finer details, using chisels, rasps, and sandpaper. When the shaping of the figure is complete, rub in some clear wax and polish with a brush.

In planning laminated figures preference should be given to pure free forms. It is permissible to go to the very limits of objective reality. Equally important is the harmonious grading of the colors when the two halves of a figure are stuck together. Guard against exaggerations and zebra effects. The general impression should not be one of overrefinement, nor should the color sequence on either side be too obviously parallel or regular.

The Christmas Pyramid

In the Erzgebirge, a mountain region on the borders of Czechoslovakia, which has long been the home of a race of skilful woodcarvers, the most original means have been discovered for giving expression to the Christmas spirit of gaiety. Long before it became the custom to deck a Christmas tree with candles, the people of the Erzgebirge used to construct magnificent Christmas pyramids, on the revolving platforms of which they portrayed a cross section of the population of the snow-bound village, including peasants, artisans, miners and huntsmen, together with all the animals from farm and forest, in a gay and glittering dance round the crib in the stable at Bethlehem.

Joining together to build such a pyramid is surely one of the most enjoyable ways of passing the long evenings of Advent. The whole family can take part in the work, and share in the anticipation of the Christmas festival.

Building a Christmas pyramid demands not only artistic skill but a definite mechanical bent, since the figures revolve around a vertical axle on one or more rotating discs. The motive power is supplied by a fan-wheel attached to the axle, which is driven by a rising current of warm air. Thus, the candles of the Christmas pyramid have a double task to perform. First, they must illuminate the whole gay carousel, and then provide the necessary "fuel" in the form of heated air. The nature of this motive force, produced by mechanical and physical means, and all its consequences, must be carefully borne in mind when the pyramid is being designed. In the first place, the framework should offer the least possible resistance to the rising air. Moreover, the pyramid must be so constructed that it can be readily set up and dismantled, and packed away in the smallest possible space. As the building material will be almost exclusively wood, we shall be able to use simple dowel joints, so that the frame will be easy to take apart.

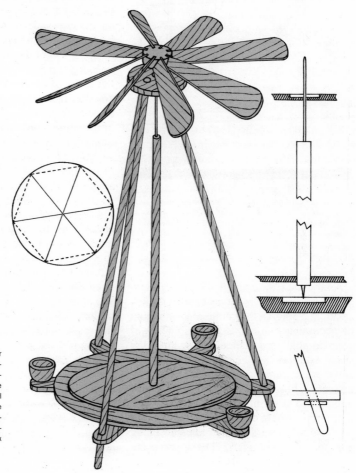

The framework of a single-tier Christmas pyramid with platform for the figures and fanwheel. The details show the two bearings for the central axle, the joint between the sloping poles and the platform brackets, and the division of the platform into six parts.

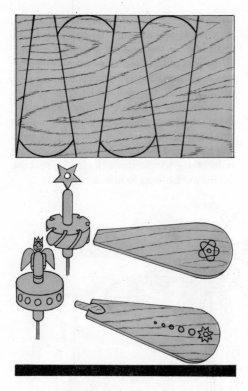

Construction of the fan-wheel. Top: an economical way of cutting out the individual vanes. Bottom: the hub of the fan-wheel with the dowel passing through it and two ways of attaching the removable vanes, by means of oblique grooves or small wooden forks.

should be pieces of plywood or beechwood $1/4''$ thick and $1 1/4''$ wide. The projecting ends of the brackets should be rounded off for the sake of a more pleasing appearance.

Three of these brackets will carry candle holders; in the other three holes are drilled to fit the three poles that form the framework of the pyramid. The poles are made of round pieces of beechwood 11'' long and $3/8''$ thick. They can be smoothed by rolling on a stretched sheet of sandpaper. A small transverse wooden pin is glued in an inch or so above the slightly rounded foot. When the pyramid is assembled, the three brackets through which the poles are passed will be supported on these pins.

At the top of the pyramid the three poles converge on a disc made of the same material as the base. This disc, however, is much smaller, being only 2'' in diameter. It has three holes drilled in it, into which the ends of the three poles will fit. The size of these holes should be slightly less than the cross section of the poles. Accordingly, the heads of the poles are filed to a slightly conical shape so that they fit tightly into the upper disk. The poles must not stand vertically, but lean sharply inwards. Therefore, the walls of the drill holes should not be vertical either. Begin by boring a vertical hole and then slope the walls with a round file, without, however, enlarging the diameter. The fixed parts of the pyramid are now ready. We must next turn our attention to the construction of the axle and the platform for the figures, which is attached to it. The diameter of this circular platform, made of perfectly smooth $1/4''$ plywood, is $3/4''$ less than that of the base. The hole drilled through it should be accurately centered and should fit the axle tightly without requiring additional support. If the hole is too large, it can be glued. This is perfectly all right, except that later, when the pyramid is put away for most

As the base for a small, single-tier pyramid take a circular disk of plywood, $3/8''$ thick and 6'' in diameter, the center of which must be accurately marked. Later this will be of considerable importance in locating the lower axle bearing. For the present it will serve as a guide in mounting the small projecting brackets (six in all) which have to be glued at equal intervals to the underside of the base (a circle can be divided into six parts by pricking off the radius six times around the perimeter). These brackets

of the year, the awkward shape will take up a lot of room.

The axle is a round rod of well-seasoned beechwood $^3/_8$″ thick. It must be perfectly straight, vertical and accurately at right angles to the platform supporting the figures. The length of this rod, in our case, is eight inches. Like the poles, the axle must be perfectly smooth.

Our candle-driven hot-air motor will not, of course, produce much horse-power. We must therefore mount the axle in a socket that offers a minimum of frictional resistance to rotation. This is not possible with wood. We shall therefore use an old steel phonograph needle driven centrally into the lower end of the axle with the point projecting only about $^1/_4$″. If a phonograph needle is not available, the shaft of an ordinary thin steel sewing needle can be used. The top of the wooden axle is extended by inserting a piece of knitting needle, about 2″ long, into a hole drilled exactly in the center of the rod, and gluing it in place.

The seat of the lower bearing will be a small coin, with the stamping filed away, embedded in the center of the base. If the recess is carefully cut out, it will be enough to press the coin into place, otherwise it must be glued down.

A far-sighted worker will have marked out the six divisions of the base not only on the bottom but also on the top. If, after inserting the coin, lines joining the marks on the perimeter are drawn in, they will intersect exactly in the center of the disc, and will therefore mark the center of the coin. Place a sharp center punch over this point and give it a light tap with a hammer. This will form a cup bearing for the end of the pyramid axle.

We shall also make the seat of the upper bearing out of a coin, inserted into the top of the small upper disk. This disk should al-

Large two-tiered Christmas pyramid with vertical poles. The upper platform is fixed to the cross-frame and does not revolve.

ready have been drilled with a hole big enough to prevent the knitting needle from rubbing against its sides. The correct bearing is provided by drilling a hole of the same diameter as the needle through the middle of the coin. It is possible to judge when the axle is vertical by moving the loose coin, with the tip of the needle passed through it, over the surface of the disk, until the axle begins to turn freely of its own accord. Then, with a sharp pencil, the position of the coin is marked on the disk and a shallow recess formed to receive it.

The only item still missing is the hot-air motor, in the form of a fan-wheel, which keeps the pyramid in motion. For the hub of the fan-wheel take a round piece of beechwood, or better hornbeam, $3/8"$ thick and one inch in diameter. The hub must be cut out of end-grain wood, that is the fibres must run parallel with those of the axle. At the central point of the hub drill a hole about $1/4"$ deep, in which the needle point of the axle is clamped. The top of the pyramid will look more attractive, however, if a round dowel $1^1/2"$ long is glued into a hole, some $3/8"$ wide, drilled through the middle of the hub. The point of the knitting needle can then be clamped in the bottom of this dowel, while an angel or a star can be mounted on top.

The fan-wheel of a pyramid of this size will need eight vanes. Larger models, with two or even three platforms, require 12 to 16 vanes. Cut the vanes individually out of beechwood $1/16"$ thick. They should be 4" in length, $5/8"$ wide at the hub and $1^3/4"$ wide at the tip. The corners of the broad ends should be rounded off. The upper and lower faces of the vanes may be decorated with designs in color.

Special care is needed in fixing the vanes to the hub. At equal intervals saw a series of eight oblique parallel grooves, into which the vanes will later be glued. Another solution is to drill eight holes radiating from the center of the hub, glue the vanes into small wooden forks, and file the ends of these forks to fit into the holes drilled in the side of the hub.

The principles applied in constructing this small model are universal. However, since the sloping poles considerably restrict the free space over the revolving plat-form, the method is not strictly suitable for larger pyramids, especially those with several tiers. The heads of figures standing vertically near the edge of the platform would strike the poles as the platform revolved.

Larger models are therefore built with four vertical poles held together by a cross-frame at the top. In this case the knitting needle passes through the center of the cross, which acts as a canopy. The circular base can be retained, except that the poles are tenoned into it directly, the extra free space being used for a larger wreath of candles. Additional candle holders can also be attached half way up the poles. If the pyramid has several revolving tiers, the diameter of the upper platforms will be reduced.

The projecting members of the cross-frame make it possible to add to the pyramid a very attractive fixed platform. This, like the revolving platforms for the figures, will be in the form of a circular disk, but will have a hole drilled through the middle wide enough for the axle to turn freely inside it. This fixed platform is suspended from the main arm of the cross by means of a pair of glued rods. On this platform we can place the crib, with Joseph, Mary and the Christ-child, in miniature. On a lower platform, the shepherds and the Wise Men from the East revolve slowly around the Holy Family, while high above the crib a choir of angels is poised.

In the case of pyramids large enough to accommodate all these decorative details, square posts and smooth axles would produce a prosaic and mechanical impression. Try, therefore, to break up these rigid lines with notches and chip carving. By painting the framework and figures in bright colors we can add to the childlike gaiety expressed in the pyramid's spirited motion.

To make a pyramid entirely in the style of the Erzgebirge, the figures should be carved out of round pieces of wood. The people of the Erzgebirge simply use the firwood found in such abundance in their native forests. For us it will be easier to use basswood or chestnut. The deceptively soft and light wood of the poplar is unsuitable for wood carving of any kind. Arms, angels' wings, and other accessories are carved separately and glued on. The bodies of the animals are also shaped from doweling, but legs, donkey's ears, and the horns of oxen have to be added. Like the creche figures, the pyramid dancers can also be carved from a solid block. The technique is the same as before, but the scale is smaller. When fitted with glued-on base pins the finished figures can be mounted in corresponding holes in the revolving platform. Take care to get an even distribution of weight. Any kind of uneven loading must be avoided, if the platform is to revolve easily and without friction.

The Christmas Nutcracker

A useful guest who is always welcome under the Christmas tree, in spite of his fierce appearance, is the nutcracker. His calling is by no means an easy one, since fate has assigned to him the thankless task of cracking the hardest nuts for other people. And while the latter enjoy the tasty kernels, he gets, at best, the shells. That sort of thing leaves its impression on his features. The nutcracker is a tough fellow and for that reason we must construct him, for better or for worse, out of a hard block of wood.

The starting material for a nutcracker manikin is a square block of the same height as the finished figure. Soft or light woods, liable to split, are unsuitable for the hard,

mechanical work demanded of a nutcracker. The best wood for the body is the indestructible hornbeam. Though, long-fibred ash is excellent for the nut-cracking lever arm.

The lever mechanism, pivoting near the manikin's throat, constitutes the main problem. The crushing chamber and the lever should therefore be constructed before any work is done on shaping the figure. In order to minimize the risk of mistakes, accurately fix the height of the crushing chamber, and the position of the seat and fulcrum of the lever, on a full-size drawing of the original block.

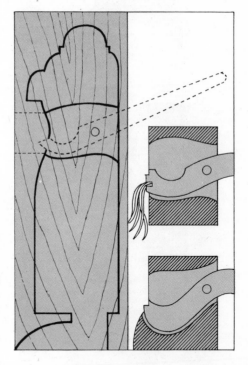

Outline of nutcracker showing the position of the crushing chamber and lever. The hollow in the bottom of the crushing chamber must match the curve of the forward lever arm.

Nutcrackers

After the correct measurements have been transferred to the wood, the opening of the mouth is chiseled out, the "gums" are hollowed, and the lever, or lower jaw, is formed. It is important to make a depression in the end of this lever so that when it is pressed the manikin does not spit out the nut, instead of cracking it. The less the longitudinal fibres of the lever are cut away the better. Those possessing a large stock of wood should look for a piece in which the curvature of the lever is already present in the lie of the fibres.

The proportions of the body can now be sketched on the block, and carved out. Pay no attention to the arms at this stage; they will be glued on later. Similarly, the legs should be left rough, or omitted entirely, so that the wood is not unnecessarily weakened. To make sure that the manikin will stand properly it can be doweled to a small pedestal. Better still select a block of wood for carving the figure big enough to allow for an integral stand. Making the whole nutcracker out of one piece not only saves the trouble of mounting, but also avoids joints, a source of potential trouble.

The accurate insertion of the lever is important. The hole for the strong hinge pin, through the neck of the figure and through the lever itself, must be drilled when the latter is already in position. If the hole is not drilled straight the nutcracker will get lockjaw!

If the long arm of the lever is made flat, when its mouth is shut the manikin will have a hole where human beings have a chin. In the old popular art this blemish was often hidden by a fierce-looking beard, actually a piece of fur attached to the lower jaw of the figure and hanging down over its chest. Skilled carvers can give the end of the lever the appearance of a fully rounded chin. The curve of the chin, however, must match the circle through which the chin moves when the nutcracker takes a bite. The radius of this circle is the shorter arm of the lever. In addition, the lower part of the mouth must project far enough for the manikin to take even the thickest walnuts between his teeth. Now nothing remains but to dip freely into the paint pots, for our nutcracker, with his robust physique, can stand being brightly colored. Spruced in this way he will make a splendid Christmas "surprise packet."

The Tinsel Angel

A pleasant contrast to the humorously grotesque nutcracker manikin from the wintry forest is offered by the tinsel angel, which looks as if it had just slipped down to earth from heaven. The best material for this delicate creature is a strong gilt tinsel. It is also possible to make silver angels, or combine these glittering materials with tissue paper or parchment, or with colored foil, in order to give the angel's robe a more life-like appearance. A good strong material for making large-sized angels is aluminum foil, in gold, silver and other colors. In this medium some splendid effects can be obtained. The foil can be treated like strong paper; it is easy to cut with scissors, though not so easy to cut with a knife. On no account must it be folded, since it consists of thin metal which will break if sharply bent. On the other hand, it is easy to trace patterns in foil with the point of a knitting needle or even a hard pencil.

The golden angel is undeniably a creature of fantasy; therefore it should be constructed as spontaneously as possible, with the imagination given a free rein. As the material is not very strong, give the figure additional support by binding two rods together crosswise. The horizontal rod will reinforce the arms, while the head can be modeled around the short upper end of the vertical rod in hardened wax. Wax is hardened by melting it together with rosin or mastic directly in the water-bath. Only pure primary colors are used to color the wax. A head modeled out of flesh-colored wax can be "made up" with red cheeks and lips using lip-stick. For finer details minute quantities of wax colors are dissolved in turpentine and put on with a very soft brush. To prepare the small amount of color required for an angel's head, it is enough to collect a few

drops of turpentine in a saucer and stir a piece of wax color in the liquid until the desired intensity of color is obtained. The color must be put on at once, since turpentine quickly evaporates. Simpler heads for small angels can be made out of wooden balls, painted in water colors.

The shoulder part of the cross, and the first inch or so of the vertical support, can be wrapped with a few turns of muslin bandage to give the figure more "body." Instead of bandage, it is equally possible to use cellulose wool, which must be firmly

Robes and wings

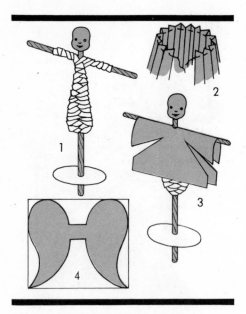

Details of the tinsel angel: 1 padded frame and cardboard disk for flaring the skirt, 2 draw-string at the waist, 3 upper garment with sleeves cut out, 4 pattern for the wings.

secured with strong thread. Over this "body" the pleated skirt can easily be attached with a few stitches. The skirt, on the bottom edge of which the angel stands, is folded in gilt paper (as for a lampshade), and the upper edge is drawn into the waist by means of a string threaded through the pleats. The attractive fullness of the skirt is ensured by a circular disk of strong cardboard with a hole drilled through the middle. This is pushed up the vertical arm of the cross until it causes the pleats of the skirt to flare out. If it is desired to decorate the hem of the skirt with bands of differently colored paper, these must be stuck on in narrow strips before the skirt is pleated. If the design of the skirt as a whole is to be set off with a second color, like that of the gold and pink angel on the previous page,

then, of course, the strips of colored paper must not be added until the pleating is complete.

Make the upper garment, with its broad, cut-out sleeves, from a doubled piece of aluminum foil, the same width as the sleeves. Be careful in forming the upper edge. In order to avoid accidental kinks or even cracks, bend the foil over a pencil or the handle of a paint brush. After the wedge-shaped sleeves have been cut out on both sides and the opening for the neck, together with a slit down the back, has been made, place the garment over the wooden "arms," and tuck in the lower part to form a "bodice," then glue together the lower edges of the sleeves. Decorate the bottom of the sleeves with a stamped pattern. Use gilt paper to cut out the doubled corsage with its neck opening and back slit. This can later be set off with a white neck-ruff or scalloped tucker.

A tinsel angel with outspread arms will usually be designed to hold candles. As only fine wax candles are suited to its delicate frame, we need not construct special candle holders. It will be enough to use a strong pin, inserted from below through the ends of the wooden arms. Before sticking the candles on the pins, place aluminum foil disks beneath them to catch the drips.

For an angel with less rigid arms, holding a scroll instead of candles, replace the wooden cross-piece with a double loop of wire, wrapped in cellulose wool and thread, and bend into an appropriate attitude. Model wax hands at the ends of the loops. Aluminum foil is not sufficiently pliable for the overgarment of such an angel, which must be made of soft tinsel, possibly brightened with glossy paper of a different color. Thanks to its greater stiffness, aluminum foil is especially suitable for the wings, the outline of which is first sketched on paper and then transfered to the foil by pricking through with a pin. If the wings are to be made of tinsel it will be necessary to stick two layers together. In order to increase their strength, both wings should be cut out in a single piece and attached to the back of the figure in the middle. Aluminum wings can be gently curved and rounded by drawing them between thumb and fore-finger while pressing lightly. Sharper curves are obtained by bending the material over a rounded piece of wood. This may be neces-

sary for example, if the angel is to wear a golden crown, which can be made out of scalloped aluminum foil. The head is best adorned with curls of spun glass, which, in fact, is sometimes known as "angel's hair." The tinsel angel will then cut such a splendid figure that he will surely be summoned by the Christ-child to preside over the distribution of presents. Moreover, he will deserve a place of special honor under the Christmas tree.

17 OUTDOOR HOBBIES

Christmas, alas, does not last all winter, but happily it isn't winter all the year round. As the days lengthen thoughts turn to outdoor activities and sports. Some of these call for equipment which the hobbyist can make in his own workshop and which he will use with doubled pleasure because it is the product of his own skill.

Archery

Archery, certainly one of the most attractive and elegant of sports, has developed into a fine art, depending less on strength than on concentration and judgement. Ammunition is cheap, while the actual shooting is virtually noiseless. Furthermore, no licenses or elaborate safety precautions are needed. You merely erect a target in some sheltered gravel pit or lonely field and your practice range is complete.

The most popular domestic wood for making bows is the tough, supple Western yew. A possible alternative is ash. The best bows are not sawn down from the log, but split off lengthwise, the object being to keep the fibres as far as possible intact. Lengths split from the outside of the trunk are generally superior to heartwood staves. If split material is not available, you will have to be satisfied with a sawn knot-free stave about $7/_8''$ thick and $1''$ wide. These dimensions correspond to a bow between $54''$ and $64''$ in length. Do not make your bow unduly long, however. A general rule is that when one end of the bow is placed on the ground, the tip should not reach above the level of the archer's eye.

When choosing material for a bow, see to

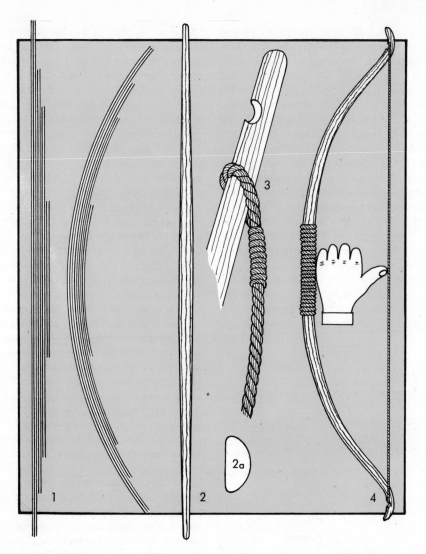

The yew bow: 1—direction of the fibres and how they are cut, 2—bow seen from in front, 2a—cross section, 3—nock and end of bowstring, 4—the braced bow. The tension is checked by inserting the fist with thumb extended.

Shaping the bow

it that as far as possible the fibres run parallel with the edge. The face of the bow turned towards the target is known as the "back." It should be planed flat and smoothed off with a spoke shave. After the edges have been rounded the back of the bow should not be touched again with the tools. As far as possible avoid cutting into the fibres or the bow may split under strain. The important tapering of the shaft towards the ends is first developed on the sides only, leaving the middle fifth intact. In the process of paring down the sides of the shaft, simultaneously round off the edges, so that the inside face or "belly" of the bow becomes gently arched. Seen from in front, the bow will then have a lens-shaped profile. All this work should be done exclusively with the rasp and spoke shave, or with the edge of a freshly broken piece of glass. Do not attempt to speed up the process by using a plane.

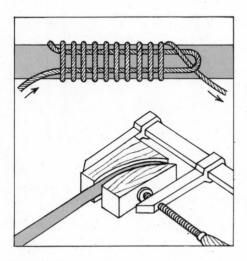

Top: securing the binding forming the handle of the bow. Bottom: press for bending the ends of the bow.

The taper must be quite even on each side, and the greater the care expended at this stage, the better the final performance of the bow will be.

Now take a round file and about $^3/_4''$ in from each end of the bow file shallow notches, so-called "nocks," for attaching the bowstring. These nocks extend only over the back and sides of the bow and should not be cut with a knife. You may now draw the bow for the first time, using a temporary bowstring made of wire or twine, and proceed to shape the "belly." The tension is just right when the archer can just insert his fist with the thumb extended between the bowstring and the middle of the shaft. Later on, this same "rule of thumb" will come in handy for testing the tension of your bow during target practice. Now pick up the spoke shave again (or the piece of broken glass) and scrape the wood away from the belly of the bow, working towards each end, until you have produced a uniformly flat curve. This scraping away of the inside face determines both the final shape of the bow and its individual tension, usually known as the "drawing weight." The more wood that is cut away—concentrate on the ends more than the center—the easier it will be to bend the bow. Thus, everyone can make a bow to suit his own strength. Excessively stiff bows should be left to the body-builders. In the long run, maximum satisfaction can be extracted from a bow, only if it can be drawn to full arrow length without overtaxing the archer's strength. In fact, it is a basic rule of archery that, regardless of whether you shoot over long distances or short, you draw the bow to the full length of the arrow.

The shaping of the "belly" completes the actual woodwork involved in making a straight bow. The tension is released, and the bow is rubbed down several times with hot linseed oil, after which it should be coated with a weatherproof synthetic-resin varnish. Finally, a grip or handle is formed by tightly winding a thin cord (fishing line) around the middle of the shaft. The end of the cord is pulled under the binding by means of a loop formed in the first turn. This will hold it neatly and firmly in place.

The bow will look more elegant and shoot somewhat further if the ends are bent slightly forward. This, however, can only be done with damp heat. About 6″ of the shaft at each end should be steeped for about an hour in boiling water, after which the wood will have softened sufficiently for it to be bent. At full heat the ends are clamped between two wooden blocks carved to the exact degree of curvature required. In 24 hours the wood will be dry enough for it to be removed from the press, and then even long usage will not produce any distortion.

For your bowstring choose fine-thread linen, hemp, or Dacron, laid in pure beeswax, or possibly a steel wire. The thinner and stronger the bowstring, the truer will be the shot. The loops at the ends of a hempen bowstring, designed to fit into the nocks, are made by turning back the ends, plaiting them in, and binding with thin twine. These loops should not be too tight and should permit the bow to recover easily after each shot. If no suitable material is available for a home-made bowstring, a ready-made substitute can be obtained from any sports dealer.

The arrows should be light, but slightly weighted towards the tip. They should be just about as long as the archer's arm (typically 26″). Very simple, though not very durable arrows can be fashioned from straight, dry reeds, weighted at the tip with a piece of green elder wood about 3″ long and rather more than finger thick. These tips are simply slipped over the end of the

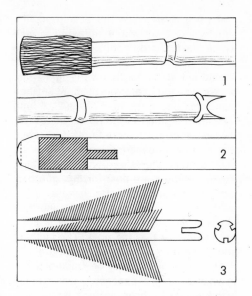

Arrows: 1—reed arrow with elderwood tip, 2—arrow with a hardwood tip and steel cap, 3—tail of arrow with nock and feathers.

arrow. The notch at the other end for attaching the bowstring, also called a nock, should be situated immediately behind a knot in the stem of the reed.

Stronger arrows can be fashioned from well-seasoned pine, maple, or lindenwood. Willow, too, is quite suitable. The shafts (diameter about $7/_{16}$″) may be either cylindrical or slightly conical, that is, slightly thicker in front than behind. Deft-fingered craftsmen can splice a hardwood tip onto their arrows and fit it with a steel cap, possibly a ferrule from a thin walking stick. This hardwood head can be replaced with a thin piece of metal tubing. For target practice a sharp, pointed arrow head is not necessary. Hunting arrows, of course, must satisfy different requirements.

The tail of the arrow is equally important.

Feathering—targets

The nock, into which the bowstring fits, should not be cut with a knife, but formed with a file. It should not be too wide. Once strung, an arrow with a properly filed nock should not fall under its own weight when allowed to hang freely from the bow. An inch and a half above the nock three 2$^1/_2$″ long feathers are glued to the shaft. Of course, they will stick much more firmly if recessed into narrow grooves cut lengthwise in the shaft, at equal intervals around its perimeter. Turkey feathers are best for this purpose, but goose quills can also be used. The feathers are cut down the middle and then glued to the shaft so that the barbs point backwards towards the nock. The feathers should be trimmed only after being glued.

The target or butt may be made of straw to which a facing of paper or canvas, marked with a series of concentric rings, is attached. Simple straw targets consist of coiled roves of twisted straw about 3″ thick. The coils are stitched together with hempen yarn. The straw is then covered with a round piece of canvas to which the actual ring target is firmly nailed using leather or cardboard "washers."

Such targets are fairly good, but cannot stand up for long to the impact of arrows launched from powerful bows. Quality targets are made of hand-threshed rye straw, the stalks being cut into 6″ lengths. The pieces are laid on a table and pressed together by means of a thick wire, or better still steel bands, to the specified diameter. The individual pieces of straw now run parallel to the direction of impact of the arrow and therefore are less likely to be chopped and broken.

Unfortunately, such a tournament target is very heavy and awkward to handle. It is usually set up on a three-legged stand inclined at an angle of 15 degrees, so that the center of the target is 48″ above the ground. The bull's-eye, which carries the highest number of points, is colored gold, so, even with a home-made bow, remember to shoot for the gold.

The Crossbow

The following story, told by travelers returning from South America, shows how accurate the longbow can be. It is said that the native Indians can shoot an arrow into the air so that it returns to earth exactly at a predetermined point. Just as the arrow begins to turn downwards at the top of its trajectory, the archer puts out his right foot and cold-bloodedly watches the needle-sharp arrow sizzle into the ground through the gap between his big toe and the rest.

We decline to conclude from this story that archers are as prone to telling tall tales as fishermen and hunters. It is true that by

Tournament butt made of chopped straw on a tripod stand. Slope of butt 15 degrees, height of center of target 48″.

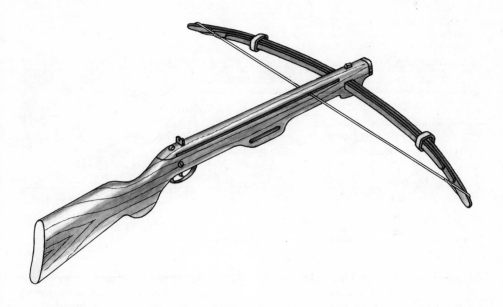

Crossbow with slotted barrel, fore and back-sights, and laminated bow.

dint of practice remarkable accuracy can be achieved. However, if you lack the time to train to this level, you may prefer to turn your skill to the construction of a weapon, the accuracy of which surpasses that of even the finest longbow.

Essentially, the crossbow is nothing other than a mechanically perfected bow. Its principal parts are the stock, butt and trigger and the bow and bowstring. This bow, similar in appearance to an ordinary longbow, is supported horizontally in the front part of the stock.

In the case of the simplest type of crossbow, the top of the stock is cut away to form a straight, open channel. It can only be used for shooting bolts or short arrows. The crossbow with a slotted stock and rifle-type barrel is superior in several ways. It can fire clay and lead balls as well as bolts. Furthermore, the slotted stock leaves room for a foresight and a backsight, which makes the weapon much easier to aim.

You can't expect accurate aiming if your crossbow has a twisted butt. Since the entire stock, including the butt, is made in

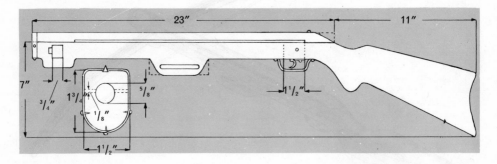

Working drawing of crossbow (bow not shown). The side view shows the barrel, butt and stock with bow slot, hand guard, trigger and trigger guard. Below: the barrel, showing the screws securing the brass muzzle strap.

one piece, we must use a high-grade hardwood that will not warp. Walnut is very good, but somewhat expensive. It is used for the butts of high-priced hunting rifles. Maple and fine-grained ash are also suitable. Fall back on beech only if you have no other choice. It splits readily and is not particularly stable, being very sensitive to moisture.

If, in return for the time and care spent on making a crossbow, you expect to collect prizes with it later on, then you should make no bones about selecting the very best wood. A reliable crossbow requires an absolutely sound, knotless and first-grade piece of timber big enough to contain both stock and butt.

The stock and butt combined make up the overall length of the finished weapon. It is true that the longer the barrel, the better the aim, but in actual practice this axiom is subject to certain limitations. The weapon must not become unmanageable. We shall

content ourselves with a piece of timber 34″ long and 7″ wide. This width is necessary owing to the angle formed between the stock and the 11″ long butt. This angle is about 10 degrees. Avoid exaggerated butt angles, otherwise the fibres will be cut into excessively, and the general strength of the stock reduced.

The thickness of the material depends on the caliber of the crossbow, that is on the internal diameter of the barrel. In this instance we shall assume that this diameter is $5/8″$. For a wall thickness of $7/16″$ this requires a total thickness of $1^1/2″$. But even if you choose a smaller caliber, say $3/8″$, don't use thin material, since the butt must be thick enough to fit your shoulder snugly.

The construction of the crossbow begins with the preparation of a scale drawing which is then used to transfer the profile of the stock and butt onto the wood. After cutting out the rough shape with a coping saw, start work on the two slots for the bow and the trigger mechanism. The further the bow is set forward, the greater its drawing weight will be. $2^1/_2''$ behind the muzzle is the foreward edge of the inch-high bow slot, the width of which depends on the construction of the bow, varying between $^3/_4''$ and 1". The top of the slot must lie at least $^1/_4''$ below the top of the stock. The side walls should be chiseled out very carefully. They should be exactly at right angles to the axis of the stock. A smaller slot, also passing right through the stock, is required for wedging the bow.

Another method of fixing the bow is to form a notch the thickness of the bow in the end of the stock, starting about $^3/_8''$ below the muzzle. The bow is then fitted into this notch and bound in position. This binding is passed through a hole drilled transversely through the stock. In crossbows of this kind, which at best can not be very strong, the extra thickness of the stock at the muzzle, designed to strengthen the bow slot, can be omitted. Don't expect too much from this particular form of construction, however, since even a weak bow when released develops a surprising amount of forward thrust.

The slot for the trigger mechanism is $^1/_4''$ wide and, as distinct from the bow slot, runs parallel to the axis of the stock. The rear wall of the narrow chamber lies flush with the rear end of the bowstring slot. A chamber length of about $1^1/_2''$ is enough, since the trigger does not have to travel very far. Thus the stock is only slightly weakened. Moreover, this mechanism has the advantage that it can be locked by means of an easily constructed safety catch.

After chiseling out these two slots, take plenty of sandpaper and a rasp and carefully shape the butt and stock, including the thickening at the bow slot and the hand guard. All sharp edges and corners should be gently rounded since the crossbow should be handsome as well as comfortable to handle. Consider carefully where to form the hand guard. Crossbowmen with a long reach may wish to move the hand guard an inch or so forward. In any case, it must lie beyond the center of gravity of the weapon. An unbalanced crossbow will tire the arm and cause eye-strain as a result of the wavering of the sights. The best crossbow will be a "custom-made" one, that is the dimensions should be adapted to the needs of the individual bowman.

The next step is to true up the two halves of the barrel. For the independent upper half use a piece of wood 23" long and $^3/_4''$ thick, of the same sort as used for the stock. The width should again be $1^1/_2''$.

Start by planing the inside faces of both halves of the barrel absolutely flat. Then, with a marking gage indicate the diameter of the barrel, which lies in the middle of the two

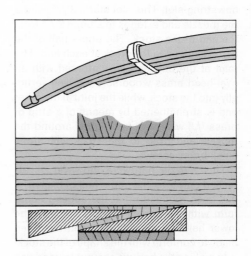

Wedging the bow in the bow slot. The width of the slot depends on the construction and thickness of the bow.

surfaces, cut out the corresponding channels with a gouge, and rub them down to the exact semicircular form, starting with the stock. This rather tedious work should be performed with the utmost care, for if the axis of the bow is twisted during the operation, it will never shoot accurately later on. The best way of ensuring an ideally straight barrel is to obtain a sufficiently long (about 12") round iron bar with a diameter slightly less than the final caliber of the bow, wrap it in emery paper, and rub down the entire length of the barrel to the required depth and the correct profile. Remember that the barrel ends at the front wall of the trigger chamber. Even if you cut through the end of the stock as well, you still won't have a breech-loading crossbow!

The upper half of the barrel is treated in the same way. Here, again, you should not cut away the last $2^1/_2$" at the end of the stock. These last $2^1/_2$" must retain their full thickness.

Then $1/_8$" is removed from the underside of the upper half of the barrel to form the bowstring slot. This slot starts $3^1/_4$" behind the muzzle and extends to a point $2^1/_2$" from the end of the stock. The upper half of the barrel is glued to the stock at each end. The joint at the butt end is reinforced with an oval-head brass wood screw driven vertically into the stock, while the joint at the other end is strengthened by means of a strip of brass $3/_8$" wide wrapped tightly around the muzzle and fixed to the stock with three small brass screws.

This muzzle hardware, however, is attached only after the upper half of the barrel has been rounded off at the edges to conform with the curved cross section of the lower half and after its rear end has been made to conform with the shape of the stock.

In making the bow we can put to good use much of what we have already learnt in making a longbow. This part of the crossbow is also made of yew or ash and it is up to the individual to decide whether to construct a bow with a one-piece shaft or a compound bow with a laminated shaft like a wagon spring. The width of the bow slot in the stock depends, as already mentioned, on the nature of the bow. It should be less for a simple bow, since we can then manage very well with a thickness of $1/_2$" in the middle. Avoid excessively long bows. In our case a span of 32" will be enough. Moreover, the shorter the distance between the bow and the trigger arm, the less the span of the bow need be. Shortening the span increases the drawing weight, but also the risk of premature fatigue and rupture.

A laminated bow requires a total of three strips an inch wide and at most $5/_{16}$" thick. The shortest strip should form the belly of the bow, the longest the back. As with the longbow, the width tapers towards the ends. Similarly, nocks are again provided for attaching the bowstring. The separate strips are not glued, but clamped together by two binders consisting of cut-down willow rods. These are glued only to the front face of the outer strip, so that the individual strips are free to move when the bow is drawn. The bow is held firmly in the bow slot by means of two flat wedges driven in from opposite sides.

Instead of yew, some crossbow designers use strips of steel. But these are heavy, apt to unbalance the crossbow, and give a very hard shot. This not particularly desirable quality is further emphasized by fitting the bow with a steel bowstring instead of the more flexible Dacron. A steel wire is certainly much more durable, but, of course, it is harder than wood and the unavoidable friction in the barrel slot quickly abrades the top of the stock. It is better to choose the lesser of two evils and occasionally pur-

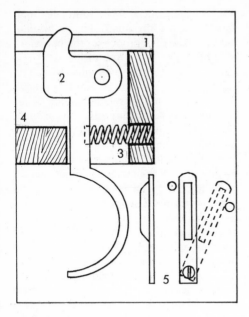

Trigger mechanism and safety catch: 1—bowstring slot, 2—cam and trigger arm, 3—trigger spring, 4—front trigger stop, 5—pivoting safety catch seen from the front and the side.

flush with the face of the stock.

The cam should be shaped very carefully. Its front edge is rounded and beveled so that when the crossbow is braced, the bowstring will slide over it smoothly and lie snugly in the notch behind.

Seen from in front the cam is also rounded. If the sharp side edges were allowed to remain, they would act on the bowstring like twin wedges and cut right through it not later than the third shot. After firing, the trigger is returned to the position of rest by a compression spring acting on the lower, vertical part of the trigger arm. This spring is mounted in a shallow hole drilled in the rear face of this component. The other end lies between two $^1/_4$″ thick wooden blocks glued to the back of the trigger chamber. In assembling the trigger the upper block with its rounded underside is glued in first. Then the entire trigger mechanism including the spring is pushed into the chamber, the pin inserted, and the lower block added. In front, a third block, acting as a stop, holds the trigger vertical in the position of rest. In constructing the trigger assembly never forget that, although small, it is nevertheless subjected to a very heavy load. It therefore needs to be built solidly. Before cutting out its metal components, make a model in plywood or stiff cardboard. Furthermore, the trigger assembly must be built in before the upper half of the barrel is attached. Otherwise you will block off the trigger chamber from above.

Don't forget the safety catch. It takes the form of a simple metal lever, pivoting about a wood screw attached to the underside of the stock, and when pushed sideways with the thumb it slides behind the trigger locking it in position. Two brass nails with round heads serve as stops. The safety catch consists of brass plate about $^1/_{16}$″ thick, onto which a lug has been soldered to

chase a new bowstring. Moreover, as with the longbow, the golden rule should be: relax the tension when the bow is not in use.

The trigger mechanism presents the hobbyist with some interesting problems. Its construction and operation should be quite clear after a close examination of the accompanying drawing. Trigger and trigger arm are filed from a single piece of $^3/_{16}$″ thick brass. The trigger pin is made from a sufficiently long flat-head brass wood screw with the originally conical shank filed into a cylindrical shape. If the screw is too long, and its point passes right through the stock and appears on the other side, file it down

provide a purchase for the thumb. You can easily make a safety catch by removing the slide from a light, straight door bolt of the type used by cabinetmakers.

The trigger guard is bent out of a strip of $1/16''$ brass. For the sake of appearance the ends of the guard are let into the stock a depth equal to their own thickness and fastened by means of oval-head brass screws. The edges of the guard are rounded from the inside towards the outside.

Finally, the crossbow is finished off by adding the sights. The greater the distance between the sights, the more accurate the aim will be. Both elements, the triangular forward-sloping foresight and the backsight with its central notch are filed in horn or a piece of beef bone. We shall need material $3/16''$ thick (slightly thicker for the backsight, since it has a dovetailed foot).

First of all, glue the foresight into a small groove formed in the barrel just behind the brass strap at the muzzle end. The sight must be located accurately in the center of the barrel without being canted in relation to the axis of the stock. Its exact height must be tested when "shooting in" the crossbow. So do not set the foresight too low, then you

will have a chance to file it down later on, if your bolts are dropping short. Chiseling out the dovetailed groove for the backsight at right-angles to the axis of the stock is a rather more troublesome business. The sight is eventually pushed into this groove from the side. It is essential that the upper edge of the backsight be perfectly horizontal. The exact position of the backsight can only be fixed by experiment. The right position is found by sliding the sight back and forth in its groove until the shots no longer veer off to right or left, but land squarely on the vertical axis of the target. When this happens, mark the correct position of the backsight by making a nick in its base and in the wood of the barrel, withdraw it from the groove, and glue it back firmly, so that the two nicks coincide. The sight can then be fixed immovably in the groove by wedging it from either side.

Making the ammunition is perfectly easy. Simply cut and smooth down 4″ long hardwood bolts to fit the diameter of the barrel. The heads are drilled out as deeply as possible and weighted with lead. Then round off the heads with a file, leaving the other end flat.

Now we have a weapon fit for the modern William Tell. Nevertheless, we don't advise crossbowmen to shoot apples from their friends' heads. Plywood shapes or, for the expert marksman, children's balloons, released on thin threads from behind good cover, are much preferable targets.

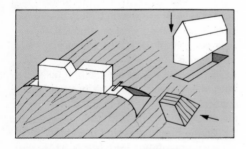

Fore and backsights, and the manner of their insertion into the barrel. The backsight is permanently wedged in place only after the aim of the crossbow has been adjusted.

The Boomerang

Even in this technical age, when we find things on earth so very boring and "old hat" that we are driven to explore strange planets and outer space, there are still things which, in spite of their venerable age, continue to hide their ultimate secrets from man's penetrating gaze.

The fabulous weapon of the Australian aborigines, the boomerang, is one of these mysteries. The name is derived from the Austrian word "wumera" which the natives apply not only to their famous returning club, but also to a device which they use as a sort of elongated arm for hurling their spears over great distances. This double meaning of the word has given rise to many misconceptions.

The boomerang produced in a home workshop is far more a matter of luck than one made in the Australian bush. A matter of luck in the sense that though it can be thrown it won't always come back. This, however, is not solely a question of how the boomerang is made. The correct method of throwing must also be mastered; in fact, technique is just as important as in shooting with a bow and arrow or with a crossbow.

The whole boomerang problem literally hangs in mid-air, in the complexities of the science or aerodynamics. It can't be solved with a hammer and chisel. But in spite of or maybe because of this, the home-made boomerang is certainly one of the most exciting and interesting projects for the hobbyist's workshop, not to mention the pleasure given by its curving flight which sometimes borders on the miraculous.

The boomerang is 24″ to 26″ long and about 3″ wide. Its outer edge measures roughly 36″. The thickness is comparatively small. At the thickest part of the curved cross section it is only 1″. The lengths of the two legs are in a ratio of 4:5. The angle at which they meet is about 140 degrees. All these measurements are approximate. One of the many peculiarities of the boomerang is that the dimensions are not particularly critical. Even the central angle is not of crucial importance. The curve may vary

within wide limits between an acute and an obtuse angle without any adverse effects. The principal features of the boomerang depend on minor modifications of the lifting surfaces.

First of all, how do we come by a piece of sound wood with the right curvature? The Australian aborigine, if not the owner of a modern gun, tramps through the bush until he lights upon a suitably contorted tree trunk. If we did not possess excellent glues and adhesives, it would be simplest for us to follow his example. We cannot saw the required shape from a straight plank, for on first striking the ground it would break at the knee. We can prevent this by gluing four pieces together at an angle. Cold glues or synthetic-resin adhesives are suitable for this purpose on account of their resistance to moisture.

Ash and pine make good material for boomerangs. We require two perfectly sound, well-seasoned boards $^3/_8$″ thick and two others $^5/_8$″ thick. They should be planed true and flat, and glued firmly together at an angle of 140 degrees with staggered butt joints, so that the two thin boards lie underneath and the thicker ones on top.

The advantages of this arrangement become clear in the course of the operation, in which the top face—which is at the same time the left side of the boomerang—is given a gentle camber, falling away smoothly towards the edges. Simultaneously the legs are tapered slightly towards the outside and rounded off at the ends. Thus the thicker board was glued on top so that the greater part of the camber could be formed in one piece. At the same time, the joint is not unnecessarily narrowed and thereby weakened. Instead of being rounded, the right side of the boomerang can be given a triangular profile, but the ridge, which should not be too sharp, should run exactly down

Designing a boomerang

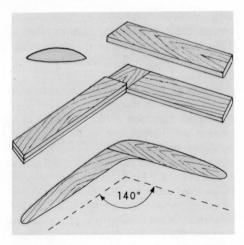

The four pieces that make up the boomerang are glued together with staggered joints at an angle of about 140 degrees.

the center.

In shaping the top of the boomerang we have to bear in mind the different lengths of the legs. Despite this difference in length, they should be equal in weight. Therefore, the longer leg should be scraped somewhat thinner and narrower than the shorter one.

This balancing of the legs of the boomerang accounts for some of its unusual properties. Most, however, are attributable to the warping of the lower, that is the right-hand, sides of the two legs. This slight, but extremely important warping—probably the boomerang's most essential structural characteristic—is achieved by gently beveling off the flat underside of the boomerang at each end, the bevel sloping from right to left in each case. Thus, the ends are spirally warped, giving the boomerang, when thrown, that twist that makes it capable of following such surprising trajectories. The reduction in thickness due to the warping

should not exceed $1/8$" or so. The wood should be trimmed away carefully with a spoke shave. Determining the correct proportions is chiefly a question of trial and error. You can get a rough idea of the orientation of the warped surfaces by drawing one guide line from the middle of the angle to the lower corner of the left-hand leg and a second to the upper corner of the right-hand leg. The bevels start close to these lines and fall away very gently to the opposite edge. This applies only to the lower half of the leg, since the warping is confined exclusively to this part of the boomerang.

The Australian aborigines do not bevel the tips of their boomerangs; both top and bottom faces are slightly curved. The twist is obtained by bending the wood over a charcoal fire, a process that is occasionally repeated during the life of the weapon. The warping obtained by beveling the ends of the boomerang may also be lost, if damp-

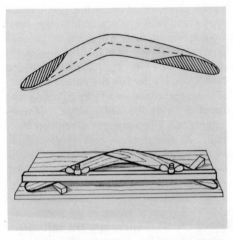

The left-handed warping of the ends. Below: stretcher for the finished boomerang.

298

ness causes the wood to work. It is, therefore, advisable to clamp your boomerang in a stretcher, like a tennis racket, using small wedges to distribute the pressure evenly over the ends. When throwing in wet weather or over sodden ground, the warped shape can be maintained by twisting the boomerang occasionally in the hands.

The performance of the boomerang, however, as already mentioned, depends as much on the throwing technique as on the way it is made. Hold the boomerang by one leg, as you would a banana, with the curved face pointing left. The throw is not exactly horizontal but aimed slightly upwards. At the same time, by means of a flick of the wrist, the boomerang is made to spin rapidly just as it is released. This spin should not be exactly vertical, but inclined slightly to the right. This is the real secret of a successful technique. The second important rule is always to throw into the wind, otherwise you may never see your boomerang again.

An especially powerful spin can be obtained by throwing slightly downwards, for example, by hurling the boomerang downhill from the top of a rise. When thrown almost parallel to the surface, the boomerang will first fly straight for about 30 yards twisting from a vertical to a horizontal position in flight. It will then go into a left-hand turn, at the same time shooting almost vertically upward. Having reached its highest point it will return to the thrower in a whirling glide; sometimes it will even circle the thrower, make a second smaller loop behind his back, and drop to the ground with a rocking movement, like a piece of sheet metal slowly sinking in a tank of water.

One flight of a boomerang seldom resembles the next. Not only does its actual construction introduce many uncertainties, but the weather also plays an important part, particularly the direction and strength of the wind, the humidity, and air currents. The most impressive throws of all are made in sunny weather. The boomerang loves hot, dry weather, such as prevails in its native Australian home.

Pictures from the Sky— the Kite-Borne Camera

We shall not try to give the ideal dimensions for a simple kite. This is something you will learn for yourself by trial and error, in the process of becoming a real kite-builder. The experiment will be very cheap. For the first trial a sheet of paper, two $1/2''$ square sticks (a longer one, say 48″, and a shorter one, say 36″), a few yards of string, and some glue is all you need. The sticks are notched at the free ends with a penknife, to provide a point of attachment for a loop of string. Then the two sticks are laid crosswise and tied together, after applying a spot of glue (not too much) at the point of intersection. The loops of string, running between the tips of the four arms of the cross, are prevented from slipping by the notches cut in the ends of the sticks. Now cut the paper to size, making it $5/8''$ larger than the kite frame all around. The wooden cross is then coated with glue on one side and stuck to the paper, leaving a $5/8''$ edge projecting on all sides. Trim this edge off at all four corners flush with the ends of the sticks. Then coat the remainder of the edge with glue and bend it inwards over the tensioning string. After the glue has set, attach a string to each corner. Then comes a really important operation: balancing the kite. Gather together the four pieces of string and lift the kite up by them. The best thing is to allow one end of the kite to rest on the ground, and raise the peak about 12″ or 16″. In raising the kite be sure that the cross brace is absolutely horizontal. Now adjust the strings carefully and knot them firmly to the long hand line. Finally, give the kite a "tail" so that it can stand up to the wind without dancing; this consists of a string several yards long tied to the bottom of the kite. Into the tail knot several twists of paper, depending on its length (find out how long it should be by testing). The end of the tail is weighted with a small nut (another paper twist is often enough). After gaining experience with a kite of this description, you can proceed to build a stronger kite capable of carrying an aerial camera.

Start by building the "airframe," illustrated in the accompanying drawing. This takes the form of a blunt, triangular kite.

Two strips of pine (a) 60″ long and $\frac{1}{4}$″ x $\frac{1}{2}$″ in cross section form the stem of the T-frame. Starting at the tail, they are glued together edgewise over about 36″ of their length, while half-way along the part left unglued they are braced apart by a strut (b) to leave a clear space about 2$\frac{1}{2}$″ wide. To prevent the joint between the two strips from opening up at this point, it is reinforced on each side with a small triangle of thin plywood (c) screwed to the stem. At the front the two strips are brought together again and held in place by another pair of plywood cover plates (d).

By separating the two strips forming the stem we have provided a stable means of mounting the camera which is supported on a thin plywood platform (e). The two narrow sides of the platform top have beveled corners. The platform is 8″ long and about 4″ wide in the middle. A tab about 1″ long is left at the tail end of the platform. This will later serve to attach the rubber bands that hold the camera in place. To prevent the camera from slipping sideways two stops are glued to the platform, one on each side, the width of the camera apart.

On this small platform the camera lies face downwards, with the lens directed through a circular opening of the same diameter as the lens holder. 2″ will generally be enough. So that the camera doesn't get scratched, the top of the platform and the inner faces of the lateral stops are padded with a layer of foam rubber.

The slope of the platform in relation to the longitudinal axis of the kite is highly important. It should be about 20 degrees. This angle ensures that the plane of the camera and the picture plane remain parallel in spite of the tilt of the airborne kite. This slope is obtained by inserting two small wedges between the back of the platform and the two branches of the split stem.

It is in making the cross brace that we first encounter the most characteristic feature of our photographic kite. This consists of the two stabilizers, mounted one on each side. These stabilizers ensure that the kite remains steady even when buffeted by sudden gusts. To perform satisfactorily, it is necessary for these two stabilizers to rotate in opposite directions, that is, both must pull outwards. Thus the right-hand stabilizer should turn clockwise, the left-hand one counter-clockwise.

In spite of these stabilizers, the kite cannot do without a tail. This is not to improve its appearance, but to enable it to be accurately "trimmed." The tail consists of a cord about six yards long with twists of paper knotted to the end.

The cross brace (f) is fashioned from a strip of pine about 56″ long with a cross section of $\frac{1}{4}$″ x $\frac{1}{2}$″ which is combined with a second member (g) that supports the stabilizer. The latter has the same cross section as the cross brace, but can be 2$\frac{1}{2}$″ or so shorter, since it runs straight, whereas the cross brace is bent in the middle at a blunt angle of 165 degrees. For a kite of the

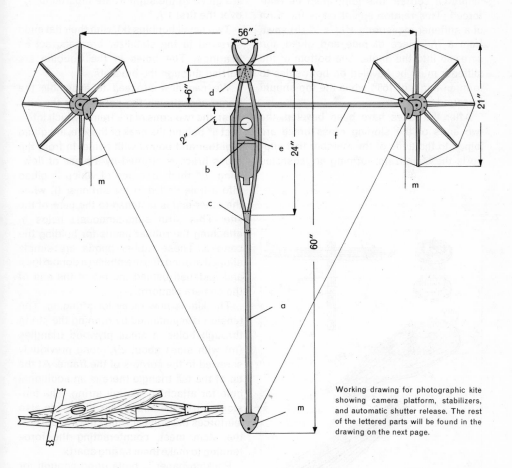

56"

6"

d

2"

e

b

c

21"

24"

60"

m

m

f

a

m

Working drawing for photographic kite showing camera platform, stabilizers, and automatic shutter release. The rest of the lettered parts will be found in the drawing on the next page.

given dimensions, this angle is of the utmost importance. Only if it is strictly observed will the kite fly as it should. To construct this angle it is necessary to cut the cross brace in the middle and rejoin the two halves after beveling off the end faces to the correct slope. Of course, this joint must be reinforced. This reinforcement takes the form of a stiffener measuring $1^3/_8'' \times 5''$ (h) sawn from a $^3/_8''$ piece of pine and glued and screwed into the angle. The bottom of the stiffener must be beveled on both sides to form an angle of 165°, while the top should be rounded off.

After the faces have been beveled, the two ends of the sloping cross brace are joined to the ends of the member that supports the stabilizers, forming an isosceles

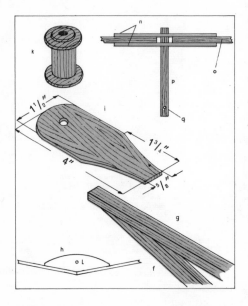

triangle with the base uppermost. Brackets for the stabilizers (i) are now glued to the ends of the stabilizer support. These are cut from thin plywood and should be 4″ long and $1^1/_2''$ wide. The outer ends of the brackets are rounded off, while the inner ends which are glued to the support are tapered to $^5/_8''$ over the first $1^3/_4''$.

Two small bobbins (k), with their flat ends screwed to the stabilizer brackets, act as bearings. The holes in the bobbins are carried through the brackets.

We can now proceed to assemble the frame and stretch the paper over the kite. First, the two arms of the frame, which intersect 6″ behind the peak of the kite, are glued together and bound with twine. In front the cross brace is strutted by a piece of doweling $^1/_4''$ thick, one end of which is glued into a hole drilled in the stiffener (l) while the other end is fastened to the peak of the kite. This strut simultaneously helps in attaching the rubber bands for holding the camera. These rubber bands are simply slipped around this member in a double loop and fastened behind the tab at the end of the camera platform.

The kite is now ready for stringing. The tension is maintained by running the string through holes in small plywood triangles (m) with sides about $2^1/_2''$ long previously screwed to the corners of the frame. At the tip of the tail triangle there is an additional hole for attaching the tail string. The tensioning triangle at the peak of the kite also reinforces the point at which the two parts of the stem meet, counteracting the force tending to make them spring apart.

Packing paper is quite good enough for covering the kite, but the strong, colored parchment sold as "kite paper" can also be used. If the kite has to be made of two sheets of paper, the joint should run parallel to the stem. Of course, the whole covering can be

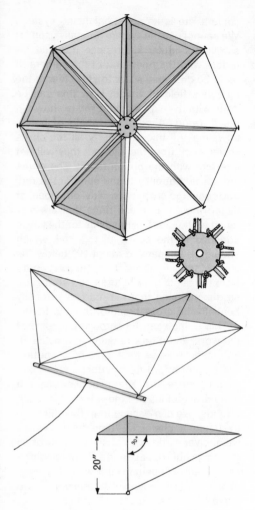

the paper are coated with glue, bent back smoothly over the tensioning strings and stuck down. The trick here consists in drawing the covering tight and smooth, without twisting the string. Special care should be taken with the area around the camera platform. Here the paper should fit snugly over the two stem members and the strut (b); it should be strengthened at these sensitive points by adding reinforcing strips. Further stiffening is also required around the peephole provided for the camera lens.

The construction of the two stabilizers is precision work. Both stabilizers should be 21″ in diameter and equal in weight. Each is based on two circular discs (n) of thin plywood, in the center of which a hole $1/_4$″ wide is bored. (Drill all four of these discs exactly vertically in a single operation.) Eight strips

Covering the stabilizers and balancing the kite. The harness lies outside the field of vision of the camera.

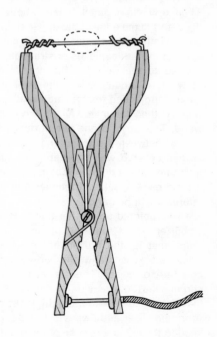

The automatic (chemical) shutter release mechanism.

cut in one piece in the shape of the kite, with the center line indicated by a crease. To cover the kite, lay the paper flat on the table, brush glue over the underside of the frame, and place it on the paper. Then the edges of

303

of pine (o) each 10" long (cross section $^3/_{16}$" x $^1/_4$") are glued radially between the two discs. Make sure that the intervals between the spokes are exactly equal. The axle of the stabilizer is a $2^1/_2$" long peg (p). This peg is glued tightly into the two holes drilled in the plywood discs and must be exactly at right angles to the plane of the spokes; otherwise the stabilizer will wobble and flutter. About $^1/_4$" from the lower end of the axle drill a small transverse hole (q) through which a small locking pin is later inserted. A washer will prevent the pin from damaging the plywood mounting as the stabilizer rotates. To reduce friction a second washer is introduced between the stabilizer and the upper bearing surface of the bobbin.

To cover the stabilizers begin by driving $^3/_4$" wire nails into the ends of the spokes, allowing the heads to project about $^1/_8$". Then drill eight small holes (about $^3/_{32}$" diameter) in the edge of the upper stabilizer disc exactly in the middle between pairs of spokes. Individual pieces of string are now knotted to the holes in the central disc, drawn tight, and fastened at the other end to the nail projecting from the adjacent spoke, which is then hammered all the way into the wood. The larger of the two surfaces thus formed between the string and the spokes is then covered with kite paper. By giving alternate panels different colors, the stabilizer is given a rather friendlier and more interesting appearance.

It was pointed out earlier that these two stabilizers must rotate in opposite directions, that is, the right-hand one should rotate clockwise, and the left-hand one counter-clockwise. This is achieved by carrying the radial tensioning cord always to the next spoke head to the right, in the case of one stabilizer, and always to the next spoke head to the left, in the case of the other.

One of the many special features of our camera-kite is its novel balancing system. We cannot use the system normally used for simple triangular kites since it would interfere with the operation of the camera. It must be designed so as to stay clear of the camera's field of vision. How this can be done with the aid of a short rod is shown in the drawing. A two-foot length of beech doweling $^5/_8$" thick will carry all the cords so far away from the kite that they will not interfere with the photography. The cords are not tied directly to the ends of the rod, but converge from each side on a pair of metal rings. It is these rings that are fastened to the rod. The hand line for the kite is attached to the center of this rod, which should be suspended about 20" below the stem of the kite frame. The strings running from the tail of the kite to the rod should be so dimensioned that the rod lies vertically beneath the cross brace of the kite frame.

This completes the aerodynamic part of the work, and it now remains to provide an automatic release for the camera shutter. We cannot afford to introduce much extra weight, since the kite described cannot carry a useful load of more than about $1^3/_4$ pounds. We can escape from this dilemma by using a chemical "time fuse," which weighs very little and consists mainly of an ordinary cable release and a simple washing peg capable of opening fairly wide. The ends of the peg are extended by means of two curved pieces sawn out of $^5/_{16}$" beechwood. Two small screw hooks are inserted in the ends of the extension pieces. The jaws of the peg are then cut away until the distance between them is enough to receive the push-button at the end of the release cable. This cable is held in a notch sawn in the end of the peg. The peg, thus modified, is fastened by a wood screw, passed through the loop of the wire spring, to the upper plywood triangle at the peak of the kite, with the ends bearing the screw hooks pointing forwards.

The chemical part of the shutter release mechanism consists of a strip of zinc about $^3/_{32}$" wide and 5" long. This strip is stretched between the ends of the peg, so as to prevent the jaws from coming together. Do this by forming eyes in the ends of the strip and slipping them over the small screw hooks. Finally, secure a wad of cotton wool around the middle of the strip by means of copper wire. The release mechanism is ready when the push-button of the cable release has been introduced between the jaws of the peg, although it will not go into action until a few drops of hydrochloric acid have been added to the wad of cotton wool. (Do not let the acid splash on your skin.) In about ten minutes the acid will have eaten through the zinc, and the peg will close, releasing the camera shutter. By then, of course, the kite must have been launched and carried by the wind to the position from which the photograph is to be taken. The delayed action effect depends on the width of the zinc strip. The acid will eat through $^1/_{16}$" in about 7 minutes. Of course, the age of the zinc also plays an important part, for whereas fresh zinc is comparatively resistant, zinc which has been exposed to the weather for twenty years is eaten through by the acid very much more quickly.

A very simple signal device will inform the photographer below when the chemical trigger has done its work. A postcard is threaded onto the zinc strip. When it flutters to the ground, it is time to pull in the kite. Unfortunately, the release mechanism must be reset after each shot.

18

LOW VOLTAGE
FOR THE CRAFTSMAN

The hobby activities dealt with in the following chapters differ from those previously described in that we shall be making use of a strange form of energy. This energy, electricity, is very mysterious in many respects. Firstly, it has properties and capabilities not shared by any other type of energy; secondly, no human being has so far been able to discover what electricity really is.

One of the many strange properties of electricity is its ability to flow in a conducting medium, like a stream of water. It is for this reason that we speak of an electric current. Like water, electricity can only flow from one place to another if there is a difference in level between them. In electricity this effective difference in level is called tension or voltage and is measured in volts (symbol = V). Obviously, the flow becomes stronger as the difference in level increases. In terms of electricity this implies an increase in voltage. In water pipes a difference in level manifests itself as water pressure, and the further we open the faucet the greater the quantity of water that flows from it. We are used to measuring the quantity of water in gallons, and we might say that what a gallon means for water an ampere or amp (symbol = A) means for electricity; this is the unit for measuring the quantity or more exactly the strength of electricity. The power of an electric current or its rate of doing work is found by multiplying V by A and is measured in watts (symbol = W), that is: W = V x A.

Electrical engineers distinguish between low-voltage and high-voltage current. Low-voltage technology uses currents with voltages of up to 60 V, mostly in communications. Currents of this low voltage are not at all dangerous for the human body and cannot cause material damage. It is therefore unnecessary to take special precautions or to provide the current-carrying wires with very heavy insulation.

In high-voltage technology very different conditions prevail; the electricity supplied to ordinary homes falls into this category. Here there are energies at work that can cause very severe damage and fatal accidents, if they are treated unprofessionally or carelessly. For this reason high-voltage systems should be left strictly to the qualified electrician. This should be our most important and inflexible rule. Work within the low-voltage range where you can exercise your skill without danger.

General Rules for Installation

The installation of low-voltage circuits is simple and requires little outlay for materials. For wiring purposes use copper bell wire. The various colors of its rubber, varnish or plastic insulation are helpful in wiring complicated circuits. For permanent wiring systems installed in dry rooms the slightly cheaper waxed cotton-covered wire is suitable. Apart from these rather stiff wires there are copper-stranded wires with a core consisting of several fine copper strands. Today these also come insulated in soft plastic and because of their flexibility they are useful where movable connections are required.

Electric wire, whether single or multi-stranded, is sold on reels by the yard. The length of wire needed for a line is taken off by turning the reel. In this way unwelcome kinks or bends in the wire are avoided. For fixing wire there are special pins for single or double low-voltage lines, but also staples, right-angle wire hooks with flat arms, and wire tacks. The tacks are hammered into the base (switchboard or other wooden support) until the head protrudes about $1/8''$. Then the wire is pulled taut and guided in a single loop around the shank of the tack which is finally driven all the way into the wood. A protective disk prevents the insulation from being damaged or the wire nipped. Wires should be laid singly. Winding several wires together and fixing them with one staple or hook is both ugly and, in the event of a fault, impractical.

In normal domestic use low-voltage lines may be fixed directly to the walls. On damp or exterior walls, however, electric wires should be carried over porcelain insulators. These keep the wire away from the wall and can be obtained in various shapes and sizes. They are fixed with wood screws. The conductor itself is tied to the roller-shaped head with thin insulated binding wire or nylon thread.

To connect two pieces of wire it is sufficient to twist them around each other and then protect the joint with insulating tape or a piece of rubber tubing. Careful electricians will solder the joints. To obtain a joint that conducts well it is important to scrape the

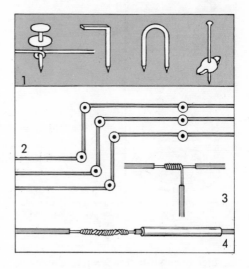

Installation of low-voltage lines: 1 pins, hooks, and staples, 2 wires should be laid separately, 3 joining two wires at right-angles, 4 twisted splice.

ends of the wires until they are quite shiny.

The same method can be used to make a branch from the main line. About half an inch of insulation is removed from the main wire at the branching point and the bare end of the branch wire is tightly twisted around the section exposed.

For our purposes we shall need three types of switches. Firstly, the ordinary rotary switch as used in domestic lighting installations, which can also take the form of a

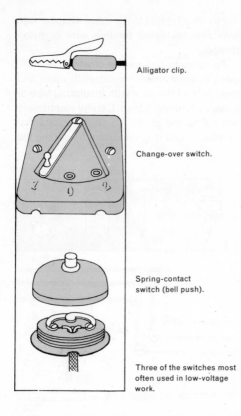

Alligator clip.

Change-over switch.

Spring-contact switch (bell push).

Three of the switches most often used in low-voltage work.

operated by the action of the push-button. The circuit is closed when the button is pushed down; when it is released the contact springs back and the current is interrupted. By inserting a match small boys can make these push-buttons into nerve-racking permanent connections.

The purpose of the switch is to produce a temporary closure of the circuit, which can be easily interrupted or reproduced. For test or experimental circuits on the work bench there is no need to introduce switches. Instead use quick-clamping devices which can be bought in any electrical store.

Low-voltage Power Sources

Before we can do anything with electrical equipment, we shall have to provide a suitable source of power, for the best circuit is useless without current. In the long run, the most reliable, cheapest and cleanest source of low-voltage current is a power transformer of the type used for electric door bells. These transformers reduce the high input voltage (primary coil) to a lower and harmless output voltage (secondary coil). As it is important in low-voltage applications to be able to use currents of varying voltage, the secondary coil of most transformers is subdivided in such a way that three different voltage steps can be tapped off, for example, 3, 5, and 8 volts. An ordinary bell transformer fed with alternating current (AC) will also provide AC at its secondary terminals. There are, however, transformers combined with a selenium rectifier which change the transformed AC to a pulsating direct current (DC). The control panels of many electric model railways are constructed on this principle. Since they are also equipped with a variable resistor acting as a regulator, the entire voltage range of the secondary coil is

tumbler or push-button switch. Secondly, the disconnecting switch which employs a pivoted arm and serves to cut off temporarily part or all of a circuit. A development of the disconnecting switch is the change-over switch. It has several contacts arranged side by side and a contact arm that can be moved from one to the other. Thus it is possible to supply power to a number of separate circuits, for example to two different electric bells.

The third type of switch, the spring contact switch, is particularly important in signal devices; it is familiar in the form of the bell-push. It has one fixed contact, above which there is a second, spring contact

made available without steps.

For reasons of safety special rules apply to the construction of transformers, and it is not advisable to try to build a transformer oneself. In any case a safe ready-made transformer is not particularly expensive. A properly constructed transformer guarantees that, even if there is a short-circuit in the low-voltage system, no accident can occur in the power-supply system.

Though the transformer offers a very convenient solution it has its limitations, particularly if AC is not available. DC cannot be transformed and if there is no AC the hobbyist will have to look for other power sources.

Among them is the voltaic cell, in its various forms, the classical source of electricity. Perhaps the best known is the Leclanché cell which was formerly used everywhere for house and telephone bells. This cell consists of a glass container with ammonium chloride solution (NH_4Cl) as the electrolyte. The two electrodes are suspended in this solution and from their terminals the electricity can be tapped off. The negative electrode, with the negative terminal, is an open zinc cylinder concentric with the glass container. The positive electrode, with the positive terminal, has a more complicated structure. Its core is a carbon rod surrounded by a compressed mixture of manganese dioxide and graphite. The whole is contained in a canvas bag and rests on the bottom of the glass container.

Apart from their other disadvantages, the power of voltaic cells is so low that a single cell is quite useless in practice. The voltage of a well-maintained Leclanché cell is no more than 1.5 V. The size of the cells has no effect on the voltage. Increasing the size of the electrodes enables us to take off a stronger current without using up the electrodes too quickly, but this method also has its limitations.

A Leclanché cell of commercial size will provide a current of 0.3 A at a voltage of 1.5 V. If we need more power, we have to combine several cells to form a battery. According to the manner in which this is done either a higher voltage or a stronger current can be obtained.

Assuming that we have four cells with a capacity of 1.5 V/0.3 A we can connect them either in series or in parallel, or in a combination of both.

In a series connection the four cells are placed side by side and neighboring positive and negative terminals are connected, i.e. carbon to zinc in each case. The current at the two end terminals, while still of the same amperage, now totals 6 volts. Notice that series connection adds the voltages of the individual cells.

In contrast, parallel connection adds the current strengths of the separate cells, while the voltage remains the same. The cells are connected in parallel by joining all the positive terminals and all the negative terminals. This type of connection is used less often than series connection. It may happen, however, that both a high voltage

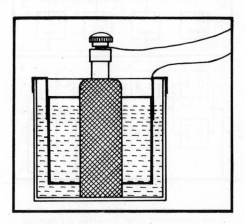

Diagram showing the principal parts of a voltaic cell.

309

and a strong current are required. For this purpose the two types of connection are combined. First, the four cells are divided into pairs and the two positive terminals and the two negative terminals of each pair are connected. These pairs are then placed in series and the positive coupling of the one is connected to the negative coupling of the other; at the other two coupled terminals a current of 0.6 A and a voltage of 3 V are obtained.

A practical application of the increased voltage obtained by the series connection of three small Leclanchè cells is found in the simple flashlight battery. Here the ammonium chloride solution has been thickened to form a paste by adding flour and wood shavings, and the zinc electrode also serves as the container. These small dry batteries have a voltage of 4.5 V and can carry a current load of 0.3 A. Working with these clean cells, which require little space and need no

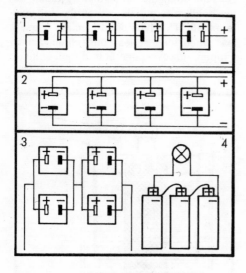

1 Connection in series. 2 Connection in parallel. 3 Combined connection. 4 Series connection of a flashlight battery.

refilling or cleaning, is pleasant, but for permanent installations they are uneconomical as the small current supply is quickly exhausted.

Apart from this method of generating current, there remains the possibility of building one's own power station, consisting of a dynamo driven by wind or water power. Wind is rather a doubtful source of energy because it often refuses to blow when it is needed. A continuously flowing stream which drives a water wheel would be more reliable, but the construction of such an expensive installation will rarely be worth while.

The storage battery, as its name implies, is not a current generator, but a current storage device. For those who build a wind-power station a storage battery will be indispensable. It offers the only possibility of accumulating the current generated on windy days so as to have it available at times when there is no wind blowing. Such a power station, however, must have a DC generator, because AC cannot be stored and has to be used as it is made. DC can be stored, and this is one of its chief advantages for the hobbyist.

Basically the storage battery consists of two lead plates suspended in dilute sulfuric acid inside a container. If the electrodes are connected to the terminals of a DC power supply, the charging current produces a chemical change at the surface of the electrodes. With the help of this charging current we can store chemical energy in the container. The reversal of the chemical reaction then generates a discharge current, which can be tapped off as required at the terminals, as with the voltaic cell. The current flows from one terminal of the battery to the load and from there back to the other terminal, thus completing the circuit.

The capacity (i.e. the discharge time) of

the storage battery obviously depends on the size of the plates. In order to avoid excessively clumsy batteries, instead of making the plates larger, it is customary to build cells consisting of several smaller plates which are connected to form positive and negative electrodes. What is important is the total area of the plates and it is worth remembering that 16 square inches of a positive plate can be loaded with up to 1 amp. The discharge voltage is independent of the plate size or of the number of plates in the cell. On the average this voltage is 2 V per cell. To charge the battery, however, a voltage of 3 V per cell is required. This brings us to the problem of how to top up our storage batteries. The charging current can be taken from the AC lighting system. The battery only stores DC, but AC is ideal for our purpose because it can be transformed. Assuming we were to charge a battery of three cells, requiring a 12 V charge voltage, from a 120 V DC supply, 108 V would have to be eliminated by a series resistance and this would be very wasteful. AC can be transformed to any desired voltage with relatively small losses. It can also be rectified easily with a copper oxide rectifier. If transformer and rectifier are combined with a rheostat or variable resistance to control the current, we shall be able to utilize about 60% of the energy supplied for charging one or more batteries.

Like voltaic cells, storage batteries can be connected in series or in parallel to form batteries of greater power. In combined connections a symmetrical arrangement of the cells is absolutely essential. In each group there must be the same number of cells and thus the same voltage. The size of the cells, i.e. the surface area of the plates, does not make any difference; each cell provides 2 V whatever its size. It is therefore permissible to connect large and small cells.

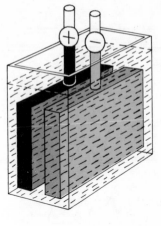

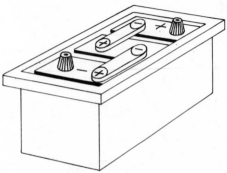

Top: the working principle of a storage battery.
Bottom: a three-cell storage battery.

The disadvantage of such an arrangement is that the battery as a whole can only be expected to have a capacity and provide a current corresponding to the smallest of the cells present. Cells of different sizes should thus be used together only temporarily and always in series, where the increase is only in the voltage and not in the current.

Although the storage battery is not a true generator, it remains very useful to the hobbyist with suitable facilities for charging it. He can then store very strong currents

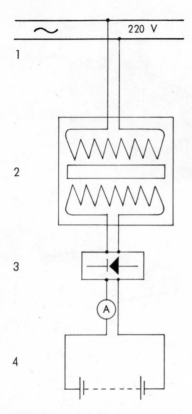

A simple battery-charging circuit: 1 power line, 2 transformer, 3 rectifier, 4 battery, A ammeter.

and cover his power requirements for many hours, especially if several batteries are combined to form a single power source.

Resistance

As soon as we begin to work with wires, generators and loads, we have to consider the important question of the efficiency of our workshop current. What voltage and what current strength should we employ?

Of course, in any circuit the strength of the current may vary. At a given moment it can be measured with an ammeter. The electromotive force (emf) that drives the current through the circuit is the voltage, which we can also measure with a so-called voltmeter. The larger the emf, the more quickly the current flows. This current, however, is confined to a conducting medium which offers a certain resistance to its passage. The conducting medium consists—at least at the hobby level—of the wiring and the device which consumes the current, or load, and it is understandable that the strength of the current in the circuit depends not only on the driving force, i.e. the voltage, but also on the resistance of the entire circuit. This resistance itself depends on the conductivity of the metal and on the thickness of the wire carrying the current. We know that copper has a high conductivity and therefore we use copper wires for our circuits; similarly we choose a particularly thick wire because thick wires have less resistance than thin ones.

As with voltage and current there is also a special unit for measuring resistance. It is called the ohm and is denoted by the Greek capital letter omega Ω. The relation between voltage, current and resistance is expressed by Ohm's law from which each of the three quantities may be calculated if the other two are known. The law states: resistance equals voltage over current or $\Omega = V/A$. Thus $A = V/\Omega$ and $V = A \times \Omega$.

Using Ohm's law we can now calculate the voltage required for any circuit in our workshop. We should not forget when doing so that the resistance of any appliance used, usually indicated on a label together with the amperage, has to be added to the resistance of the wiring. This is negligible for short distances, but it will add up to a significant factor if a long line is run for bell or alarm signal installations. Using Ohm's law it should now be possible to calculate the resistance of the filament in an electric light bulb marked 120V/100W. Since volts x amps = watts and amps = watts/volts, we obtain 100/120 = 0.83 A for the current used by the bulb. This is in agreement with the facts. If we now substitute in Ohm's law we obtain for the resistance 120/0.83 =.144.58Ω. Rather a surprising result, though actually not quite correct because our 100-watt bulb works with AC, and Ohm's law is only strictly valid for direct current.

Installation of Stage Lighting

We shall now proceed to the design and wiring of a DC lighting installation working on low voltage supplied by a transformer + rectifier unit. The problem is to produce stage lighting for the puppet theater described in Chapter 13. The installation is to be equipped with flashlight bulbs. We assume that, in view of the size of the stage, six bulbs are required as footlights and another six for the toplight ledge. Thus 12 bulbs will have to be supplied with current at the same time. One 0.2 amp bulb requires a voltage of 3.5 V, hence the power will be 0.7 W. 12 bulbs will then use roughly 10 W. This amount of power can be obtained from a 5 V transformer for loads up to 2 A (heating transformer) or from a 10 V type carrying up to 1 A.

One or the other should be provided for the lighting installation. The bulbs are then mounted on the footlight and toplight ledges and connected in series to form a so-called Christmas tree circuit. All the bulbs are linked by wires connecting the screw contact of one with the bottom contact of the next. To facilitate the dismantling of the stage, make the connection between the

footlights and the top lighting by means of two banana plugs or better an ordinary plug contact.

Because of the series connection the voltage will remain constant throughout the entire installation. At the same time if one of the bulbs fails, the circuit is at once broken and no overloading can occur. This can only happen if our calculations are wrong and we introduce more bulbs into the circuit than the volts x amps = watts relation permits. The voltage remains constant and cannot be used to correct our mistake. The only possibility for the bulbs is to extract more amps from the transformer than its coils will readily allow to pass. The transformer becomes warm, then hot and in the end fuses—just like the thin wire in the fuses of a home lighting circuit. At the first sniff of burning varnish switch off the lighting installation.

Now connect the two free ends of the wire from the bulbs to the transformer terminals and the whole stage will be illuminated. This is a rather simple installation for a fairy tale stage where modern lighting effects are expected. The installation can be extended so that, in addition to white light, it can also supply the same wattage in red light. Furthermore, we can arrange things so that the lighting does not come on or go off abruptly, but gradually dims or brightens. The original lighting system may be insufficient for some of the scenery. We can improve it by adding two side lamps with a spotlight effect.

The extended technical requirements of the new system make it necessary to construct a switchboard so that the lighting can be reliably controlled in accordance with the detailed directions of the stage manager. First, a row of red bulbs has to be fixed next to the white row and connected in series in a separate circuit. The switchboard now carries two circuits ending in two plug connections. Between these plugs and the supply transformer, which is mounted on the switchboard on an asbestos base, we now insert a variable resistance which will enable us to regulate the current according to the light intensity required. The two negative terminals of the lighting circuits are connected to the negative terminal of the resistance, while the two positive terminals are connected to the contacts of a change-over switch. The positive terminal of the resistance is connected to the contact arm of the switch so that it is now possible to close either the red or the white circuit by simply moving the contact arm from one position to the other.

The transformer can be separated from the low-voltage circuit by inserting a suitable fuse. This is introduced between the transformer and the variable resistance. A main switch is inserted in the power line between a power plug screwed onto the switchboard and the transformer. Thus the whole installation, including the transformer, can be quickly switched on and off. The main switch also controls the power supply to a secondary transformer which feeds the spotlights. For these it is a good idea to use two old bicycle headlamps built into plywood boxes. As a light source we shall need two bicycle bulbs. These differ from the flashlight bulbs in requiring a voltage of 6 V which can be obtained from a simple bell transformer. In this case the bulbs are connected in parallel, as each of them requires the full six volts. We therefore connect both bottom contacts to the positive terminal and both screw contacts to the negative terminal —or vice versa. At their rating of 2 watts the current requirements of the bulbs are so small that there is no danger of overloading the transformer.

No dimmer is required for the side-lights. They are connected to the switchboard by means of a plug, like the footlights. Easy and smooth operation of the side-lights is ensured by means of a switch mounted at the same level as the change-over switch for the main lighting and the moving contact of the variable resistance. Thus all the controls for an efficient stage lighting system can be grouped conveniently within a small space. Should the many wires exposed on top of the switchboard prove confusing, the baseboard can be mounted on a frame one inch thick. This will provide sufficient space to run all the wiring underneath the board. The various connections can then be passed through small holes drilled in the baseboard.

The Electric Bell

One of the many surprising properties of electricity is its ability to make a magnet out of a simple iron bar. Every electric bell, the points on a model railway, and the remote-control door latch all make use of electromagnetism. Like most truly great things, electromagnetism is basically simple and will help us to extend our electrical hobby activities into many interesting fields.

An electromagnet consists of a soft iron core around which a coil of insulated wire is wound. When a current is passed through the coil, the iron core becomes a magnet which loses its attracting power when the current is switched off. Because of this a door bell will only ring as long as somebody is pressing the button.

The electric bell is equipped with a U-shaped magnet, each arm of which carries a continuous wire coil. The magnet thus has two poles lying in the same plane; around them a strong magnetic field develops as soon as a current flows through the coils.

It is not difficult to wind such an electromagnet oneself. In order to avoid bending a

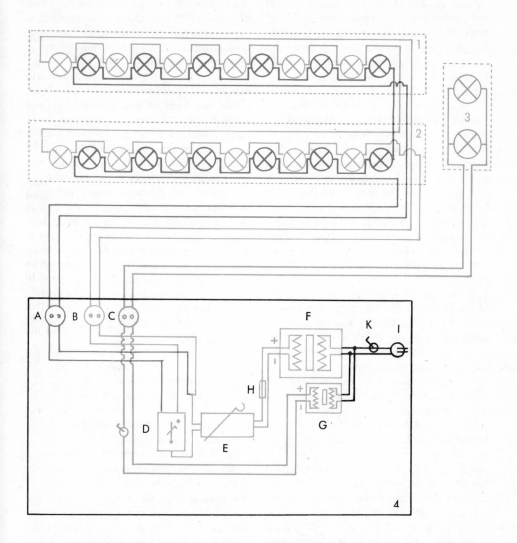

Wiring diagram for stage lighting with toplights (1) and footlights (2) in two colors, side-lights (3) and a switchboard (4) for controlling the installation. A connection for red light, B connection for white light, C connection for side-lights, D change-over switch, E variable resistance, F main transformer, G secondary transformer, H fuse, I power plug, K main switch. The footlights and toplights consist of alternate red and white flashlight bulbs connected in series.

Electromagnets

$^3/_8''$ iron rod into a U-shape, rivet the arms of the magnet to a strip of sheet iron about $^1/_8''$ thick. The magnet iron must be soft. Before the parts are fastened together, they are heated to red heat and then left to cool slowly, preferably in the ashes of a burnt out wood fire.

The coils of a magnet for an ordinary alarm or signal device require about 160 feet of insulated 24-gage copper wire. A varnish-insulated copper wire is most suitable. The wire is not wound directly onto the iron core but onto two separate bobbins, which are then slipped over the core. The bobbins are tubes made of thin, but strong cardboard. As a guide to their inside diameter use a round peg of the same diameter as the core. Close both ends of the cardboard tubes with round disks of veneer about $^1/_{16}''$ thick, through which holes corresponding to the core diameter have been drilled. The length of the bobbin has also to be considered since it must be slightly shorter than the magnetic core, the tip of which will then project beyond the coil. The end of the wire is carried about four inches through a small hole drilled in one of the two end disks in order to have a sufficient length for connecting the magnet.

Experienced workers will fit a rod, with the bobbin around it, into the chuck of a drilling machine mounted horizontally and wind the coil by running the machine at its lowest speed. Hold the wire as it comes off the reel between thumb and index finger and guide it in such a way that the turns are wrapped neatly side by side. Those who find the pace of the drill too fast can build a simple coil winder out of three pieces of wood using the rod as a winding shaft. This device is turned by hand but has the advantage that the winding and packing of the coil can be done more carefully. The packing consists of layers of thin oil paper which fit exactly into the clear width of the coil and are put down after every fifth turn. Using this intermediate packing the wire can be wrapped more regularly. If you use a wire with silk insulation it is advisable to coat each layer with shellac. This increases the stability of the coil and makes the insulation stronger.

The two bobbins are wrapped with the same number of turns, all running in the same direction. When the winding is complete, the bobbins are removed from the rod and placed on the iron core, and the two ends projecting at the bottom of the magnet are connected. Simply twisting the wires together is not good enough for this important connection, it must be soldered. It is also possible to join the two ends at the top of the magnet, but the ends should never be connected crosswise, that is upper end to lower end. Though the windings of both coils run in the same direction, the current must flow through them in the opposite sense in order to obtain a magnet of the greatest efficiency.

A U-shaped electromagnet is the main component of a door bell, and if you can wind the electromagnet you should also be able to assemble a complete bell. The principle is not difficult to understand; the electromagnet is fixed on a baseboard with the magnetic core horizontal. Immediately in front of the projecting ends of the core a small soft-iron plate is mounted on a piece of thin clock-spring steel. A continuation of this plate, called the armature, forms the gong hammer. When a current is passed through the coils, the electromagnet attracts the armature and the hammer strikes the gong which has been placed in its path. If the current is interrupted, the spring will pull back the armature and the whole device is ready for the next closing of the circuit, which can be done by pressing the contact button again. This will produce only one

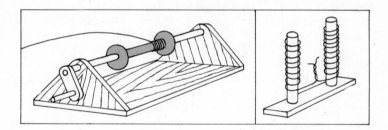

Home-made winder for winding magnet coils. The paper core of the coil is rotated by means of a hand crank. Right: connection between the two coils of a U-shaped electromagnet.

ring, but we expect the bell to go on ringing as long as the button is depressed. In order to achieve this we must include a contact-breaker in the circuit. Just opposite the spring that carries the armature an adjustable contact screw is fixed to the baseboard and connected to the power supply. The screw point, which is in contact with the armature spring, lies at the same level as the lower arm of the magnetic core.

And that is it. Whether the arrangement will work depends primarily on whether the apparatus is correctly wired. At the upper edge of the baseboard there are two screw terminals for the power supply leads. Let us call them plus and minus terminals because this type of bell works on DC. Into one of the supply leads a push-button is inserted. The coil input is connected to the plus terminal, while the output is connected to the fixed, upper end of the armature spring. When the contact screw has been connected to the minus terminal, the wiring of the bell is complete.

When the circuit is closed by depressing the button, the electromagnet is actuated and attracts the armature. This separates the armature spring from the contact screw, the current is interrupted, and the spring flies back. As soon as it touches the point of the contact screw, the circuit is closed

again and the magnet begins to act. As a result of the continuous automatic interruption of the current, the armature moves backwards and forwards between magnet and contact screw, and the bell will ring as long as the button is pressed.

The whole arrangement is very ingenious and amazingly simple. It becomes even simpler if the bell is run on AC. An alternating current changes direction sixty times a second and thus does not require a contact breaker, because in one second it interrupts itself a hundred and twenty times.

The speed at which the hammer strikes the gong depends on the length and elasticity of the armature spring; if the bell does not ring when the button is first pressed, this is probably due to the fact that the distance between the armature and the magnet is not correct. In order to adjust it, the opposite contact is made in the form of a screw so that the movement of the spring can be accurately controlled. To make the operation of the bell still more reliable, a small round copper contact can be riveted to the side of the spring just opposite the point of the contact screw.

You may have some doubts about forming the double bend in the armature spring, as shown in the diagram, for bending clock springs is not an easy task. But the spring

The electric bell

can be softened, just like the iron of the magnetic core, by heating and slow cooling. After that it is easily bent or even drilled. When the piece has been finished, it is again heated to red heat and then cooled quickly by dipping it in cold water or oil; this restores its elasticity.

With a double-contact change-over switch, similar to the one used for the stage lighting system, and a third supply terminal we can transform the bell, by a simple rearrangement of the circuit, into a device which will either give a continuous alarm or just a single ring when the push-button is pressed. The third terminal is connected to the point where the current from the coil reaches the armature spring. By means of the extra switch we can direct the current so that it avoids the contact-breaker and takes the shorter path directly to the power source. The armature is then only attracted once by the magnet and remains attached to it as long as the current flows. If we change the switch arm over to the terminal connected to the contact screw, the current has to return through the contact-breaker, and we get the oscillation of the spring which produces the continuous ringing of the bell.

Alarm and Signal Devices

A two-way switching arrangement is important if the bell is to serve as a signal device in an alarm circuit. Consider the case of a garage or boat-house door or a garden gate, which is to be protected against unwelcome intruders by means of an alarm system. We know that the bell must have a current in order to ring, i.e. a circuit has to be closed. Naturally, it would be charming, but quite useless to install a button with the request: "Intruders, please press button." We shall design an alarm system which is quiet as long as a current flows, but gives a signal to indicate an unauthorized interruption of the circuit.

For this we shall need a bell with a two-way switch and a spring contact fixed to the door to be protected. Use two strips of springy metal from an old lamp battery. One of these is fixed to the door frame, the other, bent at right angles, is screwed to the door itself. When the door is closed contact is made, when it is opened the circuit is broken. This switch is inserted into the wire leading from the end of the coil and the armature spring to the power supply, a bell transformer, which is quite inexpensive to run.

Naturally, the whole installation, which can be shut off by means of a disconnecting switch, is kept inside the house. The wires leading to the door with the safety device must be well camouflaged. When the system is switched on the current flows from the transformer to the coil, through the armature spring and across the closed door switch back to the transformer. The electromagnet is activated and attracts the armature. Thus the alarm system indicates by a single ring that it is in operation. As soon as the door is opened, and the circuit interrupted, the magnet loses its attracting power, the armature swings back and makes contact with the contact screw across the spring. Now the circuit is closed again by the contact-breaker, the bell rings until either the door with the safety device is closed or the power is switched off.

Anyone unfamiliar with the principle of this alarm system might think of putting it out of action by cutting the wires leading to the door switch. But this would not help him, because it has the same effect as if the door were opened. The circuit is interrupted, and the alarm rings. The only weak point is the possibility of shortcircuiting the leads before they reach the door switch. This would

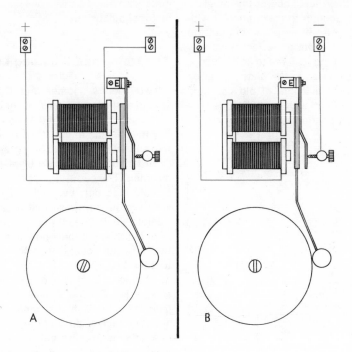

Two electric bell circuits: A without contact breaker (continues to ring only if AC is used), B with contact breaker (works on DC).

really put the whole mechanism out of action.

To avoid very elaborate circuitry we must employ a ruse. Carry two leads to the door switch and connect them in the ordinary way, but instead of bringing the return lead back to the bell cut it short some distance beyond the "danger area." If we lay the two wires separately, along different paths, the intruder will become more and more confused. If having finally located the wires, he attempts to shortcircuit them, he will use the dummy wire and end up by triggering the alarm bell when he cuts the true lead. We can succeed in misleading the would-be

intruder in this way by using the ground instead of a wire to return the current to the source. If this is a transformer, it must be of the DC type, since AC cannot be conducted through the earth.

Making a ground line is quite simple. Inside the house the terminal of the source is connected to a pipe of the water supply system. If there is a pump in the vicinity of the door to be protected, the shaft of the pump can be made to serve as a ground connection by clamping the door lead to it. This shaft reaches down into the ground water and thus makes a good connection. If there is neither a pump nor a water pipe,

A burglar alarm

it will be necessary to bury a galvanized iron plate about three feet square; this must be placed deep enough to make contact with the ground water. If the ground is not too dry, a depth of about three feet is usually sufficient. A rising lead made of thick copper wire is soldered to the plate. It can be passed through a length of old gas pipe which is then filled with asphalt. This type of ground connection is always worth in-

Bell with two-way circuit for DC alarm and safety installations. When the door contact is broken, the current flows across the contact screw and the armature begins to oscillate.

stalling if DC lines have to cover longer distances, since it saves one lead or half the material outlay.

The Relay and the Long Line

Two friends, Homer and George, are spending their vacation in a pair of summer cottages in a lonely part of the country. One day they decide to construct an alarm system so that Homer need only press a button in order to get George out of bed in the morning. They do not possess an efficient transformer, only two voltaic cells, one of which is so run down that it cannot even operate a bell. The other cell is just capable of doing this, but the long line between the two cottages would use up so much energy that the bell would only give a gentle buzz, by no means loud enough to wake a heavy sleeper like George. The whole idea would have fallen through, if Homer had not been smart enough to think of the relay.

A relay is nothing but half a bell or an electromagnet with an armature suspended directly in front of the magnetic core by a spring. The small current which Homer can send from his weak cell through the wire into George's room and through the coils of the relay is just enough to attract the armature. At its lower end, where the bell armature has a hammer, the relay armature has a copper contact. This contact is on the magnet side of the armature and just opposite it there is an adjustable contact screw fixed to the relay baseboard. From this screw a lead runs to the bell, which in our case acts as an alarm for George, and from there a wire leads to George's voltaic cell which is best placed next to the alarm. The other terminal of this cell has a fixed connection to a contact near the end of the armature spring.

320

As soon as Homer presses his button, thus closing the circuit from his weak cell, the electromagnet is actuated and attracts the relay armature. This makes contact with the screw opposite, the circuit powered by the stronger cell is closed, and the alarm rings.

If our two friends were short of copper conductor, they could also use a single wire running from the terminal of Homer's cell via the push-button to one of the relay terminals. The return connection would then be made by grounding the other terminal of the cell and the relay. However, the resistance of a ground line is much higher than that of even a very thin copper wire of the same length. A good relay is very sensitive and responds to very weak currents. This requires very accurate adjustment of the armature. The high sensitivity of the device, which also depends largely on the length and tension of the armature spring, is achieved by introducing two special regulators for the distance between the armature and the magnetic poles. Firstly, there is an adjustable screw mounted opposite the lower armature contact, and, secondly, a small spiral spring on the far side of the armature which pulls it back from the magnet and the contact screw as soon as the current in the coil ceases to flow. The end of the spiral spring is attached to an adjustable screw so that its tension can be regulated.

As we have seen, this type of relay will ring the alarm as soon as the circuit from Homer's cell is closed. By making a small adjustment, we can make it function the other way around, so that it is quiet when current flows through the coils and the alarm rings when the circuit is interrupted. We just have to transfer the wire connecting the alarm to the contact screw onto the adjustable screw on the opposite side of the armature. In order to make the relay work more smoothly the copper contact at the end of the armature should also be transfered to the opposite side. With this arrangement the circuit from George's battery is closed when Homer breaks his circuit. In combination with an alarm circuit with only one current path, such a relay could successfully replace the two-path alarm system described above.

The Morse Station

The ingenious method of communication named after its inventor Samuel Morse is based on the reduction of the entire alphabet to two signs; by combining these signs in different sequences any letter, number, or punctuation mark can be reproduced. The morse code works with dots and dashes. These can be represented by short and long current pulses respectively.

In a very simple manner we can telegraph without wires by replacing the dots and dashes of the morse code with long and short flashes of light. In order to save the lamp contacts, this is done not by working the switch but by keeping the lamp continuously alight and moving a shutter across the beam. Large navy signal lamps employ a venetian blind type of shutter lowered and raised by a hand lever.

Visual morse signaling is only possible within the range of direct vision. In the mountains, in woods, and also in strong sunlight this simple method fails, and the signals have to be transmitted to the receiver by wire. The incoming signals can be represented visually, again with a blinking light, using a battery-powered flashlight bulb, or audibly, in the form of sound. To do this with a loud rattling alarm bell would annoy the whole neighborhood. But we can still use the heart of a simple bell as the receiving station, if we remove the hammer and the gong. This leaves the contact-breaker and the armature, the rapid oscillation of which produces a clearly audible buzzing noise.

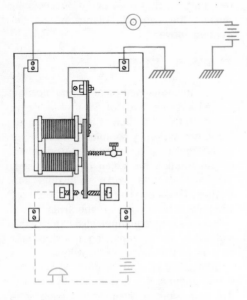

Principle of the relay. When the exciting circuit (red) is closed, the relay armature is attracted and the load circuit (blue) is also closed.

In order to transmit sound signals the receiving station will have to be manned during transmission time. If we intend to receive signals at an unmanned station we shall need a signal recorder. In this case do not use a buzzer, but remove the contact-breaker, so that the armature remains attached to the magnet while the current flows. To the free end of the armature—where the hammer would normally be—attach a bent pen and arrange for a paper tape to pass slowly underneath. Refills for ballpoint pens

can be bent quite easily, but they must not be squashed in the process. When the armature is attracted by the magnet, the tip of the pen touches the paper and, depending on the duration of the current pulse, records a dot or a dash. As a quick-acting recovery device for the pen, use a spiral spring, like the one used in the relay. The paper tape is wound on a 16 mm film spool, but the question remains how to start it unrolling at the right moment. It is wound off the loaded spool onto an empty spool driven by a small electric motor. The motor is started by the receiver via a relay circuit. This circuit is the same as George's alarm system (see above), but with a motor instead of an alarm bell. It is important for the recording pen to write on a soft support (soft lino or rubber) and for the paper tape to run in a guide (strips of aluminum foil under a loose glass plate), so that it lies flat on the support.

The signal pulses are transmitted by means of a morse key. A bell push can be used for this purpose. The elasticity of the spring, however, will not be able to tolerate continuous use and we shall eventually have to construct a proper key. This can be done in various ways.

The contact arm can either be a strip of tough clock-spring steel pivoted at one end or a rectangular brass bar (cross section $\frac{1}{8}'' \times \frac{1}{4}''$), pivoted in the middle. Both contact arms should be the same length (4"). As the brass key is so thin, we cannot drill it right through in order to fit a sufficiently strong hinge pin. We can only drill it very slightly on both sides at the pivot point and mount it between two conical set screws with lock nuts passed through the legs of a U-shaped support made of sheet iron $\frac{1}{16}''$ thick. A strong spiral spring pulling on one end of the lever arm keeps the key horizontal and resting on a counter bearing (a wooden block). When the key is depressed, the other

Morse key with balanced contact arm. The inset shows how the contact arm is supported between two conical set screws in a U-shaped bracket.

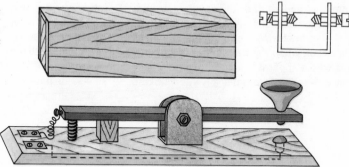

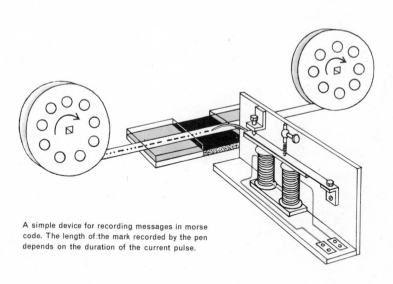

A simple device for recording messages in morse code. The length of the mark recorded by the pen depends on the duration of the current pulse.

323

end meets the contact point lying immediately underneath it. When the pressure is released, the spring pulls the key back to the position of rest.

The working end of the key requires a suitable knob. A small cabinet knob screwed onto the end of the lever with a round-headed brass screw will do. The round head of the screw forms a contact which closes the circuit when the transmitter is working. The whole apparatus is mounted on a base and covered with a small plywood box so that only the transmitting knob remains exposed.

The connection with the power circuit is made at two terminals linked respectively with the base contact and the free end of the lever arm. In order to allow for the movement of the lever, the wire is wound into a small spiral on a thin round peg. When the whole installation is ready, try it out and finish, like this chapter, with the morse signal for end of message: • — • —. If anybody answers: • • • — •, he means he has understood it all.

A PRIVATE WEATHER STATION   19

Some people shut up a caterpillar in a glass jar with a ladder made out of cigar-box wood and consider this a reliable meteorological station. If the poor insect climbs up the ladder in the hope of finding a way out of its glass prison, this is interpreted as an infallible sign of a coming thunderstorm. Others swear by the moon and claim that at full moon there is always a change in the weather. These are mere superstitions. Ancient weather lore, even at its best, consists of ambiguities.

One group of people who really do know the weather are the farmers; they can forecast tomorrow's weather from the strength and direction of the wind, from the shape and motion of the clouds, from the time when the dew starts to fall, and from many other such observations. These forecasts, however, apply only to the relatively near future and to a small area, as they have no general systematic basis.

A second group of weather-wise people consists of those for whom weather forecasting is a profession, namely the meteorologists. They can forecast the behavior of the weather by scientific methods and by means of elaborate observation systems supported by precise instruments designed to record all the processes in the atmosphere; their predictions are much more accurate.

The atmosphere supports life; its temperature, pressure, and humidity all vary. Wind strength and direction, clouds, and precipitation all play their various parts and give us what we call weather.

A private weather station will enable us to measure these meteorological factors and so provide us with data for weather forecasting, which should be valid at least for our immediate neighborhood. Although these home-made instruments do not provide the accuracy needed for scientific purposes, they do provide a very interesting and educative study of the physics of the weather.

Wind Direction and Wind Strength

The best and most rugged apparatus is needed for the measurement of wind strength and wind direction; the two functions can be combined in one wind-measuring instrument.

The instrument requires a site unobstructed by buildings or trees. A balcony is not suitable; an open field or garden is needed, in which a post (not too short) can be set up.

The combined instrument consists of a weather vane and a wind-strength indicator. The vane has a double task to perform. On

Combined wind indicator

the one hand, it shows which is the lee side, and, on the other, keeps the flap of the wind-strength indicator turned always into the wind. The bearing for this assembly takes the form of a round iron pivot rod about 12″ long and ¹/₂″ in diameter fixed in a hole drilled axially in the post so as to leave about 8″ protruding.

The end of the post is prevented from splitting, when the pivot rod is driven in, by a piece of iron (or galvanized) tubing about 2″ long; the inside diameter of this should

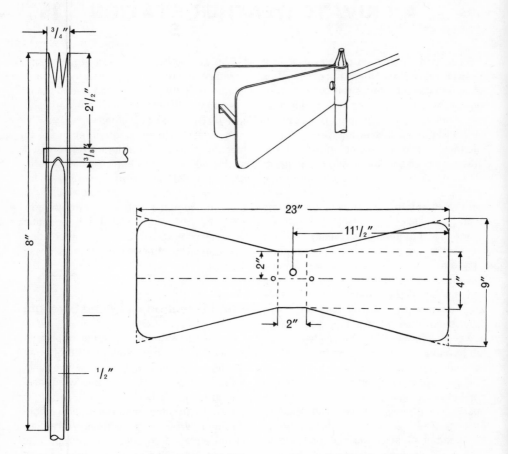

Working drawing of the bearing and weather vane of the combined wind-measuring instrument.

be the same as the diameter of the post. This tubing also acts as a mount for the arms indicating the points of the compass, iron or brass rods $^3/_{16}$" in diameter soldered into the tube at right angles. A second cross with shorter arms marks the halfway points between the principal directions. The metal letters (2" high) are cut from brass sheet $^1/_{16}$" thick and soldered to the arms, which are slotted to receive them. The entire assembly is mounted on the end of the post before the pivot rod is driven in.

Careful positioning of the pivot rod is vital to the correct functioning and sensitivity of the vane. The point must be filed to lie exactly on the axis of the rod, after which it is hardened by heating to redness and quenching in cold water.

A brass tube 8" long with a $^5/_8$" inside diameter serves to carry the vane, the wind-strength flap, the supporting frame, and the wind-strength scale. The wall thickness is $^1/_{16}$". Several slits about 1" deep are made with a metal saw in the top of the tube which is then hammered down to an internal diameter of $^3/_{16}$". The bottom end of the frame for the flap will later be inserted in this reduced section. Before this, the bow-tie shape of the tail of the vane is cut out of thin sheet zinc; the dimensions are shown in the drawing. Do not forget to drill a hole for the arrow; the same goes for the two holes $^1/_8$" in diameter on the center line, which are intended for the fixing screw.

Next, the triangular sections of the tail are turned down slightly and the rectangular middle section is bent by hand around the brass tube. The final dressing is done with a rubber hammer or mallet, and the tail is clamped in place with a brass nut and bolt.

The tail is in its correct position when the top of the hole for the arrow is $2^1/_2$" below the top (slit) end of the tube. At the rear of the vane and half-way up, an iron strut about

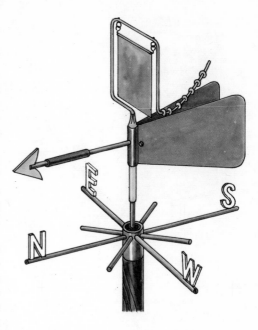

Instrument for measuring the strength and direction of the wind, mounted on a post.

5" long is soldered to stiffen the two tail sections.

We can now proceed to mount the arrow, which is a continuation of the angle between the two tail sections and must bisect this angle if it is to indicate the wind-direction correctly.

The shaft of the arrow consists of a round iron rod $^3/_8$" in diameter and 10" long. The hole in the middle of the tail section is drilled out with a $^3/_8$" drill; the end of the rod is inserted in this hole and soldered into place. A conical recess is formed $^5/_{16}$" from the end of the rod to receive the bearing pin before the rod is mounted in the tail. The other end of the rod is slotted to take the arrowhead

327

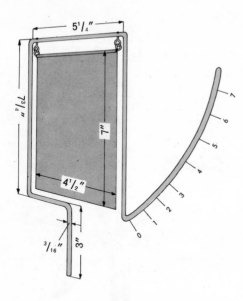

Construction of the wind-strength indicator showing flap, frame and graduated arm.

7" and can be made from the side of a tin can. The top edge is wrapped around a copper wire $^3/_{32}$" in diameter with its ends bent up into hooks to engage in eyelets, so the finished flap has an effective length of a little less than 7".

The eyelets made of the same copper wire as the hooks are passed through holes in the upper transverse arm of the frame. The top ends of these eyelets are then riveted over.

The frame and scale arm are made of a single piece of brass rod $^3/_{16}$" in diameter. The diagram gives the dimensions of the frame; a piece of rod about 36" long is needed. The rod must be bent in the vise so as to form an exact rectangle. The radius of the scale arm is the same as that of the arc described by the flap as it swings. The marks for wind strengths from 1 to 7 are rings soldered to the rod at the corresponding points. The flap is vertical at force 0; its end is displaced by 10 mm at force 1. The distance between marks 1 and 2 is 15 mm; that between 2 and 3 20 mm; between 3 and 4 30 mm; between 4 to 5 and between 5 to 6 40 mm; and between 6 and 7 35 mm. There is little point in extending the scale any further, for the deflection of the flap increases very little at higher wind speeds, so readings become inaccurate. The distance between the marks for 7 and 8 is only 16 mm, and between marks 8 and 9 only 8 mm. If the flap definitely indicates a force in excess of 9, it is high time to anchor the post firmly with wire stays.

Wind Indicator with Electrical Remote Reading

The limitation of the above simple device is that the wind speed can only be read directly from the scale. This can be very

which indicates the direction of the wind and is made of the brass sheet used for the points of the compass. This slot is best cut out with a hacksaw.

It is important to balance the two parts of the vane so that it will turn freely. This is done with a counterweight (a piece of lead tubing slipped over the arrow shaft). This counter-weight is permanently fixed in place when the two parts of the vane have been brought into balance. All that is needed is to give the ends of the lead tubing a gentle tap with a hammer.

Once balanced, the vane is complete and it remains to install the wind-strength indicator. This consists of a flap swinging freely in a frame and a graduated scale to indicate the deflection of the flap, which depends on the wind strength. This flap measures $4^1/_2$" x

inconvenient if no suitable site close at hand is available, and it is generally impossible to read the scale after dark. These difficulties are overcome in a device that converts the reading to electrical form for remote registration at any hour of the day or night in the amateur meteorologist's home.

The wind speed is represented as the voltage produced by a small propeller-driven dynamo and is read with a voltmeter. The greater the wind speed, the higher the rate at which the dynamo runs and so the higher the voltage and the greater the deflection of the voltmeter needle. The original scale of the voltmeter must be recalibrated for wind strength. This requires a little time after the instrument has been set up, but it is only necessary to accumulate a few calibration points by requesting information about wind speeds from the nearest meteorological station.

A moving-iron or moving-coil instrument is most suitable for this purpose, on account of its high sensitivity at low voltages. It is advantageous to include a capacitor in the circuit (1000 to 10,000 pF) if the instrument is very sensitive; the best value has to be determined by experiment in each particular case.

The generator is a bicycle dynamo held in a frame consisting of strips of steel $1/16''$ thick clamped at right angles to the support. This support is the front axle and hub from a bicycle; the frame is fixed to the hub by means of two clamping screws, one on each side. The dynamo is secured in this frame by metal straps $5/8''$ wide, bent to fit the dynamo body.

The drawing shows the shape of the two identical halves of the frame; they must be bent carefully in a vise to form an exact right angle. By turning over the ends of the frame at the dynamo cap and on the far side of the hub we can provide fixing points for a pro-

tective cover made of wood. The wood is made thick (one inch) to allow for rounding the edges to an elegant aerodynamic form. The front face is made from a piece with a hole drilled in it to permit the cap of the dynamo to pass. The joints are glued and screwed; a coat or two of spar varnish will make the housing weathertight.

The usual drive wheel is removed from the shaft of the dynamo and replaced with a propeller. A four-bladed propeller is used

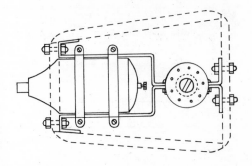

Top and side views of dynamo and bicycle hub joined by means of steel frame. The broken lines represent the housing.

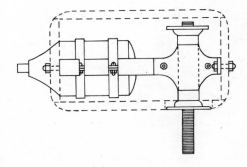

The propeller

in this device, since it is much more responsive to light winds than a two-bladed one. The essential requirement here is to make a propeller so balanced that it turns perfectly evenly in response to the slightest wind. Fine adjustments can be made by carefully filing the blades that are too heavy.

The propeller should have an overall diameter of 32″ to 48″ and should be built

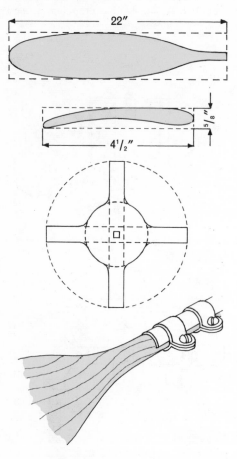

Working drawing for the construction of the propeller: profile of the blades, layout of the hub, and method of joining hub and blades.

around a metal hub; the blades can be made of balsa wood $^5/_8$″ thick. Balsa wood is available in various grades of hardness; grade III is needed here. The balsa must be made completely weather-resistant. The hub is made of stainless-steel sheet.

A propeller 48″ in diameter can be built from four pieces of wood each 22″ long and $4^1/_2$″ wide; these must be carved very carefully to the correct profile. The ends to be fitted into the hub must be cut down to circular rods $2^1/_2$″ long parallel to the axis of the blade. The blades are set to the correct angle of attack by adjustment of the clamping screws at the hub.

A paper pattern is prepared for the hub; this takes the form of a Maltese cross. The sheet is marked out with concentric circles $3^1/_2$″ and 8″ in diameter; four arms, each $^7/_8$″ wide, forming a right-angled cross are drawn in. This shape is cut from the metal, and then the central hole for the dynamo shaft is drilled and filed square. The four arms are bent to the radius of the roots of the propeller blades by hammering them over an iron rod of the same diameter. The blades are attached to these with two screw clips each.

These clips should be screwed up only loosely at first, to allow for adjustment of the blades to the correct angle of attack; then they can be tightened. The assembled metal part of the propeller can be protected by a small chromium-plated automobile hub cap. This also gives the propeller an excellent appearance.

The propeller is directed into the wind by a sheet-metal guide vane, constructed in accordance with the description given on page 327, except that the center part is made flat instead of round and is screwed to the back of the wooden housing.

The dynamo and propeller combined are balanced against the guide vane, but in this

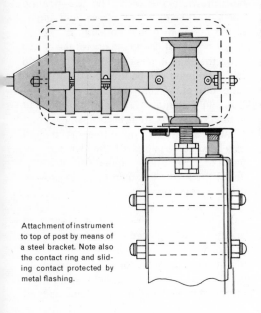

Attachment of instrument to top of post by means of a steel bracket. Note also the contact ring and sliding contact protected by metal flashing.

ping off the current generated by the dynamo; the leads must not produce appreciable opposition to the movement of the rotating head. This difficulty is simply overcome by using a contact ring made of thin copper sheet, which is connected to the live terminal of the dynamo. The contact ring is fixed to the underside of a circular plastic plate with a central hole through which the axle passes. This plate is screwed to the outside of the wooden housing. A contact brush (from a vacuum cleaner) works over this ring and connects the live terminal to the remote indicating instrument. The other (grounded) side of the dynamo is connected to the frame, so the lead may be attached at any suitable point. The sliding contact is protected from rain and snow by a piece of sheet metal open at the bottom; adequate protection is provided by the end of a large can, the top being clamped between the plastic plate and the wood housing and the lower edge extending a short way over the top of the post.

Hygrometer

The relative humidity is another important factor in weather forecasting; the variations in this can be observed and conveniently recorded by means of a hygrometer, which contains a horse hair, or (better still) a hair from the head of a blonde, to record changes in humidity.

The housing could be the round body of a can (not aluminum), in which a hair 16" to 24" long is arranged with the fewest possible bends; such bends as are necessary are made around rollers (like the ones used in tape recorders). The axles for these small rollers (they need only be quite short) can be made from hard brass wire and are soldered to the sides of the can. The rollers

case there is no need for very exact adjustment, because the relatively large ball-bearings in the bicycle hub are not seriously affected by a slight excess of weight on one side.

On the other hand, it is vital to have the supporting post absolutely upright; it must be firmly based and should be braced with three wire stays to keep it vertical. Furthermore, the complete head assembly must be mounted exactly at right angles to the post. This can be done by using a strong U-shaped steel bracket with a hole drilled in the middle to take the axle and additional holes for bolts passing through the top of the post. The entire apparatus must be very stable, because even moderate winds produce fairly large forces on the propeller and thus on the system as a whole.

A minor technical difficulty arises in tap-

331

are secured on their axles by short lengths of valve rubber. The fixed end of the hair is attached to a screw in the can. The hair then runs over the rollers and around the shaft of the needle near the far end, and is fixed to a light spring attached to the wall at a suitable point.

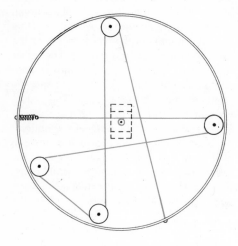

The hair (in blue), the sensitive element of the hygrometer, is stretched over a system of rollers between the walls of the instrument housing.

The spring must keep the hair under tension, but must not be so strong as to overstrain it; a suitable type is the spring from the contact brush of a vacuum cleaner. The spring and brush together can be bought from an appliance dealer. The hair must be degreased in spirit (alcohol) before use.

The bearings for the shaft of the needle may be made from brass sheet $^1/_{16}$" thick and are soldered onto the end of the can. Their height should not exceed the height of the side of the housing and should for preference be a fraction less. The shaft

itself is some $^3/_{16}$" longer and is made from hard-drawn brass wire. The two bearing holes must be drilled strictly at right angles at the midpoint of the housing. A slightly larger hole is drilled in the end of the can to allow the shaft to pass freely. The open end of the housing can be then closed with the other end of the can.

A slight change in the length of the hair should cause the shaft to turn, so the shaft must be able to turn quite freely. The shaft may be secured in place in the bearings by a piece of valve rubber slipped over the middle of the shaft; this also helps to prevent the hair from slipping.

Once the housing has been closed, the indicator needle (drilled at its center of gravity) may be placed on the exposed end of the shaft and secured with cement. Alternatively, it can be soldered to the shaft, but this can give rise to difficulties if the instrument is damaged and has to be opened up.

The indicator needle may be cut from a can or (better) from brass sheet $^1/_{32}$" thick. A housing 6" in diameter can take a needle $2^1/_2$" long, measured from the shaft to the scale. The weight of the needle is balanced by a circular counterweight on the other side of the shaft, otherwise the hair may tend to slip on the shaft. A needle $2^1/_2$" long requires a counterweight about $^{15}/_{16}$" long, as in the diagram; a counterweight $^7/_8$" in diameter will give a close approximation to balance, and an exact adjustment can be made by carefully filing down the heavier side. This balancing is essential.

The scale is made from postcard and is glued to the upper part of the end of the housing. No formula can be used for the scale, which must be calibrated by experiment. The bulletins of the local weather service can be used for calibration purposes.

We wish to measure the humidity of the free atmosphere rather than that of the room, so the hygrometer has naturally to be located in the open air. The scale and pointer must be protected from the weather. A housing can be built of strong plywood and the instrument fastened inside. The front of the box should be closed with window glass, mostly covered with paint or black paper on the inside to leave only the semicircular scale visible. Two holes in the rear of the box serve for hanging the instrument in position on the site.

The protection against the weather must not be so complete that the inside of the instrument is sealed off from the outside air. Slots may be made in the wall of the instrument and in the sides of the housing to allow the air to enter and leave the instrument freely.

If the wooden box is made somewhat larger, room can be found for a thermometer. This and the barometer are two valuable meteorological instruments, but it is impracticable to make either of these at home because the amateur cannot handle the com-

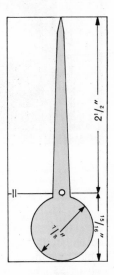

The hygrometer needle must be perfectly balanced by a small counterweight.

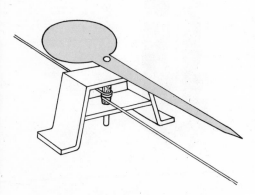

Bearings of the hygrometer needle. The shaft is held in place by a piece of valve rubber.

plicated techniques needed to produce the vacuum in the thermometer or the sensitive capsule of the barometer, especially since the latter requires a complex mechanism to convert its movements into those of a needle.

Rain Gage

A simple direct-reading rain gage can be made in accordance with the following directions.

The apparatus consists of a collector funnel, a box, and a glass cylinder, grad-

333

Rain gage

The finished hygrometer mounted, together with a thermometer, in a glass-fronted plywood box.

The right-hand wall has a door fitted with two hinges and a simple catch. A small strip of wood on the right-hand corner piece serves as a stop.

The base consists of two squares of plywood; the upper one has a circular hole in it corresponding in diameter to the bottom of the cylinder. In this way the cylinder is prevented from sliding in the box. The upper piece must be cut back by the thickness of the glass relative to the lower one, in order to leave room for the observation window, which is slipped in after the front wall has been fitted into place. The base rests on a frame made of narrow strips of wood.

The cover plate and funnel are made of thin sheet zinc. The dimensions for these parts are shown in the drawing. The blue lines indicate where parts **a** and **b** are to be bent down. Parts **a** are at right angles to the

uated to read from 0 to 100 cc. The funnel is such that 10 cc of water corresponds to 1 mm of rain; 11 cc means 1.1 mm, 12 cc means 1.2 mm, and so on. The smaller the diameter of the cylinder, the more accurate the reading.

The cylinder used in this model was 10″ high. This required a wooden box 13″ long fitted at the top with a cover plate into which the funnel is soldered.

This box was made of water-resistant plywood and four strips of pine, used to reinforce the corners of the box. The upper ends of the corner pieces were cut away slightly to allow room for the funnel. Only two of the sides remain intact. The front wall has a narrow window high enough to reveal the full length of the scale on the cylinder. The glass is held in a groove formed by the front wall and two thin strips of wood glued to the corner pieces.

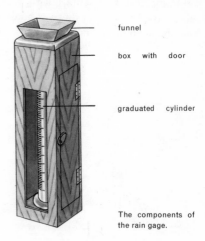

funnel

box   with   door

graduated   cylinder

The components of the rain gage.

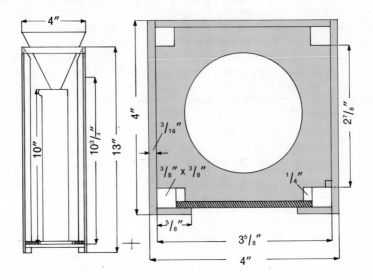

Working drawing for a rain gage showing the double bottom with a recess for the graduated cylinder.

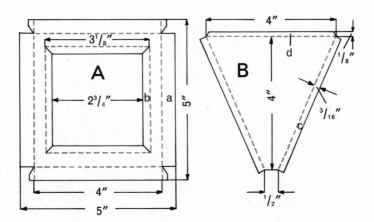

Drawing showing dimensions of the cover plate and the sides of the funnel. The flanges are bent down along the dotted lines.

top after bending and grip the edges of the box, preventing any sideways movement of the funnel.

The funnel, the top of which measures 4" x 4", is assembled from four side pieces. Only two of these have flanges **d** at the sides. These flanges are soldered to the other two pieces during assembly. The flange **d** at the top edge is present on all four; in all cases this is bent inwards before the side pieces are assembled. The outlet from the funnel is a square with sides $\frac{1}{2}$" long. The assembled funnel is soldered to flanges **b** on the cover plate, which should therefore be bent to match the slope of the funnel sides.

Finally, the wood is given two coats of spar varnish, though there is no objection to an undercoat of green oil paint as well. The finished gage must be set up in an open space, where buildings or trees will not give rise to incorrect readings. The best solution is to attach the gage to a free-standing post, with the top of the funnel at least an inch above the top of the post.

Keeping animals is a responsible business. We unreservedly reject the view that the end always justifies the means. It is quite immaterial whether the animals are kept in order to derive economic benefit from breeding them or just because it is nice to have them around, for the sheer pleasure of their company. In either case man demands a service from the animal and is indebted to the animal for it. Gratitude should not be expressed in false sentimentality. Such feelings usually do the animal more harm than good.

An animal kept in a pen or cage is held in captivity and more or less denied any free-dom. Our first duty to the animal is to see that it has ample food suited to its species and that its accommodation takes account of its natural habitat and offers it maximum freedom of movement so that it does not feel cooped up, even though the space at its disposal is bound to be small.

The Aquarium

We can go very far in providing aquarium dwellers with all the conditions for a good and healthy life.

Aquaria can be bought as all-glass tanks

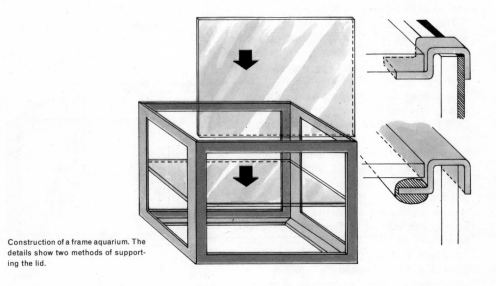

Construction of a frame aquarium. The details show two methods of supporting the lid.

or as aquaria of the frame type. All-glass aquaria, as their name implies, are molded in one piece from glass. Their advantage lies in a surface free of joints, their disadvantage in their rigid, standard dimensions, and also in the fact that the walls are often not completely flat and thus produce optical distortions. Large tanks of this type are fairly sensitive and easily broken as a result of the stresses imposed on the material.

A home-made frame aquarium is not out of the question, but it is doubtful whether it is wise for the amateur to start on one. The base and walls of the tank are not continuous, but separate panels of plate glass made watertight with putty and supported on steel angles. The opaque edges in this design detract from the appearance of the tank, but this is outweighed by important advantages: free choice of any desired size, avoidance of stresses in the glass, and plane-parallel and distortion-free walls. Moreover, the unit is not a complete loss in case of accident as individual panels can be replaced.

The greatest difficulty in making one's own frame aquarium is in fabricating the steel frame, the separate parts of which must be joined by seamless welds if the tank is going to last and be really watertight. The bearing surfaces must also be completely level and true. Even slight deviations from these precision requirements expose the glass to stresses produced by the internal pressure of the water. If the aquarium is jolted or the temperature fluctuates, such stresses may lead to breakages.

If it is possible to get a reliable workshop to make a frame of the desired size, an enterprising person can perform all the other operations himself. First of all, the frame must be thoroughly coated with red lead to protect it from corrosion. Typically, the panels for the bottom and side walls should

be $1/_4$"-thick plate glass, which must be very accurately cut to size. Whether you do it yourself is a question of self-confidence, and whether you possess a good glass-cutting diamond. Panels with ground edges are better than rough-cut ones.

Fitting the glass into the frame is the second tricky step in making an aquarium at home. A putty suitable for fixing and sealing the panels consists of lead oxide (lead monoxide or red lead) which is stirred with waterglass to give a stiff paste. Care should be taken in handling lead oxide, since like all lead compounds it is poisonous. Synthetic commercial putties are also available. The trouble with glazing with either kind of compound is that the seams must remain completely free of air bubbles, and only a very nimble worker can manipulate the putty with the thoroughness demanded by careful glazing, since it soon hardens and can then no longer be handled.

In deciding on the size of the tank one should bring one's own preferences into line with a few rules which have proved useful in practical aquarium building. The tank

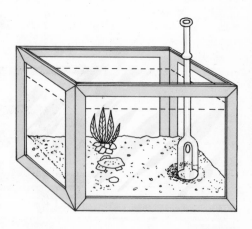

Siphon and mud pit help to keep the aquarium bottom clean.

should be neither too narrow (measured from front to back) nor too high. In either case the amount of water in relation to the area in contact with the air becomes too large. On the other hand, an attempt to increase the water surface by excessively increasing the space between front and back of the tank has the drawback of making it more difficult to observe the inhabitants of the aquarium.

The height of the aquarium should be an inch or two greater than the depth of water required, since the sand layer at the bottom takes up some space and anyhow the tank should not have the water flush with the upper rim.

The red lead priming of the steel frame is coated with varnish once the tank is ready and has successfully passed tests for water-tightness lasting several days. However, a much more elegant appearance is given by carefully boxing in the frame with thin strips of wood. The inside surfaces of these strips are coated with spar varnish and the strips themselves are neatly screwed together with oval-head brass screws. The tank is finally completed by adding a glass lid for which a sheet $1/_8''$ thick will be strong enough. In order to avoid condensation water, which accumulates on the under-side of the lid, seeping between the frame and the wood, the lid is supported on brass or zinc brackets suspended from the rim of the tank. Even better than these are molded rubber edge strips which cannot be made at home but have to be obtained from pet stores.

Bottom and Planting

Most aquarium plants draw their nourish-ment not from the ground, in which they take root, but from the water surrounding them.

Therefore, instead of a vegetable soil which would make the water cloudy, we make do with a coarse-grained river or pit sand which is wetted and transferred in layers into the still empty tank. The sand should previously be washed several times until the washing water is completely clear. The thickness of the sandy bottom is deter-mined by the size of the tank. Very large aquaria require up to four inches of sand, for smaller ones an average thickness of about two inches will do. The bottom should not be flat, but should slope gently towards the side of the tank through which one looks. It is also advantageous to make a depres-sion or "mud pit" in the bottom on one of the two narrow sides. Here, in the course of time, the unused waste products accumu-late and can readily be drawn off with a mud siphon.

If it is desired to give plants with deep roots a somewhat richer nourishment, a layer of unwashed sand or peat litter can be laid at the very bottom of the tank and then covered with washed sand.

Planting should only be done when the tank has been half filled with water. The water should be added carefully and slowly so that the bottom is not churned up. The simplest way to do this is to allow the water to run into the container through a thin tube from a bucket placed level with the upper edge of the tank. The mouth of the tube is held just above the bottom against the vessel wall and the water allowed to run onto the glass.

Biological Balance

In a well-arranged aquarium, the sub-aquatic plants, thanks to their oxygen-car-bon dioxide exchange with representatives of the fauna, help to ensure biological balance, an essential condition for a healthy habitat.

The less we interfere with this environment the better. Nevertheless, we do have to give some aid to the aquarium—not to mention the feeding of the fishes—since, after all, room conditions differ from those outside in nature. This aid consists—especially in crowded aquaria—in the artificial enrichment of the water with oxygen, and in filtering and heating the water. Home-made devices designed to take over these vital functions are in most cases of dubious value, since if they do not work very reliably, they cause more disappointment and harm than good and, moreover, necessitate meddling in the life of the aquarium with the risk of upsetting it.

The fish will be better off with a ready-made filter, ventilator and electric heater from the pet shop, as only these are suitable. It costs very little to operate these devices. The heater should lie at the deepest point of the bottom to ensure uniform heating of the water. It should be concealed behind stones or plants, but never buried in the sand.

Much experimental work has been done on filters for aquaria and it took a long time to achieve practical results. However, there are now available highly efficient internal filters which, combined with an air pump, aerate the tank and are very easy to keep clean. Such filters keep the water in a 16 gallon tank completely clear for a week. If the water starts to cloud, this is always a sign that the filter element is dirty and must either be cleaned or renewed.

Light is not a negligible factor in maintaining a biological balance. If the natural lighting is poor, additional artificial lighting should be provided. The price of fluorescent tubes may be high but as against this they are very cheap to run and have the advantage that their spectrum comes very close to that of natural sunlight. They are therefore especially beneficial for fish and plants. They are mounted either on the front ledge of the frame or — even better — on the inside of the lid, protected by asbestos.

The Terrarium

Technically it is much easier to make a terrarium by one's own efforts than to construct an aquarium, since, as the terrarium accommodates land dwellers, it does not need to be watertight, at least not all the way up its walls. The purely manual side of the work does call for some skill, however. Moreover, we must definitely decide beforehand which animals we wish to keep. If our favorites are lizards, we can manage with a so-called dry terrarium, whereas batrachia, tortoises and different types of salamander require a wet one. Finally, halfway between an aquarium and a terrarium is an aquaterrarium, which because of its wide biological scope permits the pursuit of many-sided interests. Understandably, an aquaterrarium with gradual transition from pond to dry bank demands a relatively large space but even the other types should not be too small, measuring at least 24" x 16" and 18" high.

The decision to have a dry or wet terrarium determines the building material. A point to remember is that even a dry one cannot manage entirely without moisture, since the plants and bottom always need some water. We should make the frame for the dry type from wood, but it must be hardwood (oak) and be impregnated with varnish before being given a water-repellent protective coat. A good spar varnish is highly suitable for this.

There are no fixed standards for constructing the terrarium container. The pro-

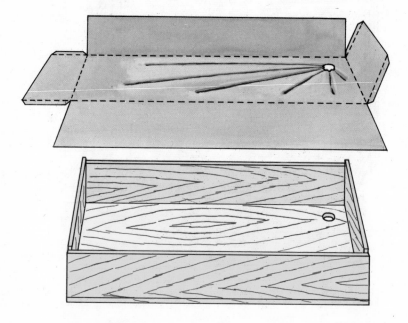

First step in building a terrarrium. Note that the front and back walls of the box-shaped base are slightly lower than the side walls. Top: construction of galvanized tray with drainage hole and radiating drainage channels.

portions and design features are largely determined by the taste of the builder and the way of life of the animal, for which the finished container must serve as a healthy abode.

Start to build it by preparing the base, which is nailed together in the form of a box measuring 20″ x 16″ (outside measurements) using $^3/_8$″ thick material. Skilled handymen concerned with quality will face the sides with zinc. The sides rest on top of the board forming the bottom. A hole $^3/_4$″ in diameter is drilled in the left or right front corner of the bottom board. If the base is made with butt-jointed corners, then in cutting the boards for the walls care should be taken to keep the narrow sides $^3/_4$″ shorter than the short edges of the bottom, since the front and back walls of the box should be long enough to conceal the end faces of the side walls. The height of the box—including the base—is four inches but only the side walls should be so high. The front and back walls are $^1/_4$″ lower. This, and the fact that the long sides overlap the short ones, is important in connection with the glazing of the terrarium walls. In addition to the wooden base, the terrarium should have glass

341

Terrarium frames

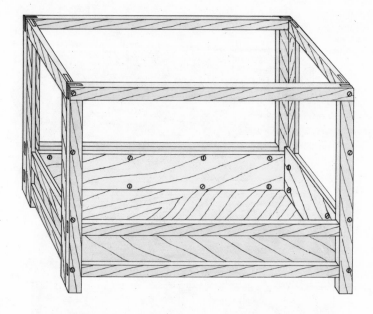

The mortised frames forming the walls of the terrarium are built independently, then assembled and screwed to the base. The wire gauze and galvanized tray are not shown. The drainage hole in the front right hand corner is concealed by the front wall.

back and front walls, while the side walls should be covered with wire gauze in order to improve ventilation.

However, before starting to construct the walls, prepare a galvanized metal tray with a base area corresponding to that of the wooden bottom. The function of this tray is to protect the wood of the box from the moisture of the soil. The height of the walls should average four inches. The tray is made from a single piece of galvanized sheet iron. When cutting leave $^{1}/_{4}''$ wide soldering strips on each side of the two shorter wall pieces. After all the edges have been bent up at right angles, the vertical corner joints are soldered. The soldering strips should lie inside the finished tray. This means that when cutting the sheet, the parts for the

shorter walls must be kept shorter than the corresponding edges of the bottom by double the thickness of the material. In both directions the bottom of the tray must be smaller than the inside dimensions of the wooden box by double the thickness of the material plus $^{1}/_{8}''$. If this is not done, the tray will not fit the box. It is often better to build the tray and then construct the wooden box around it.

Before soldering, a hole is drilled in the tray bottom corresponding exactly to the position of the hole in the bottom of the box. However, the hole in the sheet metal is only $^{1}/_{2}''$ in diameter. The purpose of both holes is to allow surplus liquid seeping through the soil to run away. In order to make it easier for the seepage to reach this drain in the bottom of the tray, take a very blunt flat chisel or even better a chasing tool, and form several drainage channels radiating outwards from the hole. If you wish to do a bit extra, solder a $^3/_4"$ long piece of $^1/_2"$ diameter iron pipe to the bottom of the assembled tray.

When the tray is placed in position this pipe will pass through the hole in the bottom of the wooden base and prevent moisture getting between the wood and the sheet metal.

The walls of the terrarium consist of rectangular wooden frames each with a single intermediate cross piece. All the members can be in $^3/_4"$ x 1" material. The members all lie in one plane and therefore must be neatly lapped. A mortise-and-tenon joint is more attractive, but more difficult to make. It has the additional advantage that it only needs to be glued. All other joints between the wooden parts of the walls need to be both glued and screwed. Nails should as far as possible be avoided, as points inadvertently hammered through and projecting inside the terrarium may injure the animals.

For a container 18" high the vertical members of the frame should be 20" long, since 2" is required at the bottom to raise the base off the ground. This is important, since the wooden bottom must be ventilated from underneath. The length of the horizontal members is 16" at the sides and 21" at the front and back. The top of all the intermediate cross pieces should be flush with the top of the wooden base.

After the upper panels of the two side frames have been covered with a strong, resilient wire gauze, all the frames are butt-jointed, the two longer ones fitting over the two shorter ones, and firmly screwed to the wooden base (screw from the inside with flat-head brass screws). Then, the bottom tray can be inserted.

The still open upper panels of the back and front walls should be glazed with easily removable sheets of glass. The glass to use is top-grade window glass about $^1/_{10}"$ thick.

The two verticals of the front frame prevent the glass from falling outwards. To the inside surface of the two adjacent verticals of the side frames glue a narrow stop to hold the glass in place from behind. Since we kept the front wall of the base $^1/_4"$ lower than the side walls, the intermediate cross piece of the frame projects $^1/_4"$ above the top of this wall. This provides a bottom stop for the glass in front. All we need to do now is to insert the glass and behind it glue a narrow bead to the upper edge of the base. This brings the front of the base to its full height and at the same time holds the bottom edge of the glass. The back wall of the terrarium is treated in exactly the same way. The terrarium walls are now in place and only the lid is missing.

The lid consists of a flat frame made of the same material as the wall frames. The corners of this frame are mitered and reinforced with a flat glued-in dowel. The lid frame should sit inside the wall frames and hence its outside dimensions must cor-

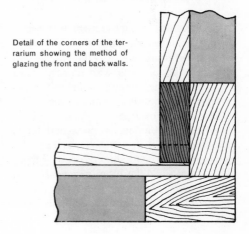

Detail of the corners of the terrarium showing the method of glazing the front and back walls.

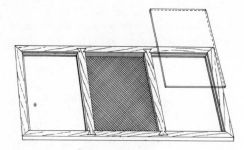

The three-part lid of the terrarium. Only the two side sections are glazed; the middle one is covered with wire gauze fixed to the inside of the lid.

respond to the clear dimensions between the walls. As hinges use two small cabinet or piano hinges. A small barrel bolt combined with a drawer handle makes an ideal lid-locking device. Make the bearing for the lid from two $\frac{1}{2}$" square strips glued to the side walls $\frac{3}{4}$" from the top. The front and back walls must remain clear, since otherwise we would block up the slots for the glass panels. To prevent any difficulty in taking out the glass wall at the back the hinges must be recessed. It is up to the individual whether he glazes the lid or covers it with wire gauze. If it is glazed, a glazing rabbet must be formed at the inner edge of the frame members before they are joined, as the lid is best glazed like a window. A lid two-thirds of which is glazed and the other middle third covered with gauze has been found practical. It is a little more difficult to make up a frame for such a lid since the total area must then be divided into three equal parts with narrow cross members. A glazing rabbet must be formed on one side of these members also. The middle section of the two long sides of the lid is left unrabbeted. A three-part lid is advantageous, if it is desired to heat the terrarium from the top on cool days with an electric heater. A far more elegant type of heating, which may be important for a container for tropical or subtropical inhabitants, is provided by an infrared heating coil mounted below the frame of the lid.

Interior of the Terrarium

Introduce the bottom soil into the tray in three layers. The lowest is a percolating layer of brick rubble or coarse broken stone, then follows a layer of dry peat litter, which is finally covered with the upper layer. It is better to cover the drainage hole in the tray bottom with small pieces of broken flower pot in order to prevent clogging.

The upper layer must suit the inhabitants of the terrarium. In a mainly dry terrarium sand predominates, but for animals fond of burrowing, provide a reserve of loose clayey earth. Very wet terraria with tropical plants need compost and leaf mold.

Flat stones lying on smaller stones will serve as a shelter for the animals. Short pieces of narrow drainage tile and flint chippings can also be successfully used for making crannies. In all cases, however, rough stones or stones with sharp edges should be avoided, since they are not very comfortable.

To prevent the terrarium becoming a dense jungle, planting should be done sparingly. Tender and tall-growing plants are unsuitable for the terrarium. Nor is it advisable to root the plants directly in the bottom soil; they should be put in sunken flower pots and bowls. With this method it is easier to change the plants and keep the terrarium clean.

Whether a water tank is necessary depends on the population of the terrarium. We do not exactly build a special marsh environment for frogs, but make do with smaller, shallow "ponds". Ceramic dishes unglazed on the inside are suitable for this, providing they do not have steep walls. However it is best to mold one's own container out of fine concrete to which a waterproofing agent has been added. With small vessels it is enough to make a mold in well-compacted, moist sand and to cast them by hand with a wall thickness of about $^3/_4$". Use wet concrete in the form of an intimate mixture of 1 part cement to 4 parts sand; knock the finished shapes hard until the perspiration water comes to the surface. Allow them to dry out slowly and well. The concrete

must be protected against direct sunlight and during the first day should be repeatedly sprinkled with a watering can. Even a shallow water tank with gently sloping edges should have a few stones to make it easier for the animals to get to the water.

Some animals are very fond of climbing "trees" made of dry wood. Use heavily branching twigs from which the bark has been stripped. Very attractively branched twigs can be obtained from the plum tree, the weeping ash or old, frequently cut-back hedges. These will stand up well if mounted in a block of wood. Driftwood may also be used.

The choice of plants and animals for the terrarium, as for the aquarium, is in itself a far-ranging subject which we cannot go into here. The two chief factors, however— the design of the house and the way of life of its inhabitants—cannot be separated and

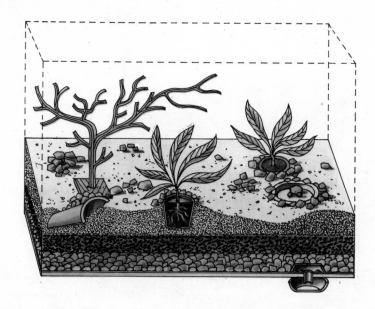

Section through a typical terrarium. The bottom material is introduced in three layers. The plants grow in pots, rather than directly in the soil.

must be harmoniously combined. The expectations of the animals must, of course, take precedence and the habitat must be arranged to suit their needs.

An Aviary in your Home

The more seldom the individual comes into direct contact with nature and its creatures, the stronger becomes his desire to bring a little nature into his home in order to enjoy it in private. The most obvious expression of this desire is a flower pot and a window box. Then follows a canary, parakeet, or bullfinch. For grain-eaters the wire cage has won general acceptance because of its suitability. The top and walls of this cage consist of wire bars, while the base, with a bottom drawer, is made of sheet metal. The rustless, jointless material has the advantage over wood of being easier to clean and provides no breeding places for vermin.

If you attempt to make yourself a wire cage

that is not only practical and durable but also attractive, you are almost certain to be disappointed with the result. However, it is quite feasible for a skilled amateur to build a box cage in which insect-eating birds are kept, for example, flycatchers, thrushes, and certain song birds. These birds are essentially bush dwellers, they readily withdraw into the shadows and feel safer and more secure in a box cage than in a wire one open on all sides. Moreover, the closed walls protect the sensitive animals from drafts.

In a box cage only the front wall is made of wire, the rear and side walls and the 2″ high base are of wood. For all the wooden parts you should use only first-class, sound hardwood, free of cracks and impregnated with insecticide. As a further protection against pests and vermin all the woodwork should be given several coats of good varnish. The inner coating should be in a bright color. As with the terrarium, the lid of the cage should be a flat frame, this time covered with a sheet of strong plastic. The lid should be built so that it can be taken out

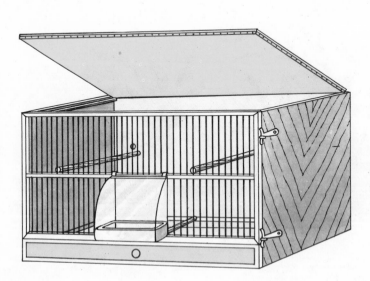

Box cage with hinged lid, removable front wall, and bottom drawer. The lid is a flat frame covered with strong plastic.

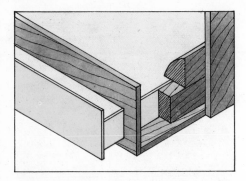

Installation of the drawer in the base of the cage. The quarter-round molding overlaps the upper edge of the drawer and helps to keep the bottom clean.

or raised.

The bottom of the cage is protected by an inch-high drawer of tin or brass plate. It is pushed through a suitable slot in the front wall and firmly guided on left and right by two wooden strips glued to the cage bottom. Narrow quarter-round molding overlapping the upper edge of the drawer prevents the scattering of the bottom sand with which the drawer is half filled.

The cage should be as large as possible. Its most important dimension is its length. The minimum size is five times the length of the body of the bird to be kept in it. Ground-dweller birds require a particularly long cage without a perch in which they have enough room to fly around. Such a cage must therefore be kept unobstructed.

The greatest dexterity is called for in building the front wire wall which should also be designed so that it can be taken off for thorough cleaning. The easiest way to do this is to build a light frame with a cross piece in the middle for stiffening the vertical bars. If the front wall is not to be too bulky the cross piece should be slightly thinner than the frame. The size of the frame should be equal to the front wall of the cage less the height of the base. The corner joints should be mitered and reinforced by glued-in dowels. However, before this the three horizontal members must be prepared to receive the bars of the cage, made of hard-drawn brass wire. The length of the bars should be slightly less than the height of the frame. The spacing of the bars depends on the size of the birds occupying the cage. The space between bars should not be too narrow nor so wide that the bird can put its head through and perhaps strangle itself.

After all the bars and frame members have been cut to the right length, vertical holes are drilled through the center horizontal corresponding to the thickness and spacing of the bars. This member then serves as a template for further drill holes in the top and bottom members. The latter are only drilled half-way through. Then the frame is put together except for the top horizontal, and the individual bars are

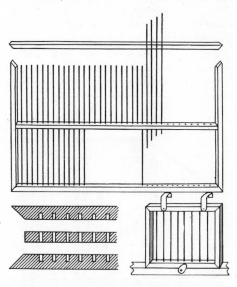

Construction of the front wire wall of a box cage. After the bars have been inserted the frame is closed at the top. Bottom: drilling pattern for the horizontal members of the frame and barred door for the bath opening.

Front wall

passed through the holes in the center horizontal to rest in the corresponding holes in the bottom horizontal. Finally, the top horizontal is fitted over the bars and the wire wall is complete.

When the center horizontal is being drilled, it is important to ensure that an area of the front wall remains free for the bird bath. The center horizontal must therefore not be drilled right through over its entire length. The bars over the bird bath should be shorter than the other bars by somewhat more than the distance from the bottom to the center horizontal. For a bath fixed on the outside, the opening formed can be closed by a small barred door made from lighter material and without a cross piece in the middle, built on the same principle as the main wall. If you find this too difficult, in one of the two side walls make a suitable little door in which a glass bird bath can be hung. The front wall is best fixed to the rest of the cage with two swivel hooks attached to the side walls. These engage in two eyes screwed at a suitable level into the side members of the wall frame. In this arrangement the wire wall

Slot-hung front wall of a nesting box. A flat piece of wood must be glued to the bottom of the box to raise it to the level of the top of the frame.

rests on the front edge of the base.

It is important to position the perches correctly. Cut them to the right length from beechwood doweling and smooth them

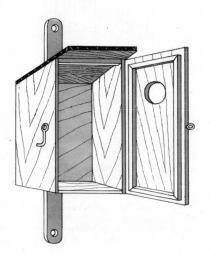

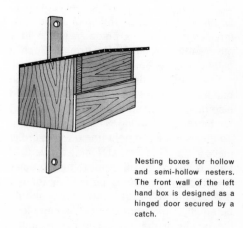

Nesting boxes for hollow and semi-hollow nesters. The front wall of the left hand box is designed as a hinged door secured by a catch.

348

with sandpaper and a spoke shave. One end is filed down with a round file to a short pin which is inserted into a suitable hole drilled in the back wall, while a shallow notch is sawn in the other end. By means of this notch the rod is fitted over a bar in the front wall of the cage. A lower perch, at the level of the base, should be placed in the middle of the cage, while two upper ones should be pushed as close as possible to the two side walls, so that the bird, if it wishes to jump from one bar to another must beat its wings. For largish cages two bars may also be fixed at the lower level, but they must be so arranged that they are not exposed to fouling from the upper perches. The same applies to feeders and drinking bowls, which are simply put on the bottom if the size of the cage allows.

Nesting Boxes

The transition from the simple pursuit of a hobby to practical bird protection can be made by building nesting boxes for wild birds. By providing good nesting facilities the home owner can attract birds to his own garden and will not only derive enjoyment from the songsters, but create for himself a very diligent sanitation force with a vested interest in keeping down garden pests.

Building nesting boxes is an extremely simple matter for anyone who knows how to handle a hammer and saw. All that it really involves is nailing together a box-shaped cabinet of strong weatherproof boards ($^3/_4''$ thick). The nails must be driven home with care so that no points protrude like thorns on the inside of the box.

Birds that nest in hollows, in particular, suffer from a lack of suitable nesting places. These include all the tits, the nuthatch, starlings, the common redstart, the woodpecker, and also the weeping flycatcher and the hole pigeon. If we wish to help them with their nest building, we can confidently offer them all—apart from the very choosy woodpecker—this type of box. Its size must not only be adjusted to the individual inhabitant, but also to its very large family. Nesting boxes for small birds should have

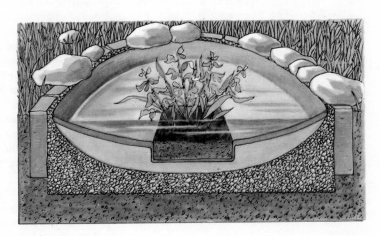

Large watering places for birds can be made of concrete bedded in gravel. Aquatic plants can be grown in the central trough.

349

a clear space inside 10″ high and 5″ square. Birds of starling size require a minimum area of 6″ x 6″ and a clear height of 12″. The circular entrance hole must also be adjusted to the size of the bird. Whereas tits can manage with a hole only 1$\frac{1}{2}$″ in diameter, starlings and wrynecks require a width of at least 2″. The entrance hole should be about 2$\frac{1}{2}$″ from the roof.

The nesting boxes for semi-hollow nesters, a category including, for example, the wagtail, the robin and the house redstart, differ from the models so far discussed in that they must be kept much flatter (clear height 5″–6″). Moreover, there is no entrance hole; instead the front wall only takes up two-thirds of the height of the box, thus forming a wide opening below the projecting flat roof.

It is not usual, however, for a starling to sit on a perch in front of its nesting box and sing. Most species fly directly to their nests. If a perch is provided, it should be wedged into a suitable hole drilled in the front wall an inch or two to the left or right of the center-line and below the entrance hole.

The roof of the nesting box is best covered with roofing felt. It should slope towards the rear and project one or two inches at the front. The front should always be built so that it can be detached without having to remove the box. This will be the more important the larger the population of the box, since in the course of time so much nesting material is brought into the box that in the end there is no room left for a new arrival. Moreover, all kinds of vermin settle in the old material. The boxes should therefore be cleaned out every fall.

The simplest way of solving the problem of the front wall is to build it like a two-hinged door secured by hooks and eyes. Such a door must have an inside seal in order to prevent drafts. This can be done with an all-round stop or better with a frame glued on the inside of the door panel. If you want to make things really easy for yourself, loosely fit the front wall into the box with a rectangular frame to act as a stop and screw two brass screws from either side into the left and right walls. This box, however, is harder to open and a screwdriver must always be used.

A slot-hung front wall looks smart, but takes quite a bit of material and work. Firstly, a frame must be firmly screwed to the front of the box. This frame must be sufficiently wide at top and bottom to take the door slot. The door slot is formed by gluing a rabbeted board to the back of the door panel. In order to insert the door, the slot at the top must be about $\frac{1}{4}$″ deeper than that at the bottom.

The finished nesting box weatherproofed with varnish and a coat of paint (only an outer coat) should be hung, as far as possible, in the shade and in such a way that its entrance hole points east or south-east. It should never face the weather side, that is, point west. Birds also do not like boxes opening to the south because of the heat. Finally, the box should not tilt backwards. It should be vertical, though it may be slightly tilted forwards. The nesting box is not nailed directly to the tree; a sturdy upright support is screwed to the back and this is used for mounting. Where it is difficult to suspend the box by the rear wall, the support is placed on one of the two side walls. A final word of advice. Do not hang too many nesting boxes. A mating pair requires a free area at least 80 feet in circumference. In this space it will not tolerate "competition" from the same species. That is why properly hung boxes often remain uninhabited.

To make birds really feel at home in a garden to which they have been attracted by good nesting facilities, one or more watering places are essential. Most species need water several times a day, especially in summer. If we offer it to them close to the breeding site, we often spare them long flights and make them less nomadic.

Shallow, unglazed dishes or artificial-stone flower bowls with a few stones peeping out of the water provide very practical watering places, providing you always make sure the water is fresh. Birds like to perch on them, especially if they are sunk in the ground and the edges covered with rock fragments.

As mentioned on p. 345, concrete watering places can be built directly into the ground. However, it is a good idea not to place the actual tank in humus but to use about $2^1/_2''$ of firmly compacted gravel as a base. Tanks made at home make it possible to get away from the rigid, commercial forms and to give the watering place a more natural appearance.

The one-piece concrete tank can easily be made quite large (about three feet in diameter), if the bottom is given a sufficiently flat curvature. Frost can lift a tank of this shape without it breaking. Large tanks should have a gravel bed at least 3" deep. This should then be covered with 3" of rough concrete (1 part cement to 10 parts pit gravel), over which a 1"-thick layer of fine concrete is laid. Only the fine concrete is waterproofed. The central part of such large tanks can be made deeper if a greater thickness of concrete is used and a wood block or board laid in the concrete when it is poured. After the concrete has set, the block is removed. We thus have room to line the tank with aquatic plants. If plants are to be grown around the edge of the watering place, which again should be camouflaged with bits of rock, a line of bricks set on edge is sunk into the earth around the tank so that the roots of the plants cannot grow below it.

Applying the same principles we can build a very nice little brook from concrete and, together with sensible planting, this can also form an ornament for the garden. Wherever conditions permit, the watering place should have inlet and outlet channels. The amount of water entering and flowing away need only be very small, but such a system provides a constant supply of fresh water.

The provision of drinking water is only one of the functions of a watering place, since in the summer it gives birds an opportunity to bathe. Birds prefer to bathe in the early morning and late in the afternoon. They do this with such relish and absorption that they readily overlook the prowling cat. The baths should therefore be scattered and stand in the open, 10 to 15 feet away from bushes and hedges, so that they do not become bird traps instead of a bird attraction.

If we take all these points to heart and, in addition, try to fit the nesting spots and watering places harmoniously into the garden scene, our efforts will be rewarded by many a profoundly gratifying experience.

INDEX

359